The Fire, the Star and the Cross

'*The Fire, the Star and the Cross* is a fascinating and pioneering account of the highly productive interplay between Muslims, Zoroastrians, Jews and Christians in Iran. Its theme has great resonance and importance in our own time.'

David Abulafia, Professor of Mediterranean History, University of Cambridge

'Aptin Khanbaghi has written an important and fascinating book which aims to present a thorough evaluation of the historical contributions made by religious minorities – Zoroastrians, Jews and Christians – to the societal and cultural physiognomy of the lands of Iran in pre-modern and early modern times. His general perspective and his broad treatment of the topic are quite new, while his use of sources and of the secondary literature is genuinely impressive. *The Fire, the Star and the Cross* makes a very significant and original contribution to our knowledge and understanding of Iranian history and civilization during an era when the foundations were laid for the emerging modern Iranian state.'

Bert G. Fragner, Director of the Institute of Iranian Studies, Austrian Academy of Sciences, Vienna

'It is rare to find unique and interesting publications on non-trendy topics; many prefer to embrace subjects that are safe; topics that would endear them to others with like-minded ideas and priories. Aptin Khanbaghi has broken that rule with courage, passion, and objective analysis. In a detailed study of the history of non-Muslims, the author reveals their trials and accomplishments through different dynastic rules of Iran. He provides a wealth of information never stated before, by using varied sources in different languages.'

Eliz Sanasarian in *Middle Eastern Studies*

The Fire, the Star and the Cross

Minority Religions in Medieval and Early Modern Iran

Aptin Khanbaghi

I.B. TAURIS
LONDON · NEW YORK

Paperback edition published in 2017 by
I.B.Tauris & Co. Ltd
London • New York
www.ibtauris.com

Hardback edition first published in 2006 by
I.B.Tauris & Co. Ltd

Copyright © 2006 Aptin Khanbaghi

The right of Aptin Khanbaghi to be identified as the author of this work has been asserted by the author in accordance with the Copyright, Designs and Patent Act 1988.

All rights reserved. Except for brief quotations in a review, this book, or any part thereof, may not be reproduced, stored in or introduced into a retrieval system, or transmitted, in any form or by any means, electronic, mechanical, photocopying, recording or otherwise, without the prior written permission of the publisher.

ISBN 978 1 78453 746 3
eISBN 978 0 85773 305 4
ePDF 978 0 85771 266 0

A full CIP record for this book is available from the British Library
A full CIP record for this book is available from the Library of Congress

Library of Congress Catalogue Card Number: available

Cover photograph: Atashgah ('place of fire') near Isfahan, Iran. Remains of Sassanian-era Zoroastrian fire temple.

Cover design: www.theoldchapelivinghoe.com

Printed and bound by CPI Group (UK) Ltd, Croydon, CR0 4YY
from camera-ready copy edited and supplied by the author

To all the wandering minorities of the world.
To their adventures and fortitude.

Contents

Foreword x

Acknowledgements xiii

A Note on the Transliterations and the Names xv

Map xvi

Introduction 1

Chapter 1: Religious Minorities under the Sassanians: The Cultural Affirmation of Jews and Christians in Iran 6
   1) The Oldest Living Diaspora: The Jews of Sassanian Iran . 7
   2) From Traitors to Loyal Subjects: Iranian Christians under the Sassanians 10
   Conclusion 14

Chapter 2: Iran under Foreign Creed: The Domination of Islam over Zoroastrians, Jews and Christians 15
   1) Non-Muslims in Early Islamic Iran: Golden Age or Decline? 17
   2) The Eclipse of Zoroastrianism in Iran: The Iranian uprisings of the 8th and 9th centuries 20
   3) The Emergence of Muslim Iranian Dynasties 27
   4) The Cultural Activities of Zoroastrians in Islamic Iran .. 29
   5) Active and Influential Minorities: The Jews and Christians in Islamic Iran 33

- 6) The Cultural Contribution of Non-Muslims to Islamic Civilization 45
  - a) The Jews and their Cultural Contribution to their Islamic Environment 45
  - b) The Christians and their Share of Cultural Contribution 47
- Conclusion 50

Chapter 3: New Hope and Bitter Deception: Iranian non-Muslims under the Mongols (1256-1336) 52
- 1) The Challengers of Islam 53
- 2) New Hopes among Christians: The Beginnings of the Mongol Rule 59
- 3) Non-Muslims in the Service of the Mongols 62
- 4) The Dusk of Non-Muslim Rule: The Recovery of Islam in Iran 69
- 5) Christians and Diplomacy 74
- 6) The Cultural Renaissance of Non-Muslims under the Mongols 79
- Conclusion 86

Chapter 4: The Post-Mongol and Pre-Safavid Period: A Brief View of Iran under the Timurids and the Aq Qoyunlu . 88
- Contacts with Europe and India 91

Chapter 5: The Safavid Period 93

Section 1: Between Economic Success and Social Challenge: Non-Muslims under the Safavids 93
- 1) The Advent of the Safavids and the Non-Muslims 95
- 2) The Social Struggle and Economic Activities of the Zoroastrians 97
- 3) The Social Struggle and Economic Activities of the Jews 102

    4) The Armenians: An Exotic Community or a Native
        Minority Group? 111
       a) The Earlier Presence of Armenians in Iran and the
          Deportations of Shah Abbas I 111
       b) The Armenians and their Monopoly of Iranian Trade . 114
       c) The Role of the Armenians in Iranian Politics and Iranian
          Diplomacy 120
       d) Christians versus Christians: The Conflict of Interest
          between Armenians and Europeans 122
       e) Expensive Prerogatives: the Armenians' Paradoxical
          Position 127
    5) The Georgians and Circassians: The Assimilated Christians
        130
    6) The Inconspicuous Christians 131

Section 2: Minority Cultures in Safavid Iran 134
    1) The Armenians and Iranian Culture: A Non-Integrated
        Minority 134
    2) The Last Glimmers of the Iranian Jewry's Culture 136
    3) An Exported Literature: Zoroastrian Writings under the
        Safavids 146
    Conclusion 155

Conclusion 159

Notes on the Text 164

Appendix 208

Bibliography 223

Index 248

Foreword

There have been several places where the great religions of the medieval world have not merely co-existed but interacted. Perhaps the best known is al-Andalus, the areas of Spain under Muslim rule. In Umayyad Córdoba and in Zirid Granada, Jews, Christians and Muslims read each other's scientific and philosophical texts, and indeed the Judaism of Sefarad (Spain) acquired an almost Islamised character, culminating in the work of the great philosopher Maimonides. Not just ideas crossed the religious divide. The Islamic conquest also brought the Arabic language to Iberia, where it left a powerful legacy in the vocabulary of Castilian and Portuguese. But there is a further fascinating and remarkable example of the interaction between Islam and the other Abrahamic religions, Judaism and Christianity, to which, in this particular case, we need to add a fourth and very influential religion, that of the Zoroastrians: this example is Iran. Even before the Islamic conquest, Iran was a land in which religious minorities were well entrenched; for the Zoroastrian Sassanid rulers had many Jewish and Christian subjects; and one of the tasks of this absorbing book is to see how far we can identify continuity in the treatment of the religious minorities from the Sassanid through to the early Islamic period. Yet, after the conquest, the Zoroastrians, like the Christians in Spain, found themselves not merely deprived of political power; they also experienced slow erosion of numbers as the old faith declined in town and country, while the ambiguous attitude of Islam towards this non-Abrahamic faith could, at times, make conditions difficult for its adherents. And yet the ancient Persian imprint on the cultural life of Iran was deep: deeper, certainly, than the imprint left by the Mozarab Christians of Spain in the same centuries. Iran's new rulers learned much from the Middle Pahlavi texts which Zoroastrian scholars translated into Arabic. In particular, the survival and Renaissance of the Persian language is testimony to the distinctive sense of identity that persisted in medieval and early modern Iran; and yet, as Dr Khanbaghi shows, the revival of Persian owed a great deal to the new Mongol conquerors of Iran in the late Middle Ages.

This book provided a marvellous overview of the relationship between the different faiths in Iran. As Aptin Khanbaghi very effectively argues, this set of relationships had many ups and downs. Thus we can observe the decline of Nestorian Christianity in Iran and the even steeper decline of Zoroastrianism, which now has its main centres in the Parsee communities of India (whose collections Dr Khanbaghi has very profitably utilised). As in other parts of the Muslim world, the status of the *dhimmi*, the protected non-Muslim, could be interpreted in a variety of ways, so that some rulers imposed the full rigour of the law, while others adopted a more lenient and pragmatic approach, in line with the practice of many other Muslim rulers in the Mediterranean world or in India. Some dynasties, such as the Safavids, understood the economic value of the non-Muslim population, and encouraged newcomers to arrive, just as their Ottoman rivals in the Mediterranean brought tens of thousands of Jews and Christians to Istanbul and lesser cities. There were periods, such as the dark days of the conquests of Timur Leng (Tamerlane), when conditions were more difficult. But there were also fruitful periods of exchange; communities such as the Armenians had links to the world beyond Iran. Yet some of the minorities, as Dr Khanbaghi aptly indicates, were far from being in any sense alien: the Jews had been in Persia since the days of Cyrus the Great, and the Zoroastrians, like the Copts in Egypt, could claim to be the heirs to even older cultural and political traditions in Iran. This is an important reminder that easily imposed categories of 'native' and 'foreigner' are often based on a deep misunderstanding of history. Pope Benedict XVI reminded his audience of a similar point in Cologne in August 2005, when he emphasized that the Jews had been in the city since the days of the Roman Empire. Thus Dr Khanbaghi's book has considerable relevance to modern times, and to present dilemmas in the Middle East and elsewhere. And this book fulfils another important role by showing that the history of the Islamic lands is not simply the history of Muslim peoples. Modern political tensions have had a nefarious effect on the world of scholarship, so that the history of the Jews and of the Muslims, whether in Spain or Iran, Morocco or Egypt, has too often been treated as two separate histories. In this book, what we have is not separate histories of Jews, Christians, Muslims and Zoroastrians, but one history of the interweaving of ideas, experiences and fates. Aptin Khanbaghi is to be congratulated on making such good sense of the vicissitudes of all the religious groups in Iran. Each, of course, has been the subject of many scholarly books. However, the scholarly work that has needed to be written is one unpartisan book that brings together these religious groups. And this we now have in the excellent chapters that follow.

David Abulafia
Professor of Mediterranean History
Cambridge University

Acknowledgements

It is not sufficient to thank all those who have dedicated several hours of their busy schedule to assist me in improving the style and the content of this book with simply two words; however at this stage I can only express my gratitude to them. There are also people who have shown no boundaries in their kindness and moral support, and have invested in me more energy than I could have ever expected. Whether a name occurs in the beginning or towards the end of these acknowledgements is more fortuitous than deliberate.

Words cannot express my gratitude to Siddharth Saxena (Montu) for having always been at my side during this tempestuous journey. His comments for improving the quality of this book were most welcome. Christine van Ruymbeke was a heaven-sent fairy, giving me unconditional and generous support all through this scholastic enterprise. Without these two guardian angels I could have never survived in this academic world, so well depicted by Eliz Sanasarian (*Religious Minorities in Iran*, 2000:XV).

I am extremely indebted to my friends Martin Worthington and William Lee for having proofed many chapters and pages of my work. My thanks should be extended to Eleanor Coghill, not only for having participated in the reading process, but also for her compassion and her support in the different stages of this work. I wish to thank her wholeheartedly for having left her Fitzwilliam flat at my disposal in autumn 2004 for preparing the final version of this book.

David Abulafia has been my mentor since the beginning of my academic venture in Cambridge. His kind support and genuine interest in my subject were vital for my continuing this research. I also wish to extend my appreciation to Bert Fragner for persuading me to have this book published. His encouragements gave me the necessary motivation to complete this work.

Ladan Niayesh deserves much credit for her careful and critical reading of my translations. I am most grateful to Omar Ali de Unzaga, and Rosemary Rodd of the Cambridge University Computing Service for patiently assisting me with the technical problems I encountered while typing in Persian. Katja Müller is another friend to whom I am much obliged: the map is the result of her endeavours.

Thanks are also due to Mari Shullaw for helping me draft the proposal for this book, and to Sister Bridget Tighe for creating the ideal atmosphere for study and research at the Margaret Beaufort Institute.

Finally, I wish to thank Shernaz Cama, the head of the *Project for the Preservation of the Parsi-Zoroastrian Heritage*, who made my field trip to India more profitable. I am also grateful to Edmund Herzig for referring me to I.B.Tauris.

This long venture would have never taken place had it not been for my mother's enthusiasm, and my father's and sister's support. No language has any words for recording my appreciation of their love and affection.

A Note on the Transliterations and the Names

All Arabic, Hebrew and Persian words at first usage are italicized. As Sunil Sharma says, 'there is no single system of transliterating Persian that satisfies everybody.'[1] I have, therefore, followed a simplified form of the Library of Congress transliteration system. For the purpose of a general readership diacritical marks have been omitted. Names of well-known Iranian or Mesopotamian towns and regions, and names of dynasties (such as Abbasid and Umayyad) and terms appearing in the Oxford dictionary (such as 'Sunnite', 'Shi'ite', 'divan', 'mulla', 'ulema', 'sharia' etc.) retain their untransliterated spelling. Terms such as *nama* are spelled without the final 'h'. For the names of some towns, their older versions have been retained, as they appear in this form in most primary and secondary sources dealing with non-Muslims in Iran and Mesopotamia. Thus, Jundishabur, Irbil and Tikrit appear in the text as Gundishapur, Arbela and Takrit. All dates are given in the common era.

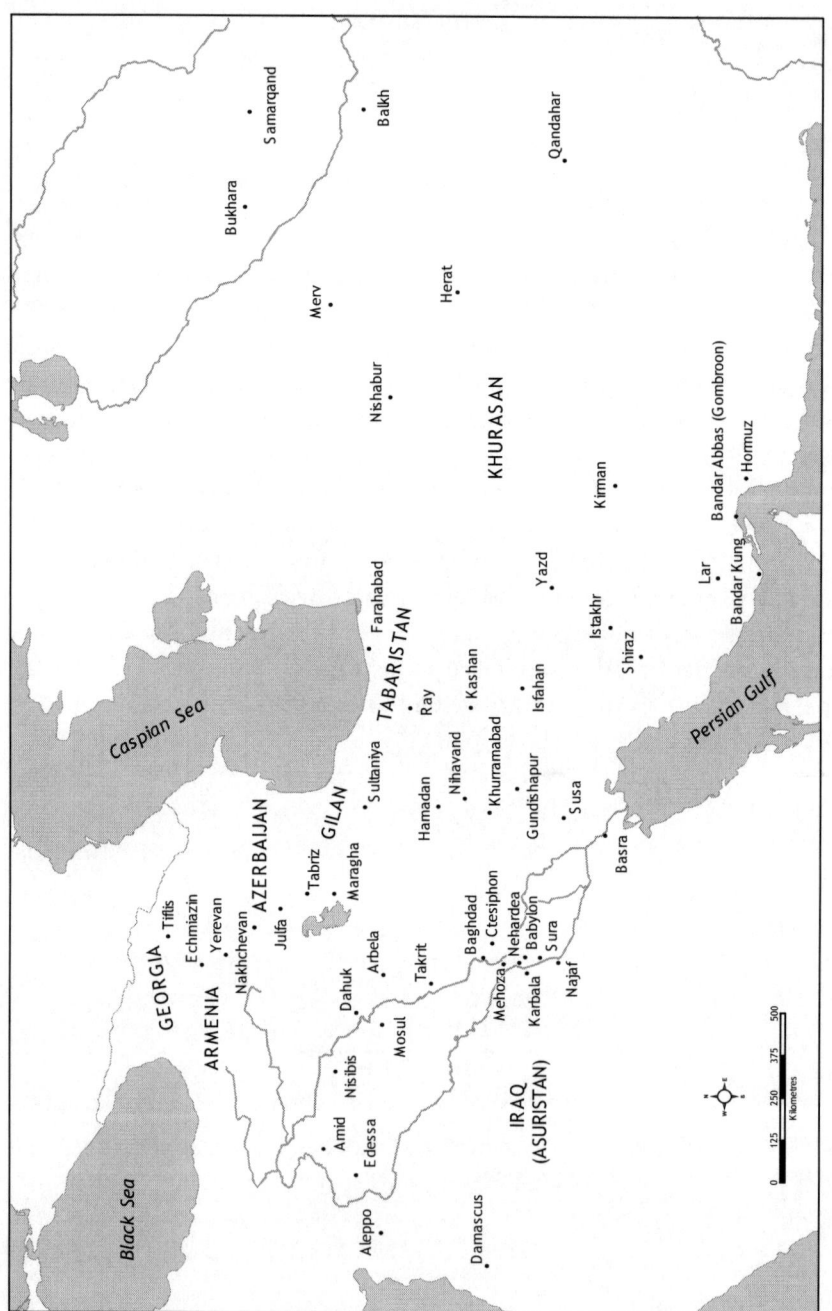

Introduction

Although the Middle East is mostly identified with Islam today, it has been home to many other great civilizations. The Islamic civilization itself is much indebted to the various peoples that the Arabs subdued in the 7th and 8th centuries. Far from fading away after the Arab conquest, the inhabitants of Mesopotamia and the Iranian Plateau occupied the main social and cultural arenas of their region. They were in fact participating in the development of a new civilization, which is now referred to by many as Islamic. The magnitude of their contribution has, however, not received the scholarly attention it deserves. Many of these groups were assimilated by their Muslim rulers and were lost to their initial communities. Some, however, chose to remain loyal to their ancestral traditions. The focus of the present research is on those groups that resisted assimilation to Islam, but nonetheless continued to participate actively in the socio-political life of their land.

Due to its complex religious history, Iran offers fascinating opportunities for studying its non-Muslim communities. The Iranian milieu, by virtue of its Zoroastrian past and its conversion to Shi'ite Islam after the beginning of the 16th century, adds a different dimension to our knowledge of religious minorities living in Muslim lands. The cultural environment in which the Iranian non-Muslims dwelt and their experiences were different from those of non-Muslims living in other Islamic dominions. Despite their historical prominence, it is striking how little the Zoroastrians have been studied as a minority community in Islamic lands. As Iran is the only region dominated by Islam and where Zoroastrian groups continue to exist, this study will provide an additional perspective on the position of non-Muslims in the Islamic world.

In contrast to the bulk of previous studies which have stressed their social restrictions, this work examines in particular the cultural and social accomplishments of Zoroastrians, Jews and Christians who lived as minorities under Muslim rule in Iran. The period on which this research focuses begins at the onset of the Mongol invasion (13th c.) and ends with the Afghan invasion of Iran in 1722. The availability of source material on non-Muslims living in this period seems to be greater than can be found for non-Muslims in Iran during earlier Islamic periods. For example, a similar exhaustive study on non-Muslims in the 7th or 8th century would not have been possible, despite the fact that in those periods non-Muslims probably outnumbered Muslims. The approach of studying a later period for which more material is available, allows a detailed study to be conducted, which can also provide an insight into the activities of non-Muslims in the earlier periods of Islam.

Although the period under study begins in the 13th century, the first section of this work provides a brief survey of the history of Zoroastrians, Jews and Christians during the Sassanian period followed by a review of their position and activities from the Arab invasion up to the Mongol invasion of Iran. An overview of the earlier periods will put in context the elements of continuity and change in this history of the non-Muslim communities of Iran.

The effect of changes that Jews and Christians felt after the Arab conquest were only manifested over a long period of time. While under the Sassanians the number of Christians had increased, under Arab rule Jews and Christians saw a gradual diminution of their populations. On this matter the sources are very revealing. Towards the end of the Sassanian period, the Zoroastrian sources refer increasingly to Christians, whereas the sources of the Abbasid period refer less and less to non-Muslims as time goes on.

There are recurrent features in Iranian History that can be observed by comparing the Sassanian period with later periods. Before the Mongols and the Safavids, the Sassanians had already chosen Christians as envoys to other Christian courts. Like the Safavids, the Sassanians had already settled Jews and Armenians in various towns, including Isfahan.[2]

Particular elements of continuity are apparent in the institutions and organizations of the non-Muslim communities.[3] The Jewish and Christian academic institutions founded under the Sassanians continued their activities for another four centuries under Islam. The relationships which the Jewish and Christian leaderships had established with the Zoroastrian monarchs were maintained with the Arab rulers.[4] The Zoroastrians who had dominated Iran before the Arab conquest provided the Muslim rulers with both intellectual and administrative tools to govern the state. The Zoroastrians were in possession of a wealth of writings on science and literature which they made available to the Arab rulers by translating them from Middle Persian (Pahlavi) into Arabic.[5] As the Arabs lacked the necessary experience for administering Iran, they took over the Sassanian bureaucratic system and allowed the Zoroastrian officials to maintain their positions.

After the 8th century, however, the Arab rulers no longer deemed it necessary to preserve the existing socio-political system, which did not represent their people. Thus, they began the Islamification of Iran by changing the official language of the government from Persian to Arabic and dismissing the Zoroastrian members of the administration. Those Zoroastrians who converted to Islam still faced discrimination by the Arab establishment. By the end of the Umayyad period, relations between Iranians and Arabs were very tense and culminated in bloody revolts under the Abbasids. These revolts caused the position of Iranians to deteriorate even more in the 8th and 9th centuries. Many of the insurgents were Muslim apostates of Zoroastrian background. The Arabs' reluctance to have Iranians in the government reached a peak during the reign of al-Ma'mun who interestingly was born of an Iranian mother. By the 9th century, the insurrections of the Zoroastrians had finally been quashed, generating massive conversions and putting an end to general apostasies. Thus, under the Abbasids, the religious pattern of Iran changed and the Zoroastrian population rapidly dwindled, turning them into religious minorities like the Jews and the Christians.

While the Zoroastrians were marginalized, this dramatic change did not prevent the Jews and Christians from holding important offices in the government and influential positions at the court. It was not until the Afghan invasion that a Zoroastrian general reached a leading position in Iran again.

At first glance, the relations that the Jews and Christians developed with the Arab Muslim majority seem similar to those they had had under the Sassanians. Generally the Jews and Christians were tolerated, although occasionally political crisis, such as wars with the Byzantine Empire, prompted persecutions of Christians.[6] By the 11th century, the decline of the Jewish and Christian communities could be felt. Numerous Nestorian bishoprics had disappeared since the 7th century. The famous Jewish Academies of Pumbedita and Sura, which had been founded under the Sassanians, closed their doors for good. Many Jewish scholars emigrated to North Africa and Spain. Positions, such as those of court physicians, which until then had been dominated by Jews and Christians, were now also occupied by Muslims.[7] However, purges from government positions caused by political troubles or economic crises, were not long lasting. The minority status of Jews and Christians made their position in society fragile and consequently they were ideal civil servants, as they could not afford to deceive those in power. In these circumstances, Jews and Christians were able to remain close to the reins of power.

The Mongols who conquered Iran in the 13th century enrolled many Jewish and Christian bureaucrats in their government. The religious tolerance of the Mongols favoured the political and cultural emancipation of non-Muslims in Iran. However, it should be mentioned that the Mongols did not offer key political positions to non-Muslims simply because of their distrust of Muslims; rather Jews and Christians had the political competence the Mongols sought. They were present in the administration of Iran when the Mongols arrived, and the non-Muslim conquerors simply gave them the opportunity to occupy higher positions. In no other period of Iranian history were political skills of Jews and Christians put to better use. Under the Mongols they not only held important offices, but a Jewish physician actually reached the most powerful position in Iran by becoming Grand Vizier. The Mongol rulers also prompted the emancipation of the Persian language, which until then had not been able to supplant Arabic as the language of science and philosophy.[8] The strengthening of the position of the Persian language integrated the Persian-speaking religious minorities in the Iranian culture of the time. This led to the growth of Judeo-Persian literature and encouraged the Zoroastrians to record their history and thoughts in 'Modern' Persian. In fact, Persian literature in general flourished under the Mongols, and Jews and Zoroastrians could not have been completely indifferent to the poetry of Sa'di and Hafiz.

The most important legacy of the Mongol period, however, was the opening of the Iranian borders to foreign diplomacy and trade. The diplomatic exchanges were undeniably most beneficial to the Christians, who acted as intermediaries between Christian Europe and Iran. The appointment of Nestorian Christians as ambassadors under the Mongols set a precedent for the recruitment of Armenians under the Safavids. The spectacular ascendancy of Armenians in trade, along with the appearance of wealthy Jewish and Zoroastrian merchants in certain regions of Iran, demonstrates the dynamism and commercial sagacity of non-Muslims in Iran. Despite this fact, the picture drawn of Jews and Zoroastrians under the Safavids has generally been grim. They are depicted as impotent victims of persecutions and the facts about their cultural and economic achievements have been ignored. Generalisations about the intolerance of the Shi'ites and Safavids have distorted the history of non-Muslims in Iran. Bernard Lewis, for example, propounds that the Shi'ites were far less tolerant than their Sunnite contemporaries in the Ottoman Empire.[9]

Sharing a similar opinion, Walter Fischel writes: 'Under no other Persian dynasty was the hatred of the Jews more intense.'[10] On the other hand, the sources produced by the Christian Carmelites during the Safavid period insist that the Shi'ites in Iran were more tolerant than the Sunnite Ottomans.[11] Were the Shi'ites really so different from the Sunnites in their policies with regard to non-Muslims? Were the Safavids really so different from other Muslim dynasties in their treatment of people of other faiths?

It appears that none of these authors have taken into consideration the changes that occurred between the reign of one Safavid monarch and another, and the variation of the non-Muslims' situation from one region to another. The non-Muslims' contribution to Iranian civilization has been disproportionate to the small sizes of their communities. The focus on persecutions has undermined the role they have played in the past 1,400 years of Iranian history. It is time to study non-Muslims from this new perspective, one which demonstrates their sophistication, their religious tenacity and their economic and political endeavours in a Muslim society despite their social handicaps.

Chapter 1
Religious Minorities under the Sassanians: The Cultural Affirmation of Jews and Christians in Iran

Iran was distinguished from the other lands conquered by the Muslim Arabs, by its religious and political situation. While the majority of the provinces that capitulated to the Islamic army were predominantly Christian and were under the rule of the Byzantine or Roman Empire, Iran was politically independent and was dominated by a Zoroastrian majority.

Indeed, in 224 AD, the Sassanians had instituted Zoroastrianism as the State Religion in Iran.[12] Nonetheless, the enforcement of Zoroastrianism at the political level had not rendered Iran a homogenous land. On the contrary, Iran was home to numerous Jewish, Christian and other religious communities. In Asuristan (Iraq), the Jews and Christians outnumbered even the Zoroastrian population. 'Iranianhood', however, was broadly defined. It embraced all the different ethnic groups settled in Iran, who were willing to integrate into Iranian society; it also included the Turks.[13] Associated solely with Iran, Zoroastrianism did not assign its followers the mission to convert 'non-Iranians'; however, this did not prevent persecutions. The grounds for these persecutions appear to have been different from those endured by religious minorities under Christianity and Islam. They were guided more by political motives rather than religious zeal. Thus, none of the known anecdotes of persecution prompted any conversions to Zoroastrianism, except perhaps in cases of apostasy. Indeed, the status of the Christians in Iran was dependant on Irano-Roman (Irano-Byzantine) relations, until Nestorianism was established as the Church of Iran in 484.[14] Moreover, Judaism and Christianity flourished at this period. Not only did the number of Christians and Christian dioceses continuously increase, but migration of Jews from the Roman provinces and Armenia had swelled the Jewish population in Iran. Putting Asuristan aside, there were dense Jewish populations in the main cities of the Zagros valley.[15] There must have been Jewish communities in the East of the Iranian Plateau, but they are mentioned on rare occasions, such as in *Shahriha i Eran*, in which we are told that 'The capital of Khwarizm was built by Narseh, the son of the Jewess.'[16] Under the Sassanians, the Jews were able to take over the leadership of World-Jewry from the Jews in Palestine, and Iran appears to have had the largest Jewish population in the world, with some towns being populated mainly by Jews.[17]

1) **The Oldest Living Diaspora: The Jews of Sassanian Iran**

The Jews had been living on Iranian soil since at least the 8th c. B.C.;[18] therefore, they were far from being an alien entity in the region. Throughout the centuries, they had been able to develop cordial relations with the Iranian court; a bond which remained under the Sassanians. Despite their predilection for Zoroastrianism, the Sassanians did not alienate Jews, even though some authors have claimed this.[19] Far from losing their right to 'govern their own affairs' as some have alleged;[20] the Talmud testifies that the Sassanian government acknowledged the validity of the Jewish courts for cases in which even non-Jews were involved.[21] The Jewish leaders were only forbidden to implement capital punishment.[22]

The purpose here is not to discuss persecutions of Jews or the tolerance of Zoroastrians, but it is important to state that Ardashir Papakan (226-241), the founder of the dynasty, did not launch a persecution of Jews or any other non-Zoroastrian group. The Syriac author Mshiha-zkha says that Ardashir had many pyres erected and strove to propagate Zoroastrianism, but neither Jews nor Christians appear to have been the objects of his proselytization.[23] The Jews were able to maintain their official positions even during Ardashir's reign.[24]

Ardashir and his successor, Shapur I (241-272), wished primarily to be assured of the loyalty of their subjects. The *Babylonian Talmud* informs us that the head of the Jews, Mar Samuel of Nehardia (d. 254), demonstrated his full loyalty to Shapur by supporting his campaigns against the Romans and by recognizing officially the Law decreed by the Shah as valid for the Jews. This strategy enabled Samuel to secure for the Jews the same privileges they had enjoyed under the Parthians, and in practice they conducted their own legal affairs independently from the Sassanians.[25] The Exilarch (*Resh Galuta*) was recognized as the head of the Jewish community. He was in charge of collecting taxes and dispensing justice, and had a function similar to that of a king's vassal.

His office was maintained long after the fall of the Sassanians, until the mid 11th century.[26]

Apart from the Exilarch, the Jews had other influential allies at the court. The disciple of a certain Samuel Mar Judah (d. 299) regularly visited Shapur I, and even spent the night at the court.[27] So close were the ties between the Sassanian court and the leaders of the Iranian Jewry that the Christian sources blame the anti-Christian persecutions launched by Shapur I on the Jews.[28] The influence of the chief rabbis is not less evident under Shapur II (309-379). They had the Shapur's mother, Ifra Hormizd, as their patron. The Jewish official, Raba, was able to elude the death penalty despite having violated the imperial law, thanks to the intervention of the Queen mother on his behalf. Ifra Hormizd even bestowed monetary gifts upon the Jews.[29] A Pahlavi source reports that Yazdgird I (399-420) had a Jewish wife by the name of Shushandukht, and that the latter was the daughter of the *Resh Galuta*.[30] The presence of a Jewish Queen at the court had enhanced the position of Jews, as at their request, they were allowed to settle in Isfahan, occupying in fact half of the city, called in the early Islamic period *al-Yahudiyya*.[31] The same Pahlavi source mentions that Queen Shushandukht established Jewish colonies in the towns of Shush and Shushtar, and that she gave birth to Bahram Gur, who occupied the throne from 420 to 438 A.D..[32] During this period, the Jewish exilarchs had a regular audience with the Shahanshah, and one of them received from Yazdgird I a belt (*kamar*), which represented then the highest sign of distinction.[33]

After nearly one thousand years of good relations between the Jews and the Iranian rulers, Yazdgird II (438-457) launched a persecution against the Jews, which was continued by Peroz (457-484). Their malevolence towards this community was unprecedented in Iranian history.[34] The factors that prompted the persecutions are unknown; however, the messianic movements at the time among both Christians and Jews, and the belief in the end of Zoroastrianism, had prompted apparently both groups to ignore the ruling power. The Jews and the Christians were numerically strong enough, especially in Asuristan to oppose the Sassanian government.[35]

The importance of the Jews (and the Nestorians) in the Persian army is evinced from the request of Kavad I (498-531), who asked the Byzantine general for a cease-fire for their sake: 'Let us respect the Festival because of the Nasraye and Jews who are with me, and because of you (other) Christians.'[36] Just as in the army, the Jews were employed in the government as officials, and their function ranged from tax officers to prison wardens.[37] The Talmud hints that the Jews who acted as government officials, were unpopular in the Jewish community, as their major duty was to collect taxes.[38] Jewish scholars in the Academies, like the Zoroastrian clergy, were exempted from these taxes.[39] All other subjects, no matter what their religion, had to pay the poll-tax (*kraga*).[40] The Jewish councils decided who would be exempt by granting them the status of scholar.[41]

The wealth of the Jewish community is also testified in the Talmud. Pumbedita was famous for its mansions, while Mehuza was famous for the exuberance of its inhabitants' garments and exquisite tables. The majority of these people were ordinary subjects.[42] Mehuza was the wealthiest Jewish town in Iran, and most of its inhabitants were involved in trade. They saved their money and invested it when possible in the purchase of land.[43] The number of wealthy Jews outside these towns was relatively important as the Talmud refers to many of them. In the 3rd century a certain Hisda and in the 4th century Papa had accumulated wealth in the brewery business.[44] The Exilarch's wealth was comparable to that of princes. He lived in a palace and often invited more than hundred people to dine at his table. The members of his family were also affluent and could benefit from prerogatives reserved to the Exilarch by being carried in gilded sedan chairs.[45] Some wealthy Jewish families abused their prerogatives. They were attached to the Persian court, and would impose their will on poorer Jews. Those who were in debt, had to pay their dues promptly or else would have had to bear the consequences.[46] The Jewish Judges were in some cases powerless and could not bring the Jewish magnates before the law.[47] However, there were also philanthropists among wealthy Jews,[48] and even more important was the well-organized system of the Persian Jewry for collecting alms through taxation of the Jewish community.[49] The Jewish magnates in Asuristan possessed a large number of slaves.[50] Their financial support of Bahram Chubin (590-591),[51] although a strategic mistake, is also good evidence of their economic power within the Empire.

The Jews were not only politically and financially influential, they were also culturally very active. The Jewish academic centres of Sura and Pumbedita flourished under the Sassanians and the *Babylonian Talmud* was completed during this period (circa 220–500 A.D.).[52] The destruction of the Academy of Nehardia in 250 A.D. by Odenarth, the prince of Palmyra, prompted the foundation of a rabbinical Academy at Pumbedita by Judah b. Ezekiel in 259.[53] It was led thereafter by the best *Amoraim* (rabbinical scholars from 3rd to 6th century) of the time.[54] The rabbinical schools of Sura gained a reputation after 219. Thenceforth the Academy of Sura attracted hundreds of students from the rest of the Sassanian Empire, but it was not until 352 that Sura overtook Pumbedita as the leading academic school and remained the repository of Jewish science for another seven centuries.[55] The *Amoraim* or the heads of the Academies of Sura and Pumbedita, also acted as judges and were influential dignitaries.[56] It is important to mention that the *Babylonian Talmud* produced in Iran is more complete than the *Palestinian Talmud* produced in the Roman/Byzantine Empire. The Jewish Academies in Iran had a longer and more glorious history. Scholars from the Roman Empire found refuge in these Academies and contributed to their success.[57] Iran offered a better environment for Jewish scholastic efforts, as despite sporadic persecutions, the Talmud testifies that they were never harassed as much as in the Roman Empire.[58] This element explains the Jews' betrayal of the Byzantines by siding with the Persians, when Khusraw II undertook the invasion of the Byzantine Empire.

2) From Traitors to Loyal Subjects: Iranian Christians under the Sassanians

If the adherence of the Byzantine Empire to Christianity had at times reinforced good relations between the Jews and the Sassanian state, it had on the contrary alienated the Christian inhabitants of Iran from the rulers.[59] Indeed, after the Emperor Constantine had proclaimed Christianity as the official religion of the Roman Empire in 325, relations between Christians and Zoroastrians in Iran had sometimes been strained.[60] It was not until Yazdgird I (395-421) sat on the throne that the lot of Christians began to improve. During his reign, Marutha, the bishop of Maipherqat obtained an edict for the official recognition of Christianity in Iran. Apart from being a good politician, we are told that Marutha was a skilful physician, and had cured Yazdgird I on one occasion.[61] This is one of the first references to a Christian acting as a court physician in Iran. This position was dominated thereafter by Christians even after the Arab invasion. Physicians were highly influential at court and were thus able to intervene on behalf of their co-religionists.[62]

Another important event, which occurred during Yazdgird I's reign in 410 was the first Iranian Christian synod. The synod established a hierarchical Christian Church in Iran, with a patriarchate at Ctesiphon and metropolitans in the capitals of five Persian provinces. The recognition of the Christian Church encouraged its adepts to proselytize freely and found new bishoprics. They were able to convert dignitaries in the government and a few members of the nobility.[63] In the synod of 422, the bishop Dadisho proclaimed the independence of the Iranian Church from Byzantium, and in 484 Nestorianism became the only standard for the Church of Iran. The new denominational affiliation established the loyalty of Iranian Christians to the Sassanian monarchs.[64] It was the Zoroastrian environment of Iran that in fact directed Iranian Christianity towards Nestorianism. Its doctrines were explicitly anti-ascetic, and its theology distinguished between the divine and human nature of Christ. In sum, Jesus was *human* on earth, and achieved unity with God only in the other world. This interpretation of Christianity was in accord with Iranian religious mentality.[65]

The position of Christians probably improved even more under Khusraw I Anushiravan (531-578) as he had a Christian wife. His son Anushazad apparently embraced the religion of his mother and hoped to obtain the support of Nestorians in Khuzistan to usurp power, without any success.[66] Anushazad's appeal to the Christians for support, shows the numerical importance of this community in Khuzistan at this time. During the same period, Maraba (540-552), a Zoroastrian apostate, became Catholicos (head of Nestorian Church) at Ctesiphon.[67] Despite the fact that apostasy in Zoroastrianism was not acceptable, the important number of Christians in the West of Iran prevented Khusraw I from killing him. He needed his collaboration to appease a revolt of Christians.[68] Following Maraba's death, Khusraw I placed his private physician, Joseph on the throne of the Catholicate (552-567). The bishops did not contest his choice.[69] Another physician, named Moses or Narses from Nisibis, is mentioned as having gone to the court in order to present to the monarch the anguish of the Christians, so that Joseph could be deposed. However, Joseph's influence on Khusraw was so strong that the bishops did not dare nominate another Catholicos.[70]

Henceforth, Zoroastrian officers who converted to Christianity were allowed to maintain their rank in the Persian army, and were no longer ostracized.[71] By the time of Hormizd IV (579-590), the number of Christians had increased to such an extant that when the Zoroastrian priests solicited the King to restrict the activities of the Christians, Hormizd replied:

Just as our royal throne cannot stand on its two front legs without the two back ones, our kingdom cannot stand or endure firmly if we cause the Christians and adherents of other faiths, who differ in belief from ourselves, to become hostile to us. So renounce this desire to persecute the Christians and become assiduous in good works, so that the Christians and the adherents of other faiths may see this, praise you for it, and feel themselves drawn toward your religion.[72]

The reconciliation of the Sassanians with the Christians generated a new social and political atmosphere, which allowed the Christians to establish intellectual centres similar to those belonging to Jews, such as the School of Nisibis and the School of Ctesiphon. The School of Ctesiphon was relatively modest, but the School of Nisibis prospered and by 575 had about 800 disciples.[73] The closure of the School of Edessa in 489 and that of Athens in 529 stimulated even more the expansion of these Christian seats of learning thanks to the arrival of scholars who were fleeing the coercive laws of the Byzantine Empire. Gundishapur, in particular, benefited from this wave of migration and emerged as the most important centre of medical and philosophical studies. Many Nestorian treatises were written at this period, one of which has reached us translated in Latin: *Instituta regularia divinae Legis*.[74] The Jacobite Mafrian[75] Denha, in his *Life of Marouta* observed that in each of the villages inhabited by Christians they had already established a school.[76]

The presence of Jacobite Christians[77] is also attested to in Sassanian Iran. Despite their religious vitality, they had not been able to secure for their Church the official status granted to Nestorianism until perhaps the reign of Khusraw I.[78] The town of Tagrit, not far from Ctesiphon, and the monastery of Mar Mattai remained their stronghold up to the Timurid period. The most notable Jacobite figure of the Sassanian period was Khusraw II's physician, Gabriel of Shiggar.[79] Khusraw II Parveez (591-628) had two Christian wives, Shirin (a Nestorian) and Mariam (the daughter of the Byzantine Emperor Maurice).[80] Gabriel converted Shirin to Jacobite Christianity and in 609 exhorted Khusraw to refuse the nomination of a new Catholicos at Ctesiphon, leaving the seat of the Catholicate empty. Gabriel was even able to arrange the confiscation of two monasteries in the district of Hulvan, from the Nestorians. He also prompted Khusraw to kill a certain Georges who had converted to Nestorianism from Zoroastrianism.[81]

It was only after Gabriel died that Yazdin, the Nestorian treasurer of the court, was able to use his influence on Khusraw. He had a substantial amount of goods extorted from the Jews, as the latter had incited the Persian army to set fire to Jerusalem.[82] In 628, after his defeat by the Romans, Khusraw had Yazdin killed, probably to appropriate his possessions.[83] According to the anonymous author of the *History of the Last Sassanians*, the sons of Yazdin, Shamta and Nehormizd used their influence in order to dethrone Khusraw and revenged themselves by killing him and conspired with the rest of the dignitaries of the empire to murder all his sons except Sheroe, who was thereafter placed on the throne.[84] This event demonstrates the waxing power of Christians in Iran. Other sources substantiate this fact by reporting that the number of bishoprics and monks was constantly rising.[85]

An anonymous Syriac author relates that in the end Sheroe had both Shamta and Nehormizd imprisoned.[86] Tabari's version of the events confirms the veracity of the story; however, in Tabari's history, Nehormizd appears as Mihr Hormuz, and he is not related to Shamta. Tabari does not mention his religion. He hints that other Iranian dignitaries also plotted with Shamta and Mihr Hormuz to kill Khusraw.[87] Khusraw II had in reality broken the bond between the Nestorian Church and the Sassanian monarchy by favouring the Jacobites and refusing to recognize the Catholicos of the Nestorians.[88]

Towards the end of the Sassanian period, Sheroe and after him, Queen Bourandokht (630-631), sent the Catholicos Isho'yahb (628-643), along with several metropolitans as their envoys to Byzantium, in order to conclude a permanent peace.[89] The truce with the Byzantines was not enough to bring peace to Iran. The Arabs were aware of the exhaustion of the Sassanian state, and yearned for the legendary riches of the Persian capital. In 634 they launched successful attacks on the Persian army and invaded Iran.

During the war that opposed Arabs to Iranians, Bar Hebraeus says that the Nestorians observed their neutrality, and were favourable to new rulers. He says that the Catholicos Isho'yahb found Christian allies among the Arabs such as the Christian prince of Najran, and assured the Arabs of his amity.[90] However, the anonymous Syriac author of the *History of the Last Sassanians* asserts that the Catholicos fled from the capital as soon as he heard about the devastation of Mahoze by the Arabs. His treaty with the new rulers was nothing more than a humble submission, necessary under the circumstances.[91] The anonymous chronicle of Guidi also shows that the Christians could not remain indifferent to the Arab invasion as they wrought destruction to towns like Shushtar, where there was a substantial Christian population, who were subject to killings.[92] Shaul Shaked says on this matter that the Jews fought the Muslim invaders on the side of the Persians, in order to defend their land.[93] Tabari ends his chronicle on the Sassanians by saying that Ilya, the Archbishop of Merv, gave the last Sassanian king (Yazdgird III) a sepulchre, because his grandmother was Christian and his grandfather had been benevolent towards Christians.[94] Based on this information, it is still difficult to deduce whom the Jews and the Christians supported, as the circumstances under which the towns surrendered were different in each case. This said, Gerö reminds us that despite persecutions during the Sassanian period, the Christian community flourished and on the eve of the Arab invasion they formed the single largest religious community in Mesopotamia.[95]

Conclusion

As Aubry Vine asserts, 'in spite of occasional persecutions, the Sassanian period was on the whole one of advancement and development for Iranian Christianity,'[96] and also for Iranian Jewry. By the end of the Sassanian period, both Judaism and Christianity were well-entrenched politically and culturally on Iranian soil. The Jewish and Christian academies had achieved fame, and Jews and Christians held office and were involved in the Sassanian administrative system and had established close contacts with the court. They had indeed received all the training necessary to cultivate and govern an empire. Their knowledge and skills ultimately benefited a new conquering people.

Chapter 2
Iran under Foreign Creed: The Domination of Islam over Zoroastrians, Jews and Christians

In the first chapter we reviewed briefly the position of Jews and Christians in Iran under the Zoroastrian Sassanians. In this period the Jews and the Christians founded vibrant schools which continued to lead their cultural life even after the fall of the Sassanians. They also developed close relations with the court, and established political institutions, such as the offices of the Exilarch and of the Catholicos, which also outlived the Zoroastrian empire.

Until the Arab invasion, the Zoroastrians dominated Iran politically and formed the majority of the population of the country outside Mesopotamia, then still part of the Iranian empire. The end of their religious and cultural hegemony after 634 made their situation at first similar to that of Jews and Christians. However, not long after Arab rule had been established, they were gradually removed from positions of influence and a century of strife ensued in Iran between Arabs and Iranians.

The Jews and the Christians, who had experience of living as minorities, were able to survive the change of power and maintained their presence in political circles. The Muslim rulers still relied on these communities for administering their lands, not always because the Muslims lacked the necessary skills, but more because the Jews and the Christians were dependent on their patrons due to their fragile minority status. There were professions, however, in which the Jews and the Christians excelled. Since the Sassanian period, the Christian academic centre of Gundishapur produced the most renowned physicians of Iran. There were also outstanding scholars among the religious minorities who provided the Islamic world with their knowledge of philosophy and science. After all, the non-Muslims were the offspring of ancient civilizations and guardians of knowledge to which Muslims desired access. They were not simply a wretched persecuted minority, as the traditional view has depicted, but were rather partners in the creation of a new civilization, called Islamic in the Modern Period.

It is a fact that, due to the virtual extinction of Zoroastrianism, not much is known about the activities of Zoroastrians between the 9th century and the Mongol invasion, except from the apocalyptic literature produced in the 10th century. However, there are numerous materials on the involvement of Jews and especially Christians in the political and cultural life of the Muslim world. Many of the historians of Islam refer to this period as the Golden Age, which benefited all the inhabitants of the Islamic lands. One should not be misled by the term Golden Age and believe that Islamic rule was always congenial to Jews and Christians. After all, these minorities were not subscribing to the religion and ideology of the rulers and, consequently were not safeguarded against persecutions. Moreover, Islam was an assertive missionary religion which forbade the prerogatives of proselytization to other creeds. Muslim rulers found different means to entice non-Muslims to Islam. In peaceful times, the latter were offered economic benefits such as exemption from the poll-tax and political opportunities such as higher administrative positions; in times of crisis many non-Muslims were simply compelled to convert. The impact of this pressure on non-Muslims had, however, positive outcomes. It ignited in non-Muslims further ingenuity as they had to find means to avoid apostasy. This was not always an easy task; however the Jews and the Christians managed to remain close to the reins of the power and used their influence to protect their community. Thanks to their skills in governing empires and their knowledge of the sciences and humanities they were able to earn the respect of the Muslim ruling classes. Throughout the reign of the Abbasid caliphs, the number and influence of the non-Muslims gradually waned, until the Mongol invasion gave them an unexpected opportunity to recover positions of authority.

The first section of this chapter depicts the political and cultural changes that affected the Iranian population between the Arab invasion and the establishment of the Abbasid dynasty in 750. It observes the elements that led to uprisings in Iran and which precipitated the transformation of the social pattern of Iran due to massive conversions to Islam. This is important for understanding the eclipse of Zoroastrians from political spheres and the lack of evidence on their cultural activities after the 9th century. Following a brief discussion of the emergence of Muslim Iranian dynasties, this chapter surveys the early political involvements of Iranian Jews and Christians under the Abbasids and investigates the elements that caused the loss of vitality in the Christian and Jewish communities before the Mongol invasion. Finally, this chapter examines the cultural activities of the Jews and Christians and assesses their cultural dynamism, which often benefited Islamic society.

1) Non-Muslims in Early Islamic Iran: Golden Age or Decline?

The Arab invasion brought abruptly to an end the religious domination of Zoroastrianism in Iran and instituted Islam as the official religion of the state. This invasion was certainly less challenging for the Jews and the Christians than for the Zoroastrians. They had lived as minorities under the Sassanians, and remained as such under Arab rule. The fact that the Jews and Christians had been religious minorities does not, however, mean that they were not affected by the change of rulers. The new nomadic masters of their land were culturally very different from the sedentary Iranians, and their religion, Islam, which regulated many of the Arabs' laws and customs, was again quite different from that of the Zoroastrian Sassanians. There have been debates on whether the Jews and Christians preferred the Arabs to the Iranians or on whether their situation improved under Arab rule,[97] but in fact all of the arguments are based on assumptions. The Jews and the Christians, as far as historical sources attest, did not collaborate more with the Arabs than did the Zoroastrians themselves.[98]

The impact of Islam on the non-Muslim population was to be felt more in the long term. Indeed, in the two centuries that followed the Arab invasion, the bulk of the Iranian population remained non-Muslim. The numerical superiority of Zoroastrians in the 7th century allowed them even to maintain positions of influence. The Arabs needed their assistance for the administration of their newly conquered lands,[99] and until the 8th century Zoroastrian bureaucrats outnumbered Jewish and Christian administrators to the East of the Euphrates.

Before 661, the Zoroastrian Iranians and the Muslim Arabs were still in a state of war. Entire regions had to be reconquered and subdued, until the Iranians resigned themselves to Arab rule.[100] It is only with the accession of the Umayyads to the throne that the participation of the Zoroastrians in the political infrastructure of the Islamic world becomes apparent. The enrolment of Zoroastrians in the administration of the country and the attitude of Mu'awiya (661-680), the first Umayyad caliph, towards non-Muslims leads us to believe that the Arabs kept more or less the existing local laws and adopted 'the Sassanian solution'[101] towards religious indifference. John bar Penkaye, a Mesopotamian monk of the late 680s noted that 'there was no distinction between pagan and Christian; the believer was not known from a Jew.'[102] He even complained about the free activities of heresies.[103]

It was in the interest of the Arabs to maintain the previous Sassanian order, and to use the local population for governing the country. Those who were a source of revenue were not to be harmed, as in the past Muhammad had sent a letter to Ala b. Abdallah, urging him to come to terms with the Magians, Jews and Christians of Bahrain so that they would pay taxes and 'save the Muslims the trouble of work.'[104] In the first century of Muslim rule, there could have been hardly any Muslim involvement in economic activities in Iran. The Muslim population was composed of Arab military men and some converted Persian soldiers and governors, who had agreed to collaborate with the former. It was incumbent on the towns to bear the tax burden and support the Muslims.[105] The caliph Umar b. al-Khattab, who had led the Arabs in their conquest of Iran, allegedly said: 'The bedouin who are the original Arabs and the mainstay of Islam (...) not a single dinar should be taken from them, nor even a dirham.'[106] Umar wished to keep the Arabs as a conquering, military caste who would live on the toil of conquered races; he had also decreed that no Arab could ever be a slave.[107]

The sources substantiate the fact that the Zoroastrians were encouraged to stay in the government.[108] The Caliph Sulayman (d. 717 AD) allegedly said one day: 'I admire these Persians; they reigned for one thousand years and never, not for one hour, did they stand in need of us; we ruled for 100 years and not for one hour could we do without them.'[109] Until the mid-eighth century, the leading positions in the administration seem to have been dominated by the same Zoroastrian families who had been involved in the Sassanian government earlier in the 7th century. Baladhuri mentions that in 698, the Zoroastrian Zadan Farrukh was at the head of the treasury in the East of the caliphate.[110] We also know from another source that his father, Piruz, had occupied the same position before him.[111] However, after ruling Iran for more than half a century, the Arabs believed that it was time for them to secure their cultural hegemony. As the Arabs dominated Iran politically, the change of the administrative language from Persian to Arabic was inevitable. Zadan Farrukh believed rightly that the new policy could only be detrimental to his family and co-religionists. He prevented his assistant Salih b. Abd al-Rahman, whose father had abandoned Zoroastrianism, from translating the records into Arabic. Zadan

Farrukh's position irreconcilable with the Arabs' political goals cost him his life in 698. Salih, with the blessing of the Arab governor, Hajjaj b. Yusuf, was able then to implement his plans for Arabicization. Distraught at such consequential measures, the son of Zadan Farrukh, Mardanshah, told Salih, 'May God efface thy trace from the worlds as thou hast effaced the trace of Persian.' The Zoroastrians tried to bribe Salih with 100,000 dirhams so that he would not continue his task, but he refused.[112]

In Iraq and some parts of the Iranian Plateau the Zoroastrians were dismissed from prominent positions. The Zoroastrian, Dadoye, who was responsible for collecting the taxes of Iraq and Fars under Hajjaj b. Yusuf, was also ousted at this time.[113] In the East of Iran changes appeared more slowly. Zoroastrians were still acting as local governors. Bahramis, the *marzuban* (governor) of Merv, was confirmed in his position in 723, during the reign of Yazid II. He ruled for the benefit of his community by exempting the Zoroastrians of Khurasan from taxes and putting the fiscal burden on the Muslims.[114] As could be expected, the Muslims with the help of the Arab authorities reversed the situation. It is striking, however, that the tax collectors named in the 7th and early 8th centuries by the Arab governors were overwhelmingly Zoroastrian.[115] Those Iranians who had converted were not acceptable for such positions, as they could have claimed an equal share in power. The Arabs did not trust the newly converted people and deemed it safer to nominate non-Muslims, who, according to Islam, were inferior to Muslims and hence had no right to claim ascendancy over them.[116]

In 741, however, the Umayyads decreed that non-Muslims be excluded from governmental positions.[117] The edict induced numerous government officers to convert in order to maintain their means of livelihood. A well-known figure who was affected by the discriminatory law was Dadoye's son, Ruzbih, better known as Ibn Muqaffa. He also converted to Islam in order to secure for himself a position in the administration, and after the victory of the Abbasids he entered the service of the Caliph al-Saffah (750-754). He was killed in 757, accused of practising Zoroastrianism in secret.[118] In Khurasan and most parts of the Iranian Plateau, the registers remained in Persian for about half a century longer than in Iraq, and the majority of the secretaries of the *divan* (or bureaucracy) were Zoroastrian until Yusuf b. Umar, governor of Iraq, wrote to Nasr b. Sayyar, the governor of Khurasan, to oust the Zoroastrians from the *divan*. Ishaq b. Tolayq translated the registers of Khurasan to Arabic in 741-742 AD.[119] The language of Isfahan's administration remained Persian, even after the fall of the Umayyads, until Abu Muslim's officials had Persian substitued by Arabic in the early Abbasid period.[120]

The pressure put on Zoroastrians does not appear to have been felt by the Christians. The latter were even able to continue spreading their religion among the Iranians. Their positions as physicians of the caliphs helped their cause. John of Daylam (724-743), after healing the daughter of the caliph Marwan II, received gold for the construction of two monasteries and one church in the province of Fars, where the population was mainly Zoroastrian. He was also permitted to conduct missionary activities in Daylam and Fars.[121]

Towards the end of the Umayyad period, the Arabs were well-established in Iran.[122] They had dominated the country for nearly a century and had had time to acquire the skills needed to rule effectively. The Arabization of the country's administration and culture had made the Iranians less indispensable to the government. Such a situation created discontent among Iranians.

The Abbasid revolution was the result of mounting hostility towards the ruling classes in Iran. While the situation of non-Muslims had deteriorated, the position of Iranian *mawalis* (converts) had not improved. Many of the Arabs who lived in Iran were also disaffected by Umayyad rule and supported the Abbasid movement. The aspirations of the Abbasids, however, was not compatible with the expectations of the non-Muslim Iranians. Once in power, the Abbasids also alienated the Iranians who had converted to Islam. Indeed, the majority of the Iranians enrolled in the government were Zoroastrians newly converted to Islam, but their background still made them suspicious in the eyes of the Arabs. The fact that Ibn Muqaffa was killed in 757, accused of practising Zoroastrianism in private, reflects the deterioration of the relations between Arabs and Iranians in the 8th century.

2) **The Eclipse of Zoroastrianism in Iran: The Iranian uprisings of the 8th and 9th centuries**

The reader of the Iranian history is usually intrigued by the sudden disappearance of Zoroastrians from the historical scene and the sudden conversion of Iran to Islam. Indeed, as Iran is integrated into the Islamic realm, we hear less about the activities of the Zoroastrians and even less about their participation in the government of the new Muslim empire, while on the other hand the Jews and Christians remain prominent in the political spheres. The fading of the Zoroastrians from the historical annals should not be interpreted as a sign of their passivity and inferiority to Jews and Christians. Rather, their sudden change of fortune should be questioned, as a people who skilfully dominated an immense empire and influenced the culture of so many societies could not have left the historical scene without a struggle.

The political turmoils of the 8th and 9th centuries are very informative as regards the fate of the Zoroastrians whose population dwindled soon after. The historian of Islam is generally focussed on the Abbasid revolution and not preoccupied by the other uprisings that occurred in Iran at this time, as none of the other movements had a long lasting effect on the entire Islamic world; however, as far as Iran and Central Asia are concerned, all these uprisings were determinant in reshaping the religious patterns of these lands. Some authors have tried to deny the ethnic dimension of these movements, while on the other hand, there are others who have overstated their 'nationalist' nature. In fact there was a mixture of factors behind these uprisings. There were social and economic motives, as Madelung has pointed out;[123] and historical sources lead us to believe there was a degree of anti-Arab and anti-Islamic sentiment behind these movements as well.

As we saw, the Arab rulers had adopted a number of radical measures for the Arabization and Islamification of Iran which created disaffection among the Iranian population. As Bulliet's study demonstrates, only a small proportion of Iranians had converted to Islam on the eve of the Abbasid revolution;[124] as a result, the new policies of the Muslims in the 8th century had had a drastic impact on the non-Muslim population, still the majority in Iran. At this time, the population of northern Khurasan was particularly rebellious. The damage caused by the Muslim conquerors in the area was considerable and still fresh in the memory of the local people who had been forced to accept Islam and who, despite their conversion were still forced to pay large tributes.[125]

It is therefore not surprising that the dissident movements began in Khurasan before spreading westwards. The earliest of these movements commenced concurrently with the Abbasid revolution and was led by Bihafrid Mahfravardan. There has been a long debate over the religion of the insurgents; however, in the case of Bihafrid Mahfravardan there is no doubt of his being Zoroastrian.[126] The opposition of the conservative Zoroastrian clergy to his political and social activities shows that Bihafrid adhered to another faction of the Zoroastrian Church. Abu

Muslim, the famous leader of the Abbasid revolution was able to take advantage of the divisions among the Zoroastrians to kill Bihafrid two years before the fall of the Umayyads.

The successes of Abu Muslim against the unpopular Umayyads had won him allies not only among the Muslim minority but also among the Zoroastrian majority, who hoped for an improvement of their condition. Abu Muslim, however, did not provide the Zoroastrians with much option other than conversion to Islam.[127] The involuntary nature of these conversion becomes manifest right after the death of Abu Muslim in 754,[128] when there was a surge in apostasies and revolts in Iran.

One of the most famous apostates is Sunbad. He also emerged from Khurasan and won the support of Tabaristan's Zoroastrian *Ispahbad* (governor-prince) Khurshid, along with numerous supporters in Khurasan and even further west on the Iranian plateau.[129] Despite having a bigger support base than Bihafrid Mahfravardan, Sunbad was defeated by the Abbasids at the hands of an Iranian convert (Jahwar b. Marrar), and his ally Khurshid had to bear the reprisals of Muslim forces.[130] As Sunbad had the blessing of a prince like Khurshid, the conservative Zoroastrian classes could have hardly distanced themselves from his movement. Thus, all Zoroastrian factions were henceforth caught in a whirlpool and became suspicious in the eyes of the Muslim rulers.

It was in Transoxania that non-Muslim leaders were most successful in destabilizing the Abbasid government and rallying local rulers. Three movements in the region were important enough to appear in the chronicles. The first movement was led by a man of Turkish ethnicity referred to as Ishaq. Zoroastrianism was widely spread in Transoxania both among the Iranians and the Turkish groups who had settled among them.[131] It is not surprising therefore that Ishaq demonstrated a great attachment to Zoroastrianism and claimed to have been appointed as a prophet by Zarathushtra.[132] Ishaq was killed by the Abbasids sometime between 756-758, but his movement was continued by a certain Baraz, who had been able to win the support of the governor of Khurasan.[133]

None of the preceding movements, however, attained the popularity of that of Ustadhsis, which shook the eastern part of the caliphate in 765. His insurrection was significant enough to be mentioned in the manuscripts of a significant number of medieval Muslim historians.[134] The size of this uprising had also attracted the attention of Christian chroniclers. Elias of Nisibis and Bar Hebraeus, who wrote quite some time after the event, have portrayed it as a very important Zoroastrian movement.[135] That the Muslim historians were interested in relating a story that shook the foundations of their Empire is not surprising; however, it is of note that of all the Zoroastrian insurrections which occurred in this period, this is the only one covered by the Christian chroniclers. The insurrection is important not only for its magnitude and the number of people slaughtered in it,[136] but also because Ustadhsis' was supported by both the conservative and innovative Zoroastrians of his region. This explains the reason he has not been labelled a Khurramdin or a heretic of another sort. This was the last time a Zoroastrian led such a vast and movement in eastern Iran.

The last of these three movements was led by a certain Hashim b. Hakim al-Muqanna. The sources depicted Muqanna as a non-Zoroastrian, but he was successful in winning the support of Bunyat, the Zoroastrian ruler of Bukhara. Muqanna's religion is unknown; however there are several interesting features regarding Muqanna and his movement. Although Muqanna's father, like Sunbad and Ishaq, had been an important supporter of Abu Muslim, his religious affiliation is also uncertain. Moreover, the description that is given of Muqanna's religion is very similar to that of the Khurramdins: we are told that he perverted people and encouraged men to share their wives between them.[137] It is therefore not surprising to read that the Khurramdins were also supporting Muqanna. These extremely negative representations of Muqanna's party and the Khurramdins do not appear veracious, but the desire to slander them demonstrates that the rulers perceived them as a significant threat. Moreover, the fact that Muqanna was not adhering to one of the traditional religions of Transoxania and yet had obtained so much support in the region, evinces only the eagerness of the local inhabitants to expel the Muslims from their territories.[138] Muqanna was executed in 783, and Bunyat a year later, for having apostatized and opposed the Muslims.[139]

By this time, the uprising had spread to the west of Iran, under the leadership of the Khurramdins. The endurance and recurrence of the Khurramdins' activities has distinguished them from the other popular movements of the period. Their movement had had time to spread all over Iran among the lower social classes. Like the previous dissident movements they rose in Khurasan. Their name appears in the Islamic historiography for the first time in 736, but their political activities become more manifest after the death of Abu Muslim in 754. Their movement spread in Gurgan and the regions between Rayy and Isfahan, and then finally to Azerbaijan when Babak appeared on the scene in 816.[140]

The most famous and charismatic leader of the Khurramdins was indisputably Babak. Babak's family belonged to the wave of Iranians who, due to the social and political pressures of the time, had turned Muslim, and who had seen the death of Abu Muslim and the successive uprisings as an opportunity to apostatize. Babak's forsaking of his Arabic name,[141] and taking of a Persian one, confirms his apostasy, as it was a common practice for those who changed religions to signal their new identity by adopting a new name. The tenacity of Babak's militancy, along with the outstanding support he received in Iran, made the Khurramdin's movement even more important then the preceding Iranian uprisings. For about twenty years Babak's legions remained victorious against the caliphate's army. Even Abdallah b. Tahir, the governor of Khurasan, feared Babak, and declined the governorship of Azerbaijan, as it was the centre of Babak's operation.[142]

Considering the religious composition of the Iranian plateau in the early 9th century, and the pervasiveness of the Khurramdin movement, the great majority, if not all of the Khurramdin militants were of Zoroastrian background. Their misidentification as Mazdakis, and the popularity of the movement among people of modest social classes[143], supports Madelung's argument that the Khurramdins belonged to the 'Low Church' of Zoroastrianism.[144] Babak's popularity among the Iranians prompted the Abbasids to chose an Iranian prince, Afshin as the governor of Azerbaijan. This was an attempt to legitimize their position in the eyes of the local inhabitants.[145] Afshin held discourses on his attachment to Iran and Zoroastrianism in order to acquire the allegiance of the people. Afshin's authority over Western Iran had for the Muslims the desired result. In 835, the battle ended disastrously for Babak's militants with a death toll surpassing the defeat of Ustadhsis. Babak's capture afflicted many.[146] Those among his partisans who survived fled to Byzantium,[147] or went into hiding. The Khurramdins manifested themselves a few other times until 913 but they were militarily exhausted and were not able to destabilize the caliphate again.[148] They participated on the side of Byzantines in their war against the Arabs in 838; however, their leader was killed and their name disappeared from the historical annals. Babak's defeat put a *de facto* end to the Iranian revolts 'conducted in the name of the old national religion'.[149]

The Abbasids still had to conquer Tabaristan where the ruler had nominally converted to Islam and his subjects were Zoroastrian.[150] After the crushing of the insurrections in Khurasan and the uprisings in Western Iran, Maziyar, the Ispahbad of Tabaristan, could no longer hope for succour from any Iranian militants as his province was surrounded by the Muslim forces of the Caliph. Maziyar was captured and killed,[151] and not long afterwards Afshin was also executed as his allegiance to the caliphate was uncertain and his sincere conversion to Islam dubious.[152]

Although the suppression of the insurrections of the 8th and 9th centuries played an immense role in the dwindling of the Zoroastrian population under the Abbasids, there were canonical reasons based on the Quran which contributed further to the marginalization and decline of Zoroastrian communities. The Quran clearly distinguished Jews and Christians from other religious groups and granted them a special status or *dhimma*[153] which it extended only to Sabians. Zoroastrians were only mentioned once, in *Sura* 22.17, only being discerned from idolaters. They thus had an ambiguous status in the eyes of the Arabs and therefore their position had to be negotiated. If at the beginning of the Arab conquest the Zoroastrians were treated similarly to Jews and Christians, their massive conversion in the 9th century demonstrates that the *dhimma* did not always apply to them. I will not expand further on the significance of the *dhimma* as Fattal and Tritton have discussed the matter in detail.[154] It is just worth mentioning that in a number of Islamic schools, the *Maliki*, the *Shafi'i*, and the *Hanbali*, the value of a Zoroastrian's life (or the price of his blood) was less than 1/4 of that of a Christian or a Jew.[155] The vulnerability of the Zoroastrians under Abbasid rule, combined with their failure to regain power, explains why Iran yielded to Islam in the 9th century, changing the religious pattern of the country.

Some time after the elimination of these 'Zoroastrian' movements and the execution of their leaders, the high priest of Fars Adurbad-i Emedan (late 9th c.- 10th c.) wrote: 'The state of affairs now evident is indicative of how Iranian rule has come to an end in the country of Iran.' Accepting the inevitability of their decline, the Zoroastrians plunged themselves into the writing of apocalyptic literature, trying to explain historical change while encouraging the steadfastness of those who chose to remain Zoroastrian.[156] This marked the eradication of Zoroastrians from most public spheres, while the Jews and the Christians still found opportunities at the court and in the caliphate's administration, although the Christians and the Jews were not shielded from Muslim pressure. This is evinced by the appearance of Jewish apocalyptic literature at that time, lamenting the end of the reign of Sassanian kings, who they believed had been good to them, and spurning the Arabs and their prophet for disrespecting them:

> I, Daniel, I saw that in their days there was to arise a king of small stature and red hue. He will have no fortune and will not consider the scripture of the Lord. He will take for himself the title of prophet. He will go forth and come upon a camel and will be a camel driver. He will come from the South and call the men to worship him. Much evil will come from him to the Israelites. Among the Israelites some will go over to his religion and his law.[157]

Similar pressure was felt by the Christians after the reign of al-Ma'mun. Thus, the Christian chronicler Zuqnin recorded in the late 8th century that Christians from the regions of Edessa, Harran, Tella, Resh'aina, Dara, Nisibis, Shengar and Callinicum went en masse to the governor at Harran and converted to Islam. The stories of martyrdom become once again the main preoccupation of Christian literature.[158]

It is noteworthy that the merciless persecution of *Zindiqs*, Manicheans and other non-Zoroastrian Iranian religious groups also began at this time. Until the Abbasid period, the Arabs seem to have treated all non-Muslim groups alike and those heretic Iranian sects which had been persecuted under the Sassanians had enjoyed a century of respite. However, the increase in pseudo-Zoroastrian uprisings in Iran and the popularity of heretic Iranian religions generated a sense of insecurity in Arab circles. As a result, the Arabs more actively suppressed these groups in order to maintain order and peace in their dominion.

The Jews and Christians were certainly affected by the socio-political upheavals that occurred in Iran at this period, although not as much as the Zoroastrians. Their activities in the government do not appear to have suffered until the reign of the Caliph al-Mutawakkil, who in 849 decided to impose restrictions on non-Muslims. Mutawakkil sat on the throne shortly after the tenacious Zoroastrian (or neo-Zoroastrian) uprisings, which were not completely overcome. These revolts, along with the constant wars with the Byzantines, were good reasons to turn al-Mutawakkil against non-Muslims. In addition to imposing dress codes and social restrictions, he prohibited the employment of non-Muslims in government offices, and ordered their dismissal from any position in which their authority could be exercised over Muslims.[159]

Nevertheless, after the reign of al-Mutawakkil, Jews and Christians continued to be hired by caliphs, viziers and governors, whereas Zoroastrians were not trusted to hold positions.

3) The Emergence of Muslim Iranian Dynasties

By the time the Iranian dynasties rose to power, the socio-religious atmosphere in Iran had completely changed. As Bulliet rightly remarked, without the support of Muslim Iranians these dynasties would have never been able to dominate territories in Iran, as neither non-Muslims nor Muslim Arabs would have supported them. Therefore the majority of the Iranians in the late 9th century must have converted to Islam. Those Iranians who sought to attain power had to be very careful not to provoke the Arabs.[160] The Jews and Christians in Iran were not confronted with such a problem, apart from the Christians living next to the Byzantine borders. For nearly two centuries bitter confrontations had opposed Iranians to Arabs, and many of the rebellions had been instigated by insincere Iranian converts to Islam. The Arab establishment was very critical of the policies of the caliph al-Ma'mun, who granted high positions to Iranians. He had appointed Hasan b. Sahl governor of several provinces in Iran and Iraq, and had made his brother Fadl b. Sahl his vizier and advisor. The Arab notables compelled al-Ma'mun to replace Hasan b. Sahl with an Arab governor in 817, and his brother Fadl was assassinated a year later, probably by the same party. The slogan of the Arab opponents was: 'We won't accept the Zoroastrian, son of the Zoroastrian al-Hasan b. Sahl, and we'll drive him out until he returns to Khurasan.'[161]

The Tahirids, who were of Iranian background, had to demonstrate their loyalty to the Arabs and Islam. They did so by distancing themselves from their Iranian identity and assimilating themselves as much as possible to the Arabs, even fabricating Arabian genealogies for themselves. Nonetheless, in order to achieve legitimacy among the Iranian population, who, it should be remembered, was only recently converted and not always wholeheartedly, they claimed to be descendants of an ancient Iranian prince, Rustam-i Dastan.[162] Thus, four generations of Tahirids (between 821-873) were able to maintain their position as hereditary governors for the Abbasid caliphs. It is also noteworthy that the Tahirids were able to rise to power during the reign of al-Ma'mun, who was relatively Iranophile; the caliphs who followed him regarded Iranians with more suspicion. This became manifest in 833, when the Caliph al-Mu'tasim decided to put an end to the supremacy of Iranians in the caliphal army by appointing Turks as military officers.

The decision of the Caliph did not have an immediate impact on the south and eastern provinces of the Iranian Plateau, where in 873 the first Saffarid, Ya'qub b. al-Layth deposed the last Tahirid governor. The Saffarids were also Iranians and they were also careful not to question the spiritual authority of the Caliphs. The Saffarid rulers conquered new territories outside the realm of Islam, and always sent presents to the Abbasids from their plunder.[163] It is however alleged in the *Tarikh-i Sistan* that Ya'qub disapproved openly of the Abbasids, and that he believed that they had duped and killed many Iranian magnates who had showed their loyalty to them. He allegedly said, 'Haven't you seen what they did to Abu Salama, Abu Muslim, the Barmakid family[164] and Fadl b. Sahl, despite everything these men had done on the dynasty's behalf? Let no one ever trust them!'[165] In order to consolidate his position in Iran he appears to have slandered the Arab rulers of Baghdad and claimed falsely to be a descendant of the Sassanians.[166] In the year 900 the defeat of the Saffarid Amr b. al-Layth by Isma'il b. Ahmad near Balkh led to the rise of the Samanids, another Muslim Iranian dynasty in Khurasan. The Saffarids had ruled for about fifty years.

Now it was the turn of the Samanids to build themselves a reputation as descendants of Zoroastrian aristocrats, constructing a genealogy going back to Bahram Chubin.[167] The Samanids were the last Iranian ruling dynasty in Khurasan; the last Samanid was overthrown by the Qarakhanid Turks in 1005. In the West of Iran, another Muslim Iranian Dynasty, the Buyids, found the chance to seize power in 945 and rule for a century. Originally from Daylam, they rose to power after the intervention in Fars of Caliph al-Radi (934-940), who executed the province's leading Zoroastrian priest, Isfandiyar-i Aturpat, and removed Zoroastrian dignitaries from all positions of authority.[168] Up till then such incidents had been seldom recorded in Fars, but more often in Khurasan. This suggests that the population of the province of Fars was probably compelled to convert to Islam later than those of the eastern provinces of Iran. These conversions to Islam in the 9th and 10th centuries, albeit superficial, initially benefitted the Muslim Iranian dynasty of Buyids, as they then had a Muslim Iranian population to rely on, like the Tahirids and the Saffarids in eastern Iran. There are certainly other reasons for the political success of the Buyids and other Muslim Iranian dynasties of the period; however, they will not be discussed here as a further examination of this subject would be beyond the scope of this book.

4) **The Cultural Activities of Zoroastrians in Islamic Iran**

The concrete Islamification of Iran which occurred after the suppression of the Zoroastrian revolts of the 8th and 9th centuries undermined the cultural activities of Zoroastrians and even of those Iranians who had converted to Islam, but still clung to their Iranian heritage. Hardly any Zoroastrian family was able to avoid conversion to Islam when employed by the Abbasids. It is already surprising that Nawbakht, al-Mansur's famous astronomer (or astrologist), was allowed to serve the Caliph as a Zoroastrian. His son, however, had to accept Islam in order not to be dismissed.[169] As we mentioned earlier, any exhibition of Iranian identity in those moments of crisis was perceived by the ruling Arabs as a sign of protest against their domination. Therefore the Tahirids did not support any form of Iranian tradition. They clung to Arabic as the language of their administration, and the literary and historical productions extant from that period are all in Arabic. The Tahirids demonstrated themselves to be the defenders of Islam and Arab civilization and acted as patrons to Arab-speaking authors and musicians, such as Ali b. Jahm, Ishaq al-Mawsili, and Ibn al-Rumi.[170] Moreover according to Dawlatshah, Abdallah b. Tahir ordered that a copy of the Persian romance *Vamiq-u Adhra* be destroyed and then commanded that all the Persian and Zoroastrian books found in his territories be burnt.[171] This anecdote sounds plausible, and Abdallah b. Tahir was probably not the only Muslim ruler to demonstrate his disapproval of 'Zoroastrian' cultural materials during that period. As a result many of the literary works written in Pahlavi disappeared.

     Nonetheless, the other Iranian dynasties that followed were not as radical as the Tahirids. As the power of the Arab rulers had waned considerably, the political situation allowed the Persian language to return to the surface, though we have to wait until the Mongol period for Persian to achieve a truly official status and supersede Arabic in Iran.[172] During this period the inability of the Saffarid governor, Ya'qub, to understand Arabic prompted the people at the court of Sistan to use Persian. There is a revealing episode during which Ya'qub had an Arabic poem addressed to him translated into Persian.[173] His successor, Amr b. al-Layth, took into his offices Persians, many of whom appear to be

Zoroastrian, or at least bear non-Muslim names.[174] Such is the case of Shapur b. Azadmard, whom Amr made his assistant and responsible for his treasury and administration in 889.[175] The Saffarids encouraged the Persian language and we are told that the poet Rudaki, who praised the Saffarid ruler Ahmad (923-963) as 'that foremost one amongst the nobles and the pride of Iran (...) just king and sun of the age (...) from the glowing orb of the stock of Sasan,' received a present of 10,000 dinars.[176]

The resurgence of the Persian language in Arabic script does not seem to have affected the Zoroastrians at this period. They were preoccupied with the rapid decline of their population especially after the defeat of the Zoroastrian uprisings in the 9th century. They continued to write in the old Pahlavi script. Not all the manuscripts bearing dates from the 9th and 10th centuries were truly produced at this period. Many of them were simply recopied. However, a series of didactic and religious literary works was written by the Zoroastrians after the Arab invasion. One of the most best-known Zoroastrian authors of this period is Aturfarnbag i Farrukhzatan. He composed his works, *Dinkard* and *Ewen Namag*, during the reign of al-Ma'mun (813-833), when Iran was in a state of social turbulence and the fate of Zoroastrianism was at stake. Aturfarnbag was concerned with preserving the Zoroastrian religion and cultural heritage, because the number of priests were diminishing apace and the religious sources were becoming scarce.[177] A descendant of his, Manuschihr-i Goshn-Yam wrote the *Dadistan-i Denig* around 850. In this book he compiled a series of answers to religious questions concerning laws which were no longer properly observed. Manuschihr was the head of the Zoroastrian community of Fars and Kirman, which appear to have been.[178] His nephew took over his seat early in the 10th century and left behind a tractate known as the *Rivayat of Emet -i Ashavahishtan*. His writings are concerned with the contacts between Zoroastrians and non-Zoroastrians, which was one of the principal dilemmas of the community. The topic is recurrent in the majority of Zoroastrian texts such as the *Dinkard*.

The third *Dinkard*, which was written by Aturpat-i Emetan, is the most important Zoroastrian collection extant today. It discusses, among other topics, marriage, medicine and other religions which the author refutes. The last significant literature known from this period is the *Shkand Gumanik Vicar*. The author of the book is a certain Martan Farrux-i Ohrmazddatan. He refers in his treatise to Zoroastrian authors of the 9th century, therefore he most probably wrote his volume in the 10th century. Like most of the treatises produced by Zoroastrians in this period, the *Shkand Gumanik Vicar* was devoted to didactic and polemical debates. Martan Farrux defends Zoroastrianism against Judaism, Christianity, and especially Islam, which was the most serious threat to the 'Good Religion'.[179]

The emergence of Classical Persian did not leave much of a readership for Pahlavi (or Middle Persian), in which these texts were written. These were the last attempts of the Zoroastrian clergy to record their cultural heritage in Pahlavi, as there were fewer and fewer people able to read the difficult script. Although the Zoroastrian scholars did not adopt the Arabic script for writing their texts until the 10th century, they did participate in works of translation like the Jews and the Christians. Not many names have been recorded, but Ibn al-Nadim has provided us with some names, such as Zadwayh b. Shahwayh al-Isfahani and Bahram b. Mardanshah (high priest of Nishapur), who translated treatises from Middle Persian into Arabic.[180]

Unlike the Jews and Christians, Zoroastrians did not feel compelled to record all the aspects of their history. As Muslim Iranians considered themselves also heirs of Zoroastrianism and pre-Islamic Iran, they produced literature relevant to both Muslims and Zoroastrians. Many treatises were produced by first and second generation Muslims of Zoroastrian background like Ibn Muqaffa (720-756) and Ibn Khurdadbih (820-912). Ibn Muqaffa, to whom we referred earlier, is a very good example of a Zoroastrian apostate who provided the Arabo-Islamic civilization with some of its most celebrated literary works, by translating from Middle Persian into Arabic the *Kalila wa Dimna* and the *Khudai-nama* (*Siyar Muluk al-Ajam*). He wrote in Arabic *Al-Durra al-Yatima fi Ta'at al-Muluk* and *Al-Adab al-Saghir*.[181] Thanks to his *Kitab al-Masalik wa'l-Mamalik*, Ibn Khurdadbih made available to the Arab speaking world a wide range of material from Persian sources. We know that he also held an important office in the Abbasid government, like his father before him.[182] Certainly, Ibn Muqaffa and Ibn Khurdadbih were not the only ones in whose literary accomplishments Zoroastrian cultural influence has been detected; however, they are probably the best examples of the new converts who acted as a medium between their Iranian heritage and the new Islamic creed established in their land.

Many of the Muslim poets and historians of this period needed the collaboration of fellow Zoroastrians who still had the knowledge of Pahlavi scripture, for deciphering older manuscripts in order to accomplish their own work. There were references to literary works in Pahlavi literature such as the *Jamasp-nama* and *Zarathusht-nama* written in

978 by a Zoroastrian author of Rayy named Kaykavus Kaykhusraw. Around the same time the illustrious Abu al-Qasim Firdawsi began writing his *Shah-nama*. As some of their themes overlap, there is a chance that they used similar sources.[183] Likewise the *Tarikh-i Sistan*, which was written at a later period (between the 11th and the 14th century), draws on many legends and stories from Zoroastrian books, and moreover, one of the authors of the book makes use of the Zoroastrian calendar for dating the events he recorded.[184] Therefore there was clearly an interaction between Iranian Muslim and Zoroastrian scholars, especially after the Saffarid period during which an interest in the Persian language and history had been fostered.

In the 11th century a number of poets and writers were inspired by stories from Pahlavi literature and transposed them into Classical Persian or Arabic. Many stories were related to the wisdom of Khusraw Anushiravan, such as the *Rahat al-Insan* and the *Khirad-nama*.[185] An even more renowned book of advice written at this period is the *Qabus-nama* of Kaykavus b. Iskandar (1080). Kaykavus was the penultimate Ziarid reigning prince of the Caspian provinces, but he had virtually no authority. He acted, like his predecessors, as a tributary to the rulers of Khurasan. The encroachment of the Saljuk Turks on Iran and the Caspian provinces had incited Kaykavus to set on paper the counsels from Pahlavi literature in order to preserve his Iranian heritage. This *Qabus-nama* is one of the earliest specimens of *andarz* (collection of advice left for posterity) in Classical Persian.[186]

Undoubtedly, political factors had repercussions on the literary productions of this period. The unsuccessful Iranian uprisings in the 8th and 9th centuries prompted the anxious Zoroastrian clergy to produce a corpus of literature for posterity; meanwhile the emergence of Iranian Muslim dynasties encouraged Muslim Iranians to take over the literature left by the Zoroastrians and develop their own version of Iranian culture. Indeed, the Saffarids and the Samanids, unlike the Tahirids, were not averse to Zoroastrianism and Iranian civilization. There are no testimonies regarding Saffarid and Samanid persecutions of Zoroastrians. Moreover the first Saffarids seem to have had no strong religious feelings.[187] On the other hand, they had no strong national impulse to support Zoroastrianism. As Amir Siddiqi argued, 'The revolt of Saffarids against the Abbasid Caliphate was not a Persian revolt against Arab domination'. In fact the Saffarids fought other Iranians for political supremacy. Moreover, the Samanids were not able to rally any Iranian national support for their battle against the Turkish Khans.[188] It is most certainly the fall of these Muslim Iranian dynasties that put an end to the cultural activities of the Zoroastrians. The Turkish Ghaznavids who seized power after them, despite their adopting many Iranian traditions and Persian as the language of their administration, had no nostalgia for pre-Islamic Iran and no attachment to an Iranian national identity; their authority depended on Turkish military force and a highly Arabicized Islamic literary establishment in the towns. These factors are probably behind the indifference of the the first Ghaznavid ruler, Mahmud towards Firdawsi's *Shah-nama*.[189]

5) Active and Influential Minorities: The Jews and Christians in Islamic Iran

The major handicap of Zoroastrians under the Arab dynasties was their link to Iranian national identity. They had dominated Iran numerically and politically for more than a thousand years. The Muslim Arabs who had had to fight them for the domination of the Iranian Plateau, considered them dangerous rivals. In the early days of their rule, the Arabs accepted Zoroastrian administrators and viziers of Zoroastrian background in their government, but after the uprisings in Iran, the only non-Muslims they relied on belonged to the Jewish or Christian faith.

This was not the case before the Abbasid revolution. The war with Christian Byzantium continued long after the defeat of the Zoroastrian Sassanians. This hostility between Muslim Arabs and Christian Byzantines caused the persecution of Christians who were suspected of allegiance to the Byzantines. Adam Mez points out that the condition of Christians under the Umayyads was even less favourable than that of the Zoroastrians and the Jews.[190] The Zoroastrian and Jewish leaders enjoyed hereditary nobility and were called kings.[191] The two communities paid their taxes to their respective leaders; this was not, however, the case for Christians. In 695 Hajjaj b. Yusuf had also forbidden the election of a Catholicos, and the seat remained empty for more than 18 years.[192] On one occasion, the patriarch of the Jacobites lamented to the Caliph that in contrast to the chiefs of the Zoroastrians and Jews, who were temporal sovereigns, he was only a spiritual leader.[193]

With the advent of the Abbasids and the transfer of the government from Syria to Mesopotamia, the policy of the Muslim Arabs towards Christians changed. As the Nestorians outnumbered the Jacobites and the Melkites in that part of the caliphate, their patriarch was chosen as the head of all Christians, just as under the Sassanians. Because of their historical animosity towards the Byzantines, they were trusted and their leader was granted the same temporal powers as those of Zoroastrian and Jewish leaders. The Jacobites and Melkites were dismayed by the caliph's decision. The relation between the different Christian communities was far from cordial and the ascendancy of a Nestorian patriarch over other Christians occasionally generated abuses. It was probably due to his influence that in 912 the Caliph al-Muqtadir forbade the patriarch of the Jacobites to live in Baghdad.[194]

The presence of Nestorians in the Abbasid government was not surprising. They had been present in the Sassanian court, and they composed at the beginning of the Abbasid period the largest community in Mesopotamia.[195] As the Abbasids had chosen the former centre of Sassanian government, they recruited Nestorians for administering their empire.[196]

These administrators were not hired wholeheartedly, as from the outset the Caliph al-Mansur (754-775) was pressurized to dismiss Christians along with the Jews. One of his dignitaries, Shabib b. Shayba, dissuaded him from such an action. He explained to the Caliph that the Christians were too influential and could as such cause trouble to the Muslims if they were dismissed all together. He advised al-Mansur to remove them gradually by dismissing a small number of them every day.[197]

The physicians of the court were not affected by this policy. Not only al-Mansur, but practically all the caliphs who followed him on the throne used Christian physicians. Al-Mansur summoned Georges son of Gabriel of the Bokhtisho family to Baghdad. He went there in 765, with two of his pupils, Ibrahim and Isa b. Shalutha, entrusting the direction of the hospital of Gundishapur to his son Bokhtisho.[198] After Georges, his son Bokhtisho, followed by his grandson Gabriel (II), became physicians at the court. The latter was at first the private physician of the influential Barmakid vizier and then served Harun al-Rashid, al-Amin and al-Ma'mun.[199] Thus began the Bokhtisho dynasty of physicians, which lasted more than three centuries. None of the Muslim viziers and governors were able to establish such a long-lasting dynasty. The Caliph al-Mansur also had a Jewish physician, named Farat b. Shahta, and he too, we are told, was very much trusted by the Caliph. We do not know if he was granted the same amount of power over his co-religionists as was Isa b. Shalutha. Nonetheless he acted as an advisor to the Caliph, and was in a position to influence him in his political decisions.[200]

The importance of the court physicians' office and that of the Catholicos not only caused confrontations with the Muslim officials, but also generated rivalry among Christians. During the reign of the Caliph al-Saffah, Surin, the Metropolitan of Nisibis, and Ya'qub, the Nestorian Metropolitan of Gundishapur, coveted the seat of the catholicate. Surin plundered the Churches of their wealth and handed it to Aban, the governor of Mada'in in order to obtain his support. Because of this, he only occupied the seat of the Patriarch for 51 days before he was removed by the Caliph al-Saffah, who had been informed of this abuse. The Caliph then gave the seat to Ya'qub (753-773). Nonetheless, Surin did not give up; he was nominated Metropolitan of Basra, and from there he tried to recover his position as patriarch, which he was able to regain for short intervals.[201]

Rivalries did not allow his successors Hnanisho II (775-779), and Georges (779)[202] to enjoy their positions as Catholicos long. They were both murdered. The seat of the catholicate was then occupied by one of the most energetic and powerful figures of Nestorian history. Timothy I (780-823) was different from his predecessors. Although he had to face the malevolence of some of his co-religionists, such as Joseph Metropolitan of Merv, his dynamism and social skills earned him the support of the Caliph al-Mahdi (775-785) and powerful Christians, such as the Bokhtisho physicians and Abu Nuh al-Anbari b. al-Salt, the Christian secretary of the governor of Mosul.[203] Timothy assured the Caliph of the Nestorians' loyalty towards the caliphate after the Caliph had been defeated by the Byzantines in 777. In return for his support, al-Mahdi allowed Timothy to rebuild several destroyed churches.[204] It is very likely that Timothy played a part in al-Mahdi's appointment of the former Nestorian, Fayd b. Abi Salih, as vizier in 782.[205]

However, Timothy owes his reputation mainly to his revival of the Christian missionary activities, which had been interrupted after the Arab invasion. Timothy urged numerous monks and priests to fill empty parishes in different regions of Iran.[206] The Christian missionaries were targeting mostly Zoroastrians and Jews, as apostasy from Islam was forbidden. His dedication to the Nestorian cause led him to send missionaries among the Daylamites and in Gilan, which were still not subject to Muslim rule. Timothy also played an important role in proselytizing Transoxania. The principality of Kashgar was converted to Christianity, and its first Christian prince was baptised Sergius. The Turkish Christians of the region had a Metropolitan consecrated by Timothy.[207]

Without al-Mahdi's benevolence, Timothy could not have been successful in his endeavours. The Caliph was not a zealot. He even freed those priests who had been imprisoned for religious reasons. Mas'udi remarked that during his reign all the heresies came to the surface.[208]

With Harun al-Rashid's coming to power, the period of respite for the Christians ended. The new Caliph reintroduced the discriminatory measures against the *dhimmis*. The war against Byzantium has been argued to be the main cause of al-Rashid's decision, as the Christians had once again become suspicious in the eyes of the rulers. The result was further defections from non-Muslim faiths.[209] Timothy, who was still in office during that period, had the support of al-Rashid's mother, al-Khayzarun.[210] Timothy had either to appeal to her to appease the Caliph's antagonism towards the Christians or to the court's physician, Bokhtisho, who then became al-Rashid's private physician after an 'impressive diagnosis'.[211] He was able to secure the position of al-Rashid's physician for his son Gabriel, who went on to become a valuable asset for the Christians. On several occasions, he approached Harun al-Rashid on behalf of his co-religionists in order to conciliate him with his community and have the discriminatory laws abolished.[212]

The intervention of these highly influential Christians, although useful, was not always sufficient in eliminating all the obstacles encountered by their community. The pressures put on the Christians during the first half of Harun al-Rashid's reign had reduced their number, and as a result, Timothy was no longer able to build new parishes. In 795, the Catholicos nominated Serge as the bishop of Elam, hoping that he would be able to preserve the Christian Church in Iran, but Serge was not able to find priests. In Fars, Timothy and Serge faced the disobedience of many bishops who, according to Timothy, were following the laws of Zarathushtra and the customs of pagans (i.e. Muslims). Securing the support of the Caliph, he compelled them to yield to his requirements. Nonetheless, Bar Hebraeus testifies that in his time the Christians of Fars were still reactionary and that their behaviour was more Zoroastrian than Christian. They believed themselves to have been converted by the apostle Thomas in person and because of this felt entitled to disregard the authority of the Catholicos of Baghdad.[213] Their clergy married, ate meat and wore white clothes similar to those of Zoroastrian priests.

These dissensions between the patriarch and the Christians of Elam and Fars demonstrate the vulnerable position of the Christians in Iran. With the death of Timothy, the power of the Nestorian Church waned even more. The seats of Daylam and Gilan did not survive his death.[214]

The disturbances in the 9th century prompted a large number of Christian Iranians to leave Iran for India. Documents written in Pahlavi and Arabic have been found in the south of India dating from 824, granting some rights to these new settlers.[215] The behaviour and customs of the Christians of Fars betray their Zoroastrian background. Moreover, the migration of Iranian Christians to India suggests that they were affected as much as the Zoroastrians by the massive conversions to Islam after the defeat of the Iranian uprisings in the 9th century.

Undoubtedly these uprisings had reverberations on Iranian Jewry. There may be no records of Christian uprisings in Iran during this period, but there are sources that testify to the rebellion of Iranian Jews against the Arab-Muslim establishment. Already in 720, the Jewish masses of Mesopotamia, thanks to their large population, had defied the Arabs.[216] Their revolt was suppressed but it was followed by a more significant movement led by Abu Isaac b. Jacob al-Isfahani. He rose during the chaotic period when the Umayyads and the Abbasids were troubled by the Zoroastrian uprisings. Abu Isaac claimed to be the messiah and desired to amend the Judaism of the *Rabbanim* (traditional Judaism). He gathered many disciples in Isfahan and instigated a revolt against the Muslims. He also acquired many followers in Rayy, Hamadan, Qum and Arrajan. Wasserstrom asserts that his messianic movement was the most important to occur between the second century religious agitation of Bar Kochba and the 17th century movement of Shabbetai Tzvi.[217] His rebellion reached its peak under al-Mansur (754-775). As expected he was defeated, but his movement did not die. His followers were known as the *Isawiyya* or *Isfahanians*, and a number of them were still encountered by Muslim scholars in the 10th century. The fact that Muslim authors mentioned this movement evinces the importance of the *Isawiyya*.[218]

Contemporary to Abu Isaac's activities, a serious conflict broke out between the *geonim*[219] and the Exilarch, the most important Jewish figures of Iran and Mesopotamia. The Caliph al-Mansur intervened in the dispute and chose as Exilarch a candidate of 'Persian lineage', a Karaite by the name of Sayyid Anan,[220] who had converted many Rabbanites. The movement had apparently a strong following in Iran. It was then led by Daniel al-Qumisi and David al-Mukammas.[221] In gratitude, the Exilarch transferred his seat to Baghdad. From this period onwards the schism between the Karaite and the Rabbanite sects became permanent.[222]

Like the Christians during this period, the Jews attempted to reinforce their position on the fringes of the caliphate. The Jews of Khurasan played a prominent role in trade, participating in the Silk Road traffic.[223] They also distinguished themselves from those of the rest of Iranian Jewry by rebelliousness towards their religious leaders. The Exilarch and *Geonim* were concerned to reaffirm their supremacy in Khurasan, which was far from their centres, and despatched Jewish representatives from Mesopotamia to Khurasan. With the support of the Muslim authorities, they forced the Jews of Khurasan to pay the taxes for maintaining the Exilarch and the *Geonim*.[224]

These coercive measures were far from successful in uniting the Jews in the caliphate. The litigations between the different parties among the Jews and Christians prompted al-Ma'mun to proclaim in 825 an edict, which gave the right to any group of ten non-Muslim men to form an independent community. Al-Ma'mun was prompted to enact such a decree by members of the Jewish and Christian communities. Abraham David affirms that al-Ma'mun took such measures in order not to alienate the Karaites of the Academy of Sura. The Caliph had recognized the Rabbanite David b. Judah as Exilarch, and without these additional political safeguards the Karaites and their candidate, Daniel, would have been in a vulnerable position.[225] Members of the communities who had close contacts with the court were able to influence the policies of the Caliph. The Patriarch Denys, for example, was able to have the Jacobites excluded from the edict after complaining to al-Ma'mun.[226] The Caliph manifestly wished to accommodate all parties and has been recognized for his religious tolerance in interfaith gatherings, in which even the chief of the Manicheans, Yazdanbokht, participated without being compelled to convert to Islam.[227]

It appears that al-Ma'mun's decree mainly concerned Jews, as the sources do not mention how much the Nestorians were affected by it. The Nestorian Catholicos was too powerful a figure and the Nestorian population too important in Mesopotamia to be alienated by al-Ma'mun. He, like other caliphs, relied very much on the support of the Catholicos and even requested that he accompany him to the battlefields.[228] The Nestorian physicians at the court were also in a position to manipulate the caliphs against other religious or political figures, and even the Catholicos was usually invested by the caliph in accordance with the advice of his Nestorian physician. This suggests that the Catholicos and the favourite court physicians were usually on good terms.

On the other hand, the court physicians were not always working harmoniously together. Even the famous and influential Bokhtisho family during its three centuries at the Abbasid court, saw its position occasionally challenged by other Nestorian physicians, such as Salmawayh b. Banan, with whom Bokhtisho II had to share the seal of the Caliph. It appears that Salmawayh was the more influential figure, thanks mainly to his brother, who was the treasurer at the *divan*,[229] and his ally the Nestorian Fadl b. Marwan, who had converted to Islam in order to become the vizier of al-Mu'tasim (833-842). Thus, Salmawayh was able to place his own candidate Abraham, bishop of Haditha, on the seat of the Catholicate despite Bokhtisho's disapproval.[230]

Another well-known political figure who converted to Islam under al-Mu'tasim was Ali b. Sahl b. Rabban al-Tabari. This physician served as a secretary to Maziyar b. Qarin and then became an administrator at the court of al-Mu'tasim, who compelled him to become Muslim. He remained thereafter the private physician of al-Mutawakkil. Bar Hebraeus refers, however, to a Nestorian physician who acted as a scribe in al-Mu'tasim's court, who most probably was Ali al-Tabari.[231] Ali al-Tabari was probably Christian, nonetheless other non-Muslim communities have also claimed him. He was important enough to be mentioned by Muhammad al-Tabari, Ibn al-Qifti, Ibn Abi Usaybi'a, Yaqut and Ibn Khallikan.[232]

Although the Zoroastrian revolts had reached their peak under al-Mu'tasim and were suppressed during his reign, it was the caliph al-Mutawakkil (847-861) who took the strongest measures against non-Muslims. Many of them became Muslim in this period, including political figures such as Isa b. Farrukhanshah and Ahmad b. Isra'il al-Anbari.[233] Al-Mutawakkil's discriminatory laws against non-Muslims, heretics and Shi'ites are well-known and have been discussed by many authors.[234] On the other hand, al-Mutawakkil's shift of attitude after 837 is usually not mentioned. It seems that the loss of his favourite Christian physician, Bokhtisho (III), affected him to such an extant that he ceased to persecute the Christians.[235]

He had another favourite physician, Isra'il b. Zakariya al-Tayfuri, who like Bokhtisho came from a medical dynasty.[236] Al-Mutawakkil's affection for this physician, along with al-Jahiz's testimony on the fate of Muslim physicians, confirms the prestige that the Christians and Jews enjoyed as medical experts in the caliphate. Al-Jahiz supported al-Mutawakkil's policies against non-Muslims, as he believed they were given too much power. He deplored the high position and wealth possessed by the Christians. He added that, while the Muslims disliked Jews and Zoroastrians, they appreciated Christians and refused to visit a Muslim physician 'because his name is Asad instead of Gabriel, and he has an Arab accent instead of the Persian accent of Gundishapur.'[237]

The successor to al-Mutawakkil, al-Musta'in (862-866), does not appear to have taken Jews and Christians into his service. On the other hand, Muhammad al-Tahir (862-873), who was ruling over eastern Iran, had two Christian secretaries, one of whom was invested with full powers in the caliphal estates on the borders of Tabaristan.[238]

It was only under al-Muhtadi (869-870) that his vizier Abdallah b. Sulayman reintegrated the non-Muslims in the *divan* of the caliphate. The social restrictions imposed during the time of al-Mutawakkil were no longer enforced. The trust that al-Mu'tadid (892-902) had in his Christian secretary, Abdallah b. Sulayman, attracted the enmity of many Muslim administrators. The Caliph saved a eunuch accused of blasphemy against Muhammad, because he belonged to one of his Christian physicians.[239] The Muslims concluded that the Caliph preferred the Christians. The Caliph retorted to this accusation:

> I have not entrusted any government to a Christian, apart that of al-Anbar to Umar b. Yusuf. And I have not allocated government to to Magians and Jews other than that of the *jahbadh* (perception). I did this, because I trust them, and not because I am fond of them. (And he told Abdallah b. Sulayman) If you find a Christian who meets your requirements, hire him, because Christians are more trustworthy than Jews, since the Jews hope that the power will return to them, and also more trustworthy than Magians, to whom the kingdom once belonged.[240]

The presence of Christians in the administration did not check the gradual decline of Christianity. Many bishoprics in Western Persia disappeared between 900 and 1000. Ram Hormizd and Dinawar were no longer mentioned after this period in the ecclesiastical chronologies.[241] Many more were to be eradicated from the map in the following centuries.

As we saw earlier, the Jewish institutions were not immune to crisis. The position of the Exilarch had been undermined since the reign of al-Ma'mun, when religious dissension had divided the Jews of the caliphate between the Karaites and Rabbanites. The situation was further exacerbated when a dispute broke out between Kohen Zedeq, *Gaon* of

Sura (838-848), and Ukba the Exilarch, as the latter had decided to withhold money sent by the Jews of Khurasan from the *Gaon*.[242] The wealthy Jews, who were close to the reigns of the power, were often tempted to interfere with the leadership of the Jewish institutions, just like the Christian court physicians who meddled with the Catholicate. In 917, the Exilarch David b. Zakkai was not able to appoint Kohen Zedeq b. Joseph as *Gaon* of Pumbedita. The powerful court bankers Aaron b. Amram and Joseph b. Pinchas *(jahbadh)* supported another candidate. Aaron and Joseph were the most wealthy financiers of Mesopotamia and Western Iran. Not only was the vizier Ubaydallah b. Yahya financially indebted to them, the administration of the province of Khuzistan was in the hands of Joseph b. Pinchas, as is testified in a letter written by the vizier Muhassin b. al-Furat and Ali b. Isa. The salary of the army depended on him.[243] Mubashshir Kahana won the official title of *Gaon*. Kohen Zedeq was granted the position only after Mubashshir's death in 926, despite the fact that Zedeq had the support of the esteemed Saadia b. Joseph.[244] The fate of Kohen Zedeq's son, Nehemiah, was not much different from his own. Amram's son, Bishr, thanks to his powerful contacts, was able to become *Gaon* in Nehemiah's stead. Nehemiah too had to wait until Bishr Amram's death before occupying this prestigious position at Pumbedita. Till the last years of the Academy, the descendants of Kohen Zedeq had to struggle with the wealthy and powerful Jewish members of the Abbasid *divan* to occupy the *gaonic* seat. Nonetheless, the influence of the Jewish court bankers was not always negative. In 987, as we will see later, they provided the means to revive the Academy of Sura, which had been shut 43 years earlier. One of the providers appears to have been Abraham b. Netira II, the grandson of the famous court banker Netira.[245]

Unfortunately the only information available on Iranian Jewry is generally limited to the relation they held with their co-religionists in Mesopotamia. The political developments in Baghdad certainly had repercussions in the Iranian plateau, but as the Abbasid Empire was gradually disintegrating, the Jewish leaders close to the Abbasid capital had more difficulty affirming their supremacy over the Jews living further east. The Jewish communities in eastern Iran were particularly far from the political centres of the caliphate, and thus were able to develop independently. The most radical Jewish scholars, like Hiwi (Hayawayh) al-Balkhi (second half of 9th c.) appeared in Khurasan. The success of Hiwi's unconventional ideas among Jews of Khurasan prompted the *Gaon* of Pumbedita, Judah b. Samuel (906-918) to call upon them to conform to Babylonian *Halakha* (Jewish law). Nonetheless, the success of the heterodox movements, such as *Karaism*, among Iranian Jews demonstrates the difficulties of the Exilarch and the *Geonim* in wielding power over them.[246]

The 10th century was a turning point in the history of the non-Muslims in the caliphate. On one hand, they were able to reinforce their position by being close to the reins of power, on the other hand, the decline of their population was making their community more vulnerable. In the year 923, the Caliph al-Muqtadir sought to help them by issuing an edict which gave the belongings of a heirless *dhimmi* to the members of his own community, while those of a Muslim went to the treasury.[247] His vizier, Ibn al-Furat, attempted to abolish the edict, but abandoned his plan after the interference of the Catholicos Abraham. On the other hand, at his discharge in 924 Ibn al-Furat was criticized for selecting Christian secretaries at the head of the army.[248]

Christians continued to hold important positions at the *divan* to the end of the reign of the last Abbasid caliph holding temporal power, al-Radi, but their influence did not end there.[249] After al-Radi's reign (934-940), the true power passed to the hands of Buyid amirs. The latter took over the Abbasid administrative system and the Christians even reached higher positions. The vizier of the second Buyid amir Adud al-Dawla Fana Khusraw (949-982), was the Christian Nar b. Harun.[250]

The Bokhtishos continued to practise at the court henceforth serving the Buyids. Gabriel II Abidallah Bokhtisho was summoned by Izz al-Dawla (967-973) to practise at the new hospital of Baghdad, as he was considered to be one of the best physicians of the caliphate.[251] As the main centre of the Buyids' power was in Fars, we hear also of a Zoroastrian physician who had converted to Islam in order to practise at the Buyid court.[252]

The position of non-Muslims had deteriorated by the close of Buyid rule. While in the East of the caliphate the Sultan Mahmud Ghaznavid (997-1030) had entrusted the administration of his court to a Jew, Isaac Yahudi of Ghaznin, in the Buyid west the Academies of Sura (1034) and Pumbedita (1038) were shutting their doors for ever. The situation deteriorated even further with the coming of the Saljuks. In 1058, the caliph's vizier Jalal Abdallah had Hezekiah the leader of the Jewish community executed. Hezekiah was the grandson of the Exilarch David b. Zakkai. His sons fled to Spain. Later on, Nizam al-Mulk, who became vizier of the Saljuks in 1072, wrote his *Siyasat-nama* saying that non-Muslims should not be appointed to any state office. He praised the

Saljuks for having an administration devoid of non-Muslims. His complaint was directed at the caliphal administration, in which non-Muslims still had positions. Nonetheless, Nizam al-Mulk maintained cordial relations with several Jewish bankers and financiers.[253] Furthermore, Ibn al-Athir informs us that he and the Sultan shared a Jewish steward by the name of Abu Sa'd b. Samha.[254] On the other hand, after the fall of Baghdad to the Saljuks, the civil power no longer intervened in the election of the Catholicos, as the latter no longer had much power.

The destruction of the ancient Jacobite community of Takrit (north of Baghdad) also occurred in this period following a fatal riot that had been instigated against them. All the Christians of the town were forced to flee. Takrit had been a Jacobite centre since 629.[255] This was the culmination of a wave of persecutions that had begun in 1091, which had caused many non-Muslims to abandon their religion. Abu Sa'ad al-Musilaya, who had been the Chief of the Chancellery (*Katib al-Insha*), was compensated for his conversion by being offered the vizierate, and was given the title of *Amin al-Dawla* (trustee of the state). His nephew became the Chief of the Chancellery, and upon his conversion he was given the title *Taj al-Ru'asa* (Crown of the Chiefs).[256]

Fourteen years later in 1105, the Saljuk Malikshah II relaxed all the discriminatory laws regarding non-Muslims, and in 1138 the Caliph al-Muqtafi (1136-1160) renewed the charter of protection granted to Nestorians. For the Christian physicians of the court these laws did not bring about much change, as they had been spared the earlier restrictions imposed on their co-religionists. The physician Abu al-Hasan Hibatallah succeeded his uncle Ibn al-Tilmiz and served the caliphs al-Muqtafi (1136-1160) and al-Mustanjid (1160-1170). His influence earned him the hostility of the Grand Vizier, who tried to deprive him of his trade revenues, though without any success. Abu al-Hasan Hibatallah had also a Jewish rival at the court called Hibatallah Abu al-Barakat. The latter, however, was compelled to convert to Islam. This he only did after his children were granted the permission to remain Jewish and inherit his wealth.[257]

It was during the reign of al-Mustanjid that Benjamin of Tudela visited Baghdad and some other towns in Mesopotamia and Iran. He testifies that the Exilarch was a very respected figure, with a spiritual authority that encompassed all Asia with the exception of the Levant. The Muslims, we are told, were compelled to honour him and call him 'Our Lord', or else they would have received one hundred stripes. This suggests that the office of Exilarch had recently been revived after the defeat of the Saljuk sultan by the caliph al-Muqtafi.[258] Benjamin of Tudela also informs us that there were many Jews in the *divan* of the Caliph, and that the Caliph knew Hebrew. The last remark seems rather doubtful, but reflects the sympathy of the Caliph for his Jewish subjects. Benjamin's description of the Talmudic academies in Baghdad confirm that the Abbasid capital had replaced Sura and Pumbedita as the main centre of Jewish learning. Regarding the Jewry of Baghdad, he mentions that they were very prosperous and learned and possessed 28 synagogues. The information he gives on Iranian Jewry is less detailed, although he mentions that the chief rabbi in Isfahan was Sar Shalom and had been appointed by the Exilarch as the leader of all the Jewry in the Iranian Plateau.[259]

Benjamin of Tudela did not reside long enough in Baghdad to be able to recount the poisoning of the Caliph al-Mustanjid by his Christian physician and secretary Ibn Safiya. The latter had been prompted to kill his master by the vizier Qutb al-Din Qaimaz.[260]

The Caliph al-Nasir (1180-1225) gave the *coup de grâce* to the power of the Christians by decreeing their discharge from all official positions. Amont those affected were the al-Nizam and al-Ashqar families. At least one from the al-Ashqae family, one Abu Galib converted in order to keep his position. Abu Abdallah b. Yahya b. Fadlan, who obtainedthe *diwan al-mawali* under al-Mustansir (1226-1242), wrote to the Caliph al-Nasir in order to have the *dhimmis*' humiliated during the ceremony of the payment of the *jizya*[261], as had been the custom in the past. Some Christian physicians close to the throne were able to delay his plan,[262] but eventually Ibn Fadlan was able to impose the humiliating measures, as the influence of the Christians had considerably waned. Henceforth, even their position as court physicians was no longer assured. Bar Hebraeus recounts the misadventure of the physician Hasnun in 1227, who was not granted a position at the court because he was Christian, although he excelled in his profession.[263]

Thus, by the end of the Saljuk period, prospects of advancement for non-Muslims in the social and political life of the caliphate had diminished, and the future looked increasingly difficult. However, the hope remained that a change in ruler or dynasty would bring about a turn in their fortunes.

6) The Cultural Contribution of Non-Muslims to Islamic Civilization

While it was not easy for non-Muslims to maintain their position at the *divan*, as physicians they had virtually no competitors until the 13th century. Indeed, the Muslim Arabs appreciated their knowledge and skills and granted them opportunities in a wide range of professions. Furthermore, the non-Muslim administrators and physicians owed their position to *dhimmi* scholars, whose knowledge and competence enhanced the prestige of Jews and Christians in the Islamic world.

This prestige had been earned prior to the advent of Islam. The Jewish centres of Mesopotamia and the Christian centres of Western Persia had flourished under the Sassanians. Once the Muslim rulers had transferred their capital to Mesopotamia, they were able to appreciate at first hand the Iranian civilization, as well as that of Christian and Jewish communities who belonged to the Iranian cultural sphere. Indeed, the Academies of Sura and Pumbedita, near ancient Babylon, produced the great majority of the Jewish scholars, while Gundishapur in Khuzistan provided the Christian physicians and translators for the Abbasids.

a) The Jews and their Cultural Contribution to their Islamic Environment

The direct contribution of Iranian Jewry to Islamic civilization is less perceptible than that of the Christians; nonetheless, their cultural dynamism in Iran during the Abbasid period is still remarkable and reflects their ingenuity in adapting their Jewish heritage to their Islamic environment. Indeed, the first known documents written in "New" Persian were produced by Jewish tradesmen in the 8th century in Hebrew characters. As the Zoroastrian scholars of this period continued to write their documents in Middle Persian, it seems that Iranian Jews were pioneers in employing the new language that emerged in Iran after the Arab invasion.[264]

Among the Jewish cultural figures of this period, the most interesting to our topic is Masha'allah b. Sariya [or b. Athari] (active cir.750-815), a Jewish astrologer from Basra. With the assistance of two other astrologers, he chose the date and place 'favourable to the foundation of Baghdad'.[265] From the sources he used it is clear that he mastered Persian and Syriac. There has been some speculation that he was from Egypt, but his Persian name (Yazdankhwast), and the pro-Iranian and anti-Abbasid sentiments detected in his writings, leave little room for doubt that he was Iranian. His predilection for the Iranian militants who fought the Muslims and his hope that they would bring an end to Arab rule demonstrates clearly that Iranian Jewry was concerned and directly affected by the political upheavals in Iran.

The massive conversions to Islam which followed the end of the Iranian uprisings in the 8th and 9th centuries, triggered new religious movements, not only among newly converted Muslims, but also among Iranian Jewry. While the *Mu'tazila*,[266] and the *Shu'ubiyya*[267] movements, found a great echo among the new Iranian Muslims,[268] the Karaite movement manifested itself among the Jews in Western Iran.

This anti-Talmudic movement was launched by Anan b. David (active cir. 754-775).[269] For the Karaites, the Talmud was responsible for weakening the Torah and corrupting its laws. The leaders of the movement put their understanding of Biblical Law above that of the *Rabbanim* and the *Geonim*, who were the leaders of the Jewish Academy.[270] The early leaders of the movement were all from Iran and Mesopotamia. Benjamin b. Moses Nahawandi (from Nihavand, cir. 830-860) consolidated the position of *Karaism* and was the first Karaite writer to use the term *Kara'im*. The movement spread westward in the 9th century, after Karaite figures like Daniel b. Moses al-Qumisi (from Damghan, Tabaristan cir. end of 9th century) settled in Jerusalem.[271] A very renowned Karaite figure was Ya'qub b. Yishaq al-Qirqisani (Qirqisan is a town near Baghdad). He composed the *Kitab al-Anwar wa'l-Maraqib* in 927 and is the most important source from this period for the Karaite sect. He had a very good knowledge of the *Mishnah*, the *Gemara* and also of the New Testament and the Quran. He was the last important Karaite figure from Iran (or the Iranian cultural sphere), as by the end of the 10th century the Karaite movement had lost its importance in the region. It had not been able to obtain the support of influential court officials.

Certainly, Jews influenced and were influenced by their environment; however, contrary to Christians they did not associate much with Muslim scholars. They followed a separate course outside the mainstream Islamic cultural activities until the appearance of Saadia b. Joseph, the most prominent Jewish scholar of the Abbasid period. Saadia began his career in Fayyum (Egypt), and arrived in Baghdad under the reign of al-Muqtadir (908-932). The Exilarch of the time, David b. Zakkai, recognized his administrative abilities and his intellectual skills and appointed him in 928 to the head of the Academy of Sura. Saadia strove to revitalize the decaying Academy of Sura and dispatched emissaries to Egypt, Spain and Iran to gather the necessary funds for its maintenance. The decline of the languages and cultures of Iran and Mesopotamia, overpowered by the domination of Islam and Arabic at this time, is well manifested in the person and work of Saadia. He did not assimilate to the culture of the Irano-Babylonian Jews, but instead used Arabic and believed in integrating the Jewish learning of the area into the Arab academic world. He translated the Torah into Arabic and wrote treatises refuting *Karaism*, criticizing among others the work of Hiwi al-Balkhi.[272] In Sklare's words, he was the founder of the 'Judeo-Arabic literary culture'.[273] Conflicts between different factions led Saadia to leave Sura in 943, and by 948 the Academy no longer had the budget to function.[274]

Samuel b. Hofni (d. 1013) was the academic successor to Saadia. He appears to have been the most intellectually active of the *Geonim*. He produced 65 titles, all in Judeo-Arabic.[275] He wrote biblical exegesis, Talmudic commentaries and legal treatises related to Jewish civil law.

As the Jewish academic centres of Mesopotamia declined and assimilated the Arabo-Islamic culture of their environment, Muslim Iranian scholars developed an interest in Judaism and Jewish History. Many of them sought the aid of Jewish scholars for their research. Hamza al-Isfahani (10th century) mentions in his *Annals* a Jewish chronology produced by an otherwise unknown Pinhas b. Bata al-Ibraniyya, which he had consulted for his work. Biruni (d. 1048), who according to Fischel is the greatest Muslim Hebraist, pays tribute to a Jewish scholar named Jacob b. Musa al-Nikirsi of Gurgan for his help. Kirmani (d. 1013), Nasir Khusraw (d. 1083), the celebrated poet and scholar, and Shahrastani of Ghazna (d. 1153) were other scholars who appear to have consulted learned Jews.[276] This collaboration between Jewish and Muslim scholars, at a period when Jewish scholarship was in crisis, was rendered possible mainly due to the fact that Jews had begun writing in Arabic, rather than Hebrew.

b) The Christians and their Share of Cultural Contribution

It was not long after the settlement of the Abbasids in Mesopotamia that the Nestorian physicians of Gundishapur were summoned to court. In 765, the Caliph al-Mansur (754-775) abducted Georges b. Gabriel of the Bokhtisho family, who was the head of the hospital of Gundishapur, in order to be cured. Once Georges arrived at the court, he lauded al-Mansur in Persian, his mother tongue, and Arabic.[277] He wrote many treatises in Syriac and upon the order of the Caliph translated medical books from Greek to Arabic.[278]

The major cultural activities which led to the flourishing of Islamic civilization began after the accession of al-Mahdi to the throne (775-785). As mentioned earlier, he was favourable to non-Muslims and encouraged Christians to translate many volumes from Greek and Syriac to Arabic. Al-Mahdi's astrologer, Theophile b. Toma, translated the works of Homer and Aristotle from Greek into Syriac, and soon after Abu Nuh al-Anbari b. al-Salt translated them from Syriac into Arabic. He was the scribe of the governor of Mosul and apparently the first Nestorian to translate documents into Arabic for a Muslim audience. The dynamic Catholicos, Timothy, who was his contemporary, produced a series of books on different subjects, including history. However, only his canonical tractates are well-preserved.[279] Timothy even encouraged other Nestorian scholars such as Isho Bokht, the metropolitan of Fars, to translate documents. The latter gave himself the mission to translate Middle Persian sources into Syriac.[280]

Under Harun al-Rashid (786-809) the Persian vizier Yahya al-Barmaki founded a hospital in Baghdad and appointed a Jacobite pharmacist and oculist from Gundishapur, Masawayh b. Yuhanna, as its director. The Nestorians also produced accomplished astronomers and mathematicians, such as Sahl b. Raban of Tabaristan, who translated Ptolemy's *Almagest* from Greek into Arabic at this time. His son Ali b. Sahl b. Rabban al-Tabari, whom we mentioned earlier as the secretary of Maziyar Qarin, was a well-known physician and the teacher of Abu Zakariya al-Razi. Under al-Mu'tasim he wrote two famous medical treatises, *Firdaws al-Hakim* (Paradise of the Physician), where he referred to Indian medicine, and *Hifz al-Sihha* (Preservation of Health).[281]

Al-Ma'mun further encouraged the translation movement which had started under al-Mansur. The Caliph sent an Arab delegation to Byzantium to collect manuscripts in Physics, Geometry and Medicine. Beside the 'Library of Wisdom' (*Khizanat al-Hikma*) which had been created by the Barmakids, he founded the great translation institution called 'House of Wisdom' (*Bayt al-Hikma*) in 830, encouraging further intellectual interactions. He had been inspired by the ancient Academy of Gundishapur, founded by the Sassanians.[282]

The majority of the translators until the 11th century were Christians, mostly Nestorians, but there were also Melkites and Jacobites. The greatest translator among them was Hunayn b. Ishaq (809-873), a Nestorian Christian from Hira, who is reputed to have translated some 100 books from Greek and Syriac into Arabic. He was appointed as the head of the *Bayt al-Hikma*. He took his nephew Hubaysh al-A'sam under his wing, as he was an excellent translator and had mastered Syriac and Arabic. Hunayn's son Ishaq assisted him and remained in office after Hunayn's death, serving the vizier Qasim b. Ubaydallah during the reign of al-Mu'tazid (892-902). Gabriel II Bokhtisho, who was the chief of the physicians, respected him and probably encouraged Ma'mun to support his translation works. Hunayn gained a lot of fame in Baghdad and became the most celebrated Nestorian in the Muslim literature. His son and Hubaysh produced a number of medical treatises and translated many philosophical books.[283]

Gabriel Bokhtisho spent a part of his salary on hiring translators. As well as Hunayn b. Ishaq he hired Yuhanna b. Masawayh, Abd Isho b. Bahriz and Job of Edessa.[284] Like Hunayn, Yuhanna was sent to Byzantium in order to gather manuscripts.[285] Apart from producing translations, Yuhanna also wrote Christian apologetics such as the *Book of the Demonstration (Kitab al-Burhan)*.[286] Yuhanna served four caliphs: al-Ma'mun, al-Mu'tasim, al-Wasiq, and al-Mutawakkil.[287] The other translator hired by Gabriel, Abd Isho b. Bahriz, was a Persian Nestorian bishop. Like Yuhanna he translated medical and philosophical books from Syriac to Arabic and produced religious tractates.[288]

The majority of the philosophers in the 10th century, as testified by Ibn al-Nadim, were still Nestorian. It is interesting that many of them were from eastern Iran, but only those of them who went to Baghdad achieved fame, such as Israel of Kashgar (870-960), Yuhanna b. Haylan and Abu Yahya (Ibrahim) of Merv. In the reign of al-Muqtadir (908-932), the Nestorian philosopher Yuhanna b. Haylan came from Merv to Baghdad. He was the master of the famous Muslim scholar al-Farabi. A contemporary of Haylan was the Jacobite philosopher and physicist Abu Zakariya b. Adi, whom Mas'udi eulogized as the most knowledgeable person he had ever met.[289] By this time, the majority of the Christian scholars no longer wrote in Syriac. Among the famous Christian physicians who wrote their medical tractates in Arabic were Abu al-Husayn b. Kashkaraya (of Kashgar), Abu Ya'qub al-Ahwazi (of Ahwaz), Isa Abu Sahl al-Gurgani (of Khurasan) and Gabriel (III) of the celebrated Bokhtisho family, who emerged in the reign of al-Ta'i (974-991).[290]

The fact that, by this time, the Christians wrote their scientific work in Arabic shows that Syriac (and by the same token Pahlavi) had by now been supplanted as the language of scholarship. Thus, the Muslims were no longer dependent on non-Muslim scholars for enhancing their knowledge. The previous generations of Zoroastrians, Jews and Christians had already initiated them into the art of administration and now, through their translation work, they conveyed the learning of their ancestors to the Muslim Arabs.²⁹¹ By the end of the 12ᵗʰ century, they were no longer playing a leading role in the culture of the Islamic world. As mentioned earlier, even in the field of medicine they had lost ground to Muslims, who had by now acquired reputations as physicians. The last Nestorian to distinguish himself under the Abbasids was the Patriarch Elie III (Catholicos 1176-1190). We are told that he was elected because there was no one else. He was an accomplished literary figure, but earned his fame mostly for being close to the poor.²⁹²

Conclusion

While the Abbasid period has sometimes been perceived as an Golden Age for the non-Muslims, it has also been seen as a period of decline for the Zoroastrians, Jews and Christians. These communities were highly appreciated by the Muslim Arabs for their skills in the fields of administration, science and literature. The latter encouraged them to use their skills and gave them the opportunity to rise to high positions. However, politically they were in a delicate situation. As long as they were needed and favoured by Muslim rulers, they were able to take an active part in public life. Once they lost the support of the caliphs or viziers, their careers came suddenly to an end.

While the Zoroastrians disappeared from the political scene after the reign of al-Mu'tasim (833-842), the Jews and the Christians continued to play important roles in the administration of the caliphate. They functioned as advisors to viziers and caliphs, and also participated in the gathering of taxes from their own communities. Their minority status, with all the handicaps it entailed, was an asset to them, as viziers and other government magnates did not feel threatened by them. As a result they were preferred to Muslims for some positions of power. Nonetheless, their influence depended strongly on their numerical importance in Islamic lands. As their populations decreased their number in the government also waned.

In addition to this economic and administrative cooperation, without which the Arab empire could not have functioned, they contributed to the building of Islamic civilization. Their longest-lasting achievement was in the fields of science and literature. The Jews and the Christians produced a vast quantity of theological, philosophical and legal works. However, the field in which they were most valued was medicine. Thanks to their skillfulness and knowledge, they were able to overcome discriminatory laws and come close to the throne. At times their close relation to the caliph attracted the envy and enmity of Muslims and even the hostility of their own co-religionists, but it was also in such positions that they were able to help their own community and maintain its cohesion. This solidarity within non-Muslim communities assured them their high positions. Thus, a long succession of physicians from the School of Gundishapur were able to monopolize the office of the Caliph's private physician. Nonetheless, their knowledge could also be a factor in their forced conversion. Some caliphs and viziers believed that the conversion of an eminent scholar would enhance the prestige of Islam. Two scholars who were converted for this reason are the Christian born Qudama (10th c), author of the *kharaj*, and the Jewish physician Hakim Da'ud al-Tabib (d. 1087).[293] Such incidents accelerated the transition from indigenous civilizations to an Islamic one.

This wave of conversion of non-Muslims to Islam generated movements within Islam such as *Shu'ubism*, where Muslims of non-Arab background desired to promote their own identity. These Islamic movements also had repercussions on non-Muslim communities and generated movements within Judaism and Christianity. The Karaite movement, which found a great echo among Jewish Iranians, is one example. Nonetheless, the progress of Islam after the 10th century occurred at the expense of non-Muslim civilizations. As the population of non-Muslims declined and their positions in public offices waned, their intellectual activities were marginalized and they no longer visibly participated in mainstream culture. In the 13th century there seemed no hope for the revival of the Jewish and Christian communities of Iran. The secondary status of the Persian language and Iranian civilization during the Abbasid period was a major reason for (and result of) the detachment of the Jews and Christians from the declining Persian culture. The Mongol invasion, with all its atrocities, was a reunifying force, which not only gave a second chance to non-Muslims to reenter the political leadership in Iran, but also drew them back towards the Persian culture.

Chapter 3
New Hope and Bitter Deception: Iranian non-Muslims under the Mongols (1256-1336)

In the 13th century Iran was struck by another formidable invasion. After the Greeks and the Arabs, it was the turn of the Mongols to wreak havoc on the land. Initially, the Mongols seemed no different from the Arabs. The Iranians regarded their arrival as a catastrophe. If the cultural upheaval the Iranians had to bear was not as radical as that provoked by the Arabs, the physical damages were, according to some, of another magnitude.[294]

It is noteworthy that the immediate reaction of Jews and Christians was different to the two invaders. While they do not appear to have been awed by the Arabs, they were alarmed at the deeds of the Mongols.[295] Once the period of conquest was over, the attitude of these religious minorities changed towards their new rulers. In the 7th century, the Jews and Christians did not express much joy over the fall of the Zoroastrian Kings,[296] but in the 13th century they were exhilarated by the defeat of the Muslim rulers. The reason is evident. The Muslim Arabs were not more tolerant than their Iranian predecessors towards the Jews and Christians,[297] while the Mongols delivered the religious minorities from Muslim discriminatory laws. The Armenian chronicler Kirakos of Gantzak, at the fall of Baghdad, summarized the Muslim and Arab rule in these words:

> Pendant tout le temps qu'elle conserva l'empire, pareille à une sangsue insatiable, elle avait englouti le monde entier; elle rendit alors ce qu'elle avait pris... Elle fut punie pour le sang qu'elle avait versé, pour le mal qu'elle avait fait, lorsque la mesure de ses iniquités fut comble devant Dieu (...) La domination violente et belliqueuse des Tadjik avait duré 647 ans.[298]

The arrival of the Mongols was perceived as a disaster by the Muslims. For the first time in history, Islam was seriously threatened by a strong conquering nation. This generated an entirely new situation, allowing the Jews and the Christians to come to the forefront of the political and cultural scene. During the preceding Muslim governments they had been gradually removed from administrative positions in the country; however, their reappearance in politics demonstrates that they had not completely lost touch with the governmental institutions. Soon after the Mongol conquest, the Jews and Christians were invited to fill the empty political positions left by Muslim bureaucrats. This did not mean that the Muslims were eradicated from the country's administration, but many Muslim officials found themselves subordinate to non-Muslim bureaucrats.[299]

Zoroastrians did not appear in the bureaucracy; nonetheless, after a few centuries of silence they now expressed themselves in literature. They wrote in Modern Persian, which to the detriment of Arabic became the norm for scholarship in Iran under the Mongols. Unlike the documents produced by the Jews and Christians, their testimonies fell into oblivion, only to be read by few. On the other hand, the literature produced by the Jews and Christians became important reference sources for the study of Iranian history. This literature reveals that, despite the picture painted of them by some modern historians as bloodthirsty savages, the Mongols were capable of appreciating science and learning.[300] For Jews and Christians, their arrival caused much optimism, as they were perceived as liberators from oppressive Islamic rule. What the Jews and Christians failed to see was that the first Mongol rulers' hesitation to support a religion did not exclude conversion to Islam at a later stage, and that Iran's period of religious tolerance was going to be shortlived. Nonetheless, this is an extraordinary period, in which foreign people and communities not commonly associated with Iran collaborate in recreating the country politically and restoring its lost identity.

1) The Challengers of Islam

By the 13th century, the religious minorities in Iran had resigned themselves to the domination of Islam. Muslim dynasties succeeded one another, and non-Muslims saw no alternative but to seek the sympathy of the new rulers.

It is not always clear whether the fall of Saljuks at the end of the 12th century changed the situation of religious minorities. In the west of Iran the Saljuks were in competition with the Abbasid caliphs such as al-Muqtafi, who in 1152 expelled the Saljuk officials from Baghdad, and al-Nasir who assumed full power in Iraq in 1180-1225. The Caliph al-Nasir decreed the discharge of non-Muslims from official functions. The Saljuks had already cleansed their administration of Christians and Jews a century earlier. Consequently, the fall of the Saljuks in the East must have overjoyed the non-Muslim communities. The Chinese Qara Khitais, who defeated the Saljuk Sultan Sanjar in 1141, were not Muslims and had no strong religious inclinations, and therefore did not discriminate on a religious basis. Nonetheless, the non-Muslims were not given much time to benefit from the rule of the Qara Khitai, as by 1212 they were completely evicted from Transoxania by the Muslim Khwarazmshahs, who struggled to dominate central and eastern Persia between 1156 and 1215.[301]

While the realm of Islam seemed unshakeable, in outer Mongolia in 1206 a very capable chieftain called Gengis Khan imposed himself as the leader of the Mongols. Three of the tribes he had rallied to his cause were Nestorian, converted by missionaries from Iran a few centuries earlier.[302] Gengis Khan relied heavily on them for the administration of his country.[303] Juwayni tells us that he ordered the Mongols to learn the Uighur script (which emanated from the Syriac script of the Nestorians) from them, and had their legal code written down in that script.[304] This markedly increased their influence and prestige among the Mongols. As a result, Gengis Khan and his followers held the Christians in high regard, but we know from the sources, such as Juwayni's and Rashid al-Din's works, that Muslims were also appreciated for their skills. When Gengis Khan's son, Tolui, captured the town of Merv, he spared the lives of four hundred artisans, but his army and the people of the rival neighbouring town of Sarakhs were allowed to slaughter the rest of the population.[305] The brutality and intransigence of the Mongols in battle has brought some western authors, such as Wilhelm von Rubruck, to call the Mongols savages and depict them as indifferent to religious matters.[306] However, Bar Hebraeus, a Jacobite Christian and witness to the events of the period, admired their religious tolerance:

> With the Mongols there is neither slave nor free man, neither believer nor pagan; neither Christian nor Jew; but they regard all men as belonging to one and the same stock... They entrust to [anybody] whatsoever office he seeketh, whether it be great or whether it be little... All they demand is strenuous service and submission...[307]

He acknowledged that none of the so-called civilized Christian, Muslim and Jewish communities of his land were as forbearing, 'for every one...

soundly revileth his fellow, and judgeth him [to be] an unbeliever [or one who is not of the true faith].'[308] Gengis Khan's *yasa* of 1218 is another testimony to the Mongols' religious tolerance:

> Pour ce qui est des hommes de religion, bouddhistes, nestoriens, taoistes et musulmans, qu'on ne leur applique ni taxes foncières, ni taxes commerciales, ni à aucune sorte de réquisition, mais qu'ils invoquent le ciel et demandent le bonheur pour l'Empereur.[309]

Rashid al-Din and Bar Hebraeus, who wrote a few decades after the reign of Gengis Khan, describe him as respecting Islam and desiring to protect his Muslim subjects.[310] Juwayni goes so far as to describe the Khan's conquest of Khotan as a liberation for the region's Muslim population, noting that they had suffered ill treatment from their previous ruler, Kuchlug.[311] However, these historians cannot be consulted uncritically on the issue of Gengis Khan's relations with Muslims, for they were writing at a time his descendants had converted to Islam, and it would not have been political to dwell on any anti-Islamic tendencies of his. The actual historical facts mentioned in the same historians' accounts tell a different story. Juwayni reports that in Bukhara the Mongol soldiers trampled the Qurans with their horses and made the imams and sheikhs tend to their animals, while in Samarqand they singled out the Friday mosque for destruction.[312] Reading in between the lines, it emerges that the Mongol invaders were not as well-disposed towards the Muslims as the historians claim, and the reason for antagonism is evident: Muslims were the rulers of territories the Mongols coveted.

It should be noted, however, that the Mongols did not initially spare any part of the Iranian population. Jews, Christians and Zoroastrians suffered along with their Muslim neighbours. Apparently, until the Mongol invasion Sistan had a noticeable Zoroastrian community, still in possession of an impressive fire temple which was admired by travellers. After the 13th century, there is no mention of Zoroastrians in the area. The Mongol invaders are presumed to have exterminated them.[313] Even the Christians of Tagrit, who were initially spared during the Mongol invasion of Mesopotamia, were sentenced to death in 1258 once the Mongols found out that they had not handed over the possessions of the Muslim victims.[314] The anonymous author of the *Chronicon ad AC 1234 Pertinens*, said that the invaders had pity for no one, but he admitted they were particularly unrelenting towards the

Muslims.[315] The fact that the Mongols were putting an end to Muslim domination and granting religious freedom attenuated the fear of non-Muslims.[316] The Christians were further reassured as they saw many co-religionists among the Mongols.

Consequently, the Christians seized the chance to gain the sympathy of the Mongol emperors. By the time Gengis Khan's son Ugeday (1229-1241) sat on the throne, many Christians were dispatched from Mesopotamia and Persia to the Mongol court. The Eastern Syriac chronicles attest to the influence of the Nestorian physician Simeon on Ugeday.[317] Simeon's prestige among the Mongols had even impressed the Armenian historian Kirakos of Gantzak.[318] The Armenian chronicler's sympathy for Simeon is not surprising as the latter had persuaded the Mongols not to harass the Christian population of Caucasus.[319] According to Rashid al-Din, Ugeday was a merciful ruler who did not make distinctions between people of different creeds. He cites a series of instances during which Ugeday had spared the lives of Muslims who had infringed Mongol laws with regard to the use of rivers and the slaughtering of animals. Rashid al-Din also records that Ugeday distributed money to both Mongols and Muslims without discrimination.[320] While Rashid al-Din aimed in his *Jami' al-Tawarikh* at demonstrating the Mongols' benevolence towards the Muslims, he also furnishes us with information explaining the non-Muslims' preference for the Mongols.

The Mongol law or *yasa* was not a law particularly favourable to Christians, but it did not impose the restrictions of the Islamic law (*sharia*) on them. This generated a situation in which the Christians, although not in power, had hopes of attaining it. They had to call upon their political ingenuity in order to keep the Mongols' sympathy. Ugeday's son Guyuk (1246-1248) was brought up surrounded by Christians. His mother was a Christian, and so was his tutor Qadaq, the *atabeg*. He had also another Christian vizier called Chinqay.[321] To observers in faraway Europe, Guyuk's adherence to a religion other than Christianity appeared odd, and they formed the opinion that the fault for his non-conversion lay with his Christian officials, who had not put enough pressure on him to bring him to the right faith. It was this perception which prompted the Pope to send Guyuk a letter instructing him to accept baptism. Guyuk refused, believing that the world had to submit to him, not he to the religious authority of Rome.[322] Despite his refusal to embrace Christianity, Guyuk clearly demonstrated his favour towards the Christians. Juzjani says that these people urged Guyuk to emasculate the Muslims, but a miracle prevented the Khan from implementing this plan. In another instance, a Muslim *imam* was brought to the court where his prophet was denigrated as just an ordinary man with a great sexual appetite.[323] Rashid al-Din alleges that Guyuk had handed the affairs of his Empire to the two Christian viziers (Qadaq and Chinqay) and as a result the cause of Christians flourished.[324] Key positions, such as the Command of the army in Iraq, had been given to Christians, and as one might expect Christians were also chosen as Mongol ambassadors to Western courts. King Louis IX (1226-1270) of France received two such Christian ambassadors who described to him the liberalism of Mongols towards Christians and told him that all Christians were exempted from taxation.[325]

Guyuk's reign lasted only two years. Juzjani said that God killed him because of his injustice towards Muslims. After three years of strife, his throne was occupied by his cousin Mongke (1251-1257), who like Guyuk had a Christian mother. His mother, we are told, was very benevolent towards Muslims, and so was the son. The Christians at this time, as during the entire rule of Mongols before their conversion to Islam, had a strong presence in Mongol courts. Their importance is manifest in the words of Shams al-Din Qazwini, the Muslim *qazi* who appealed to Mongke for help in fighting the Ismailis. In order to receive Mongke's help, he was careful to include Christianity among the three religions endangered by the Ismaili activities, the other two religions being Islam and the religion of the Mongols themselves.[326] Nonetheless, Mongke did not let himself be influenced by his Christian surroundings and as a result did not discriminate against Muslims. He confirmed the *yarlighs* (Mongol ordinances) of Gengis and Ugeday Khan, that those belonging to the priestly class, and those unable to earn a living were exempted from taxes. Juwayni tells us, however, that the Jews were displeased, as their clergymen were not included in the edict.[327] It should be added that neither were the Zoroastrians. After the 9th century, the Zoroastrian population had drastically decreased, and it is not certain how much bigger the size of the Jewish population in central and eastern Iran was. Undeniably, the Zoroastrians had been eradicated from positions of power after their revolts in the 9th and 10th century, whereas the Jews had been able to maintain theirs throughout Muslim rule. Their absence from the political sphere may explain why Juwayni refers to the vexation of Jews without mentioning Zoroastrians.

As well as enforcing his predecessors's *yarlighs*, Mongke Khan also nominated a person responsible for the internal affairs of each of the religious communities mentioned in his edict. Juwayni insists on the fairness of Mongke, because all those people who harassed the Muslims were punished by him.[328] Mongke also granted the Muslim *qazi* Jalal al-Din Khujandi large sums of gold and silver just for having prayed for him.[329] On the other hand, we are told that Mongke abolished the tax exemptions for all those Buddhist, Taoist and Christian priests who were married as this was not sanctioned by their own ecclesiastical laws.[330]

Despite Mongke's liberality, neither the Christians' nor the Muslims' position was certain. As long as the Christians were under non-Muslim rule, they could still obtain power and use it against Muslims. Under the reign of Qubilai Khan, they were given such opportunities. On one occasion, some Muslim merchants offended Qubilai Khan (1260-1294) by calling the food he offered 'unclean'. Qubilai Khan reacted by decreeing a law forbidding the Muslims (and non-Muslims) to slaughter animals other than in the Mongol fashion. Those who infringed the law were to be slain along with their family. The Mongol authorities, of whom many were Christians, made sure that these laws were properly implemented. The Muslims, we are told, were not able to circumcise their children for four years, and for seven years they were not able to kill sheep. They were subject to the same type of harassments to which the non-Muslims had been exposed under Islamic rule, suffering financial extortion, being spied on by their slaves, and even losing their lives. Many of them left the country of Khitai.[331] The Jews must have also suffered from Qubilai's decree, as apparently they had no protector in the court of the Great Khan, but for obvious reasons Rashid al-Din omits to mention this. To increase the predicaments of Muslims, the Christians brought to Qubilai Khan's attention a verse from the Quran, which condemned the polytheists and demanded their death. The Muslims were saved from the Khan's rage by a certain Hamid al-Din, who assured the sovereign that the Muslims did not consider him a polytheist since he believed in God.[332]

These religious affairs had repercussions in the rest of the Empire, including Iran, as all Mongol rulers maintained close relations with Qubilai Khan until his death. Rashid al-Din testifies that Hulagu (1256-1265) complied with the recommendations of his brother Qubilai and that Hulagu's son, Abaqa, obtained Qubilai's benediction before he occupied his father's throne.[333] However, the events occurring in other Mongol courts should have been a warning to the non-Muslims of Iran. By 1256 the Mongol rulers of the Golden Horde (controlling the Russian steppes) had already begun to abandon their ancestral religion. Sartaq

Khan (1256-1257) had converted to Christianity, but after one year of reign he was killed and replaced by Berke (1257-1266) who was the first important Khan to convert to Islam.[334] At the political level these conversions had heavy consequences as they determined the alliances and hostilities between the different ruling parties. By converting, Berke had broken the unity of the Mongol Empire. His accession to the throne also coincided with the complete submission of Iran to the Mongols, which culminated in the slaying of the Abbasid caliph.

At the socio-religious level, this was a blow to the Christian population living in Transoxania. The Muslims henceforth had Berke to intervene in their favour, and they requested his help in Samarqand against the Christians who, probably after the fall of the Muslim power, refused to yield to the rule of the Muslim majority. In one case, the Christians who had killed a Christian convert to Islam were slaughtered on the orders of Berke, and the Christian church in the town was razed to the ground.[335]

2) New Hopes among Christians: The Beginnings of the Mongol Rule

In Iran proper the Mongols did not convert to Christianity or Islam. Until 1260, they were still waging war in the area and their rapid successes probably gave them a feeling of superiority over the inhabitants of the country. Hulagu (1256-1265) had managed to subdue Iran entirely and destroy the forces of the Ismailis, the Kurds, the Lurs and of all other rebel elements in the area. He started off in 1253 ordering the various rulers of Iran to come to his assistance, and threatening that those who failed to do so would suffer the consequences. He conferred the command of his army on Kitbuqa, a Nestorian Uighur,[336] who remained at the head of the Mongol army until his death at the battle of Ayn Jalut. The Mongols were fighting in unison, as for the time being it was in the interest of all of them. Hulagu received contingents from all over the Empire, including the Golden Horde, and assailed the fortresses of the Ismailis.[337] Baghdad was Hulagu's next target. Having heard of the Christians' influence, the Caliph al-Musta'sim sent the Catholicos Marikha II (Patriarch of the Nestorian Church) to intercede on his behalf. Indeed, Hulagu's mother, Sarghaghtani Beki was a Christian, and so was his wife Doquz Khatun. Both were influential women, and on this occasion, Doquz Khatun could have met the Catholicos and upon his request supported the Caliph.[338] However, there was no reason for her to do so. It was the life of the Caliph that was at stake, not that of Christians. Thus, shortly after the fall of the city, in 1258, Hulagu had the Caliph slain.[339] Berke, who had recently converted to Islam, now had the pretext he had been waiting for to break his relations with Hulagu. He ordered his troops to leave Hulagu's army. There is reason to believe that Berke's decision was not solely based on his religious beliefs, but also on his territorial ambitions in the Caucasus and Azerbaijan controlled by Hulagu.[340]

During Hulagu's Il-Khanate or more precisely, before the conversion of the Mongols to Islam, religion and political interest were still strongly interrelated. Until 1295, the Mongol rulers of Iran were neither Christian nor Muslim, but it is noteworthy that the political circumstances prompted them to favour different religious factions. This was particulary evident during the sack of Baghdad. According to the sources, the lives and possessions of the Christians of Baghdad were spared, and apparently, the Shi'ite population was also spared the carnage suffered by the Sunnites of the city. The Mongol army included a large Christian contingent, mainly Georgians.[341] The Mongols did not have to beg for their assistance, as the Georgians had suffered tremendously from the cruelty of the Muslims during the invasion of Jalal al-Din Khwarazmshah a few decades earlier. Their churches had been razed and the population of Tiflis massacred.[342] During the sack of Baghdad, the Mongols gave the Georgians a chance to take their revenge on the Muslims.[343] This may explain why the majority of Christians were not harmed, but in addition, Doghuz Khatun had also requested immunity for all Christians, even those who were not Nestorians like her.[344] The Shi'ites also had an important protector in Hulagu's entourage: the astronomer Nasr al-Din Tusi. He, along with al-Musta'sim's Shi'ite vizier, Ibn al-Alqami, encouraged the execution of the Caliph, but asked that the Shi'ites be left unmolested.[345]

Although it exceeds the scope of this chapter to discuss the Shi'ites, it should be emphasized that *Twelver*[346] Shi'ites benefited fortuitously from the Mongol invasion, and indeed the Mongols unintentionally strengthened their position by destroying the Ismailis and the caliphate of Baghdad. Because of their intrinsic bias, the testimonies of the Christian chroniclers should be interpreted with caution. Incidents such as Hulagu forcing Muslims to eat pork or Doghuz Khatun destroying mosques as narrated by Grigor of Akanc and Vartan may be isolated incidents or overstatements,[347] as the Mongols did not systematically persecute Muslims, and their preference for the Christians never reached the point of making neither the Mongols nor the Muslims wish to convert to Christianity.

On the other hand, the Christians were convinced that the Mongols had come to extinguish Muslim rule for ever; therefore, in some instances they intentionally provoked the Muslims by their triumphalism. The Muslim historian Maqrizi recounts that after the Mongols' conquest of Damascus there was euphoria among the Christians:

> Ayant obtenu de Hulagu un diplôme qui leur garantissait une protection expresse, et le libre exercice de leur religion, ils buvaient du vin publiquement dans le mois de Ramadan, et en versaient au milieu des rues sur les habits des Musulmans, et sur les portes des mosquées. Lorsqu'ils passaient, portant la croix, ils contraignaient les marchands de se lever, et maltraitaient ceux qui refusaient de le faire (...) Les Musulmans indignés, allèrent porter leurs plaintes au gouverneur établi par Hulagu; mais cet officier les traita avec mépris, et plusieurs d'entre eux reçurent, par ses ordres, la bastonnade. Il comblait d'honneurs les prêtres chrétiens, fréquentait leurs églises, et protégeait hautement leur religion.[348]

The governor in question is Kitbuqa, who was a Kerait and a Christian.[349] The fact that Kitbuqa was leading the Mongol army in Syria may explain the excesses of Damascene Christians. Due to a smaller Chrisitain population in Iran, such exhibitions of joy were not expressed in Tabriz or other major Iranian towns. Nonetheless, as in Syria, the Mongol invasion had generated such a favourable atmosphere to Christianity that ambitious Muslim administrators, such as the Syrian Sa'id Hasan of Banyas and the Persian Izzidin Muhammad b. Muzaffar,[350] became Christian in order to be assigned to more prestigious offices in the Mongol bureaucracy. The sources have generally been silent on Muslim apostasies, and indubitably the Mongols' defeat at Ayn Jalut in September 1261 halted this short-lived tendency in the Il-Khanate, and erased the Mongols' image as indestructible warriors. The Mongols' failure to retain Syria had a dramatic effect on the Christians' spirit; nonetheless, those of them who remained under Mongol dominion, continued to hope that their new rulers would convert to their religion. After all, the Mongols were favourable to them and had given them opportunities they could not have obtained easily under Muslim rule. The

Mongol invasion had opened for them a new era, which they wished to last.

3) Non-Muslims in the Service of the Mongols

Incontestably, the Christians reached high positions under the Mongols to the detriment of the Muslim majority. The phenomenon was so conspicuous that it was recorded even by poets. A well-known verse from Sa'di's famous *Gulestan*, which has not caught the attention of historians, manifests the Muslim spirit of the time:

ای کریمی که از خزانه غیب   گبر و ترسا وظیفه خور داری

دوستان را کجا کنی محروم   تو که با دشمنان نظر داری ³⁵¹

The poet only mentions the Christians (*tarsa*) and Pagans (*gabr*) in this verse. It is obvious that by Pagan he is referring only to the Mongols and not the Zoroastrians, who did not have any share in ruling the country.³⁵² It is the rule of non-Muslims over Muslims that distressed our poet, and this can explain why he recited this verse right at the opening of his book. Indeed, it appeared for a while that the Shamanist Mongols were using Christians to rule the country. The Mongols, however, were pragmatic rulers; they took advantage of all those communities who were willing to collaborate, and these were mainly religious minorities, including Muslim Shi'ites.

As in the 7th century, the new invaders of Iran needed the assistance of the local people for administering the country. As the Sunnite population had been alienated, the Mongols could not count on their loyalty. On the other hand, the local Christians were willing to associate themselves with the new rulers. If the Mongols' religious policy was liberal, that of the Christians or Jews who ran their bureaucracy was not. The Christians had high hopes that the Shamanist and Buddhist Mongols would soon join their faith, and therefore they did not hesitate to provoke the Muslims. Right after the fall of Baghdad, the Catholicos Makkikha II took over the Palace of the Caliph and its neighbouring buildings including the *harem*. He had the Arabic inscriptions erased and replaced by Syriac. He also had a Church constructed on the site where he beat the *nakus*³⁵³, which was undisputedly unacceptable to orthodox Muslims. In the same year, that is in 1258, the Shi'ite Lord of Mosul, Badr al-Din Lu Lu, named the brother of Safi Sulayman (a renowned

Armenian physician), Mukhtas, as the governor of Arbela.[354] Nonetheless, the Mongols did not allot freely these positions of power to Christians. Those who obtained them were involved in the usual political imbroglios and ambitiously fought their way to the top. The Bishop Hanon Isho who became governor of Jazira b. Umar, visited Hulagu and collaborated with the Mongols in his town. Another Christian, named Zaki, had been politically active before he was nominated governor. In 1264, he had seized the chance to denounce the Muslim rulers of Mosul as traitors and as Mamluk agents. Consequently, he was able to take over their position.[355]

Yet the Christians could not assume all the dominant administrative positions under the Mongols. Their population was concentrated in certain regions only. Unfortunately for them, by the 9th century Iran had become one of the most Islamized countries in the region. Thus, the Mongols needed the assistance of the Muslims in order to collect taxes from the majority of the provinces of the country, which means that most of the country remained under Muslim administration. As a result, it was at court and in diplomacy that the Christians had to concentrate all their energy. The location of the Il-Khanate's capital made their task easier, as Maragha and later on Tabriz were close to Northern Mesopotamia, where the majority of the Christians dwelled.[356] They could easily gain access to the court, where they had many influential Central Asian co-religionists, the principal one being Doghuz Khatun as already mentioned. Another important Christian protector in the Mongol court was the Armenian King Hethum I. His name recurs throughout the annals, as he outlived many Mongol sovereigns. He had become the 'ecclesiastic advisor' of the Mongol Khans since capitulating in 1243 to Batu (1237-1256), the master of the Golden Horde. He encouraged Hulagu to invade Aleppo and secured him the support of the Armenians of Cilicia.[357] There is also no surprise in finding influential Christian physicians in Mongol courts; even the Muslim Caliphs had them in their service until the 13th century. Bar Hebraeus' father, Aaron, a Jewish Physician converted to Christianity, was already in the service of the Mongols in 1244. Bar Hebraeus also refers to the physician Simeon, whom we mentioned when discussing Ugeday's reign. He was still present at the Il-Khan's court, serving Hulagu and subsequent Il-Khans until 1290. Bar Hebraeus wishes us to believe that he was a Jacobite.[358]

Because of this strong Christian presence in the court, the Christians were convinced that the Khan was eventually going to embrace their faith. They began spreading rumours on the subject; nonetheless, his funeral in 1265 was held in the Mongol fashion.[359] His son Abaqa (1265-1282) who replaced him on the throne was a committed Buddhist, and even promoted the religion in Iran, where he had numerous Buddhist temples erected. Rashid al-Din and Bar Hebraeus mention them only at the moment of their destruction under Ghazan.[360]

Being a Buddhist did not prevent Abaqa from continuing his predecessor's tolerant religious policy. All the Buddhist, Shamanist, Christian and Muslim dignitaries remained exempted from the Mongols' heavy taxation. Once again the Jews and the Zoroastrians seem not to have benefited from this edict, although there were Jews serving the Mongol rulers. The future Grand Vizier Rashid al-Dawla was already present at the court, attending to Abaqa as a physician. During this period he had still not left Judaism, and hence had not taken the Muslim title Rashid al-Din. It is also noteworthy that Rashid al-Din's grandfather, Muwaffaq al-Dawla, had also been in the Mongols' service after being delivered from the Assassins in 1247.[361]

For the Muslims, a mere tolerance of their religion was not sufficient. They formed the majority of the population and could not accept the development of Christianity and Buddhism in Iran. The construction of Buddhist temples and the Christians' freedom to proselytize and build churches had heightened the anger of the Muslims, who were always on the verge of sedition.[362] In 1268 the Muslims rioted when the Catholicos Denha I (died 1281) had a number of Christian converts to Islam drowned. The Catholicos had to flee Baghdad.[363] It is also worth mentioning that in the same year Frankish rule collapsed in Syria, after the Mamluks attacked the area once again. Antioch fell into Muslim hands and was laid waste. As their Christian allies were fading away, the Mongols began to show more leniency towards their Muslim subjects.[364]

Facing the hostility of the Muslims, the Christians could only count on the benevolence of the Mongols for their survival. They had influential protectors in the court such as Despina Khatun, Abaqa's wife and the illegitimate daughter of the Byzantine Emperor Michael VIII Palaeologus, but the deeds of some prominent Christians and the strong animosity of Muslims undermined their cause. At the beginning of Abaqa's reign, Isaac, a Christian secretary of Qara Bogha, governor of Baghdad, was involved in a conspiracy. By 1268, the Bishop Hanon Isho, governor of Jazira b. Umar had also become unacceptable to the

Mongols. Likewise, Zaki, the Christian governor of Mosul was removed from office. Hanon Isho and Ibn Umar were beheaded.[365] In 1271, Ismailis attempted to assassinate the *Sahib al-Diwan*, the Grand Vizier Juwayni. The Muslims spread the rumour that the murderers were Christians sent by the Catholicos. Numerous monks and Christian notables were arrested in Baghdad, Kutlu Beg, the Lord of Arbela and the Catholicos were also seized and held in prison until a royal edict ordered their immediate release. After the incident, Bar Hebraeus says that the Catholicos moved from Mesopotamia to Azerbaijan.[366] Furthermore, in 1274 a monk of the convent of Mar Mikail was found with a Muslim woman. He converted to Islam to save his own life. The monks put him behind bars and appealed to the Mongol authorities. However, the uprising of the Muslim population dissuaded them from intervening, and the monks had to release the apostate. In the same year the Muslims disrupted a religious procession led by the Catholicos, in which mounted Christian Mongol soldiers were also participating.[367]

Just a decade after the fall of Baghdad to Hulagu, Mongol rule appears to have slackened. The Muslims had recovered their courage and tried to reestablish their own order, and sometimes they were successful. Earlier, there seem to have been many Nestorian generals in the Mongol army who supported the local Christians, but at this time the Mongol army appears to have lost its anti-Muslim fervour, leaving the Christians to their fate.[368] As a result, the Christians needed to consolidate their position further. In 1281, the Nestorian Christians elected an Uighur as Catholicos, for he was acquainted with the language and traditions of the Mongols. It did not matter to them that the new Catholicos Yahballaha III spoke neither Syriac nor Arabic.[369]

Not long after the election of Yahballaha III, Abaqa passed away in Hamadan, where we are told he had assisted at a Christian Easter ceremony in 1282.[370] His brother, Teguder (1282-1284), prevented Abaqa's son acceding to the throne, and became the new Il-Khan. Although he had been baptised as Nicholas by his mother Qutai Khatun he was converted to Islam and was given the name Ahmad.[371] Two bishops had accused Yahballaha of conspiracy against the new sovereign. He was arrested but released after the intervention of Qutai Khatun.[372] In the year of Teguder's accession to the throne, Susa disappeared from ecclesiastical records.[373] According to the annals written by Bar Hebraeus, the Jacobites had been reduced to an insignificant community at this time.[374]

Hayton, the Armenian chronicler,[375] claimed that Ahmad Teguder sought to reinstate Islamic laws and improve his relations with the sultan of Egypt. Apparently he also promoted the destruction of churches.[376] Arghun allegedly notified Qubilai Khan of Teguder's intentions and wrote: 'He is not of our creed, and worships Muhammad. Is it acceptable that an Arab rule over Mongols?'[377] The Muslims had still not recovered the strength necessary to retain Teguder on the throne. He was eliminated less than two years after his accession to the throne and Arghun took his place in 1284, thanks to Boqa, a Mongol general, who was made treasurer and subsequently Grand Vizier. Boqa's brother Arok was granted the governorship of Azerbaijan and Mesopotamia.[378] Arghun reappointed the Christian, Mas'ud of Bar Qatwa, as the governor of Mosul, but on the day of his accession to the throne, the Uighur monk Ashmut, who had acted previously as the ambassador of the Mongols and was Mas'ud's administrator, was assassinated by Muslims who coveted his position.[379] The assassination of the monk was not an isolated case. The Muslims were determined to put a stop to the Christians' ascendancy, and whenever possible they eliminated those ruling over them.

Arghun's reign marked the last days of the Golden Age for Christians. The Il-Khan rebuilt the churches that had been destroyed, and in 1289 the Il-Khan had his son baptised as Nicolas after the Pope. Moreover, Bar Hebraeus averred that Arghun trusted the Jews and Christians more and had advised his governors not to recruit Muslim secretaries.[380] Many Christians attained high positions. They were at the peak of their confidence. It was a time when the Armenian clergy could afford to ignore the Papacy, even to the extent of declining its invitation to attend the Council of Lyon in 1274, whereas prior to the Mongols' capture of Baghdad they demonstrated less resistance to the conditions of Rome.[381] The Grand Vizier Boqa, who was a Buddhist or a Shamanist, also favoured Christians and Jews. He and his brother Arok had been ruthless in their policies. Like most viziers of the epoch, Boqa's role was to exact as much money as possible from the common people, which had made him numerous enemies.[382] His Muslim and Mongol opponents instigated Boqa's and Arok's execution in 1289. Many of the Christian governors and administrators, who supported him, were also killed. The governor of Mosul, Mas'ud of Bar Qatwa, was arrested, tortured, and executed. The Armenian Taj al-Din Isa, son of Mukhtas, who was the governor of Arbela, was taken to Mosul to be executed, but managed to escape. A year later, Arghun named him governor of Mosul again, adding to his jurisdiction Mardin and Amid (Diyarbakir). But not long after, in 1290, the Armenian governor of Mush was killed by men sent from the Amir of Mayyafariqin, who according to Bar Hebraeus abhorred Christians. The Christians were no longer at peace in any part of Mesopotamia.[383]

While the Christians were facing difficulties in the west of the Il-Khanate, where their population was concentrated, the Jewish physician, Sa'd al-Dawla was named governor of Azerbaijan and Iraq. He was able to gain the Il-Khan's confidence thanks to his administrative and social skills. As a result he obtained the position of *Sahib al-Diwan* in 1289, putting him above all other dignitaries after the Il-Khan.[384]

The Grand Vizier Sa'd al-Dawla was very authoritative and favoured his co-religionists, distributing the high positions to his relatives and other Jews. One of his brothers was appointed governor of Baghdad and another of his brothers was made governor of Northern Mesopotamia along with Taj al-Din Isa, but the former was given more power.[385] The Muslims were infuriated by his demeanor and waited for an occasion to eliminate him. Noble Mongols who had seen their revenues reduced and had not been treated as they wished disapproved of him and, according to David Morgan, so did the Christians.[386] He had, indeed, mistreated a number of the Christian potentates.[387] Bar Hebraeus depicts Sa'd al-Dawla's rule over the Il-Khanate as the greatest punishment inflicted upon Muslims.[388] Although Sa'd al-Dawla's rule exasperated both Christians and Muslims, it did not diffuse the tensions between them. If the Muslims had the superiority in number, the Christians had a stronger presence in the army and in the court. The Christian soldiers took advantage of their power to harass the Muslims.[389] On the other hand, Muslims assassinated Christian leaders and governors. In 1290, Amir Matta, chief of the Christians of Karamlaiss (near Mosul) was assassinated.[390]

Finally in 1291, Sa'd al-Dawla's enemies took advantage of Arghun's illness to kill Sa'd al-Dawla. According to Morgan, he had been the most efficient Grand Vizier since Shams al-Din Juwayni. Even his contemporaries, Vassaf and Bar Hebraeus, who disliked Sa'd al-Dawla, acknowledged his administrative skills.[391] Furthermore, Arghun's favourite Jewish and Christian officials suffered similar fates. The Christian governor of Mosul and the Jewish governor of Baghdad were also executed in 1291. As Arghun had passed away nothing could prevent the plundering of the Jewish quarters of Baghdad. In Tabriz, the Jews saved themselves by paying a substantial amount of money to the authorities. It is interesting to read that the Jews in Baghdad were able to retaliate against the Muslims. Bar Hebraeus says that 'The Arabs killed and were killed;' which suggests that the Jews were present in Baghdad in significant numbers, or else they would not have been able to resist. Moreover, the Mongol rule had given the Jews the confidence to fight back against the Muslims. They would probably not have resisted physically if all power had been effectively in Muslim hands. The Jewish communities of Mesopotamia and Iran managed to survive the crisis, although they were never able to recover the level of influence and power they had reached under Arghun.[392]

The situation did not improve for the non-Muslims under Gaikhatu (1291-1295) despite the fact that he was favourable to them. He assisted at the Christian ceremonies and made many donations to their cause: 20,000 dirhams to the Catholicos and a similar amount for the construction of a magnificent convent (St John Baptist) in Maragha. His economic policies, however, were extremely unpopular and his scandalous behaviour added to the disaster. He paralysed the commercial activities of the country and emptied the central treasury. Bar Hebraeus tells us that Gaikhatu called upon a certain Rashid al-Dawla, who was of Jewish confession, to straighten out the precarious economic situation. Rashid al-Dawla is most probably, as Netzer pointed out, none other than Rashid al-Din. He thus entered politics under Gaikhatu.[393] Nonetheless, Gaikhatu was not able to save his throne despite his new political strategy. He was beheaded in 1295 by Baydu, who succeeded him.[394]

Baydu was favourable to Christians, and apparently wore a cross. Hayton and Marco Polo go even further and say that he was a Christian.[395] However, the circumstances had changed. According to Bar Hebraeus the majority of Mongols, whether noble or common, had converted to Islam.[396] Fra Ricoldo of Monte Croce asserted that the Muslims lured the Mongols into their religion by giving them money, and that the Christians had not been as generous.[397] There are few mentions of Mongols converting to Christianity in Iran. Those who were Christian, had been born in the faith or had converted in their original land. By the end of the 13th century, even the Mongol Il-Khans were persuaded to convert to Islam. Ghazan, who had erected Buddhist temples in Khurasan, was lured by the opportunities that Islam offered, such as the support of the majority of Iranians. His generals followed his example en masse. Rashid al-Din does not refer to Baydu as a Christian and apparently he was very attached to Mongol traditions and disapproved of the Mongol Amir Nawruz who had converted to Islam.[398] At the end of his reign, Baydu, like Ghazan, converted to Islam for political reasons, but Baydu's decision to convert had come too late. He was killed and Ghazan (1295-1304) seized the throne.[399] Spuler believes that these conversions were precipitated by the death of Qubilai Khan in 1294.[400] Qubilai was certainly an influential and talented politician, but it is unclear whether or not he invested any effort in the politics of Western Asia. The Empire had already lost its cohesion with the conversion of Berke three decades earlier. His death, however, was a good opportunity for the Mongols of Persia to change their relation with the other Mongol rulers and convert to Islam.

4) The Dusk of Non-Muslim Rule: The Recovery of Islam in Iran

If earlier Ahmad Teguder lost his throne partly because of his conversion to Islam, from this moment all those who rejected it were likely to experience a similar fate. Browne asserts that, 'The Mongol dominion had hitherto been of this last and cruellest type; by Ghazan's conversion it was ameliorated at once.'[401] But this should be considered with some reserve. Most likely his opinion has been influenced by Rashid al-Din, who as Christensen points out 'had an obvious interest in exaggerating the administrative chaos and the extortionate taxation of Ghazan Khan's predecessors.'[402] He aimed to legitimize his patron's rule and by the same token his own, as he had come to power with Ghazan's accession to the throne.

Ghazan's conversion may have improved the situation for the Muslims, but it certainly did not bring any benefits to the non-Muslims. There was a brutal purge of non-Muslim Mongols from the political scene. Therefore it is far from certain that the level of cruelty had really decreased, as the number of victims under the new Mongol regime was still significant.

The Muslim Mongol Amir, Nawruz, on whom Ghazan had relied for his power, abhorred the non-Muslims.[403] Once in power, he made Islam again the religion of state and proclaimed a *yarligh* for the destruction of churches, synagogues, pagodas and fire temples.[404] The *jizya* and even dress codes, that had been in place only under some caliphs, were reimposed. In Mosul, Christians succeeded in saving their churches from destruction by paying the authorities. In Arbela, they were too poor, and their churches were destroyed. In Baghdad, the palace of the Catholicos was reoccupied by the Muslims and the statues and the Syriac inscriptions were removed. The cemetery containing the bodies of the patriarchs Makkikha II (died 1265) and Denha (died 1281) was also appropriated by the Muslims. In Hamadan and Tabriz, the residence of the bishop and the main church were razed to the ground. In Maragha, the Catholicos Yahballaha was arrested and tortured, but his persecutors' aim to have him apostatize failed. He paid his captors a substantial amount of money in order to save his life, but was unable to save the Mar Shallita church. He then escaped from Maragha and went to Tabriz to visit the Khan, but the latter refused to grant him audience. As a result, he had to hide, but was found by two Mongol agents, one of whom was a Christian converted to Islam. He was rescued by his disciples and one of his messengers succeeded in seeing Ghazan in 1296. The Armenian King Hethum I saved the church of Rabban Bar Sauma by paying from his treasury, and complained to Ghazan about the tribulations inflicted upon the Christians. Ghazan, who had married the niece of the King, responded that he had not consented to such abuses, and took measures to stop them.[405]

On the other hand, he did not remedy the agony of the Buddhists and Shamanists, who suffered the most from Nawruz's religious zeal. They were given a choice between conversion or exile. The reason for Ghazan's intransigence with the Buddhists appears to be political, as those who had remained of that creed were Mongol soldiers, and they could not tolerate Ghazan's adherence to Islam and wished to eliminate him.[406]

During this period, Ghazan needed to restore order in the country, and therefore selected two promising viziers from among his officials: Sa'd al-Din of Saveh and Rashid al-Din Fadlallah. It seems that Rashid converted at this point. Some authors argue that Rashid al-Din's conversion was sincere.[407] The clearest evidence against such an argument is that his conversion occurred around 1295-96, when Nawruz imposed Islam on the country and compelled high ranking officials to convert. Moreover, Rashid al-Din had surrounded himself with Jewish bureaucrats, of whom a few have been named: Najib al-Dawla, a certain Johudak (little Jew), and Johary (whose father was a banker from Tabriz).[408]

It took Ghazan more than a year to establish his authority. Once in control, he issued an edict putting an end to the discrimination against Christians, demanding that 'none should be obliged to leave their religion."[409] Soon after he agreed to receive the Catholicos. Nawruz was infuriated and had an edict circulated which announced falsely the conversion of the Catholicos. His edict instigated riots against the Christians in Maragha. Mongol Amirs fought each other for the control of the town. During the chaos, many monks were killed and churches were sacked, along with the residence of the patriarch. A Christian queen, Burgesin Argi, hid the Catholicos who then succeeded in visiting the Khan near Hamadan. He obtained an edict against the inhabitants of Maragha, but because of the Islamification of the government and the army, the edict was not applied. Finally, in 1297, Nawruz was arrested and executed, most certainly not because of his anti-Christian behaviour, but for treason and plotting with the rulers of Egypt.[410]

Discriminating measures such as the payment of the *jizya* and the dress codes, applied by the Grand Vizier Nasir al-Din, did not last long. Ghazan had them revoked. In 1298, he refused to punish the Christians of the fortress of Arbela who fought against the Kurds. On the contrary he had the Muslim mobs of Tabriz who had plundered churches pursued. He also sojourned three days in the patriarch's residence in 1300 and a year later he invited the Catholicos to the Mongols' New Year celebration near ancient Babylon.[411] During his lifetime, he had also supported Shi'ite institutions and had even visited their shrine in Karbala.[412]

With the advent of Uljaytu (1304-1316), the situation became more difficult for the Christians. The new Il-Khan had been baptized by his mother Uruk Khatun, but as soon as she passed away, he apostatized and converted to Islam without even remaining attached to a particular Islamic denomination. One reason advanced by scholars for his conversion to Islam was his upbringing in Khurasan, which, since the Arab invasion, was a region populated by militant Muslims. Despite his Christian upbringing, we are told that he was not favourable to Christians, and even desired to turn the new convent of Maragha and the church of Tabriz into mosques, but there were still Christian Mongols in the court and they prevented the Il-Khan from implementing his wish.[413]

Not surprisingly, under Uljaytu pressures weighed also on Jews. Less than one year after his accession to the throne, the Jewish official Najib al-Dawla converted to Islam along with several Jewish physicians. Like that of many non-Muslim dignitaries in Iran, his conversion to Islam appears not to have been sincere, and therefore Rashid al-Din, owing to discords with Najib al-Dawla, had him transgress the Mosaïc Law by making him eat non-kosher food.[414] Najib al-Dawla was able to attain the position of governor and a few years later found a chance to settle old scores with Rashid al-Din. It is during his plot that the presence of Jewish officials is mentioned by the sources. They are not mentioned in other accounts. The anonymous continuator of *Jami' al-Tawarikh* says that Najib al-Dawla duped a certain Johudak, a subaltern Jewish official, to write a letter in Judeo-Persian on behalf of Rashid al-Din to Jawhari, a highly ranking Jewish official, advisor to Uljaytu. The letter proposed an attempt against Uljaytu's life, but Rashid al-Din was able to prove his innocence, and escaped death.[415] In another version written by al-Kashani (*Zubdat al-Tawarikh*), Rashid al-Din himself was involved in the conspiracy, and his aim was to bring into disrepute the defunct vizier Sa'd al-Din. Therefore, the letter was written on Sa'd al-Din's behalf to Jawhari. It also appears from this version that Rashid al-Din was known as the protector of the Jews, as Najib al-Dawla tells the Johudak, that the Grand Vizier (Rashid al-Din) would protect him in case he was caught.[416] The information given by Rashid al-Din's continuator suggests that Sa'd al-Din might also have been a Jewish convert like Rashid al-Din.[417] Blochet believes that his wife was definitely Jewish, because she was involved in plots with Najib al-Dawla and Rashid al-Din.[418]

On the Christian front, the Catholicos had to struggle to maintain his church. In 1306, he was not able to have Uljaytu revoke the *jizya*, but in 1308, after experiencing the hospitality of the monks in the convent of John the Baptist, Uljaytu agreed to abolish the humiliating poll tax.[419] Not long after, Uljaytu opted for Shi'ism and persecuted Sunnites, which was a factor in the tarnishing of the Il-Khanate's relations with Egypt. The Mongol generals even contemplated a return to Shamanism, but did not undertake any actions.[420]

The Catholicos had settled in Arbela, where there was a strong Christian community, controlling also the citadel of the town. However, in 1310 it was no longer acceptable to the Muslim rulers of the area to have a neighbouring Christian stronghold, especially where they had also a military contingent. They decided to attack, plundering the Christians of the lower town and the Christian villages in the region. The Catholicos was caught and held hostage. The local Muslims tried to prevent any communication between the Christians of Arbela and the royal court. In the end, the Arabs and the Kurds were able to convince Uljaytu that the Christians had rebelled against him. On 26 June 1310, the Christians of the citadel of Arbela had to surrender. The forces sent by the Grand Vizier, Amir Chupan, arrived too late. The majority of the Christians were massacred, and the Metropolitan of Arbela was only able to save the Catholicos.⁴²¹ Massacres also occurred in Maragha. The Catholicos visited the Il-Khan to discuss the horrific events but the latter refused to consider the matter and shortly after had the *jizya* imposed. There was not much left for the Catholicos to do. The last seven years of his life were spent without much activity. He died in 1317, a year after Uljaytu. That year the Christians of Amid also suffered a riot against them, and the same year, in 1318 Gundishapur disappeared from the ecclesiastical records.⁴²²

That year, the famous Grand Vizier of Jewish background, Rashid al-Din, was executed, due to the intrigues of the other Grand Vizier Ali Shah who had already caused the death of Sa'd al-Din of Saveh.⁴²³ The physician who testified against him was a Jew named al-Hazan. Rashid al-Din's head was paraded all over Tabriz with the slogan: 'This is the head of the Jew who profaned the word of Allah; may Allah's curse be on him.'⁴²⁴ It was the end of the prosperous years for Christians and Jews.

The advent of Abu Sa'id (1316-1335) marked the end of an era for the Christians. He was the first Mongol ruler with a fully Islamic name, which reflects the full integration of the Mongol dynastic families to Islam. Two years later, in 1318, there took place the last Synod registered by the Eastern Syriac Church, during which the Metropolitan Joseph of Arbela was elected Catholicos under the name of Timothy II. He was the last Catholicos enthroned on the site of the Sassanian town of Veh-Ardashir near Ctesiphon.⁴²⁵ The Christians benefited for a few more years from the protection of Amir Chupan, who was at the service of the Il-Khans. Informed of Amir Chupan's benevolence towards Christians, the Pope sought to establish relations with him.⁴²⁶ Nonetheless, he was also the main cause of rupture between the Latin states and Persia, as he reestablished Sunnism as the official religion, which improved the relations between Mamluk Egypt and the Khanate of Persia. It culminated in a definitive peace treaty in 1322.⁴²⁷ Five years later, in 1327 Amir Chupan was executed, and the Christians lost an important protector in the government. Heavy taxes were imposed on them (in 1330) and in many areas they had to observe special dress codes. Churches were destroyed and the Muslims exhumed the body of the Catholicos Yahballaha III from the convent of John the Baptist and turned the place into a mosque. Many Christians apostatized during this period.⁴²⁸ Despite these reactions against non-Muslims, in 1333 a Jew from Baghdad named Mansur b. Abi al-Aron, won a high ranking position next to Abu Sa'id, with the title Sadid al-Dawla. In the Arabic sources he is named 'Rukn li'l-Yahud' (the pillar of the Jews) of Baghdad. He was able to build himself a mausoleum before his death. He was an important figure in his own community. At the end it seems that another crisis appeared and that he converted along with several Jews in Baghdad. He then had churches transformed into mosques. His son Mas'ud also attained high positions, and he had probably converted too as he had inherited his father's wealth; nonetheless, he had his father's Jewish name engraved on one of the walls of a *madrasa* (Muslim college).[429] Whether all these converts remained *anusim* (concealed Jews) or not is an enigma.

5) Christians and Diplomacy

As briefly mentioned earlier, one of the most important roles played by Christians during the Mongol period was in their missions to Europe. Their function as ambassadors enhanced their value for the Mongols, who considered them the best intermediaries between themselves and the Western Christian sovereigns.

Moreover, because of their wars with the Muslims, the Mongols could not trust local Muslim officials as their representatives. Thus, the Mongols dispatched Christian emissaries even to the Muslim princes of Mesopotamia. But Muslim rulers approved neither of the Mongols nor of their Christian diplomats. The ruler of Mayyafariqin crucified the Jacobite legate sent by Hulagu. Hulagu avenged his death by massacring the Muslim population of the town and sparing the Christians.[430]

Initially, Western Christian powers feared the Mongols due to their ravages in eastern Europe. In 1259, Poland and Hungary were still suffering from Mongol attacks. That year, Pope Alexander IV even condemned the Christian prince of Antioch for siding with the Mongols. Moreover, Hulagu's first attempts to establish relations with the West were not a brilliant diplomatic stroke. For example, in a letter of 1262 to King Louis IX, he mentioned that his army had slaughtered 200, 000 people in Baghdad.[431] However, towards the end of his reign, the Mongol advances in Europe had ceased and the Mamluks' attacks on Christian possessions in the Levant brought the Pope and the Franks closer to the Mongols. It was only about 1263-1264 that the Europeans were disposed to receive envoys sent by the Mongols. Brother David seems to be the first one to have seen the Pope on the Mongols' behalf, and he assured the sovereign pontiff about Hulagu's future intention to embrace Christianity, which seems to have been believed also by the Armenian chronicler Vartan.[432] The arrival of this envoy in Rome reconstituted the old relations between Iran and the West which had ceased after the Arab invasion. Numerous envoys were dispatched from the Ilkhanid court to the Christian courts and vice-versa, trying to find a common strategy for fighting the Muslims. The aim was to co-ordinate military forces and defeat the Mamluks.[433]

It is not certain how determined the successive Popes were to fight along with the Mongols against the Muslim Mamluks. Pope Urban IV, for instance, employed more efforts in increasing the sphere of his influence and bringing the Christian communities of the Mongol Empire under the 'spiritual domination' of Rome than in mobilizing the European armies.[434] He sent a series of missionaries to Iran and the majority of them settled in areas where there was a local Christian community. As it was more difficult to convert Mongols, the Catholic missionaries left that task to the local Nestorians.

Abaqa (1265-1282) continued his predecessors' endeavours to maintain close relations with the Latin powers. In 1274, he sent a large group of Christians to the Council of Lyon. Some of the representatives embraced Catholicism in order to demonstrate their sovereign's goodwill. The envoys returned to Abaqa the following year bringing nothing but a letter from the Pope Gregory X urging him to become Christian. Abaqa himself was preoccupied by the attacks of the Golden Horde, and could not dedicate his army to the war in the Levant to satisfy the European princes.[435]

If these contacts did not bear any fruit at the military level, they did have economic and religious consequences. Numerous Italian merchants established themselves in Tabriz during Abaqa's reign. Their presence is attested to in 1264, right after the first contacts between the Il-Khans and the Pope. All those for whom records are available travelled with Christian missionaries. Most of these merchants did not enjoy high social status, and so needed the assistance of Christian dignitaries to enter the court. The presence of these Italian merchants facilitated the stay of Dominican and Franciscan monks in the country: they could rely on a Catholic community and at the same time justify their presence in Iran after the conversion of the Mongols, who after their conversion to Islam did not tolerate any missionary activities targeting Muslim Iranians. Convents and monasteries appeared in all the major cities of the Empire where the Italian merchants had trading posts. These merchants also served as intermediaries between the European princes and the Mongols of the Il-Khanate, as their business often caused them to travel between Europe and Asia. It is noteworthy that they usually settled in a town where there was a local Christian community, such as Merv (though this had the additional attraction of being an important silk supplier at the time). Little has been found on the interaction between the local Christians and the Italian merchants. There is evidence that some merchants settled for good in Tabriz where they finished their days.[436] We know from various sources, such as the one written by Odoric of Pordenone, that European travellers and missionaries stayed in the residences of their co-religionists during their journeys.[437] These interactions would have prompted the local Christians to learn European languages, hence making them ideal diplomats. This is a quality that was appreciated in the Christian Armenians from the Safavid period onwards.

Indeed, one of the most famous ambassadors sent to Rome was the Nestorian monk Bar Sauma, who had been chosen for his linguistic skills, and probably also because he was an Uighur and a close companion of the Catholicos Yahballaha III. He was sent two years after Isa Kelemchi's mission, which had already promised the joint sovereignty of the Pope and Qubilai Khan over the Levant upon their victory. Thus, Bar Sauma went to Europe in 1287 with four other Nestorian ambassadors. In Rome he repeated the words of his predecessors, offering a military alliance with the Christian princes to defeat the Egyptian Mamluks and emphasizing again the favour of the Mongol sovereign for the Christians. He also promised that the day Jerusalem would be liberated from the Mamluks, Arghun (1284-1291) would convert to Christianity. He concluded his speech by saying 'Since I am a Christian, my word should be credible to you.'[438] Unfortunately for Arghun, the only European sovereign who showed enthusiasm for the Mongols' cause was Philippe IV le Bel of France. Charles II of Naples and James II of Aragon had exhausted their armies in a recent war in which James II had destroyed Charles II's fleet. Edward I of England simply made no promises to Bar Sauma.[439]

A year before his death, Arghun sent another series of Christian ambassadors to Rome. In order to demonstrate the goodwill of the Il-Khan, all of his representatives accepted baptism in the Roman rite. The Pope Nicolas IV then had them sent to King Edward of England. Letters were sent back to Arghun and his sons by the Pope, advising all of them to be baptised. Even Arghun's general, Tagachar received a similar letter. The Pope did not omit to send letters to influential Christians at the court such as Arghun's Christian wife, his Christian son, Nicolas, the

Nestorian bishop Bar Sauma, and the Jacobite bishop of Tabriz, Denys. He probably solicited them to defend the cause of the Roman Church in Iran. Fra Ricoldo de Monte Croce, who was visiting Iran in that year, had offended the Nestorians of Baghdad by preaching Catholic theology in their Church.[440] However, the relations with the Latin states were intense at all levels. The Franks had sent 900 skilled Genoese to help the Mongols construct a fleet to fight the Mamluks.[441]

If Ghazan's conversion was a turning point in Iranian religious history, it did not have a drastic impact on the relations between the Il-Khanate and the Latin powers. Upon his conversion, the diplomatic exchanges were interrupted for a while, but did not end completely as with the Eastern Mongols, who no longer sent High Commissioners from China. Ghazan's openness towards Christians, and his expedition against the Mamluks in 1299, reopened the military negotiations between the Persian Khanate and the Latin powers once again.[442] The Il-Khan displayed his closeness to the Christians by taking the Catholicos Yahballaha with him on the expedition to Syria. After his military successes he sent envoys to the Western Sovereigns hoping for a new alliance. The Pope and the King of Aragon prepared their fleet, but they were not followed in this enterprise by any other Christian princes. Once again the attempt at an alliance failed, but the relations between the two parties resumed again. That year Ghazan took the Catholicos back with him to Azerbaijan. Yahballaha was not required to accompany Ghazan on the subsequent expeditions to Syria which took place in 1301 and 1302. He was confident that the Latin sovereigns regarded him henceforth as an ally.[443]

Important diplomatic exchanges occurred in 1302. Ghazan sent his vizier Sa'd al-Din to the Pope for the negotiation. Sa'd al-Din, was probably deemed trustworthy for such mission because of his aversion to Sunnism; however, he still needed the blessing of the Il-Khanate's Christians, whose recommendations mattered to the European ecclesiastics. Sa'd al-Din carried several letters from the bishops of Iran and Mesopotamia to the Pope.[444] Ghazan also used the diverse influential Christians to promote his image as the 'friend of Christianity'. King Hethum I was one of them. The Byzantine Emperor Andronicus II (1282-1328) also sent an ambassador to Ghazan, offering him the hand of one his daughters in marriage and seeking the Il-Khan's protection against neighbouring hostile Turks.[445]

Upon the death of Ghazan in 1304, Yahballaha must have felt insecure, and sought external protection. He wrote to the new Pope

Benedict XI, accepting his proposition for union with the Roman Church. However, he mentioned that the task would be very difficult as he needed the approbation of his suffragans.[446] It is interesting that the Jacobite Bishop, Denys, had already yielded to Pope Nicolas IV's exhortation for Uniat Status in 1291, the year the non-Muslims were afflicted with a new crisis following the execution of the Jewish Grand Vizier, Sa'd al-Dawla.[447] As we saw, the Jacobites had been reduced to a very small community by that time.[448] Therefore, Denys was probably hoping to save the remnants of the Jacobite Church by acquiring the Pope's support.

Uljaytu's lack of consideration towards Christians had damaged the relations between Persia and Europe. Uljaytu (1304-1316) continued to send letters, but the Pope and the kings of France and England no longer showed the Mongol sovereign any enthusiasm. King Edward II responded to his letter in 1307, saying that the distance between his Kingdom and the Levant made any cooperation impossible. The Pope responded in 1308 that he would write to the Il-Khan whenever a decision was planned for the invasion of the Holy Land. Iran vanished from European literary works, and missionary activities declined, leaving only the commercial activities of the Italian traders.[449]

In 1319, during Abu Sa'id's reign, Pope John XXII divided the Franciscan diocese of Khan Baliq (China), and created a new ecclesiastical seat in Sultaniya, to which he confided Western Asia, India and Ethiopia. The first incumbent was Francis of Perugia, who was granted six suffragans; he was followed by William Adam in 1323. There were Catholic bishoprics established in Tabriz, Maragha and Dehkhwarqan. The atmosphere of insecurity persuaded a group of Armenian monks to join Rome in 1319.[450]

Knowing the benevolence of Amir Chupan towards Christians, the Pope wrote to him in 1321 to recommend his Franciscan missionaries and all the Christians residing in Persia. It appears that he listened to the Pope's exhortations, at least to protect the Christian Armenians from their Muslim neighbours.[451] But two years later, a definitive peace treaty was agreed between the Persian Khanate and Mamluk Egypt, and the political relations between Persia and the Latin states deteriorated, if they did not actually temporarily cease.[452] By 1328, Barthelemy of Bologna was the only Catholic bishop left in Persia, in the town of Maragha.[453] The Nestorians had lost so much of their influence and presence at the court that the ambassadors were henceforth chosen from the Italian merchants established in Iran, who had certainly acquired the local language, now making non-Iranian Christians ideal representatives.

6) The Cultural Renaissance of Non-Muslims under the Mongols

One of the most important effects of the Mongol invasion was the 'secularization' of the cultural atmosphere in Iran. For the first time in centuries Islam was abolished as the official religion, and no other state religion was imposed. Consequently, not only were non-Muslims politically and socially emancipated, they were also culturally 'demarginalized'. As Islam was not supported by the new rulers, its language, Arabic, lost its cultural dominance to Persian.[454] The Mongols used Persian extensively in their diplomatic exchanges. Even the rulers of the Golden Horde sent letters in Persian to the sovereigns of other states besides those of Iran.[455] The emergence of Persian as the language of art and science, although not falling directly within the scope of this study, had a notable impact on the non-Muslims and their participation in the new developing culture. Persian, unlike Arabic, did not challenge their tradition, as it had no religious value. Thus, it could be used without inhibition.

The first non-Muslim group to manifest itself in Dari Persian, appears to have been the Zoroastrians. During the 9th and 10th centuries, a series of Zoroastrian religious texts were produced in Pahlavi scripture, and one Zoroastrian author, Kay Kavus, even wrote his story in Classical Persian, but after the tenth century no Zoroastrian documents are preserved until the Mongol invasion.[456] This scarcity of sources makes the evaluation of the Zoroastrians' cultural activity difficult; nonetheless, some inferences maybe drawn from the works of Zarthusht Bahram, and his father Bahram Pajdu.

A year after Hulagu acceeded to the throne (i.e. 1257), Bahram Pajdu, wrote a treatise in Persian titled *Bahariyyat*. His son, Zartusht Bahram, tells us that he was an astrologer and a scholar well-versed in Pahlavi and Dari Persian. However, his work *Bahariyyat* was not outstanding and he may owe the survival of his name to his son, whose work achieved a certain degree of popularity thanks to his *Arda Viraz Nama*.[457]

Zartusht Bahram wrote *Arda Viraz Nama*, along with *Changranghacha-nama*, and *Qissa-ya Umar Khattab va Shahzada-ya Iran-Zamin* during the reign of Abaqa (1265-1282).[458] He was wrongly held to be the author of *Zartusht-nama*,[459] which he had in fact recopied as he considered it a pious deed to revive a story related to Zoroastrianism and the memory of its deceased author Kaykavus. Zartusht Bahram could relate to Kaykavus, as like him he wrote in difficult times. Kaykavus seems to have written his story during a period when Turkish dynasties were taking over the rulership of eastern Iran, and not long after the Caliph al-Radi had a leading Zoroastrian priest executed (cir. 935). Zartusht Bahram witnessed the destruction wrought by the Mongol invaders. Both Kaykavus' *Zartusht-nama* and Zartusht Bahram's *Arda Viraz Nama* contain passages which reflect the political situation of the time. Iran was going to be delivered from its enemies and a Zoroastrian king would again occupy the throne.

Zartusht Bahram should have been all the more captivated by the *Zartusht-nama* as the text contained prophetic verses which predicted the Mongol invasion:

> From the country of the Turks, of Baikand, Khutlan and China, an army will invade Iran. The kingdom and the fortune of the rulers will come to an end, and the crown and the throne will fall to the hands of the vassals. They will gather considerable wealth and treasure, and will squander them utterly.[460]

In his *Arda Viraz Nama*, Zartusht Bahram laments over the situation of Iran in his time. The verses were written under Mongol rule, but the author cautiously avoids naming the new invaders:

> In the days of irreligion they flocked in their thousands, destroying without measure like demons. Lord, in this misadventure we are to be blamed in every way. As a result we have been tormented by demons, through the hands of irreligious Turks. From end to end, the world is turned into a cemetery; houses and possessions have been blended with corpses.[461]

It is evident from this *Arda Viraz Nama* that the Zoroastrians were immensely afflicted by the Mongol invasion. Zartusht Bahram refers to them as irreligious Turks who turned the world into a field of corpses. As mentioned earlier, one of the last ancient fire temples, which according to Qazwini were extant in the 13th century, was apparently destroyed by the Mongols when they passed through Karkuye in Sistan.[462] Thus, even if they were no longer under Muslim rule, Zoroastrians were still not benefiting from the security and good fortune gained by other non-Muslim communities under Mongol dominion. They had no protector among those in power. As we saw in our historical analysis of the period, there is no mention of any Zoroastrian official in the Mongol courts. Because of the fact that Zartusht Bahram wrote in the Arabic script, he found an audience beyond the Zoroastrian community. His works have been preserved along with the verses of Attar in manuscripts copied by Muslims for audiences in Bukhara.[463]

Another important effect of the Mongol conquest had been the dissolution of the borders of Islamic lands in Asia, encouraging cultural exchange between Iran and the rest of the continent. Thus, Rustam Mihraban was able to visit India in 1269, which previously would have been difficult for a Zoroastrian. At that time, Gujarat had still not been integrated into the Persian cultural sphere, and thus Rustam Mihraban provided the Parsis with only Pahlavi manuscripts, which he copied himself. Fifty-four years later (in 1323), his great-great nephew Mihraban Kaykhusraw also travelled to India, and like his uncle copied texts from the Pahlavi literature for his Indian co-religionists.[464] While, the two Zoroastrian travellers did not produce any work of their own, they nonetheless lay the foundation for further cultural contact between the Zoroastrians of Iran and India, who after the Tughluq's conquest of Gujarat in the 15th century,[465] adopted Persian as language of belles lettres.

The Zoroastrians were not the only non-Muslims to use Persian as a cultural language in the 13th century. The Jews also admitted the 'standard Classical Persian' into their literature at this period.[466] The only surviving pre-Ilkhanid materials in Judeo-Persian are commercial and legal documents of which samples have been found dating back to the 8th century, and some biblical translations and exegeses dating from the 11th and the 12th centuries. Although the Jews living in Iran spoke the local language, and the Jewish religious dignitaries from Baghdad communicated with them in Persian,[467] before the Mongols' rule they used a Persian 'with its own linguistic peculiarities'.[468] Until Persian had displaced Arabic as the language of the elite and savants, the Jews were not inclined to write their literature in Persian.

Incidentally, along with the Mongol rulers, one of the first learned men to foster Persian as the medium for science and literature was of Jewish extraction. Indeed, Rashid al-Din wrote one of the most important medieval historical works in Persian. It is true that he converted to Islam; nonetheless, Judaism was an integral part of his formation and its influence on his work is visible.[469] Moreover, he converted quite late in his life, along with his patron Ghazan Khan (1295-1304), whose conversion we argued earlier to have been prompted by political considerations.

Rashid al-Din was conscious that he was closely watched by the Muslims because of his Jewish background, and this is reflected in his book. Throughout his work, he was very careful to adhere to the Muslims' mentality, and for instance he referred to Ananda, the Emperor of China, as a Muslim.[470] Furthermore, Rashid al-Din omitted an anecdote in which Jews were wronged, even though we know that he drew extensively on the work of Juwayni,[471] who had not hesitated to cite the occasion when Ugeday had exempted Muslim, Christian and Shamanist clergymen from taxation, leaving out the Jews.[472] Rashid al-Din apparently deemed mention of the affair compromising.

Rashid al-Din knew Hebrew, so that it was possible to accuse him of having written a letter in Hebrew characters against the Il-Khan. He had a profound knowledge of Judaism, which is evident in his advice to the Il-Khan with regard to the Jewish diet and the religious laws emanating from the Exodus 34:26, Leviticus 11:4 and Deuteronomy 14:7. His works also include biblical citations and explanations of Hebrew words.[473]

Another field to which Rashid al-Din greatly contributed was science. It is said that he was a pharmacist himself, but he reached fame as a physician.[474] These were fields which attracted many Christians and Jews. As late as 1329, Ibn al-Ukhuwwa attested that many towns had *dhimmi* physicians,[475] which demonstrates that the Muslims were not able to supplant them in this field. Elgood says that Rashid al-Din was the scholar who made Persian into the language of science, to the detriment of Arabic. He developed the hospitals of Shiraz and Hamadan, his native town and sought to eliminate corruption in the hospital administrations so that patients would receive proper treatment.[476] In Tabriz he established a medical centre for training physicians and healing patients.[477] Rashid al-Din also encouraged works of translation and invited foreigners and local Christians to collaborate with him in such tasks. He requested that a book called the *History of Franks* be translated for him into Persian from Latin.[478]

It is remarkable that the celebrated Jewish literature from the Mongol period, did not appear until the reign of Abu Sa'id, after Rashid al-Din was executed. There are a number of documents from that epoch, such as the manuscript of a Judeo-Persian Pentateuch written by a certain Joseph b. Moses in 1319, and held in the British Library. The author of that manuscript refers to a number of treatises written around the same period, namely the *Biur Milot Ha-Torah* and the *Perush Ha-Milot* dedicated to lexicography. There are also two Bible dictionaries composed at that time and still extant. One of them was produced by Salomon b. Samuel in 1339 from the city of Urgenj in Transoxania. His dictionary was copied in Merv, and sent to Samarqand.[479]

The works of famous Jewish poets from Spain such as Judah Ha-Levi, Salomon b. Gabriol, Israel Najara were translated into Judeo-Persian in the 14th century. Many famous Persian poets were highly appreciated by the Iranian Jews, and the poems of Nizami, Rumi and Sa'di were all transliterated into Judeo-Persian. However, the man reputed to be the pioneer in Judeo-Persian poetry is Mawlana Shahin, who was born at the end of the 13th century in Shiraz, and displayed his talent during the reign of the Mongol Il-Khan Abu Sa'id Bahadur (1316-1335). Shiraz was then a renowned cultural centre, which as we know produced important poets such as Sa'di and later Hafiz, and at the same time the town had a flourishing Jewish community. Shahin was a near contemporary of Hafiz (d. 1389) and began his career not long after Sa'di. Babai b. Lutf, the Jewish Iranian chronicler of the 17th century has compared him to both poets for his literary talents.[480] Shahin wrote two major collections of poetry. One gathers together his pentateuchal epics: *Bereshit-nama* (Book of Genesis), *The Tale of Job* and *Musa-nama* (Book of Moses), and his other work consists of epics based on the *Book of Esther* (*Ardashir-nama*), and the prophetic books of Ezra and Nehemiah (*Ezra-nama*).[481] He employed Jewish themes, but set them in a Persian garb. His reconstitution of the Jewish past was modelled in the fashion of Firdawsi's epic of Iranian kings. Moses, for example, is turned into an epic hero; in his *Ardashir-nama*, Cyrus the Great becomes the offspring of Esther and Ardashir son of Isfandiyar. Shahin was also influenced by Nizami for the poetical structure of his *Ardashir-nama*. For obvious reasons, Shahin was in contact with Muslim learned men of his time, and his knowledge encompassed the Bible and rabbinic literature (*Talmud* and *Midrash*); he fully mastered the forms and conceits of classical Persian poetry. It is not certain whether the miniature paintings in his manuscripts were drawn by Jewish artists or whether Muslim Persians collaborated with the poet.[482]

The excerpt selected here is a panegyric to Sultan Abu Sa'id, who was the last Mongol ruler descending from Hulagu:

> In Praise of Bahadur Abu Sa'id, Monarch of Shahin's Realm:
> Upon the great Shah, monarch and son of monarchs, Bahadur Bu Sa'id,
> Reigning Khan, generous lord of the universe, let the company of victory and good fortune fall.
> He is the Faridun of the age, the Alexander of our time;
> May the evil eye never glimpse his face!
> He is generous to the kingdoms of the world;
> He wears Faridun's crown upon his brow.
> Endless arrays of soldiers, entire armies he musters through justice and right action.
> 5   Kings of the world, from one end to the other, bring him tribute from every direction.
> Since Jamshid's time such a radiant sun
> Has not been seen in the world.
> He made justice and equity abide everywhere;
> All creatures rejoice through his good fortune.
> If in ages past, in Nushirvan's fabled times,
> Lambs and wolves drank from the same spring,
> Now in the monarch's age,
> No blood-thirsty wolf dares even to appear at the gates of a house.
> 10 The Shah rids the world of all seeds of oppression;
> He tears the ears of enemies to shreds.
> The world flourishes through his good fortune;
> Whoever hears his name cannot but rejoice.
> Through all the regions in which he rides,
> He scatters happiness from his stirrup;
> Happiness's happiness is Bu Sa'id;
> May his happiness increase daily,
> And may the royal crown never depart from his august brow.
> May God Himself be his friend everywhere, and may misfortune never harm his throne and crown.[483]

The combination of religious freedom with the desire to reach a wider audience prompted even Nestorian Christians to use Persian. During the reign of Gaikhatu (1291-1295), a certain Iwanis (John) of Tabriz desired to strengthen the ties between the Christian communities in Iran and visited the Armenian and Nestorian communities of Khurasan and Tabaristan. Seeing that Syriac was not understood by the majority, he translated the Diatessaron of Tatien and had four copies made and sent to Herat, Mazandaran, Nishapur and Tus.[484] This was not the only Christian volume to be written in Persian at this period. It seems that the Nestorian Mongols in Iran, like the majority of the Mongols in Western Asia, had adopted Persian for expressing themselves in literature and diplomacy. Thus the account of the travels of Bar Sauma and Yahballaha, discussed above, was originally written by the former in Persian, and then translated into Syriac.[485]

Nonetheless, the most impressive Christian literary work from the Mongol period was written in Syriac and then translated into Arabic by Bar Hebraeus (d.1286). It should be mentioned that Bar Hebraeus began his literary career before the completion of the Mongol conquest, and therefore before the new cultural trend generated by the Mongols, which encouraged the usage of Persian. Moreover, Bar Hebraeus spent only the last twenty years of his life in Iran (i.e. Maragha) and had lived mostly in Mesopotamia where Persian was not the dominant language. Bar Hebraeus also produced treatises on Medicine and Syriac grammar, and wrote commentaries on sections of the Bible and the Jacobite canon. Although Gillman believes that he was not anti-Nestorian, he rarely alluded to Nestorians as honourable people. One reason why he approved of the Catholicos Yahballaha was that he was not a dogmatic Nestorian, if indeed he did not just belong nominally to that denomination.[486] Bar Hebraeus' *Universal History* remains to this date the most important primary source for the study of Christians in Persia up to the 13th century.

The last notable literary figure among the Nestorians was Abdiso b. Berikka (d. 1310). He also produced important literary works like Bar Hebraeus. After him, the Ancient Church of Iran declined dramatically, ending Christian scholarship in Persia. Even Gundishapur, which had been for centuries a centre of Christian medical education, no longer produced Christian physicians, as by 1318 there seem to have been no more Christians in that town.[487]

At the architectural level, the Christians were, for obvious reasons, also very active during the Mongol period. In 1282, an oratory was constructed in a church in Tabriz. The event was important for Bar Hebraeus, and apparently he was the one who had instigated its building.[488] Bar Sauma (d. 1294), famous for his missions to Europe, was another active clergyman who had an important church built in Maragha, intending that it should replace the mobile church of the Mongol camps. Thanks to the many endowments he received from the court, the Catholicos Yahballaha also had a 'magnificent' convent (of John the Baptist) built in Maragha. These edifices represented the Christians' architectural masterpieces. Not many names of Christian architects have survived, and little is left of their craftsmanship. The monk Jibrail of Bartelli was one of those architects. He constructed the convent of John bar Nagore on the orders of Bar Hebraeus. Sculptors (Ibrahim and Abu Salem), engravers, and silversmiths (Da'ud b. Salama) also contributed to the embellishment of these Christian edifices. The great majority of the churches were destroyed, and therefore their splendour cannot be appreciated today.[489]

Conclusion

The appearance of non-Muslims on the political and cultural scene of Mongol Persia was not a sudden phenomenon. Christians and Jews had been present in the courts of caliphs and sultans since the Arab invasion. But their presence had been waning rapidly and they were being marginalized. The Mongol invasion gave them fresh impetus.

The Christians had numerous co-religionists among the Mongols, including queens and military generals. This factor prompted them to support the Mongols, the majority of whom were Shamanist or Buddhist, against the Muslim establishment. The Jews were another group capable of winning the Mongols' confidence. Admittedly they had no powerful supporters, but their disaffection toward the Muslim majority and their medical and administrative skills opened the door of the Mongol court to their community. Their efficiency procured them even higher positions than Christians: two Jewish men, Sa'd al-Dawla and Rashid al-Din were made *Sahib al-Diwan* or Grand Vizier. By contrast, the Zoroastrians did not attain any high state positions. Under the Muslim domination their community had been weakened to such an extent that they were not able to reemerge at the political level. However, they benefited from the Mongol rule at the social level, as like other non-Muslims they were freed from the Islamic restrictions and, by the same token, exempted from the *jizya*.

At the cultural level, however, all the non-Muslim communities were stimulated by the Mongols' arrival and made important contributions to the newly regenerated Persian culture. Even Zoroastrians, who had kept themselves politically isolated, experienced a 'literary renaissance'. The Jews at this time were becoming reintegrated into Persian culture, and one of their apostates (Rashid al-Din) even contributed to the flourishing of the Persian language. The Jews' decision to write their literature in Classical Persian coincided with the expansion of the Persian culture and language in the non-Arab Islamic world.

The Christians were the non-Muslim community who introduced the most exoticism into Persian culture. Nestorian Turks and Mongols coming from the East and accompanying their Nestorian comrades to the West certainly brought many new ideas, and opened Iran to European and Chinese art and science. As intermediaries between Iran and other nations, they were able to enhance their image and position inside the country. At the same time the Christians contributed to the reestablishment of diplomatic relations between Persia and Europe, which according to Boyle were ruptured by the Arab invasion.[490]

However, the rivalries between Christians, the intrigues and litigations between Jews, and the religious liberalism of the Mongols, who allowed the Muslims to continue professing their religion freely, made the non-Muslim communities extremely vulnerable. The Shamanist and Buddhist Mongols, unlike the Jews and the Zoroastrians, had no religion attached to their ethnicity, and therefore they were not only religiously tolerant, but even open to proselytization. This in the long run was detrimental to the Christians, who had not been able to convert the Mongols, and lost the rulers of their country to the Muslims, who were more successful.

The short domination of the government by Christians had provoked the Muslims, to whom they had not been always benevolent. On the conversion of the Il-Khans to Islam, the Christians had to pay dearly for having dreamt of a Nestorian kingdom. They were henceforth held in suspicion by the Muslims, who a century earlier had deemed them as the most trustworthy of their compatriots.[491]

Furthermore, the 14th century marked the last wave of Islamification in Central Asia, which commenced under the influence of Tarmashirin in the Khanate of Chaghatai.[492] A few decades earlier, European travellers had testified that Christianity was still flourishing in Samarqand and Merv,[493] but the conversion of the Mongols precipitated the closure of many dioceses. Awdisho of Nisibis is the last ecclesiastic to mention the metropolitans of Rayy, Merv and Nishapur in 1316. Christianity vanished also from Nihavand after the 13th century. In 1339, Mustawfi Qazwini alluded to an old church (and also a fire temple) on the outskirts of Herat, between the fire temple of Sirishk and the town. The text in Persian is already written in the past tense.[494]

Chapter 4
The Post-Mongol and Pre-Safavid Period: A Brief View of Iran under the Timurids and the Aq Qoyunlu

Between the death of the last Mongol ruler Abu Sa'id (1316-1335) and the establishment of the Safavid dynasty in 1501, not much has been recorded on non-Muslims in Iran except the massacres and calamities endured by Nestorians and Jacobites. While the Nestorians were being pushed to the margins of the historical scene, the rise of contacts with Europe and India during the Timurid period paved the way for new political and economic opportunities from which non-Muslims benefited.

A brief summary of the events which followed the collapse of Mongol rule will help us understand the socio-political and economic situation of non-Muslims under the Safavids. From 1336 until the end of the 15th century, Iran was torn between different factions who strove to rule the country. The chief protagonists were four local dynasties, whose respective areas of influence comprised the entire country: the Muzaffarids took control over Central Iran, the Jalayirids imposed themselves in Mesopotamia and Azerbaijan, the Karts continued to rule in Khurasan, and the Sarbadars in Western Khurasan. Except for the Jalayirids, all of them were eliminated by Timur Lang.

Timur Lang was Mongol in origin but his tribe had adopted both the Turkish language and Islamic religion. His career appears very similar to Gengis Khan's; however, Morgan notes that Timur Lang surpassed his predecessor in cruelty. His ruthlessness is all the more remarkable as he was not an alien in the region like Gengis Khan, but a Muslim. He tortured and slaughtered his own co-religionists on a massive scale.[495] He began campaigning in 1361, after affirming his position as leader of his own tribe. By 1370 he had become the undisputed master of Transoxania, and was thus encouraged to continue his conquests. He subjugated Iran, and then plundered Syria and India. Like the Mongols, he showed some signs of pragmatism in Iran, where he spared cities and people when economic interests were at sake. Thus, the wealthy dignitaries of Herat (in 1381) and the craftsmen of Tabriz (in 1386) were spared. Even Yazd was not destroyed, despite its having defied Timur's rule in 1396, because the town was an important centre of textile manufacture.[496] His pragmatism might have prompted him to overcome his intolerance and employ non-Muslim administrators, had the latter been still involved in the state bureaucracy; however, as we saw, the Muslims had been outraged by their ascendancy under the early Mongol rulers and had instigated the dismissal of the Jews and Christians after the conversion of the Mongol rulers to Islam. Since the non-Muslims were barred from positions of influence, they had no sympathetic party close to the rulers to intercede on their behalf. As a result, the general picture of their condition under Timur is quite grim. Timur did not have much trust in the Persian bureaucrats either. He distributed the key administrative positions to Turko-Mongol military figures in order to keep the bureaucracy tightly under his control.[497]

In this respect, both the continuator of Bar Hebraeus and Sharaf al-Din Ali Yazdi have had more to say on Timur's atrocities than his philanthropic deeds. One of the first non-Muslim peoples to suffer from Timur's onslaughts were the Georgians. By 1387, Timur had already subjugated Azerbaijan and was busy devastating Georgia. The Georgian king, Bagrat V was forced to accept Islam in order to save his life, but apostatized after Timur's departure. As a result Georgia was afflicted with more calamities in 1392, 1394, 1399, 1401 and 1403.[498] One rebellion against Timur was remarkable in that one of its leaders Gudarz was identified as a Zoroastrian by some sources. The revolt was crushed at Sirjan in 1396 and Gudarz suffered the same fate as other rebel leaders such as Sultan Muhammad (son of Abu Sa'id).[499] If Gudarz was truly a Zoroastrian, this shows that even after the tenth century, the Zoroastrians were not completely politically marginalized. We will see later that another Zoroastrian reached a high rank during the Afghan occupation,[500] thus, in periods of turmoil, it was possible to see a few non-Muslims play political roles.

According to Bar Hebraeus' continuator, Takrit, a town mainly populated by Christians and earlier the centre of Jacobites, was completely destroyed in 1392 and its inhabitants were carried off into slavery. Then, Timur marched towards the Euphrates and slaughtered the people of Amid (Diyarbakir) and Edessa.[501] Timur's son, Miran Shah arrived in the area of Tur Abdin (Midyat) where he burnt a village, and then headed for Gazarta of Beth Sharwaye, where he looted the Great Church of the Jacobites.[502] Miran Shah had inherited his father's dislike for non-Muslims. While his father was occupied with campaigns in the East of the country, he had the body of Rashid al-Din, Ghazan Khan's famous vizier, exhumed and buried in the Jewish cemetery.[503] Timur himself invaded Anatolia and Mesopotamia. Once he conquered Sivas (Sebaste), he buried all the Christian soldiers alive, but spared the Muslim ones.[504] He sacked Mardin before reaching Damascus in 1399 (1400).[505] Thus, all the regions with important Jacobite and Nestorian concentrations suffered immensely from the Timurid invasion. The description of Timur's massacres prompted the Mamluk king of Egypt to send a letter to him in Damascus asking:

> I [say] tell us [what] is thy Faith? If thou art a Christian, behold thou havest no mercy to the Christians. And if thou art a Jew, behold thou dost not suffer the Jews [to live]. And if thou art an Arab, behold thou hast wiped out the Arabs utterly and hast rooted up their mosques, and thou hast slain their judges and burnt their religious teachers. There is no way for us to see and meet each other except with the sword.[506]

But political plots in Egypt prevented the Mamluks from resisting in Syria, and Damascus was sacked. Despite sparing the Muslim orders in Transoxania,[507] in Syria Timur Lang spared neither mosques nor Muslim clergy,[508] the reason being perhaps that Damascus had revolted after a first capitulation and its clergy had not supported Timur.

On his way back to Iran, Timur looted another series of Christian villages (i.e. Guzia, Beth Abishai, Kaphar Shama, Beth Ishak) and monasteries (e.g. Monastery of Kartamin) and the inhabitants of Nisibis and Ma'ara were also slain. We are told that those of the village of Arbu in Beth Risha were spared because their bishop Behnam Shabhti humbled himself in front of Timur's son.[509] Timur died in 1405 at Utrar in Transoxania, without fulfilling his wish to conquer China.[510] Anarchy followed his death. Iran along with its Nestorian population continued to suffer tremendously. After having been ravaged by Timur's army, the Mesopotamian provinces were hit by severe plagues in 1403 and in 1411, which killed 400 monks in Beth Kudsh. The region was also exposed to Kurdish raids. In 1414 the church of the village Keprath was plundered and in 1415 the patriarch Behnam was killed. There are more reports of plagues devastating the area in 1418 and 1422 and 1447. Beth Sebhiryana suffered on all these occasions. In 1432, its inhabitants were taken as captives and in 1460 it was plundered by the Kurds. In 1440 the village of Nahrawan near Baghdad was sacked and in 1444 Baghdad itself was looted. Until 1469, the area had to endure brutal Kurdish raids, and in

1491 a series of monasteries (e.g. Monastery of Mar Ya'kub of Salh) were destroyed again.[511]

As a result of these military raids and natural calamities, many of the Nestorian parishes were destroyed. Those Nestorians who were not able to escape to the Kurdish mountains and the banks of Lake Urumia were killed. None of the dioceses of Fars survived the onslaughts and epidemics.[512] By the end of the 15th century, the Nestorians were no longer conspicuous on the Iranian historical scene. The seat of the Patriarchate was moved from Baghdad to Mosul, where it remained until the 18th century, and finally ended in the Hakkari mountains, also known as Julamerik, on the borders of Persia.[513] A small population of Nestorians survived at the west of the Lake Urumia and in the Kirkuk region of Iraq.[514] Outside those regions, nothing much is recorded of the Nestorians after 1413, as they were no longer close to the centres of power and their numbers had shrunk. If the Arab invasion had sealed the fate of Zoroastrianism, the Mongol and Timurid invasions has fortuitously suppressed Nestorianism in Iran.[515]

Contacts with Europe and India

Before the Safavids, the Mongol and Turkic rulers had already established contacts with the Pope and European monarchs; however, due to the carnage wrought by Timur Lang and the turmoil that ensued after his death, diplomatic and commercial relations remained limited. By 1377, Nakhchevan already had a Catholic bishop by the name of Johannes de Galonifontibus. Under Timur he was ordained archbishop of Sultaniya by Pope Boniface IX (1389-1404). At the same period, Henry III of Castile (1309-1406) sent envoys to Timur, who reciprocated by sending an envoy named Haji Muhammad al-Qazi.[516]

The fall of Constantinople to the Ottomans in 1453, and the Ottomans' conquests in Europe made the European powers look to the Turkic rulers of Iran as potential allies against the Ottomans. The dominant Turkic dynasty in Iran at this time was the Aq Qoyunlu headed by Uzun Hasan (1453-1478). He was married to a Byzantine princess, and until the interference of the Muslim clergy in 1470, his administrative staff included a large number of Christians. His good relations with his Christian subjects and the political tensions with the Ottomans encouraged the Venetians, who had suffered the most from the territorial expansion of the Ottomans, to send several envoys to Uzun Hasan's court at Tabriz.[517] The most famous of these ambassadors were Ambrogio Contarini, Giosafat Barbaro and Caterino Zeno, who also acted as a military advisor.[518]

These military alliances and diplomatic exchanges encouraged commercial relations with Europe. The discovery of the Cape of Good Hope by the Portuguese in 1488 increased commercial opportunities. This resulted in more Europeans travelling to Iran,[519] and we will see in the following chapter that those who in the end most benefited from the new economic conditions were the Armenians, who played a pivotal role in the foreign trade of Safavid Iran.

Apart from commercial exchanges with Europe, by the 15th century there was already a dynamic trade between Iran and India,[520] and traffic between Hormuz and the other ports in the Indian Ocean was thriving. In 1442 Abd al-Razzaq described Hormuz as a cosmopolitan port, where there were merchants from all over Asia.[521] It is no coincidence that the Portuguese took possession of the place in 1507 and 1515.[522]

India had a special relation with Iran, as Muslim rulers of Turkish background and Persian culture were ruling over the northern half of the subcontinent.[523] Indeed, after 1297 the province of Gujarat in India was brought under Muslim rule and the new rulers began fostering the Persian language and culture in the region. Trade contacts along with the flourishing of Persian in India generated more interest in Iranian civilization. Thus, there were many incentives for the Parsis to visit their historical fatherland. One of the first Parsis to travel to Iran was Nariman Hushang. He arrived at Yazd in 1477 and obtained religious guidance from the *dasturs* of Sharifabad and Turkabad. These texts were collected in the *Rivayat*s named after its bearer.[524] After Nariman Hushang, travels from Iran to India became more frequent and continued even after the fall of the Safavids. As a result, Zoroastrians in India were able to establish long-lasting relations with their co-religionists in Iran. Along with the cultural flourishing of Persian, the commercial activities were a decisive factor in attracting Zoroastrians, along with other Iranian religious dissidents, to India.

In sum, the political and commercial developments under the Turkic dynasties paved the way for new conditions and opportunities for non-Muslim Iranians after the advent of the Safavids.

Chapter 5
The Safavid Period

Section 1
Between Economic Success and Social Challenge: Non-Muslims under the Safavids

There is no need to prove the importance of the Safavid period in Iranian History. It has already been established by many historians that the Safavids played a key role in shaping Iran as we know it today.[525] Roger Savory asserts that their advent in 1501 was as important as the Arab and Mongol invasions in changing the course of Iran's history.[526] This may be somewhat exaggerated, as the Safavids were not invaders, like the two aforementioned groups; moreover, at the religious level, the changes they triggered were not as dramatic as those generated by the Arabs. However, it is a fact that after 1501 a new religious orientation was imposed on Iran by Shah Isma'il I (the first Safavid king). The official religion of the country became *Twelver* Shi'ism. This ideological transformation has usually been argued to have affected all Iranians, non-Muslims and Muslims alike. However, it has not been determined with clarity how the status of the non-Muslims was redefined.

Few historians have written on the topic, but most will agree that, by virtue of its Shi'ite character, Iran offers a new perspective for the study of non-Muslims in Islamic lands. Theoretically, Shi'ism and Sunnism did not enshrine identical views of non-Muslims, nor did the different Sunnite schools always agree about their status.[527]

Certainly, the territorial losses under Safavid rule and the earlier disruptions, after the conversion of the Mongols to Islam had the effect of changing the distribution of the non-Muslim population and weakening their communities more than ever. The most conspicuous occurrence was the reduction of the Christian population. Geographically, Mesopotamia with its various Christian populations was lost to the Ottomans. Moreover, as the Mongol rulers had failed to give them protection, the Nestorians had been exposed to many brutal attacks, some of which had been provoked by the Christians' temporary ascendancy over the Muslims. Timur Lang's carnage in Iran and neighbouring lands wrought much harm to what had remained of the Church of Iran.

The decline of the Christian population seems to have generated a vacuum in society, and, as is well known, the Safavids imported many skilled Christians from the Caucasus to Iran to compensate for this. The Armenians were to take over the role which Nestorians had played earlier as intermediaries between Iran and other states, distinguishing themselves in commerce, but the majority of the Georgians and Circassians converted and enrolled in the army. Moreover, as in the Ottoman Empire, many Christian women from the Caucasus were taken into the *harems*. As a result, Christians had some advantages compared with other religious minorities, who only rarely had a co-religionist in the court. Nonetheless, at the cultural level, both Jews and Zoroastrians were as active as the Christians. They were also less isolated than in the previous centuries, thanks to the numerous contacts that had been generated between Iran and the rest of the world.

The interactions with other nations, the settling of a new religious minority among the Iranians, and the change of Islamic dogma in Iran, all tend to complicate the status of religious minorities in the Safavid period. Unfortunately, there is a tendency in scholarship to simplify the issue, and many modern writers have hastened to describe Safavid rule as a period of harsh persecution and to characterize Shi'ism as the most intolerant form of Islam. In fact, in this chapter we will see that life for the religious minorities did not solely change because of the switch from Sunnism to Shi'ism. Their situation changed because of the wars with the neighbouring Muslim lands, and the lucrative commercial exchanges with Europe and India. Thus, the geographical location of Iran and its Mongol legacy played a more important role in defining the non-Muslims' position than the newly imposed Shi'ite creed. As under the Sunnite rule, there were times when the non-Muslims were able to secure for themselves the benevolence of the rulers, while during periods of socio-economic crisis they were victims of persecutions. In principle, according to Shi'ite creed, the Shi'ite ecclesiastical dignitaries, or the *mujtahids*, ought to be in charge of legal and political matters rather than the sovereign, and in times of political chaos the *mujtahids* did succeed in usurping power and persecuting religious minorities. However, they were able to dominate Persian politics only towards the end of the Safavid period. Initially, the new political, social and religious changes in Iran were not at all to the detriment of non-Muslims. As after the Mongol invasion, the preoccupation of the new masters of Iran was the Muslim majority who had the potential to overthrow them, not the religious minorities who would settle for mere toleration.

Despite the silence of the Muslim authors on these groups, we will see that non-Muslims played key roles in the economy of Safavid Iran. They were even able to leave traces of their literary and artistic talents. This is an interesting period full of contradictions, when religious fanaticism appears together with the beginnings of nationalism and the secularization of foreign diplomacy.

1) The Advent of the Safavids and the Non-Muslims

Some historians have tended to exaggerate the changes that occurred in Iran during this period. As we observed earlier, the advent of the Safavids did not generate a formidable political and cultural upheaval. The Safavids were not foreign invaders like the Arabs, the Mongols or Timur Lang. They rose to power from within Iran. In fact, Shah Isma'il I, the founder of the Safavid dynasty, was related through his father to the Turkmen dynasty that ruled Iran before them: Shaykh Haydar (Isma'il's father) had married Uzun Hasan's daughter Marta.[528]

The establishment of Shi'ism and the enhancement of a strong state by the Safavids had more significant social consequences than it did political ones. The Ottomans and the ruling class of Iran were more affected by such a change than the non-Muslims. As far as the non-Muslims were concerned, the Shi'itization of Iran did not alter dramatically their lives. In fact, the most significant religious hostilities that followed the arrival of the Safavids were between Shi'ites and Sunnites.[529] As in all periods of war between Muslim factions or nations, less animosity was shown to non-Muslims than in peace time. They suffered through the tumult like the Muslims, without their religion causing them significant problems in addition. Unfortunately, there are not many documents on the non-Muslims in Iran at this period, therefore it is very difficult to evaluate their situation during this period of religious disturbance.

The first Safavid monarch, Isma'il, was strongly attached to Islam, and like the Sunnites, viewed the non-Muslims as 'infidels'. Nonetheless, he did not have the opportunity of his Sunnite predecessors, or even his father and grandfather, to cause havoc in the Christian Caucasus. Alvand, the sultan of the Aq Qoyunlu dynasty, had mobilized against him while he was fighting against the Shirvanshahs in the Caucasus. Therefore, in 1501 he had to return south. Husayni says that he plundered Georgia on his way back to the Araxes valley, where he was successful against Alvand.[530] However, as he had to reach his destination swiftly, Georgia was spared destruction. Even his later campaign of 1522 in Tiflis, unlike the battles of his son, Tahmasp, did not leave an indelible mark in the memories of the Georgians. Therefore, it appears that Isma'il had to dedicate most of his time fighting other Muslims in order to impose his hegemony in Iran. In these conditions, Isma'il could not concentrate on warfare against Christian principalities, and was even less interested in harassing the non-Muslims under his rule, as he had not much to gain from it.

Shah Tahmasp followed in his father's footsteps and invaded Georgia on several occasions. He led four campaigns against the Georgians between 1540 and 1554. On his first incursion in 1540, Shah Tahmasp's army poured into Tiflis and plundered the city, taking women and children as captives. Gulbad, one of the chief nobles of Lawasun, converted to Islam in order to have his life spared, but all those in the fort of Birtis who did not convert to Islam were slaughtered. After plundering Georgia in 1546, Shah Tahmasp invaded the country again five years later and captured numerous Georgian nobles. He took many of them to his court, but had Lawasun Shir Mazan Ughali and Wakhush killed. He then made Kaykhusraw son of Qurqura governor of the Georgian territories under Safavid jurisdiction. In 1553 Shah Tahmasp sent a punitive expedition to Georgia and once again deported and eliminated a number of Georgian nobles.[531] The *Chronicle of the Carmelites* says that during these deportations, Shah Tahmasp carried more than 30,000 young men and women from Georgia to Iran.[532] These deportations changed the ethnic composition of the Iranian army, court and population in general. From Tahmasp's reign onwards until the end of the Safavid period, the royal guards and even the commander of the army was commonly chosen from among Georgians.[533] This was a strategy to undermine the power of the Turkmen military aristocracy, which the Safavids perceived as a threat.[534] As we shall see, the Safavid *harems* also held many Georgian and Circassian women who exerted much influence on the Shah and his viziers. All those Georgians who were enrolled in the army or given prominent positions at the court were forced to convert to Islam. The rest of them were allowed to maintain their religion and were tolerated, though they were labelled as *gabrs* (pagans) when they were resisting the Muslim invaders.[535]

2) **The Social Struggle and Economic Activities of the Zoroastrians**

The aggression against the infidels, then, was conducted outside Safavid territories. For those non-Muslims living in Iran, nothing much had changed, although after Shah Isma'il's victory over the Aq Qoyunlu and the further consolidation of the Safavid hegemony under Shah Tahmasp, the non-Muslim communities were anxious to establish amicable relations with the new rulers of the country. Aware of the new ruler's zealous support for the Shi'ite creed and the cult of Ali, they were apprehensive about new forms of religious discrimination. Islam clearly recognized Judaism and Christianity, but its attitude towards Zoroastrianism was ambiguous.[536] There are sufficient historical testimonies to show that under the Safavids, the Zoroastrians were the least well accepted of all the non-Muslim groups.[537] This factor prompted them to find strategies in order to avoid more discriminations or forced conversions. The accounts in *Mino Khirad*, which were written during the Safavid period, demonstrate that the Zoroastrians sought textual proof in defence of their religion. The samples provided here display Ali, the figurehead of the Shi'ite faction, as a defender of the Zoroastrians and their religion.

> Then he (the *Mubid*) produced a letter,
> In the handwriting of Zardusht of pure religion.
> The entire letter was full of meaning,
> It was written in the Pahlavi script.
> As the reciter chanted (the verses) of the letter serenely.
> The meaning thereof he sprinkled on him (Ali).
> Everything that was to occur in the world,
> He read and his (Ali's) two ears heard.
> All the presage on Muhammad's time,
> Were mentioned in that orderly letter.
> How from Mecca he was to appear,
> And how blacks and whites alike were to become his followers...
> As the *Mubid* chanted the stories for him,
> And Ali heard them, he was struck with amazement.[538]

In these verses we are told that Zarathushtra had predicted the advent of Muhammad, and that Ali was stupefied by such a prophecy. It is clear that such a story was not meant for a Zoroastrian audience, but was written by Zoroastrians in order to show Muslims the divinatory abilities of their prophet Zarathushtra. As could be expected, the Muslims have kept no record of such texts, as lauding Zarathushtra did not serve any of their purposes. These verses were probably preserved by religious or community leaders, and were presented to Muslim authorities whenever their religion was questioned.

In the following verses, we are told that Ali wished to destroy the buildings erected by the order of Khusraw Anushiravan, until he heard about his wisdom and read about a special *dakhma* (tower of silence) which he built near Mada'in. Ali was intrigued by this mysterious place and decided to visit it, hoping to see Anushiravan in a vision. It should be remembered that Anushiravan is evoked in Iranian texts as one of the most pious Zoroastrian kings, and his devotion to the Iranian faith remains unchallenged. Once again, the author of the text aims to demonstrate Ali's respect towards an important Zoroastrian figure.

> In the fire temple of Pars I read the following,
> That Nushiravan, the praiseworthy king,
> Built a *dakhma* on the mount Mada'in,
> A building whose top touched the sky.
> To that mountain shall I now find my way,
> So that I may have a glimpse of it.
> Maybe then I will receive something of his wisdom,
> By envisioning his rite and lore.[539]

Acknowledging the sanctity of the *dakhma*, Ali and his Muslim followers dismount from their horses:

> As they were approaching the magnificent *Marquzan*,
> The amir (Ali) said to his worthy followers:
> 'That near this renowned *dakhma*,
> It is not proper to be mounted on the saddle.'[540]

Once in the *dakhma*, Ali repents of his initial intention to destroy the place and then has a vision of King Khusraw Anushiravan.

> Ali ran towards the King of Justice,
> As soon as his eyes fell on Nushiravan.
> And as he saw him full of glory and strength,
> He bit his lips in repentance.
> By his throne he paid him tribute,
> A tribute to his very spectre.

'Why did I hold grudges against him,
And wanted to destroy his edifices?
I regret those (vile) intentions,
O God forgive me, as I am tormented.'

Then Ali read the tablets left by Khusraw Anushiravan:

Thus had the righteous King written to them,
'When I will leave this world,
Many years after my time,
A king among Arabs,
Will come to visit me at *Marquzan*,
And as he will see my accomplishments and my righteousness,
He will behold me with benevolence,
And will give endowments to this *dakhma*.'[541]

In the following verses, Ali undertakes a pilgrimage to Mecca after his visit to the *dakhma* and discloses his astonishment about the wisdom of Anushiravan. He is then presented as an enthusiast defender of Zoroastrians. We are told that he wrote an ordinance, in which he asked Muslims not to harm or oppress Zoroastrians if they wished not to experience Hell in the afterlife.

For three days he (Ali) rested at Mada'in,
On the fourth day he stared off towards Mecca.
He went to the house of the Almighty,
And did his pilgrimage there as he had yearned.
Wherever appeared the *Lion of God* (Ali),
Blessings were increased upon the fair ones.
He spoke about the wisdom of Nushirvan,
He was always honouring his memory.
He wrote a covenant with piety and justice,
And honoured in every way the *Good Religion*[542] :
'May the Zoroastrians be spared
May the oppressor of this community suffer.
If anyone terrorizes this community,
May his place be in the deep hell.
Whoever has good intentions for this community,
Will not be reprimanded by the offsprings of the *nabi* (Muhammad).
May he meet happiness in both worlds,
As promised by the *rasul* (Muhammad)[543] and by the covenant of Ali.'

Thus again he made the *Good Religion* prosper,
And destroyed and dislodged oppression from its roots.[544]

Recapitulating the content of the five extracts of *Mino Khirad* cited here, it appears that the Zoroastrians were subject to harassment by the Shi'ite majority, and that at times their shrines and temples were under threat of being destroyed. It is not known how successful they were with these testimonies in their attempts to stop the abuses. The last excerpt mentions a covenant (*ahd-nama*), that the Zoroastrians claim was given to them by Ali. More than two centuries later, the count de Gobineau visited Iran and says that the Muslims doubted the authenticity of the document.[545] However, on the evidence of available sources, it appears that the Zoroastrians were usually able to negotiate their cases and were not persecuted on a regular basis, although they were subject to discriminatory laws.[546] The difficulty they experienced depended on the time and the location in which they lived.[547]

The majority of the documents and testimonies available on Zoroastrians are from the 17th century. The little information we have from earlier times comes mainly from the letters written by the Iranian Zoroastrians for the Parsis in the late 15th and the 16th century. Before the arrival of Nariman Hushang in 1477, there had not been any contacts between the two communities, as in his letter the Zoroastrians of Iran express their surprise about the existence of the Parsis in India.[548] This demonstrates the isolation of the Zoroastrian community until the 15th century.

The development of commerce had played a key role in bringing the two Zoroastrian communities together. Both Yazd and Kirman, where the bulk of the Zoroastrians of Iran were concentrated, were important textile centres.[549] The north-western Indian coastlines where Parsis lived were also important trading centres. Therefore, once the Mongols had opened the doors of Iran and foreign merchants had discovered the Iranian market, the Parsis were encouraged to visit Iran. The sources from the Safavid period do not allow us to see whether the Parsis were involved in 'international' trade. We know, however, that they benefited from a more pluralistic and tolerant environment than the Zoroastrians enjoyed in Iran.

Albeit subject to hardships in Iran, the Zoroastrians were not always victims of religious fanaticism. The sultan or the shah could have launched persecutions, but the local governor had the power to mitigate or implement the orders given by the monarch. The Safavid period was no exception.

The situation of the Zoroastrians of Yazd was not identical to those of Kirman. In both regions, however, they seem to have been relatively tolerated. The *rivayats* given to the Parsis in 1511, tell us that there were Zoroastrians also in Sistan and Khurasan.[550] We are also led to believe that Fars too had a Zoroastrian community in this period, as Mubid Azar Kayvan (1533-1618), a Zoroastrian high priest, was from this province. It is difficult to find any sources referring to Zoroastrians in these provinces. Jean de Thévenot, during his travels in Iran, encountered Zoroastrians at the confines of Khurasan, in Qandahar, where they were in a miserable state.[551] Most probably, in provinces like Sistan, Khurasan, and Fars, as later Isfahan, where their community was small, the Zoroastrians had had to endure more hardship and as a result migrated or converted. There is more information on Zoroastrians in Isfahan than anywhere else in Iran. As the city was the capital of the Safavids, it was the destination of many Western travellers and missionaries who were intrigued by the Zoroastrians' traditions and beliefs.

Shah Abbas I (1588-1629) had brought these Zoroastrians to Isfahan from Kirman and Yazd.[552] Their activities in Isfahan suggest that only the poorest ones had been deported to the capital. Unlike the other non-Muslim groups, they were not involved in trade, but were mostly gardeners or cultivators,[553] but excellent ones according to Nicola Hemmis.[554] Chardin eulogized them for producing the best grapes and wine in Isfahan.[555] Like Pietro della Valle, he was struck by their poverty but was impressed by their hard work. He wrote that Iran would have been in a better state if it were ruled by Zoroastrians and Armenians.[556] Most of these travellers, who visited Iran before the reign of Shah Sultan Husayn (1694-1722), convey to us the impression that the Safavid government generally tolerated the Zoroastrians. The justice system did not appear to discriminate against them, as the Zoroastrians had even their own magistrates.[557] Nonetheless, in the writings of Chardin, they still appear to be the least tolerated of all the non-Muslim groups in Iran.[558] By 1707, when Le Bruyn visited Isfahan, the Zoroastrians were no longer practising their religion freely. He complains that he could not find a single knowledgeable Zoroastrian. This should not be surprising as the most deprived Zoroastrians had been brought to Isfahan, and in addition, had been forced to become Muslim three years earlier.[559]

The socio-economic situation of their co-religionists in Yazd and Kirman was different as the Zoroastrians in these regions were involved in the thriving textile trades of the region.[560] In one of the *rivayats* sent to

India, a certain Behdin Kavus Yazdi, asserted that he was a tradesman and travelled very often for his business.[561] Tavernier affirms that the Zoroastrians controlled the production of the best wool in Kirman. He was in a good position to judge as he was involved in the wool trade himself. He also informs us that a wealthy Zoroastrian had a fire temple constructed at his own cost at Kirman in 1644. These facts demonstrate the better condition of Zoroastrians in Kirman. Tavernier estimated the Zoroastrian population of the town to be about 10,000 in 1654, seemingly the largest in Iran.[562] As remarked by E. G. Browne, the population of Kirman were more tolerant than that of Yazd.[563] This factor could explain the Zoroastrians' relative prosperity in this town.

We do not hear about mass conversions in Yazd and Kirman as in Isfahan. Therefore, generalisations about the precarious situation of Zoroastrians in Iran should be read with caution,[564] as in each of the three towns mentioned above their situation was different. Moreover, even in Isfahan, where their condition was not enviable until the reign of Shah Abbas II (1642-1666), they were usually left in peace. With the advent of Sultan Husayn (1694-1722) the socio-religious situation changed and the Zoroastrians were forced to become Muslim, but their conversion still appears to have been nominal, as Le Bruyn (1707) could still distinguish them from the rest of the population, and adds that they were still living in extreme poverty.[565]

Due to their social condition, the Zoroastrians of Isfahan were most probably the least culturally active of all the Zoroastrian communities of Iran. Most evidence from the Safavid period shows that the main centres of Zoroastrian religion and culture were located at Yazd and Kirman.

3) **The Social Struggle and Economic Activities of the Jews**

As with the Zoroastrians, it is difficult to evaluate the situation of the Jews during the earliest phase of the Safavid period. The only record we have of their treatment comes from Tomé Pires, who visited Iran between 1512-1516, during the reign of Shah Isma'il (1501-1523). He said that 'Sheikh Isma'il (...) reforms our churches, destroys all houses of all Moors who follow Muhammad (Sunna) and never spares the life of any Jew.'[566]

Incontestably, Shah Isma'il I was a zealous Shi'ite. Apart from imposing the Shi'ite creed on the Sunnite population, he waged war against the Georgian Christians, as mentioned above. In view of this political scene, it is possible that Shah Isma'il had some non-Muslims killed along with the Sunnites. Shah Isma'il was fully engaged in his struggle against the Sunnites and establishing his own hegemony. As a result, the Jews most certainly suffered along with the rest of the population. Nonetheless, there are no other sources that refer to his harming Jews and even Tomé Pires does not provide any specific examples, so their suffering may have been a side effect rather than the result of persecution.

The later Safavid period, until the reign of Shah Sulayman I, seems to have been a time of relative tranquillity for non-Muslims. Fischel portrays Shah Abbas I as a tolerant monarch, and says that the Jews of Zagrum or Zagam (in Georgia) willingly settled on the Caspian coast after helping him in his expedition of 1613 against the Ottomans.[567] However, Shah Abbas is renowned for having deported and resettled many communities, including Muslims. There were some parts of Iran in particular, which Shah Abbas wished to populate with non-Muslims, namely Isfahan and the Caspian area. Thus, he deported the Jews of Zagrum to the Caspian coast in the hope of benefiting from their commercial, agricultural and handicraft skills, as they were already involved in the silk culture and trade.[568] Shah Abbas had no intention of losing them to the Ottomans.

Despite assertions that Shah Abbas was a tolerant monarch, the position of the Jews in his reign was ambiguous. This was mainly due to the rivalry among the Jewish leaders, which may or may have not been instigated by the Muslim authorities. The main Jewish source for studying the Iranian Jewry of this period is the chronicle produced by Babai b. Lutf, the *Kitab-i Anusi: The Book of the Events of the Forced Conversions of Persian Jewry to Islam.*

Through a study of this book and the analysis of the information provided by other sources, we will determine whether Iranian Jewry was a passive and impoverished community, repetitively subjected to persecutions, as they have been traditionally viewed; or a dynamic community, with social and economic assets which allowed them to play an important role in their country.

Babai b. Lutf reports two cases of apostasy during this period which caused hardship to the Jewish community. The first occurred in 1619 when Mulla Abu Hasan Lari, who had been the leader of the Jews of Lar, converted to Islam in the wake of a disagreement with the Jewish community. The Jews of Lar were exasperated by his determination to monopolize the official functions of ritual slaughterer and distributor of the slaughtered meat, which meant that the meat could not be inspected according to the laws of *kashrut* (ritual cleanliness). His Jewish customers decided to boycott his meat, and seeing his business ruined, he retaliated by converting to Islam and convincing the *ulema* (the Shi'ite clergy) to declare a *fatwa* (religious edict) against the Jews, setting them a discriminatory dress code. He then visited Shah Abbas I and succeeded in having the *fatwa* extended to all the Jews of Iran, as well as in obtaining permission to be the sole provider of the compulsory garment. Allahverdi Khan, the governor of Fars, who was a Georgian converted to Islam, refused to implement the law. As he was the favourite of the Shah, he did not suffer any reprimand. During his visit to Farahabad, Mulla Abu Hasan was assassinated by some Jews, and as a consequence the lives of the town's Jews were in jeopardy.[569] To save their lives they had to convert en masse, but after an alleged mystical experience of the Shah at the tomb of Sarah bath Asher, they were allowed to return to their faith. Even so, the dress code seems to have remained in force forty-five years later, as attested by Thévenot who visited the town about 1663-1666, and Fryer who stayed there in 1676.[570]

Not long after the first apostasy, the Jewish community experienced a similar plight in the same year of 1619. Simon Tov Mumin, Jewish *nasi* (leader) of Isfahan, who was also a butcher by profession, stole money from the communal funds. As a result, his leadership was challenged and he was removed from office. Angry at his community, he apostatized and accused the Jews of practising magic against the person of the Shah, which resulted in the Jews of Isfahan and nearby towns being forced to convert to Islam. They remained Muslim between 1619-1620 and from 1625 until the reign of Shah Safi (1629-1642), who allowed the community to return to its original faith.[571]

The reign of Shah Abbas II was also marked by forced conversions in many of the provinces of Iran. This time, the conversion of the Jews was instigated by the Grand Vizier, Muhammad Beg. This incident must have been quite dramatic, as Arakel of Tabriz, the Carmelite missionaries and even the Muslim author Muhammad Tahir Wahid Qazwini report it alongside the *Kitab-i Anusi*. The crisis lasted six years from 1656 until 1662.[572] The acuteness of the situation depended on the distance from Isfahan and on the disposition of the local governor. In some towns, like Gulpaygan and Khurramabad, the Jews were able to avoid conversion.[573] The governor of Khunsar, Khalil Khan, also refused to implement the edict on the Jews, until a Jewish jeweller from Khunsar appeared at the court of Isfahan and refused to do business with Muhammad Beg on a Saturday. Thus, the Grand Vizier discovered that his decree had been ignored in Khunsar and obliged Khalil Khan to comply to his orders. The Jews of Farahabad strongly opposed the edict, and informed the authorities that they would rather die as martyrs than turn Muslim. The Jews in Yazd were the most fortunate, as the Muslim authorities of the town supported them in circumventing the edict of the Grand Vizier.[574] Matthee brings to our attention the fact that Muhammad Beg had not acted on his own initiative, but that the messianic movement which had appeared in the Ottoman Empire had had repercussions in Iran, and this had irritated the Shi'ite clergy, who pressured the Grand Vizier to take such radical measures.[575] According to the Jesuit Alexander of Rhodes, who visited Iran in 1659, the Jews had publicly promised to convert if their expected messiah did not appear. Once their hopes did not materialize, they were forced to abjure Judaism. In order to avoid any strong protest, the Shah paid every Jewish man two *tumans* and every Jewish woman a *tuman*.[576] Once the period of crisis had elapsed and the Muslims realized that they had failed to convert the Jews genuinely to Islam, they accepted their return to Judaism provided they paid back the money distributed to them by the Shah.[577] A decade later when John Fryer visited Iran, he reported that the Jews were able to practise their religion without any disturbance.[578]

Reassessing the information provided by the sources, it is a mistake to draw a simple conclusion like most modern scholars and say that the Jews were just a persecuted community, or else that Islam was relatively tolerant with them when compared with Christianity in Europe. Such interpretations commonly display the Jewish communities as passive and helpless. Considering all the reverses that the Iranian Jewry managed to surmount in its long history, it is evident that they had the political skills and the economic means to defend themselves in periods of crisis. Thus, three centuries earlier, they had overcome the fury that ensued following the fall of the Jewish vizier, Sa'd al-Dawla, by remaining politically active and producing another great vizier: Rashid al-Din.

The political ingenuity of the Iranian Jewry is rendered manifest in this period of religious intolerance when they were forced twice to embrace Islam. Islam being intransigent with those who forsook it, the Jews certainly needed financial power and demographic strength to do so. Iran had a large Jewish population, probably reaching 100,000 souls.[579] In addition, they had efficient leaders who were able to negotiate their religious status. Farahabad is a very good example of a town where the Jews were able to resist the royal edicts for conversion.

In these reports of forced conversions, there are notable details that evince the socio-economic condition of the Jews in Iran. The instance of Farahabad is one of the most revealing and intriguing. We see that on the first occasion in 1619, they outwardly accepted Islam, practising Judaism in secret (as *anusim*), but the second time in 1656, they felt safe enough to refuse outright the orders of the Grand Vizier to convert to Islam. Eight decades later, in Kashan, the notable figures of the Jewish community ingeniously had the Jews of the town convert to Islam in order to escape from financial extortion and impoverishment, but after a period of seven months the Jews renegotiated the religious status of their community and returned to Judaism again.[580] In all these cases, they were unmolested and were allowed to preserve the Jewish faith. There are two important factors which explain their ability to negotiate and refute Islam. One was the political organisation of Safavid Iran, and the other the economic role played by the Jews.

Under the Safavids, contrary to the Abbasid period, the Jewish leadership was territorially defined. The Iranian Jewry was no longer under the jurisdiction of a *Resh Galuta* or a *Gaon*. The local leader was chosen from among respected Jewish personalities, and was usually a rabbi, but occasionally, as Fischel points out, it could have been also a Jewish apostate. This was the case of Hanukka, the leader of the Jews of Zagrum, who were settled in Farahabad. The conversion of the leader could have been used as a strategy for easier negotiation with the Muslim authorities.[581] Secondly, the welfare of the Jews depended on the local Muslim governor, who was able to protect them even when they travelled to another province. There are two examples of this in Babai b. Farhad's chronicle. During Tahmasp Quli Khan's occupation of Kashan, the Jews of the town decided to convert in order to escape from heavy taxation. Abraham Yazdi, who was a Jew from Yazd, boldly refused to convert as he was not from Kashan. In another case, such policy worked to the disadvantage of Jews visiting Hamadan, as they could not benefit from the immunity granted to the local Jews during the Ottoman occupation.[582] Thus, as can be observed from the sources, the local governors had the power to free the Jews from restrictions imposed by the court.

The tolerance of the local rulers was not the only factor that determined the condition of the Jews. The Jews' impact on the local economy was another important element which regulated their relation with the Muslim authorities. Again, Farahabad is a very good example of a town where the Jews' financial strength enabled them to earn and benefit from the respect of their Muslim neighbours. Babai b. Lutf tells us that Shah Abbas I built Farahabad for the Jews on the Caspian coast, just as the Shah had built New Julfa for the Armenians.[583] Despite Moreen's protest, Babai b. Lutf's assertions are very plausible. The Shah may not have built an entire town for them, but could have certainly erected a special quarter for the Georgian Jews, like New Julfa, which was also just a neighbourhood of Isfahan.[584] Moreover, the lenient way in which the Jews of Farahabad were treated during both periods of crisis, in 1619 and 1656, substantiates the fact that they had a position similar to that of the Armenians of Julfa and likewise were valued by the Muslim rulers for the capital they generated. Arakel of Tabriz asserts that they were rich and opulent and were involved in the trade of textiles and silver.[585] The Muslim author, Iskandar Beg Munshi, conveys to us that at least numerically the non-Muslim population of the town was as important as the Muslim population.[586]

As the Caspian coast was an important centre of silk production, it is not surprising that the Jews of Farahabad were involved in the silk trade. Dutch sources and the *Afzal al-Tawarikh* mention powerful Jews who led the silk trade in 1619 and 1632. Their contact with Jews in the Ottoman Empire enabled them to export silk beyond the borders of Iran. The thousand Jewish families of Farahabad had been given exclusive rights over the silk production and trade in the province of Gilan. We are told that Khwaja Balazar (or Lalazar) Yahud was appointed as their delegate.[587] Elsewhere in Iran they were also implicated in this business, and the Jews of Farahabad could have well been their primary suppliers. Olearius testifies that the Jews had silk girdles in Lar,[588] and so does Father Schillinger, who asserts that the silk manufacture of Lar was mostly run by them.[589] Tavernier confirms this and adds that they were also involved in the wool industry and produced very refined belts.[590] Indeed, Lar was a prosperous town and there have been more reports on the mercantile activities of the Jews of this town than anywhere else in Iran.[591] Lar was on the crossroads between the Ottoman Empire and the trading posts of the Persian Gulf. Therefore, it was well situated for commercial traffic. Giosafat Barbaro related already in 1472-1473 that Lar was a trade centre, with fertile agricultural soil.[592] Lar definitely had an important Jewish community. In fact, according to Tavernier, Lar was mainly a Jewish town. Many other travellers referred to the Jews of Lar, such as Antonio Tenreiro (who was himself of Jewish descent and visited the area in 1560), John Newbury (cir. 1579), and Thomas Herbert (cir. 1628).[593]

In 1559-1561, the Jesuit missionary, Gaspar Barzaeus, testified to the existence of an organized Jewish community, which included Jews of Persian, Portuguese and Spanish descent at Hormuz. They were indeed involved in the silk trade, but they also traded live stocks. Like the Armenians and the Baniyans (Indians) they were involved in the overseas trade, but probably at a more modest level.[594] The Iranian Jewry had the advantage of having co-religionists in other lands, and as a result could establish commercial links with less difficulty than the Muslim Iranians. We know that they carried out transactions with the Jews of the bordering Ottoman Empire.[595] They also conducted trade with India, where there were small Jewish communities living near the trading posts such as those of Cochin. The Spanish traveller Moses Pereyra de Paiva had met two Iranian Jews in the region; one was from Shiraz and the other from Hamadan.[596] The Jewish merchants followed the same trajectory as the Armenians from Iran to India. Pietro della Valle conversed with one of them during a journey which had began at Hormuz.[597] Indeed, these commercial ships generally left from Hormuz, where in 1596 there dwelled about 150 Jewish families.[598] Their number seems to have remained unchanged by 1617, when Garcia de Silva Figueroa visited the trading post. He mentions a certain Isaac, who spoke Spanish and Hebrew, and was the tax collector of the government.[599] This last observation of the Spanish traveller is important as this demonstrates that the commercial activities of the Jews had won them some political influence. This is further corroborated by the *Chronicle of the Carmelites*, in which a Jew is mentioned acting as an Iranian ambassador to Europe. His name was Joseph and he was probably chosen for his linguistic skills. His task had been to carry letters to Pope Gregory XIII and the Iberian kings on behalf of the Persian court and the missionaries in Iran.[600]

Joseph's fluency in Spanish lets us deduce that the Jews of Spain had not only immigrated to the Ottoman Empire, but that the economic prosperity of Iran had also attracted a few of them. Antonio de Gouvea mentions his encounter with one of them.[601] Moreover, there were a few Jews from the Ottoman lands who had settled in Iran, such as Mulla Massih, who was originally from Palestine, but was born in Iran. In 1618, he was the physician of the Shah. We hear about another Jewish physician at the court, under the reign of Shah Safi. His name was Hakim Davud. He had accompanied David of Abarquh during his audience with the Shah in 1629 for reversing the decree that had forced Jews to embrace Islam.[602] Medicine was a profession in which the Jews excelled since the appearance of Islam in Iran, and the Jews were illustrious in this field at least until the end of the Mongol period. There are references to other Jewish physicians in the Safavid period, like Yehudah b. El'azar, but as they were not connected to the court, there has not been much elaboration on their situation.[603] The Jewish presence at the court was not limited to physicians, as Chardin testifies that there were Jewish women in the *harem* acting as midwives and fortune-tellers. Therefore, as during the Abbasid period, the Jews could gain access to the court and defend the interests of their community.[604]

Moreen believes that Chardin's statements are spurious and that he invented these episodes, basing them on his experience in Europe.[605] However, there is no reason for us to disbelieve Chardin. Indeed, there were times when the Jews would appeal to the court to act in their favour, therefore Jewish women could well have been visiting the royal *harem* regularly.

The presence of the Jews is attested in the two other important trading posts of Iran, such as Gombroon (Bandar Abbas) and Bandar Kung. Chardin noted a relatively significant Jewish community in Gombroon and Abbé Carré mentioned their presence in Bandar Kung.[606]

Apart from Hormuz and Lar, Shiraz, Kashan and Yazd were the other towns where there was a significant and active Jewish community. Shiraz had about six hundred or seven hundred Jewish families, most of which earned their living by selling wine.[607] The well-to-do families of the community were engaged in silk manufacture.[608] Kashan, according to Chardin, had ten synagogues, but Babai b. Farhad provides us with the more reliable figure of sixteen synagogues. It is certain that Kashan was a prosperous town in the 17th century, thanks to the flourishing commerce of silk, textile and rug weaving. The Jewish elite, of which Babai b. Farhad names several individuals, must have been involved in one of these trades to build a fortune. There is an allusion to their participation in the silk trade, as on one occasion some wealthy Jews are mentioned distributing fine silk in order to win the authorities' sympathy.[609] Financially, they were wealthy enough to succour their co-religionists in Hamadan, when the Jews of Hamadan were put under pressure by the Ottoman occupying forces (cir.1730). Babai b. Farhad says that a certain Meir Levi, Aharon Khunkar and Eliyahu brought several purses of coins to Hamadan for this purpose.[610]

Undeniably, the Jews of Yazd also played a significant role in the town's economy. Their importance is evidenced in Babai b. Lutf's narration of the crisis which forced many Jewish communities of Iran to become temporarily Muslim between 1656-1662. The Muslims of the town told the Shah that they were financially dependent on the Jews, as they had lent them important sums and employed numerous Muslims. They also were involved in the lucrative trade of silk and textile production.[611] Yazd was renowned for its wine production, which was exported to Lar, where the consumers were Jewish, and to Hormuz, where the consumers were from diverse backgrounds.[612] The sale of wine generated a good revenue for both the Jews and Zoroastrians of the area, as they monopolized its production.

Another commerce in which the Iranian Jewry was successful was the trade of precious gems. The chronicle of Babai b. Lutf cites many Jewish jewellers, some of whom frequented the court. One of them was Khan Khalil who had travelled to Isfahan to sell a large ruby to Muhammad Beg, but refused to negotiate on a Saturday.[613] According to Tavernier, Isfahan had a small Jewish community, which superficially looked wretched, but had affluent members. The trade of the most precious jewels were in their hands. If one needed to sell such jewels, one had to contact them.[614] A notable Jewish jeweller was Sa'id, a leader of the Jews of Isfahan. When Muhammad Beg decided to have the Jews of Isfahan converted, he promised to give two *tumans* to each new convert, but we are told that Sa'id received a caravanserai for his apostasy, as his wealth and status required a greater compensation.[615]

Tavernier also says that while the foreign trade was in the hands of the Armenians, the trade in the country was shared between the Jews and the Muslims.[616] It is noteworthy, however, that they competed with the Armenians in providing caravan services to European traders who needed to transport their merchandise from Iran to the Mediterranean coast.[617] Chardin adds that the Jews acted as moneylenders and bankers, but had lost much of their business to the Indian Baniyans.[618]

As with Zoroastrians, the situation of the Jews varied from one region to another. In some provinces they were well off and well treated, in others they were not wealthy and subject to the caprice of the clergy and whims of the governors. In Kashan, our Jewish eyewitness (Babai b. Lutf), says that there were rich and poor among the Jews of the town. During the conversion episode of 1656, he says that the poorer Jews were given clothes, the wealthier ones were given slaves and money.[619] His grandson refers to eleven eminent figures in Kashan who were notorious for their wealth. They were invited to a banquet by Tahmasp Quli Khan (Nadir Shah).[620] Poor people, whether Jew or Muslim, were never invited by the potentates of the country. We also are told that during the time of Nadir Shah, important sums were collected from the Jews of Lar, Shiraz, Isfahan and Kashan.[621] Finally, the Jewish élite of Iran was involved in the trade of precious gems and silk. The latter was the most lucrative commerce in the country. Thus, not all the Jews were poor weavers and destitute farmers as it has been sometimes argued.[622] On this matter, John Fryer has provided us with another interesting point. During his visit to Isfahan in 1677 he noted that all the druggists of Isfahan were Jews. They may have monopolized this profession in some other towns.[623] Thus it is clear that the Iranian Jewry were involved in a variety of businesses and their dynamism certainly benefited the rest of the Iranians, who relied on their endeavours and skills.

4) The Armenians: An Exotic Community or a Native Minority Group?

a) The Earlier Presence of Armenians in Iran and the Deportations of Shah Abbas I

The existence of a geographic Armenia to the north of Iran has prevented students of pre-Safavid Iran from treating Armenians as an Iranian minority. Undeniably, the Armenians form a distinct nation, and this is not going to be contested here. Nonetheless, they represent an old established element in Iran. Their history has been intertwined with that of Iranians since antiquity. Armenia was conquered by Iranians on several occasions, and population movements from Armenia to Iran have occurred since the Achaemenid period.[624] Like the Jews, they have been living among Iranians and mingling with them for centuries, but their easy access to their neighbouring motherland distinguished them from Iranian Jews, who albeit part of a greater Jewish nation, were much more assimilated and *Persianized* than the Armenians.

Until the Safavid period, the number of Armenians in Iran was smaller than that of the Jews and Zoroastrians. Under the Saljuks, the Mongols and the Timurids, Armenians had been carried to Iran, but not on the scale of 1603, when thousands of them were deported by Shah Abbas I and settled all over the country. Long before the deportations of Shah Abbas, Tabriz had a sizeable Armenian community. In 1334, there were two Armenian churches in the town, named Surb Astuacacin and Saint Sargis.[625] Considering the distance between Tabriz and Armenia, it is more likely that the Armenians had settled in the town for mercantile reasons, as Tabriz had become a flourishing town under the Mongols. Giosafat Barbaro had met a wealthy Armenian merchant in 1487, while visiting the town. His name was Khwaja Mirak.[626] In 1514, the Ottomans occupied Tabriz and deported the population of the town to Istanbul. Along with the Muslim population, they took 3,000 Armenians. It is noteworthy that the non-Muslims were not the only victims of deportations, and that entire populations living in Iran or the Ottoman Empire were subject to mass relocations.[627] By 1574, Tabriz had apparently recovered from the Ottoman aggression, and the Armenians were once again active in the economic life of the town. The Carmelites refer to a very wealthy Armenian merchant whose house had been robbed in that year, and who had had 4,000 bales of silk stolen.[628]

The presence of Armenians is documented in other important cities of 15th century Iran, such as Samarqand and Hormuz. Clavijo had met Armenians in Samarqand whilst the city was the centre of the Timurid empire. In 1490, Hormuz was already a prosperous notable trading centre, where Armenians were noticed by European travellers.[629] These references to Armenians demonstrate that before the advent of the Safavids the Armenians were already playing a conspicuous role in the trade of Iran. The English merchant Arthur Edwards, who was an agent of the Russia company visiting Iran in 1566, complained that it was very difficult to compete with the Armenians and the Venetians in the country, as they were not ready to surrender their commercial privileges.[630] Arthur Edwards also said that the inhabitants of the Armenian village Gilgal alone carried yearly between five hundred and a thousand mules loaded with silk bales for trading purposes.[631]

The first massive deportation of Armenians under the Safavids occurred in 1530.[632] There are not many sources that discuss these deportees, therefore it is difficult to know where they were settled. However, there are many references to the major deportation of the Armenian population to Iran which occurred in 1603-1604. Arakel of Tabriz narrated forcefully this tragic episode, but he adds that the Safavid monarch planned to deport Christians, Muslims and Jews alike.[633] Without any doubt, this deportation was a dramatic event; nonetheless, if the subject is discussed objectively, it is clear that this act of Shah Abbas I was not motivated by religion, but was part of a military and economic strategy. Arakel of Tabriz testifies that before Shah Abbas' intervention, the Ottoman incursions had prompted the Armenians of four villages to emigrate to Iran. The Ottomans were planning to plunder the area and their main objective was, according to Arakel of Tabriz, Julfa. The Shah did not wish to lose this wealthy region of Caucasus to the Ottomans. Encouraged further by the animosity of the Armenians towards the Ottomans, he led his army into Armenia. Taken by surprise, the Ottomans had only the opportunity to ravage Nakhchevan.[634] The Shah, for his part, devastated the area and enforced his 'scorched-earth policy' in order to prevent the Ottomans from controlling the Araxes valley.[635] Moreover, Shah Abbas ordered the massacre of the inhabitants of Nakhchevan, as they were Sunnites.[636] Considering the fate of the Muslims in that region, who were being killed either by the Safavids or the Ottomans according to their denomination, the Armenians were more fortunate.

Even though their lives were spared, common Armenians suffered greatly during this deportation and many of them perished on their way to Iran.[637] Large numbers of them were sent to the Caspian coast (27,000 families to Gilan and 24,000 families to Mazandaran), where not many of them survived due to the insalubrity of the climate. Some of them were settled in Farahabad along with the Georgian Jews we discussed earlier.[638] Some 500 families were taken to Shiraz. The wealthy Armenians of Julfa had a much better fate.[639] Shah Abbas I reckoned them a valuable economic asset.[640] He had the Julfans taken to the new Safavid capital, Isfahan.[641] Shah Abbas granted them lands not far from Isfahan, and the place was named Julfa[642], after the original Julfa in their homeland. It is noteworthy that Shah Abbas had Muslim peasants removed from villages surrounding Isfahan, such as Saghabad, Falashan and Marbanan, for the settlement of the Armenian population, and on the Caspian coast he had the Shi'ite peasants evicted for the same reason.[643] This demonstrates further that Shah Abbas gave more importance to his purse than to Islam. He wished to have the Armenians involved in the silk trade under closer control,[644] and therefore both Christians and Muslims had to suffer deportations.[645]

This deportation changed the pattern of the Christian population in Iran. From this time onwards, the Armenians formed the largest Christian population in Iran.[646] After Timur's onslaughts, the Nestorians, who had composed the main Christian population in Iran, had been reduced to an insignificant minority. As a consequence, the arrival of the Armenians had in effect 'resuscitated' Christianity in Iran.

b) **The Armenians and their Monopoly of Iranian Trade**

By the end of the 13th century, Iran had already replaced China as the supplier of silk to Genoese manufacturers.[647] The increasing demand for silk in Europe opened new commercial opportunities for the Armenians and the Azeri merchants who lived close to the silk production areas of the Caucasus and the Caspian sea; however, they had to compete with the Italian merchants from Venice and Genoa.[648] The Italian merchants had been involved in the silk trade since the establishment of the Mongol Empire and had a strong foothold in the European markets.[649] As both Venice and Genoa were mercantile city states, the Italian merchants benefited also from the active support of their statesmen. The Armenians of Julfa lacked such protection; nonetheless, they had managed to build a fortune which had caught the attention of both the Safavids and the Ottomans, who were fighting for supremacy in their region. In the endless war (1578-1588) which opposed the two belligerents, the entire region was devastated, but Julfa was not destroyed.[650] The Julfans had bribed Shah Abbas I to spare their town from ravages. One of the wealthiest merchants of Julfa, Khwaja Khacik, had offered him trays full of gold coins.[651] The sight of the Julfans' wealth had prompted Shah Abbas to plan their deportation to Isfahan. In 1590, he had already selected a wealthy suburb of the city beside the Zayanda Rud for them.[652] A number of Julfan nobles and ecclesiastics of Julfa who were heavily indebted to the Ottomans had also encouraged the Shah in his decision. They wished for the Iranians to take over Armenia, so that they would not have to pay the Ottomans back. Arakel of Tabriz laments that Shah Abbas was 'an infernal dragon' who deceived these Armenians after he conquered Armenia by taking away their wealth.[653]

The treatment the Shah had reserved for these wealthy Armenians was very different from that which he assigned to the rest of the Caucasian population deported to Isfahan. He regarded them as a valuable property. Indeed, the Armenians of Julfa had a long history in trade. They had built a dynamic network, purchasing their silk from Gilan, Shirvan and Qarabagh and then selling it in the trading houses they had established in market towns of the Ottoman Empire and trading posts on the Mediterranean and Indian coasts.[654] Baghdiantz alleges that their commercial organisation equalled that of the European East India companies. Such trading associations did not exist in Iran.[655] This enabled the Julfans to amass a fortune unmatched elsewhere in the area. They were the richest merchants of Western Asia, and because of their financial status, they had been able to obtain privileges from Safavid monarchs even before the reign of Shah Abbas I.[656]

After deporting the Julfan Armenians to Isfahan, Shah Abbas waited until 1619 before confirming their ownership of the lands in the neighbourhood of the New Julfa. This was a condition for the Armenians' agreeing to the Shah's price for the purchase of silk. Shah Abbas had decided to control the supply of silk, since he knew that all silk producing areas were under his jurisdiction. His prices were not appealing to foreign merchants, and so the Armenians became the sole purchasers.[657] Shah Abbas relied on the Julfans' commercial contacts in the Ottoman and European markets, where they sold the Shah's silk and brought back silver. The Shah taxed both their export of silk and their import of silver. Thus, the Armenians, as the main supplier of the country's silver, had become the backbone of Iranian foreign trade.[658]

Owing to the capital the Julfans generated, Shah Abbas had granted them privileges, which were usually denied to other non-Muslim communities. For example, they were allowed to ride horses and adorn them like the Muslims. They were also permitted to hold their religious processions in the sight of the Muslims, and were protected by the royal guards during their ceremony. Moreover, Muslims were strictly forbidden from taking abode in New Julfa.[659] These privileges made New Julfa virtually a state within the state, where Christians could evade Islamic laws ordinarily enforced elsewhere in Iran.[660] The Carmelites add that Shah Abbas I did not even pay heed to the Shi'ite laws of purity (*najasat*) in the presence of Armenians:

> Nowadays, because the Shah shows great regard for Christians, passes his time with them and sets them at his table, they have abandoned all this [laws of *najasat*] and act towards them as they do towards their own people.[661]

The Christians (and the Jews) in Farahabad benefited from similar privileges granted to the Armenians of Julfa. Pietro della Valle says that Shah Abbas I valued them so much that he had pigs sent to them from Isfahan, despite the disapproval of the Muslims. As they were the main suppliers of silk in the country, Shah Abbas was well-disposed towards them as well.[662]

There are a few speculations with regards to Shah Abbas' choice of Armenian merchants instead of Muslim ones. After Shah Abbas had conquered the major silk growing regions of Qarabagh and Shirvan at the beginning of the 17th century,[663] he had already attempted to sell Iranian silk in European markets without the help of Armenians. On this matter, Tavernier reports that Shah Abbas had suffered from the ineptitude of the Muslim Iranian merchants, who instead of fructifying the Shah's capital, had squandered his money.[664] As a result, the Shah called upon the Armenians to take over the silk trade, which he had decided to monopolize.[665]

Baghdiantz argues that Christian European travellers, such as Tavernier, were prejudiced against the Muslim population, and that their assertions should be considered carefully.[666] Tavernier claims that the Shah's appeal to the Armenians demonstrates that they were more diligent and more shrewd than the Muslim Iranians.[667] In order to be fair, it should be mentioned that until the beginning of the 16th century, the majority of the merchants selling silk to the Italians in the Ottoman markets, were Muslim Iranians from Azerbaijan. These were members of the Turkmen aristocracy, whose economic and military power was regarded by the Safavids as a threat. Thus, the Safavid monarchs resolved to substitute them with Armenians and Georgians, who had no chance of winning the support of the Muslim majority and whose survival depended on the Shah.[668] Furthermore, at the beginning of the 16th century, the Ottomans forbade their subjects from conducting trade with Iranians, exempting, however, the Jews and the Armenians from this restriction. Whatever were the motives behind such a policy were, the Armenians and the Jews of Iran benefited from it.[669]

As such, the political circumstances were not favourable to Muslim Iranian merchants. On the other hand, the competence of the Julfan Armenians in the commercial sphere is incontestable,[670] as Shah Abbas did not select any other minority group, except them, for conducting his commercial affairs. After the death of Shah Abbas I, Shah Safi relinquished the royal prerogatives for the purchase of silk, leaving it henceforth in the hands of the Armenians.[671] The Safavid shahs, however, continued to rely on Armenians for carrying out their business.

Silk was not the only commerce in which the Armenians were involved. As they were the principal tradesmen of Iran,[672] it is not surprising that they conducted all sorts of business,[673] including the lucrative trade in precious stones. In this respect, they were competing with Jews at the court. The Shah relied on them for assessing the value of the jewels he wished to purchase, and sold his own jewels through their intermediary. Their travels abroad made them the principal distributors of imported merchandise in Iran. They introduced new goods and new fashions into the country such as cloth-stockings, card games, bowling, and tennis. The most coveted imported items appear to have been watches, which the Armenians took to the court to bribe senior government dignitaries. They also established the first printing house in the country and brought the first turkeys to Iran.[674]

The prerogatives they had obtained from the Safavid monarchs and their trading skills had enabled the Armenians to monopolize the Western foreign trade of Iran after the 16th century. As could be expected, they were the principal intermediaries for the commerce between the Ottoman Empire and Iran.[675] During the reign of Shah Abbas I, the Portuguese had thwarted the Iranians' use of the maritime routes. The Armenians were able to negotiate the passage of Iranian merchants through the Ottoman territories, despite the uneasy relations between Iran and the Ottoman Empire. The large Armenian population in the Ottoman Empire was definitely an asset to them in such negotiations. The Ottoman Armenians were themselves much involved in trade and played a major role in the silk weaving industry of the empire. Their connections in the Ottoman Empire enabled the Armenians to avoid the use of European vessels, when the English, Dutch or Portuguese companies refused to agree to their terms.[676] The Ottomans benefited from the Armenians' conduct of trade from Iran, as the transit of the silk through the Ottoman lands to Europe generated a considerable revenue for the *Sublime Porte*.

The geographical position of Armenia had also made the Armenians trade intermediaries between Iran and Russia since the 16th century. After their deportation to Iran they maintained their privileged position between both kingdoms. During the reign of Shah Abbas I, they played an active role in the economy of Astrakhan. In 1660, ten Armenians were sent from Isfahan to the Russian court, and in 1666 this number had quadrupled. These merchants attended the Russian court in order to negotiate commercial settlements. Thereafter, other commercial treaties were signed between Russia and New Julfa. During these accords, the *kalantar* (governor) of New Julfa virtually acted as a head of state. At the close of the 17th century, Peter the Great (1682-1725) was determined to modernize Russia. He appealed to the Armenians who had begun emigrating from Iran,[677] and granted them privileges which he refused to other Iranian merchants.[678] Thus, he wished to regain control over the Russian economy, as its foreign trade was run by Western European companies.[679]

Their involvement in the European and Indian trade demonstrates that their organisation was as important as the European

East India Companies.[680] They competed successfully with European trade groups beyond the confines of Asia. Iran was their trading base, just like the European East India Companies, which were also based in England, the Netherlands or France. Surprisingly, the Iranian Armenians have been ignored by the majority of the books treating of trade in Europe and the world in the Medieval period.[681] Yet, they were as active as the European traders, and were even the 'preferred trading partners and agents of European Levantine merchants.'[682] Their commercial activities in Venice have been alluded to in the *Chronicle of the Carmelites*, where it is mentioned that in 1610, Shah Abbas sent one of the most distinguished Armenian merchants, Khwaja Safar Azaria, to collect his goods from the Republic. From Venice, Azaria headed for Rome, where he was made Count and Knight by Pope Paul. His visit to Rome had some diplomatic purposes, but Azaria certainly wished to negotiate further commercial agreements. Not long after, we are told that the Armenians sought to establish trade houses in the Papal States and solicited the Pope to furnish them with letters which would press other Catholic sovereigns to sanction commercial transactions of Armenian merchants from Iran.[683]

The support of European sovereigns was not always sufficient to secure them trade opportunities, as their commercial successes aroused at times the animosity of local merchants. This was the case in France, where in 1621 the French merchants petitioned their king to put an end to the commercial activities of 'Persians' (in fact Armenian Iranians).[684] In the Netherlands they were given better opportunities as the Dutch concluded a reciprocal treaty with Shah Safi, according the same privileges to their merchants in Iran which were given to Iranian Armenian merchants in the Netherlands.[685] The Armenians had also established trading houses in England, after the English East India Company had expressed its desire to consolidate its trade links with Iran. At the end of the 17th century, the company had encountered difficulties with the Mughal authorities, and thus looked for alternative markets. The English merchants sought desperately to convince the Armenians to trade exclusively with them, but the deal was not advantageous to the latter.[686] The Julfan Armenians, however, continued to use the vessels of the English East India Company along with those of the Dutch between Gombroon (Bandar Abbas), Surat and Europe. They had created a network between Iran, India and Europe. Many of them, such as Khwaja Minas, operated from Surat. In the 1660's Khwaja Minas had become the principal buyer and creditor to the English East India Company. He owned many ships himself. Another Julfan family present in Surat and associated with the English East India Company, were the Callendars.[687] François Bernier who visited India between 1659-1667, says that the Dutch had difficulty competing in trade with the Armenians.[688]

The French East India Company wished to conclude similar agreements with the Iranian Armenians, but the restrictions imposed by the French government on their trade activities rendered such association difficult.[689] Nonetheless, the Armenians' network and success in Indo-Iranian trade was important enough to make Colbert choose in 1664 a Julfan Armenian, Marvara Avanchinz, as the head of the first French factory in India despite the animosity of the French merchants against them. Colbert wished to benefit from Avanchinz's influence in Surat for obtaining trade advantages from the local rulers. This was not a difficult task, as Avanchinz had relatives at their court.[690]

The European East India companies sought the association of the Julfan Armenians, as they too were aware of the Armenians' experience and network in the Indian trade. They had been involved in the Indian trade before their settlement in Iran, thus by the time the European East India companies had arrived in the area, they had already secured for themselves a prominent place in the subcontinent for themselves. India's economy depended considerably on them, as they were the main providers of the region's silver.[691] Although their supremacy in the trade between India and Iran was challenged by the Indian Baniyan tradesmen, the latter commonly appealed to Armenians in order to deal with European merchants in Iran.[692]

As in Europe, the Armenians had highly reputed merchant families, who acted as financiers and bankers of the court.[693] Baghdiantz says that the Shafraz family of New Julfa was the equivalent of the Fugger family in Germany, and the Grimaldi in Italy and Spain. They were the bankers of their country's sovereign. The affluence of the Shafraz family enabled them to dominate the politics of New Julfa. A member of this family was always appointed by the Shah as the *kalantar* (governor) of New Julfa. There were other famous and affluent Armenian families, such as the Shahrimanian, Lazarian, Minasench and Velijian. None of them, however, was able to challenge the power of the Shafraz. The Velijian, who attempted to take their position, were obliged to depart for Surat (India). Even at the end of the 17th century, when the economy of New Julfa was on the decline, Chardin estimated the fortune of the *kalantar*, Agha Piri, to be around two million *livres tournois*, whereas at the same period, the wealthiest trader in France possessed about

163,000 *livres tournois*. Agha Piri was one of the twenty (sixty according to Chardin) richest Armenian merchants of Iran.[694]

c) The Role of the Armenians in Iranian Politics and Iranian Diplomacy

There is no surprise in the Armenians' influential position in Iran. Their affluence won them contacts in the court and elsewhere in the country. We saw that the most wealthy among them had been able to dominate the leadership of their community. The power of the Julfan Armenians had enabled the transfer of the jurisdiction of the Archbishop of Echmiazin in historical Armenia to the Archbishop of New Julfa during the patriarchate of *katholikos* Moses (1629-1632). As such, they made their town the centre of the Armenian Apostolic Church, with a jurisdiction over all the Armenian churches in Iran, India and other places with Armenian colonies outside the Ottoman Empire.[695] The diocese of New Julfa was renamed *Iranahindkastani tem*, i.e. the diocese of Iran and India.[696] Manifestly, the Armenian church had taken over the place of the Nestorian Church in Iran. This religious authority of New Julfa over the Armenian colonies in India allowed the Julfan Armenians to consolidate their commercial ties with their community in the subcontinent. Baghdiantz depicts the Armenian settlements in India as satellites of New Julfa.[697]

The political power of the Julfan Armenians stemmed from their close relationship with the Shah. They could not have dominated the economy of Iran otherwise.[698] Both their wealth and the Shah's support gave them a highly privileged political status and a great amount of autonomy.[699] It should be remembered that Shah Abbas I had Muslim populations deported in order to offer one of the nicest neighbourhoods of Isfahan to them.[700] He had also ruined the trade of Muslim Iranians by handing the most lucrative trade to the Armenians.[701] For these privileges, the Armenians had to disburse a substantial amount of money to the Shah.[702]

Their position was also reinforced by the presence of Armenian converts at the court. Many of the viziers and military commanders were Muslim converts of Armenian background. The most famous ones are Qarchay Beg, Allahverdi Khan (not to be confused with the Georgian Allahverdi Khan) and Muhammad Beg. Qarchay Beg played a key role in Shah Abbas' campaigns in the Caucasus. He was nominated commander-in-chief of the Iranian army in 1613. Allahverdi Khan, son of Khusraw Khan, was a favourite of Shah Abbas II, who appointed him as Master of the Hunt in 1644. Allahverdi Khan used his influence at the court to install his protégé, Muhammad Beg, who had recently converted to Islam, as the vizier of Shah Abbas II.[703] Until then, Muhammad Beg had been the *kalantar* of New Julfa,[704] and after becoming vizier, he encouraged the persecution of Jews and Christians. It is difficult to explain Muhammad Beg's intransigence with the Armenians. However, his coming from a modest Armenian family of Tabriz could explain his rancour towards the wealthy Armenians of Julfa.[705]

There were other Armenians attached to the court, who had not been obliged to apostatize. But these were mostly Armenian artisans, who did not occupy military or administrative positions, such as the head of the court's carpenters (the *najjarbashi*) during the reign of Shah Abbas II (1642-1666).[706] In the same period, the chief of the court's painters (the *naqqashbashi*) was also an Armenian called Yakobian. If they were valued by the Shah, they could have indirectly influenced his decisions. Yakobian for example was granted authority over the Armenians living in Isfahan, and it seems that henceforth this prerogative remained in the hands of the following *naqqashbashis*. New Julfa, however, was never subject to their control.[707]

The Safavid monarchs had many Christian wives in their *harem*. However, the majority seem to have been of Georgian or Circassian stock. The absence of Armenian women from the royal *harem*, as we saw, did not prevent the Armenians from influencing the court. The Safavids commonly selected Armenians as envoys to Europe as their linguistic and commercial talents made them ideal diplomats.[708] Even prior to their deportation to Iran, they had been sent as royal envoys to Europe. The Italian d'Alessandri had met one of them at Venice in 1571,[709] and the Carmelites recorded the arrival of an Armenian messenger at Kashan, sent back by the viceroy of Naples in 1582.[710] They acted as ambassadors for the Georgian kings as well.[711] They were the interpreters who most suited the court, and were usually asked to accompany important foreign merchants or traders acting as diplomats to the court.[712] Tavernier confirms that this was the custom. At his arrival in Iran, the *nazir* (the head of the Shah's court) had sent the New Julfa's *kalantar* accompanied with eight other Armenian dignitaries to escort the French merchant to the court.[713] Robert and Anthony Sherley were the other European merchants escorted to the court by Armenians.[714]

The everlasting wars with the Ottoman Empire were another factor which prevented Shi'ite Iranians from acting as ambassadors, for Armenians on the other hand could traverse Ottoman territory as Iranian agents and negotiate with interested parties in Europe, including Istanbul.[715] Many of the Armenian merchants were asked to carry letters from the Shahs to the Pope or other European monarchs, who in turn requested the Armenians to take back their messages to the Shah.[716] Pietro della Valle met one of the Armenian envoys at Qazvin. His name was Ya'qub and he carried a letter from the king of Poland to archiduke Ferdinand and Italian princes.[717] The first contacts between Shah Abbas I and the king of Poland, Zygmunt III Waza, was through an Armenian merchant called Sefer Muratowicz.[718] As discussed earlier, the Armenian merchants had also acted as intermediaries between Iran and Russia,[719] but not always in matters of trade. Shah Sulayman used them as his envoys. By sending Armenian merchants he wished to avoid any kind of suspicion on the part of the Ottomans, especially when military negotiations were involved.[720] In trade posts such as Livorno, where the Iranian silk trade thrived, Armenians acted as Iranian consuls.[721] Occasionally, Armenian priests from Iran were selected by the Pope as representatives of the Vatican to the court of Iran; however, these Armenians had to convert to Catholicism in order to be eligible for such a position. This was the case of Mathieu of Avaniac, bishop of Nakhchevan, who, after being consecrated in Rome, was sent back to Isfahan as the representative of the Pope and the king of France from 1668 until 1674.[722] By the time Father Krusinski visited Iran in the 18th century, Armenian merchants acted even as ambassadors of the Russian Czar in Iran. Thus, they were exempt from paying any customs and excise while doing business in Iran.[723]

d) **Christians versus Christians: The Conflict of Interest between Armenians and Europeans**

In the diplomatic field also, the Armenians had replaced the Nestorians as intermediaries between Iran and the rest of the world. Nonetheless, there were elements that distinguished the former from the latter. The Armenians dominated the economy of Iran at a time when world trade was flourishing and competition with European traders was intense. This factor exacerbated the relations between the Iranian Armenians and their European 'co-religionists' whose economic interests diverged.

As we saw, the Armenians did not want the foreign trade companies to be accommodated in Iran, as this did not suit their interests. In 1618, Thomas Baker presented himself to the Safavid court as the ambassador of England. He wished to obtain commercial privileges and trading posts in the port of Gombroon (Bandar Abbas).

The Armenians opposed such a treaty as they would have lost their control over the silk trade. As they had overland access to Europe through the Ottoman Empire, the English vessels were not vital to them.[724] More than a half century later in 1688 and 1693, the English made further attempts to obtain trade concessions in Iran. By this time, they had understood that they had to come to terms with the Armenians; however, their efforts were in vain.[725] In 1708, Sultan Husayn refused to grant the French similar trade privileges to those granted to the Armenians. He told the French ambassador, Sieur Michel, that the Armenians were subject to his laws and his fiscal requirements, whereas he did not have the same authority over the French merchants. Nonetheless, the French did manage to obtain some concessions, which incited the Armenians to visit Shah Sultan Husayn in order to have them revoked.[726] The Armenians' antagonism towards the French merchants must have been all the stronger because a few decades earlier the latter had pressurized the French government to stop the Armenians' commercial activities in France.[727] Their commercial success had also embittered their relations with the Portuguese, who created many obstacles to their operations in Hormuz. The hostile attitude of the Portuguese towards them made the Armenians accuse them of not being Christians.[728]

After Shah Abbas I, Shah Safi ended the royal monopoly of the silk supply. Henceforth the European companies had to deal with the Armenians for obtaining silk. Apart from the Dutch, the Europeans were not able to come to terms with them, as the Armenians preferred to transport their merchandise through Ottoman territories rather than use European vessels and lose their control over the silk trade.[729] The merchants from the Catholic countries seem to have suffered the most from the Armenians' domination of the Iranian silk trade, as the latter had persuaded Shah Abbas II to avoid deals with sovereigns of Catholic countries. Instead they obtained his support at the end of his reign for negotiating commercial treaties with the Tsar.[730]

It is interesting, however, that while the Armenians occasionally accepted commercial alliances with the Baniyans (Indian tradesmen), they refused similar deals with European merchants.[731] Their lack of sympathy towards their fellow European 'co-religionists' may explain Raphaël du Mans' comment that 'the Armenians despite their nice clothes look vulgar like the rest of the Iranians.'[732]

The denominational differences between the Armenians of Iran and the European merchants cannot be advanced as a reason for the commercial disagreements. Nonetheless, religious issues did embitter the relations between the Armenians, who belonged to the Apostolic Church, and the Catholic missionaries who wished to convert them.[733] The Islamic laws in Iran forbade apostasy to Muslims, and the population of the Nestorians in Safavid Iran was too insignificant to be the target of missionary activities. As a result most of the efforts of the Catholic missionaries were directed into converting the Armenians. In fact, the principal Catholic mission to Iran was launched in 1604, after the news of the Armenians' deportation reached Europe.[734] Arakel of Tabriz describes the Catholic priests as thieves who stole the relics of Armenian churches in order to deprive them of their holy character and lure the Armenians to their own churches.[735]

As might be expected, the Armenian clergy did not wish to lose their parishes to another Church. Moreover, the Julfan Armenians were a wealthy and self-aware community, who did not see any reason for accepting the spiritual authority of the Pope. There were some Armenians who were enticed by the idea of receiving the protection of Catholic sovereigns if they converted. However, in reality this protection never materialized as Catholic countries were quite far from Iran, and the conflicts between Portugal and Iran in the Persian Gulf damaged even further the position of Catholics in Iran.

Since their settlement at Hormuz in 1508, the Portuguese had claimed jurisdiction over all the Christian Iranians living in the area. The majority of these Christians, as can be surmised, were Armenian. Furthermore, during the conflict with the Ottomans, Shah Abbas I was letting the Catholic sovereigns of Europe believe that, if he obtained their support, he would order all his Christian subjects to submit to the Catholic Church. However, the conflict between the Iranians and the Portuguese and the economic power of the Armenians, who belonged by a great majority to the Apostolic Church, made it unlikely that the Shah would make his Armenian subjects Catholic. The Carmelites tell us that the Armenians had stirred Shah Abbas I against the Augustin Fathers, telling him that the Augustins wished to make the Armenians Portuguese subjects.[736] The peace with the Ottoman Empire made the Shah even less obliging towards the Catholic missionaries, and for a period he even refused to grant them an audience, as the conversion of the Armenians was an issue he did not wish to discuss.[737]

The Catholic missionaries, however, persevered in their evangelical activities.[738] They established schools to which they invited the Armenians to send their sons. The Archbishop of New Julfa did not wait long to threaten with excommunication all those who had their children tutored by Catholic missionaries. He even had Shah Abbas II expel Father Ambroise from Iran, as he was deemed to be an assertive Catholic militant.[739] The Armenian ecclesiastics had even succeeded in obtaining an edict prohibiting the Augustin missionaries from officiating for Nestorian Christians.[740] In 1654 they simply forced the Jesuits, Carmelites and Capucins to leave New Julfa.[741] Many Armenians in Nakhchevan had been converted to Catholicism by a Dominican from Bologna, but Chardin says that the persecution by the Armenian patriarch had brought them back to the Apostolic faith. The Dominicans sent letters to the Safavid court from the Pope and the Catholic monarchs of France, Poland and Italy, asking the Shah to protect the Catholics in Iran.[742]

After the death of Shah Abbas II, the struggle between the Armenians and the Catholic missionaries intensified even further. Agha Piri, who was the *kalantar* of New Julfa and probably the wealthiest Armenian of Iran, was staunchly opposed to the activities of the European missionaries. His conversion to Islam in 1673 increased even further his influence at the court,[743] which he certainly used to frustrate the Catholics. During this period, the Armenians persuaded Shah Sulayman (1666-1694) to ban marriages between Armenians and Catholics.[744] Knowing the delicate situation of the Armenians, the French missionaries and merchants lured the Armenian *katholikos* to appeal to the Pope and acknowledge his authority, but the Carmelites and the Augustins, seeing that they could not play any part in this political reconciliation, advised the Pope to ignore his appeal.[745]

The Catholic missionaries had in fact damaged the fragile unity of the Armenian community. There were as a result occasional discords between the Church and the secular leaders of the Armenians. In 692 the bishop Nahapet Edesaci obtained the seat of the *katholikos*, with the support of the *kalantar* of New Julfa, Khwaja Awet. The Armenians forced both men out of their office and elected a new *katholikos*. Khwaja Awet and the bishop Nahapet Edesaci decided to avenge themselves. The former converted to Islam, and the bishop Nahapet, through Khwaja Awet's assistance and the support of the Jesuits, had the *katholikos* elected by the Armenians arrested by the Safavid officials.[746] A year earlier, in 1691, the Carmelites tell us that the *kalantar* of New Julfa calumniated the Armenian Catholics to Shah Sulayman, preferring to see them convert to Islam.[747] The Catholic missionaries admit that Shah Sulayman had no predilection for the Armenians,[748] therefore the Armenians were skilled negotiators, as despite the cordial relation the missionaries maintained with the court, the Julfan Armenians were able to thwart their plans for settling and building churches in New Julfa by obtaining edicts from Shah Sulayman forcing them to abandon their plans.[749] The Carmelites expressed their confusion about the behaviour of the Armenians, saying that the Armenians and their *katholikos* put themselves under the authority of the Iranian king voluntarily and incited him against the Catholic emissaries.[750] The Christian missionaries retaliated against the Apostolic Armenians by having the Pope and other Catholic monarchs send envoys to Iran, in order to win Shah Sultan Husayn's favour for the Catholic missionaries and denounce the hostility of the Armenians.[751] In 1695, the Carmelites took advantage of the arrival of the Portuguese ambassador (Gregorio Pereira Fidalgo) to present their petition to Sultan Husayn. However, at that time, the Armenian *katholikos* enjoyed the support of the Queen mother, and therefore the Carmelites saw their attempts fail. Two years later, to the consternation of the Armenians, the Portuguese ambassador was able to obtain from the Shah the right for the Carmelites to establish a Catholic church at New Julfa.[752]

The Armenian *katholikos*, Aleksander, was exasperated by the attitude of the Catholic missionaries. However, he wished to open a dialogue with Pope Clement XI. He sent him in 1709 a letter which reveals the situation:

> We can state in the clearest possible way that we live among such people who do not accept Christ as God (...) Also our King (...) who is a non-Christian (...) cares for us and protects us (...) But the fathers who have come to our country behave differently by opposing us and by creating obstacles for us. And when we complain against their behaviour, they present to your greatness false and groundless reports. Being unaware [of the reality] you believe them. In the presence of non-Christians, they call the Armenians schismatic and heretic.[753]

The Pope paid no heed to the grievance of the *katholikos*,[754] so the Armenians had no other alternative but to appeal to the Shah. They obtained further royal edicts against the Catholic missionaries. This prompted the Catholic bishop of Baghdad to complain about the Armenians in 1711, because the latter had the privileges of the Catholics revoked.[755]

e) **Expensive Prerogatives: the Armenians' Paradoxical Position**

The Christian Iranians have sometimes been depicted as the most fortunate of the non-Muslim groups in Iran. Such a statement is not based really on the financial success of the Julfan Armenians, but on an erroneous assumption that the Armenians, as Christians, enjoyed Papal support. The support in question was nothing more than a letter written by the Pope to the Shah, which 'had little or no effect at the Safavid court.'[756] In 1672, for example, Louis XIV sent a certain Sieur de la Jonchère to petition Shah Sulayman against the persecution of the Armenians. Sieur de la Jonchère died during his journey, and the protest of Louis XIV was never heard. It is worth noting, however, that Louis XIV was solely interested in the fate of the Armenians who professed the Catholic faith.[757] Chardin confirms that the European Christian ambassadors did nothing to improve the situation of the Armenians, and in fact worked against them.[758] Indeed, many Christians were forced to abandon their faith in this period.[759] Even the European travellers were indifferent to the Armenians' problem. Chardin and Tavernier praised the Grand Vizier, Muhammad Beg, despite his persecution of Armenians, as he was well-disposed towards foreign merchants.[760]

In the foregoing pages, we explained that not only did the Pope and the European monarchs not support the Armenians, but that their economic and religious ambitions in Iran were detrimental to the interests of Armenians. On some rare occasions, the Armenians did receive support from the missionaries. This happened in 1609, when Shah Abbas I demanded that the non-wealthy Armenians of Isfahan return him the 400 *tumans* he had lent them after their deportation. The Augustins, hoping to convert them to Catholicism, provided them with the required sum. Shah Abbas was vexed by the Augustins' interference and forced many Armenians to embrace Islam, which most of them managed to leave discreetly.[761] Similarly, the Ottoman Jews, as we saw earlier, had also intervened on behalf of the Iranian Jews whilst they were in trouble. Consequently, the Armenians had no stronger a foreign support than Iranian Jewry.

At other times, we are told that the French and the Dutch had requested safeguards for the Armenians in their service. However, in these cases they had asked for similar guarantees for the Baniyans and even the Muslim Iranians working for them. They were not truly concerned about the welfare of the Armenians, but were worried about their own commercial interests.[762]

In sum, the Armenians, like the Jews and the Zoroastrians, could not count on exterior support, and had to rely on their own negotiating skills.[763] During the crisis of 1619-1621, when there was pressure on the Armenian community to convert, all the Carmelites could do was give moral support. The Armenian merchants, on the other hand, had the financial means to threaten Shah Abbas I. They simply refused to return to Iran and hand him his share of profits until he had relieved the Armenians from the menace of enforced apostasy.[764]

This wave of persecution was not an isolated case. Shah Abbas I had already put pressure on the Armenians 1613. Around 1624, he had also issued an edict granting the possessions of Christians to any of their relatives who turned Muslim. In 1651 they borrowed 150 *tumans* from the Jesuits in order to appease Shah Abbas II.[765] They do not seem to have been very successful: the Carmelites say that by 1654 about 50,000 Christians had turned Muslim in order to avoid beggary.[766] According to Matthee, the Julfan Armenians were not affected by this decree.[767]

Towards the end of the 17th century, the situation of the non-Muslims had begun to deteriorate rapidly. This was mainly due to growing power of the *ulema* (Shi'ite clergy) at the court. During their youth, Shah Sulayman and his successors had been kept secluded in the *harem*, and as result had not acquired any political experience. As a result, they greatly depended on the guidance and assistance of their entourage, enabling the *ulema* to interfere increasingly in the affairs of the country.

The result of such interference was the deterioration of the position of non-Muslims' situation in Iran. The *ulema* pushed Shah Sulayman to revoke the privileges of the Armenians. New Julfa's tax exemptions were abolished.[768] In 1671, a royal decree forced the Armenians of Isfahan to pay taxes on their churches. This put the Armenians in a difficult situation, as the Armenian suburbs of Isfahan had approximately 71 Armenian churches. We are told that the rivalry within the Armenian community had aggravated the situation, as an Armenian cleric whose ambitions had not been satisfied had induced the Shah to believe that the Armenian churches were full of gold.[769] Shortly afterwards, according to the Carmelites, the Shi'ite clergy had convinced Shah Sulayman to kill the leading rabbis of the Jews and extort money from both the Jews and the Armenians. This was probably one of the reasons that drove Agha Piri, the wealthiest Armenian merchant and *kalantar* of New Julfa, to convert to Islam. This enabled him to intervene on behalf of the Armenians in 1678, when they had become scapegoats for the drought. Nonetheless, five years later, Shah Sulayman selected some 27 Armenian women, some of whom were already married, and distributed them to his subalterns. Some of the relatives of these women were compelled to become Muslim in order to preserve their possessions, as Muslims had the right to claim the wealth of their non-Muslim family.[770]

These abuses prompted the emigration of wealthy Armenians to safer havens like India, Russia and Venice.[771] The Armenians made overtures to the Tsar Alexei Mikhaelovich. They were even willing to accept Catholicism in order to obtain the protection of Louis XIV,[772] but the precarious situation of the Catholic Armenians shows that these appeals were of no avail. Their adherence to Catholicism had encouraged them to emigrate to Europe even before the harsh persecutions which occurred during Shah Sulayman's reign. Between 1567-1667, the Catholic Armenians had lost six bishoprics in Greater Armenia alone, leaving just one in Nakhchevan.[773]

At the close of the 17th century, the position of the Julfan Armenians was not much different from that of the rest of the non-Muslim inhabitants of Iran. The most wealthy among them, such as those belonging to the Shafraz family, had left Iran.[774] New Julfa itself was no longer a wealthy neighbourhood.[775] Shah Abbas II had forced poorer Armenians and the Zoroastrians of Isfahan to move to New Julfa.[776] Later on, there were a few Muslims settled in the suburb in order to spy on the non-Muslim population.[777] The English merchant, Jonas Hanway, wrote that by the time of Sultan Husayn (1694-1722), all the privileges of the Armenians had been taken away.[778]

In conclusion, the affluence of the Julfan Armenians had distinguished them for a few decades from the rest of the non-Muslim population of Iran. As we have seen, there were also wealthy Jews and Zoroastrians, but their role in the economy of Iran was much more modest than that of the Julfan Armenians. Nonetheless, as demonstrated, their control of the silk trade and their fortune did not save them from persecutions. Contrary to general belief, they did not benefit from European protection. Moreover, the majority of the Armenians living in Iran were not opulent. Most of them were artisans, labourers and farmers. They encountered many hardships and did not benefit from the privileges granted to the Julfan community. Unfortunately, there is much less information available on these groups of Armenians.[779]

5) **The Georgians and Circassians: The Assimilated Christians**

The Armenians were not the only Christians deported to Iran. The Safavids had led campaigns against other Christian people in the Caucasus, namely the Georgians and the Circassians, and had carried many of them to Iran. The position of the Georgians in the Iranian army was as important as the position of the Armenians in the Iranian economy. In order to circumscribe the power of the Turkmens, the Safavid monarchs enrolled Georgian soldiers and appointed them to the highest military posts.[780] In the Ottoman-Safavid wars of 1603-1604 the commander-in-chief of the Iranian troops was the Georgian Allahverdi Khan.[781] As the Georgians were a foreign element, they did not have any local support and were entirely dependent on the monarch. Thus, the Shah was assured of their loyalty. Until the end of the Safavid period, the Georgians 'formed the backbone of the Persian fighting forces'.[782] Le Bruyn, who visited Iran in 1707, attests that the governor and the head of the army of Tabriz was a Georgian prince called Rustam Khan.[783] The Carmelites testify that in 1711 the Iranian force sent to Qandahar for curtailing an Indian attack was composed mainly of Georgian soldiers.[784]

There were also many Georgians and Circassians taken as slaves to the court.[785] After the reign of Shah Tahmasp (1524-1576) the number of Georgian and Circassian women had increased to such an extent that all the Christian relics brought by the European missionaries to the court were sent to the seraglio.[786] The mother of Shah Abbas I was a Caucasian Christian, and he himself had Christian wives, one of whom was the daughter of Simon Khan, a Georgian prince.[787] Father John Thaddeus asserts that Shah Safi (1629-1642) had not been circumcised. His mother was Georgian, and he too had many Georgian wives.[788] Shah Abbas II (1642-1666) had also married Caucasian women. His son, Shah Sulayman (1666-1694) was born of a Circassian slave.[789]

The large presence of Christian women in the royal *harem* and of Christian slaves at court certainly had some repercussion on the political level.[790] Indeed, many of these Caucasian women were of royal descent and wanted the court to comply with their wishes.[791] It is difficult, however, to evaluate how beneficial this Christian presence was to the Armenians, for the doctrinal differences between the different creeds of the Armenians and Georgians had historically made the two groups hostile towards each other.[792] The intervention of the Georgian princesses apparently served more the purpose of foreign Christian merchants or missionaries, who wished to obtain commercial concessions or intended to establish convents in Iran.[793] Along with the Georgian princesses, Georgian princes were also taken to Isfahan. The Shah chose from among them the heir to the Georgian throne, and made the chosen prince the governor of Isfahan after having converted him to Islam. He was put on the throne of Georgia after the death of the ruling Georgian monarch.[794]

It should be mentioned that not all the Georgians ended up in the army or the court. Savory says that in 1614 alone, there were 130,000 Georgian prisoners brought to Iran. They were scattered all over the country, and unlike the Armenians, who were able to preserve their religion, they were assimilated to the local population.[795] The European missionaries had endeavoured to win a number of them back to Christianity,[796] but their successes were temporary as the Georgian and Circassian communities were dispersed in such a way that it was difficult for them to maintain their ethnic cohesion.[797]

6) **The Inconspicuous Christians**

About two centuries before the advent of the Safavids, the political scene of Iran had been dominated by Nestorian emissaries and influential dignitaries at the court. By the time the Safavids had taken over power, the Nestorians had been reduced to a tiny community, numerically even less important than the Zoroastrians. The seat of the Nestorian patriarchate at Baghdad, which had survived all the peripeteia of history since the Sassanian period, had not been able to overcome Timur Lang's onslaught in 1392. Timur Lang's assault caused the dramatic decline of the Nestorian population and the removal of the Nestorian seat from Baghdad. The Nestorian Patriarchate then became a hereditary office until 1551, when the cohesion of the community was destroyed.[798] There were certainly many factors which had created this division, but the two most important ones were the meddling of the Catholic missionaries and the division of the territories inhabited by the Nestorians between the Ottomans and the Safavids. The missionaries say that the Patriarchs residing in Azerbaijan claimed authority over the Nestorians living in Ottoman territory. However, their power had dramatically waned since the 13th century, and there was not much left of the glorious days when they had spiritual jurisdiction over most of the Christian churches in

Asia. By 1606, there were hardly any contacts between them and the Nestorians in India.[799]

The only Nestorians left in Iran were gathered around the town of Urumia. According to the Carmelites, in the 17th century there were about 5,000 Nestorian families living there, and a few families scattered in Maragha and near the town of Solduz.[800] A number of them were deported to Isfahan along with other non-Muslim groups by Shah Abbas I at the beginning of the 17th century. Tavernier and Pietro della Valle confirm their presence and say that there were also some Jacobites in the town.[801]

In Isfahan, their fate was very similar to that of Armenians. Certainly, the part they played in the Iranian economy was much more modest; however, the Nestorians were also very active at the commercial level and had built themselves a reputation for their craftsmanship.[802] Shah Abbas' interest in them confirms their abilities in those occupations. Like the Armenians, they also suffered from the edict of Shah Abbas I which made any of their Muslim relatives the sole proprietor of their possessions. In 1621, which appears to be the year the edict was proclaimed, about thirty Nestorian families converted to Islam and seven left Isfahan.[803] The Catholic missionaries strove to convert those of them who had remained Nestorians. They were quite successful, as the Nestorian religious establishment was not as powerful or influential as that of the Armenians,[804] and therefore there was less resistance towards the activities of the Catholics. Nonetheless, the Armenians not only wished to protect their own community from the Catholic missionaries, but also desired the Catholic population not to increase. In 1650, they obtained an edict prohibiting Catholic missionaries from officiating to Nestorians.[805] This proves further that the presence of the Catholic missionaries was not politically beneficial to the Armenians, and that the Armenians considered themselves the leaders of all the Christians in Iran.

In Azerbaijan, during the same period, the Nestorians were suffering from the persecutions of the local governor (Taj al-Din). Therefore, they sent a representative to Isfahan in 1652, hoping that Shah Abbas II would intervene on their behalf. The Catholic missionaries promised their assistance if the Nestorians converted to Catholicism.[806]

The situation of the Nestorians does not seem to have improved, as four years later Shah Abbas II decided to expel all non-Muslims from Isfahan, grouping the Christians and the Zoroastrians in New Julfa. A year later, in 1657, he ordered the conversion of all non-Muslims, obliging the Jews, Mandeans, Armenians and Nestorians to embrace Islam.[807] As discussed earlier in the chapter, many were able to evade the edict and some were able to recover their original faith after the crisis.

Despite the strict religious policies of Shah Abbas II and that of his less tolerant successors, in 1692, both Patriarchs, Mar Shamun (residing in Azerbaijan, Iran) and Mar Eliyya (residing in Mosul, Ottoman Empire) renounced Catholicism.[808] The difficult atmosphere of Iran had pushed many Christians to migrate at the close of the 17th century, but those who had chosen to remain no longer wished to associate themselves with foreign missionaries as this had not brought them any advantages and had at times provoked the Muslims or indigenous Christian ecclesiastics. Such remained the situation in Iran until the 19th century.

Section 2 (to Chapter 5)
Minority Cultures in Safavid Iran

1) The Armenians and Iranian Culture: A Non-Integrated Minority

Putting the 20th century aside, at no other moment in the second millennium have the non-Muslims of Iran appeared as culturally active as during the Safavid period. Following the fall of the Safavids, the non-Muslims entered a period of cultural stagnation which was due to the social and political circumstances that followed the Afghan invasion.

The economic and political circumstances of the Safavid period were particularly favourable to the development of new ideas as the exchanges between different countries had increased dramatically since the discovery of new trade routes and the rise of mercantilism.

The Armenians played a unique role in this respect. As in the 20th century, they were culturally the most avant-garde group in Iran. Their successful mercantile activities had broadened their horizons more widely than those of other Iranians. Thus, they brought back exotic ideas and new fashions.[809] As mentioned above, they were able to impress the court with European merchandise such as watches and stockings, but none of these items had the revolutionary impact of the printing press. It is true, however, that the first attempts by Khachatur Kesarachi to establish a printing house, in 1636, were not very fruitful. After printing the first book ever in Iran, *The Psalms of David* (Salmos Davte), he was obliged to stop his printing activities due to the protest of the scribes whose livelihood he threatened.[810]

The true cultural impact of the Armenians did not reside in the materials they imported, but in the fresh ideas they introduced to Iranian art. Their churches in Isfahan today are evidence of the blending of Persian and Western styles. When Le Bruyn visited New Julfa, he reported that there were three important churches. The largest one was called *Surpa Tomafa*. The one which contained the largest number of paintings was *Surpa Kroop*, and Le Bruyn added that it had a fine dome (probably similar to those of Isfahan's mosques). However, the principal

Church was *Anna Baet* or Church of the Bishop. This church also contained many paintings.[811] The Armenian paintings reflected a new trend, which was adopted later by Muslim Iranian artists.

New Julfa had several famous painters. Chardin met one of them, called Avadick. He was a wealthy Armenian merchant who had resided in Italy for some years. On his return to Isfahan, he produced a number of paintings in the Armenian churches of the town.[812] Another illustrious painter was Minas, who trained in Aleppo under European masters. He was much appreciated by Shah Safi, who had seen his paintings at the residences of notable Armenians. Yakobian was another famous painter. His skills had made him *naqqashbashi* at the court of Shah Abbas II (1642-1666). The Shah appreciated him to the extent of granting him the governorship of New Julfa.[813] Another painter of high repute, Yovhannes Mrkuz, belonged to the clerical class. He has been credited by Khachatur Julayechi with the decorations of *All Saviour's Cathedral*.[814]

New Julfa had twenty-five small churches, which may have also contained some pieces of art, but there is no allusion to them in the sources. The European travellers were more impressed with the mansions of the prominent Armenians, which like the churches were well ornamented. The house of one of New Julfa's governors, Hodshe Minozes, had an amply decorated large hall. The front gates of these houses were usually very small in order to prevent people from seeing the magnificence of the interior.[815]

During this period, the Armenians produced some religious literature, as well as books that reflected their commercial talents. A certain Kostand composed a treatise on the basic rules of trade and on the different types of measures and currencies used in other countries. In the 1640's, Simeon Julayechi produced an Armenian grammar book for the use of his community.[816] None of these books were written in Persian. Although there were groups of Armenians living in Iran before the Safavid period, they were not assimilated linguistically, as the bulk of their population had been brought to Iran relatively late. Nonetheless, it seems that their interest in the Persian literature was ignited once they had migrated to the Mughal court. A certain Alexander nicknamed Mirza Zul-Qarnain, reached fame as a poet at the court of Shah Jahan. Unfortunately, none of the verses he composed have reached us.[817] Another poet, who migrated from Iran to India and has been thought by some to be Armenian, is Sarmad.[818] However, he has generally been referred to as a Muslim convert of Jewish background, so we will discuss his work in the following section, in which Jewish literature in Iran is discussed.

2) **The Last Glimmers of the Iranian Jewry's Culture**

Despite the assertions to the contrary by some European travellers and modern historians, the Iranian Jewry was still culturally very active during the Safavid period.[819] It is true that the scholastic centres of Sura and Pumbedita no longer existed in the 15th and 16th century, but there were still Jewish academic institutions in Iran. The Italian traveller Giambattista Vecchietti (1552-1619) records that both Kashan and Lar were centres of Jewish learning. During his visit to Iran, Vecchietti acquired Judeo-Persian manuscripts, which he brought back with him to Europe.[820]

The end of the medieval period witnessed the appearance of Jewish Iranian scholars who were held in high repute outside Iran. This was the case of Jacob b. Joseph Tawus (1490-1576), who was called to the Jewish Academy of Istanbul, where he translated the Pentateuch into Judeo-Persian in 1546. The Jews distinguished themselves from other non-Muslim groups in Safavid Iran by choosing to write Persian in a script other than Arabic, and transliterated into the Hebrew script the works of the Muslim Iranian poets, such as Nizami, Sa'di, Hafiz, Jami and even the less known Sa'ib of Isfahan.[821] This demonstrates that the Jews were not culturally isolated. They knew how to read the Arabic script and their knowledge of Persian literature, as their poetry attests, equalled that of their Muslim neighbours.[822] Their usage of the Hebrew script shows that there were Jewish centres of education, where they were principally taught religious texts and trained to use the Hebrew script.

Nonetheless, the usage of the Hebrew script by the Jewish poets rendered their work inaccessible to the Muslim majority. It is probable that they did not see much reason to write their poems in the Arabic script, as their work is unlikely to have been appreciated outside Jewish circles. Indeed, the famous Jewish poet Imrani (1454-1536), like his predecessor Shahin (14th c.), is not mentioned in any Muslim Iranian source. Both poets were from Shiraz, which is a town that produced many celebrated Persian poets, such as Sa'di and Hafiz. Imrani, like Shahin, had been inspired by his Muslim peers.[823]

Imrani was not a pioneer like Shahin, but he is the most important literary figure of Judeo-Persian after the latter. Following the footsteps of Shahin, he made the five books of the Pentateuch the subject of his poetry and adopted many Persian and Islamic features. He contributed much to this unique and eclectic genre of Persian literature by producing two important books: the *Fath-nama* and the *Ganj-nama*.[824] While writing the *Fath-nama* he was supported by a patron who held an official position with the honorific title of *Amin al-Dawla* (trustee of the state). Once his patron died, he had to face the hostility of the Jewish community of Isfahan. As a result, he had to leave for Kashan. This event had an immense impact on his work, which is dominated by the theme of exile. Imrani made extensive use of midrashic sources, and like Shahin he emulated Firdawsi's epic style in composing his prose and poetry. This demonstrates his sense of attachment to his Persian heritage. He was not however isolated from his Islamic environment, for his *Ganj-nama* reflects influences from Attar (d. 1220) and Sa'di (d. 1292).[825] It is interesting to observe in Imrani's minor works, *Hanukkah-nama* or *Zafar-nama* (The Book of Victory), an effort to bring hope to the community. He strives to show the strength of his ancestors, who were able to resist their "infidel" enemies despite their small number:

The infidel cried:
31 'O shah, Israel fled;
    You have succeeded in your wish.
32 I have destroyed the choicest homes,
    All ramparts and all towers.
33 I have attacked with confidence,
    Turned my attention to every province.
34 Wherever Israelites are found,
    We annihilated or turned them into heathens.
35 This people's name we scattered,
    Their heads we severed from their bodies.'
36 When Mattatiah[826] heard yet again,
    Of this army's tyranny and injustice,
37 He summoned his sons once more,
    Seated them gladly by his side,
38 And spoke: 'I've had another revelation;
    The divine voice called to me thus:
39 "This army, all these princes,
    And this host, none other than the shah has mustered.
40 Yet shall they all fall by the sword,
    To find a resting place in Hell..."'
    [At the end, the people of Israel were victorious]
212 When they beheld all the uncircumcised ones annihilated,

The Israelites gathered, all thanking God;...[827]

In his last work, the *Ganj-nama*, Imrani was, according to Moreen, influenced by Sufi ideas. His work also reflects familiarity with Judeo-Arabic and Ladino literature. For example, he makes a reference to Maimonides' *Mishneh Torah*. Like many of the documents written by the Iranian Jews and Zoroastrians, the *Ganj-nama* is a collection of didactic poetry. The advice given in it reflects the difficulties that the community had to face (discussed earlier in the chapter). These were mostly cases of apostasy, and situations where Jews betrayed their co-religionists. Thus, the author seeks to avert such incidents by exhorting the Jews to preserve their traditions and remain united.[828] Imrani quotes advice from a well-known rabbi of yore:

	Rabbi Yose the Priest[829] says:
1	If you wish not to depend on people, Become the crown of princes;
2	You must be trustworthy, Incapable of treachery.
3	Whatever a friend entrusts to you, Protect it according to the Torah;
4	For it is trust that upholds the world, And the heart of him who is always,
5	Openly and secretly, mindful, Of the living Bestower.
6	He takes not a barley grain's worth from anyone; He burdens no one.
7	The man whose dealings are clean, Why should he fear plaintiffs?...
52	Heed my advice, [O friend] [As learning brings humility]....
66	Take heed; say not, 'My son studies; He will earn credit for the father,'
67	Or, 'My father is a learned man; My need for knowledge is already satisfied.'...
73	The sage expressed this thought most fittingly; Sweet is his speech if you would comprehend.
74	'Granted your father was a learned man, How do you benefit from it?'[830]

By 'sage', Imrani is referring to Sa'di. There are actually two quotations from his *Gulestan* (couplets 7 and 74).[831] These quotations evince clearly that Imrani was familiar with Muslim authors and was well instructed in classical Persian poetry.

The Judeo-Persian background of our poet appears clearly at the end of the *Ganj-nama*, where Hebrew terms along with the Persian festival of *nawruz* are cited:

> In the Year *Atatmah*,[832] after divine guidance,
> The Almighty bestowed upon me this favour.
> O God who may ever intervene in this world,
> May he always fill the hearts of mortals with joy.
> In sum, may everyone be blessed and victorious,
> And be embellished like nawruz;
> O God may *guevala* (redemption) arrive soon,
> So that the tired hearts will be *refua* (healed);
> A hundred times may mercy from the Lord,
> Descend on the soul and spirit of Ibn Imran.[833]

Imrani's passion for the Jewry and his sympathy for Iranians are in evidence in the *Qissa-ya Haft Baradaran* (The Story of Seven Brothers). These verses gather stories from the Bible and the *Shah-nama*. Imrani evokes the historical event which intertwined the fate of the Persians and the Jews after the Persians delivered the latter from the hands of the Babylonians. He then narrates the misfortune of both peoples after the Greeks invaded Iran.

> Hear one (story) of how the sons of Yaqub,
> Were treated by those perverted pagans;
> See what those pious exalted ones
> Experienced at the hands of those infidel pagans;
> What misery and pain they suffered,
> (And) experienced in each corner of this world;
> From Babylon and oppressive Adonites,
> What came upon those pious tribes,
> One by one they offered their lives in their hands,
> But did not lose faith in the right religion;
> First Nebuchadenezzar, that *arel* (uncircumcised) pagan came from Babylon;
> He burnt first the *miqdash* (temple) of God,
> Then the Chosen Land of God Almighty,
> Dislodged the Torah out of Israel,
> Turned the world upside down.
> In one day, that destructive oppressor
> Killed countless numbers from the people of religion...
> As seventy years passed again,
> The munificent God, who knows all the secrets
> Manifested his mercy,
> (And) looked at the state of those wretched (children of Israel)...
> Through the hands of the Persian and Mede army,

He destroyed totally those dogs.
The king of Persians and Medes, that Just one,
Who was called Cyrus, the Wise man;
When the entire world was conquered,
The Guardian of the world further inspired him.
He proclaimed in every kingdom and country,
Where anyone from the progeny of Hebrews was to be found,
That they may return to their land again,
(And) rebuild the chosen kingdom of God;
They shall rebuild the sacred *miqdash* (temple),
(And) be freed from the sorrows of the world.
Then this prudent man sent word
To those commanders who were there;
That the children of Israel should not be harassed again (...)
When four hundred years passed,
Luck once more turned away from us.
On the basis that we were given to *aavun* (sin),
And had turned away from the path of *mithva* (good deeds);
As the period became filled with guilt,
From Rome (i.e. Greece) came an army with many horsemen.
They were all like Nebuchadenezzar, that cruel pagan,
Their commanders were murderous and malevolent.
They set out for the Chosen Kingdom,
And from there headed towards the *miqdash* (temple);
As the foot of those *aarlims* (uncircumcised) and *tamiims* (impure)
Was set there, they decided there;
They ruined the *miqdash* (temple) once more,
May a hundred curses be upon those pagans.
From that time onwards they established tyranny,
And oppressed the Ya'qubites (the descendants of Ya'qub).[834]

Another interesting author of didactic poetry is Yehudah b. David. His most recurrent *nisba* (attribute) is Lari, which suggests that he was from Lar. Occasionally he is also called as Shirazi. He lived around the end of the 16th or beginning of the 17th century and he composed *Makhzan al-Pand* (The Treasury of Advice).[835] Many of his maxims are similar to those appearing in the didactic literature of Muslims and Zoroastrians. Some of them reflect the perpetual concern of the non-Muslim communities, whose members were sometimes lured to abandon their faith by the prospect of lucrative positions:

41	Flee from shahs and lords;
	Become a hermit when faced with an army.
42	Don't be their guest at gatherings,
	For you will stray if you eat their bread.
43	If you have acquired a lot of wealth,

	You have acquired anxiety and grief.
44	Eating a slice of barley bread in peace
	Is better than having a platter full of food but lacking peace of mind.[836]

In 1692, Aharon b. Mashiah composed the *Shoftim-nama*. He was from Isfahan but, probably owing to the wave of persecutions taking place at the end of the 17th century was compelled to move to Yazd. Aharon claims that Imrani was his teacher, but he can only have been inspired by his work, as Imrani died about 1536. His only extant work is a versed form of the Book of Judges.[837]

More interesting for our topic is the work of Babai b. Lutf, *Kitab-i Anusi* (The Book of a Forced Convert). This book is not only an excellent example of the literary activity of the Iranian Jewry, but also possesses great historical value. As Babai b. Lutf died sometime after 1662, his writings cover events from the reign of Shah Abbas I (1571-1629) up to the last years of Shah Abbas II (1642-1666).[838] Although his text focuses on tales of persecution, it provides us with details about the socio-economic position of Jews (as discussed in the first section of this chapter). Babai b. Lutf, like the other Jewish literary figures, uses the stylistic norms set by Muslim Iranian poets. He includes his signature (*takhallus*) and uses *masnavi*[839] as his literary style. His occasional quotations from other Persian poets demonstrate that he was acquainted with the works of Nizami, Jami, and Firdawsi in particular.[840] Below is an excerpt from the introduction to the *Kitab-i Anusi*, which displays Babai b. Lutf's poetic skills:

1	O, Lord, by the truth of those whose gaze is fixed upon your threshold,
	And by the sun, Jupiter, Venus, and the moon;
2	By your exalted, glorious throne,
	And by the truth of Your elect of old;
3	By all the ministering *mallakh* (angels),
	And by the truth of Heaven and Earth and [Adam's offspring];
4	By the truth of Noah, Abraham, and all the chieftains,
	The prophets Ishaq, and Ya'qub,
5	By the truth of poor, righteous Yusuf,
	Who was always a candle, faithful,
6	By the truth of *Moshe*, Harun, and *Pinhas*,
	The noblest at Your noble threshold,
7	By David and Solomon's power,
	And by the valour of Yahushu' ben Nun,
8	By the truth of Yormia, that patient sage,
	Remember, Lord, Caesar's oppression![841]

Babai b. Lutf's grandson, Babai b. Farhad, continued the work of his grandfather in his *Kitab-i Sar Guzasht-i Kashan* (The Book of Events in Kashan). He narrated the situation of the Jews during the Afghan invasion from 1722 to 1730. The impact of the dominating Shi'ite environment on the Jewish community is noticeable by the terms used by Babai b. Farhad. Islamic words such as *mahdi* (the twelfth imam of *Twelver* Shi'ites) and *qibla* (direction to Mecca) are used for referring to the Messiah and the Jewish direction of prayer.[842] It is also interesting to see that the Jews spoke of the Shi'ites in the same way that the latter referred to the Jews. Babai b. Farhad uses the word *pasul* (v. 220-225) for them, which in Hebrew means 'ritually unfit'. The word is deployed in reply to the Shi'ites' usage of the Arabic word *najis* (unclean) for non-Muslims. Jews in other Muslim lands do not use such a term. This demonstrates a noteworthy impact of Shi'ite Islam on Iranian Jewry.[843]

Another Jewish Iranian author who emerged in the 17th century is Yehudah b. El'azar. In 1686, he wrote *Hobot Yehudah* (The Duties of Judah), which according to Moreen is the most important philosophical text we have from the Iranian Jewry.[844] Like Imrani, Babai b. Lutf and Babai b. Farhad, Yehudah b. El'azar came from Kashan, which in the 17th century was a prosperous town thanks to the commerce of silk, textile and rug weaving. Yehudah b. El'azar was a physician himself, and beside this philosophical treatise he also wrote a book on astronomy, *Taqwim al-Yehudah* (The calendar of Yehudah), and a short text about the hazards of wine. He was referred to by Refu'ah b. El'azar as *rabbi* and *dayyan* (Hebrew for 'religious judge'), which reflects his level of scholarship. He had a good command of Hebrew, Aramaic and Arabic in addition to Persian. He was acquainted with rabbinic sources (such as the Talmud and Zohar)[845], Greek and Islamic philosophers and Persian poetry, not to mention Jewish philosophers, and Kabbalists.[846] In his tract he debated the ideas of Moses Maimonides (1135-1204)[847] and David Messer Leon (1470-1526).[848] Yehudah b. El'azar also lived during the period of forced conversions, resulting in his polemic against Jewish apostasy.[849]

A very interesting poet from the end of the Safavid period is Amina (Benyamin Mishael Kashani). Although he originally stemmed from Bukhara, his panegyric to the Afghan monarch Ashraf (d. 1730) and his title Kashani show that he lived in Iran as well. He too followed the style of Shahin in his poetry.[850] Moreen doubts whether his panegyrics ever reached the monarch, because they were written by a non-Muslim.[851] However, as we saw, the Jews of Kashan were bribed by

Ashraf, therefore they had certainly met him. Moreover, Ashraf must have been kind to Jews, otherwise Amina and Babai b. Farhad would not have eulogized him. Moreen sees Amina as the greatest Jewish Iranian lyrical poet. According to her, Amina's favourite poet, like the majority of Iranian Jews and Muslims, was Hafiz.[852] Amina may have lived during a period of relative peace, for he was able to dedicate himself to writing poems about his sentimental life: *She Is the Rose Garden's Cypress, The Story of Amina and His Wife*. However, there are also poems in which he laments and seeks God's protection, such as: *In Praise of Moses, Our Master; Peace Be upon Him* and *A Prayer*.[853] Below is Amina's panegyric to Shah Ashraf:

> O just Shah Ashraf, your dower will certainly grow,
> First Egypt and India second, third Rome, and China fourth.
> May God be your refuge and protector; because of you endure
> First Justice and faith second, third honour, and religion fourth.
> Through the blessing of your good fortune, in Iran perished,
> First war and anger second, third rage, and vengeance fourth.
> Your generosity is greater than any source of water, than
> First the Tigris and the Oxus second, third Oman, and Zan fourth.
> Through the intrusion of your spiritual body these appeared in the world,
> First fire and spirit second, third water, and clay fourth.
> Through contact with your body all these became filled with light,
> First the horseshoe, the mount second, third the gallop, and the saddle fourth.
> Come, O world-burning Shah, consider Amina's state,
> First look and learn second, third find, and see fourth.[854]

Our survey of Judeo-Persian literature cannot be complete without any mention of the Jewish authors of Bukhara. This city produced a number of Jewish literary figures, one of whom was the famous Yusuf b. Ishaq b. Musa (18th c.). However, the most celebrated Bukharan Jewish poet of the 17th century is Khwaja Bukhara'i. His only surviving work is a *masnavi* called *Daniyal-nama* written in 1606. His poem indicates that he was an accomplished scholar and was acquainted with Firdawsi's *Shah-nama*, the Torah and the midrashic and apocalyptic texts. *Daniyal-nama* gathers messianic stories and anecdotes from Persian history:[855]

> How Sezavvol was sent by Balshasar around his country in order to gather an army and how he mounted in order to wage war on Dariush the Iraqi and Kurosh the Parsi.

When the afflicted said this speech in front of the Shah, the monarch
was agitated by its sense;
Like a man he put his dress around his waist,
And put an eagle's feather on his golden crown,
On each side, Sezavvol made a way,
That assembled the people following the kingly order.
As the army of the Shah heard this edict,
They ran to him without any delay.
...
With strong arms, stature and thick neck,
Like young Suhrab, and Rustam Zal.
Each of them another Bizhan, when it came to horsemanship,
While in the past there had only been one Bizhan.
All of them brave on the day of battle,
Like Bahman and Som of Nariman.
All of them were virile in equal measure,
Like *Barzou*, Faramarz and Fereidun.
They shunned nothing,
At war, as each was another Afrasiyab.[856]

Yusuf b. Ishaq b. Musa is another famous Jewish poet from Bukhara, better known as Mawlana Yusuf Yahudi. According to Fischel he was born in 1688 and died in 1755, but Moreen believes that he died in 1788. Yusuf Yahudi authored a well-known ode, *Mukhammas*, in which he praises Moses, and wrote another popular poem called *Haft Baradaran* (The Seven Brothers), which is based on a story from the Midrash. Another of his famous works is a *tafsir* on the *Megillat Antioch*.[857] Below is an excerpt from this *tafsir*:

1	I am going to give a testimony on this subject,
	If there comes any help from the Almighty.
2	A story now about Antiochus,
	Which I am going to tell now.
3	Brave was that tyrant king,
	Whose army was innumerable.
4	Unexpectedly, he attacked India,
	Which that king conquered before returning.
5	He took a large army to Rome,
	Seized Rome, and returned satisfied.
6	He subjugated many a city;
	Before returning once again to his own land.
7	He sat mirthfully on his throne,
	Happy was he night and day, free from sorrow.
8	To him tribute from all over the world,
	Was paid by the kings from low to high.[858]

It is interesting that the works of the Jewish poets of Bukhara were known
by some Muslim scholars of their city. Both Khwaja Bukhara'i and Yusuf Yahudi were mentioned in *Muzakkir al-Ashab* (The reminder of companions) written by Muhammad Badi b. Mawlana Muhammad Sharif Samarqandi.[859] This demonstrates at least that in Bukhara Jewish and Muslim literary figures associated with each other, whereas in Iran at the same period we have no concrete proof that Muslim poets were interested in the poetry written by Jews.

Before closing this section, it is worth mentioning that, like Zoroastrians and dissident Iranians, there were Iranian Jews who migrated to India. One of them was the famous Jewish poet Sarmad, whose conversion to Islam has intrigued the scholars of Judeo-Persian. He was a successful merchant who while on a trade mission in India abandoned his possessions and became a *dervish*[860]. He went to Delhi in 1654 during the reign of the Mughal Emperor, Shah Jahan (1627-1659). He wrote many *rubais* (quatrains) in his new settlement. Amnon Netzer, unlike Fischel, believes that Sarmad should not be studied as a Jewish cultural figure as he had left Judaism. Asmussen says that he had not truly embraced Islam, and had his own concept of God and religion.[861] He thus recited:

> I submit to Moses's law,
> I am of thy religion, and the guardian of thy way.
> I am a Rabbi of the Yahuds,
> A Kafir (an infidel), a Muselman.[862]

Seth is even more convinced of Sarmad's non-adherence to Islam, and cites one of the verses he recited in front of Aurangzeb:

> O King of Kings, I am not a hermit like thee, I am not nude. I am frenzied, I am distracted, but I am not depressed. I am an idolater, I am an infidel, I am not of the people of faith, I go towards the mosque, but I am not a Muselman.[863]

Sarmad's knowledge of Judaism, as displayed in the *Dabistan-i Mazhab* (The School of Creeds), demonstrates that he was of Jewish background.[864] As we will see later, this literary collection gathered many non-Muslim authors from Iran who had settled in India.[865]

The Iranian Armenians' claim that Sarmad belonged to their community does not appear to be completely unfounded. It seems that he was an Iranian Armenian Jew. This would explain his involvement in the trade with India, which was dominated by Armenians and not by Iranian Jews.[866]

3) **An Exported Literature: Zoroastrian Writings under the Safavids**

Among the non-Muslim groups of Safavid Iran, the Zoroastrians were the most culturally linked to India. The majority of the texts written by them at this period were sent to India either for religious or cultural purposes. It is difficult to find any Safavid-period literature written by the Zoroastrians, which was meant for an audience in Iran.

Both the style and the content of these texts are interesting as, like the historical documents written by Jewish Iranians, they are written in poetical verses and illustrate the situation of the Zoroastrians in the 16th and 17th centuries. However, the information conveyed by the Zoroastrians about their condition is less explicit than the accounts provided by the Jewish authors. One explanation is that the documents sent by the Zoroastrians to India could have been intercepted. They were written in the common Arabic script and so were intelligible to the Muslims, and while the Zoroastrians usually avoided vilifying them, on rare occasions they did. In principle, the aim of these texts was to provide the Parsis with religious instructions, but sometimes they included details of historical interest.

As mentioned in the first section of the chapter, the exchanges between the Iranian Zoroastrians and the Parsis began, according to the *rivayat*s of 1477, when the Parsi Nariman Hushang travelled to Iran in order to gather religious material for the benefit of his community back in India. Indeed, Lord Henry, who visited India before 1630, attests that the Parsis had lost much of their ancestors' religious and cultural heritage until the Zoroastrians of Iran assisted them by providing them with historical accounts and religious guidance.[867]

More than nineteen *rivayats* were sent from Iran to India. Nineteen of them bear the name of the individuals who carried them, but there are also a few documents that were taken from Iran to India and which do not bear the name of their messengers. The majority of the *rivayat*s consist of religious treatises, and also contain answers to questions asked by the Parsis. Some of the accounts in these volumes are legendary, whilst others recount episodes of Iranian history but do not stem from any authoritative sources. Finally, information sporadically appears in these documents which reflect the activities and the condition of the Zoroastrians in Iran, and today is of historical value. One example is a letter co-authored in 1635 by Dastur Bahram and Dastur Ardashir, addressed to Dastur Kamdin Padam and Behdin Asa Jamshid. It refers to the persecution launched by Shah Abbas I in 1628 in which he killed two prominent figures of the Zoroastrian community and confiscated several books.[868]

The style of the *rivayats* and the poetry included in these volumes demonstrate that the Zoroastrians, like the Iranian Jews, had a good knowledge of the literature produced by the Iranian Muslim authors and probably studied them in their seminaries. A perfect example is a verse recited in the *Rivayat-i Dastur Darab Hormazdyar*. This was composed by the famous 11th century poet Nizami and was quoted to encourage Zoroastrians to maintain the cohesion of their community:

> Dove with dove and falcon with falcon,
> Birds of a feather flock together.[869]

The *rivayats* also reflect the predilection of the Zoroastrians for Firdawsi's masterpiece. It seems that the Zoroastrians of the period considered Firdawsi to have been Zoroastrian.[870] Many of the verses in these volumes are inspired from the *Shah-nama*:

> Thus until the time of Siyavush,
> That *deav* was still hanging, waiting for a deliberation.
> As he is freed from the chains,
> The Dragon will soon be killed by Som.
> This is how Fereidun, using his wisdom,
> Has managed to chain him to Mount Damavand.
> From then the intelligent sage,
> Will inquire again about the *Mino Khirad*.[871]

The importance of Fereidun lies in the role he plays in Iranian mythology. Fereidun delivered Iranians from the hands of the Arab king Zahak. He epitomizes the Iranian king par excellence. Pictorial representations of him can be found in most fire temples in India.

After many pages dedicated to legendary Iranian kings, the authors of the *rivayats* dedicate a number of pages to Sassanian monarchs, but the information used by the authors emanates from Muslim sources.

One of the most interesting features of the texts produced by the Zoroastrians in the Medieval period is their belief in their apanage of Iranian identity. Iranian and Zoroastrian are synonyms in these texts and it is only in the 20th century that Zoroastrian authors accept their non-Zoroastrian compatriots as Iranians. The following is a very good example of their view on the matter:

> Zarathusht looked on them at that time,
> That all had a *koshti*[872] on their waist.
> Non-Iranians and Iranians cannot be distinguished,
> So I will say it that you may find out.
> When Zarathusht Spitaman appeared in the world,
> He saw the people of Iran all tied with a *koshti*.
> There is a difference between Iranians and non-Iranians,
> The Iranians have a *koshti* knotted.[873]

The *rivayats* convey the preoccupations of the Zoroastrian communities, whether in Iran or India, who lived under Muslim rule. These concern their freedom to practise their religion and their interaction with Muslim neighbours.

> From the *Rivayat* of *Kamdin Bahreh* - the question is:
> An ancient *ostudan* (place where the bones are collected) is on the land of non-Iranians (non-Zoroastrians), and whenever that land is watered, the bones of the dead float on the water and the non-Iranians would not sell and would not allow us to build a wall around the gathered bones. We fear that they will take the *ostudan* to the sown field and that those bones will end under the earth and become part of it.
> The answer is:
> The king has to be begged so that the bones be taken from the water.
> The enquirer said that this has been done but, due to the shame felt in the face of people and fear of the king, we have abandoned that place. Yet we cannot indefinitely rely on mere hope.
> The answer:
> Bad and good periods are just temporary, and one has to struggle and keep hope in a better fate. The day may come that that land will be taken back from the non-Iranians, and if one exerts oneself and that effort is fruitful, an immense *kirfeh* (boon) will be obtained, and if it is in vain, your sin will be small therein.[874]

> From the *Rivayat* of Nariman Hushang - the question is:
> Question: Any fruit that is grown by Muslims and given to you by them, can it be eaten or not; and is it suitable to sit and eat with infidels and non-Iranians.
> The answer is:
> Any fruit that gives off moisture, that in it has seeds, if it is washed it can be eaten when brought by their hands, but if it is seedless,

> according to the Good Religion one cannot [eat if brought by them], and sitting and eating with them is not to be done under any circumstances and is a sin.[875]

The delicate subject of conversions is tackled here too. The Zoroastrian *mubids* of Iran who were preoccupied by the decline of their parish encouraged their co-religionists in India to convert people who showed interest in the faith. In Iran, the Muslim clergy would have severely punished any missionary activity on their part, whereas the liberal Muslim rulers of India would have tolerated at least the conversion of Hindus to Zoroastrianism.

> With regards to a non-Iranian whose heart is in the religion (Zoroastrianism), and has become impure (in Zoroastrianism), can one perform the *barashnom* (ceremony of purification) or not. The truth:
> From the *Rivayat* of Kama, the result of the question: the non-Iranian who has his heart in the Good Religion, and is unclean and polluted, and from the fear of others one cannot perform the *barashnom*, the *Dadestan* (Persian books produced by the high priest of Pars) answers from the 8th *Pargard* (Fargard) of the *Jedivdad* (Vendidad), that whoever has performed sixty *parsangs* (a sort of measure for distance), and is impure and becomes impure, somebody should bring a *neday* (a perfume composed of musk, ambergis and the wood of aloes), perform the *padyab* (ablution with prayer), and then dry and then perform the *padyab* with the *neday* of cow and the (other) *neday* should be poured on his head so that everywhere he would get wet. He must then dry himself with earth. And thirty times he must wash with *padyab* and dry with earth. And the non-Iranian whose heart is in the (Good) Religion and is impure should be washed in this way.[876]

As in Judeo-Persian literature, there are many didactic texts in the *rivayats*. In the extracts selected below, the author explains why one should not walk barefoot, and advises the reader to avoid ill temperament. He choses Muslims as archetypes of misbehaviour.

> With regards to the fact that God (Izad) has created a remedy for each ailment and the truth about it.
> From the *rivayat* of Kavus Kama
> You should know that the remedy to Ahriman is the people of religion, and the remedy to the sword of wrath and fire and rancour is great knowledge to beat Ahriman. If hatred enters the body, the way of religion will be closed...

> Since hatred appeared among Muslims, from then they became seventy-three groups, and their quarrel is in nothing about religion, and their hatred solely originates from the killing of Hasan and Husayn. These two have died, but the hatred has remained in the world, so it is better not to allow hatred to enter our body, for abstinence (control over passions) is better than taking medication; and the purpose intended here is that the remedy (medication) of any badness is goodness and the remedy to hunger is bread, and the remedy to thirst is water, and the remedy to nakedness is clothing.[877]

The Zoroastrians demonstrate also their bitterness over the loss of Iran, and discuss their religious disagreements with the Parsis:

> The multitude of *dasturs*, *mubids*, scholars and learned men of this community bear witness, every single one of them, that the following is true:
> Such a discussion among the people of clear judgement sounds most improbable, and if they believe that the fall of the government and the Arab conquest is not true, they are mistaken. The truth is that after the change of Iran's government, we the true inhabitants of Iran ended up in divided kingdoms. And for a long time carnage and horrible battles took place. After 400 years the kingdom of Iran gradually became subjected to perpetual rulers among the Arabs and this truth has been amply written of and referred to in the books and chronicles. Yet, maybe these have not reached the attention of the people of that area (i.e. India). And they have also announced that because a number of *mubids*, and circles of *Behdins* (Zoroastrians), have entered a dispute due to a month difference between their calendar and ours, doubt has appeared in the minds of most people, who are led to believe that religious affairs have become subjected to wordly diversions. Therefore, these differences have been changed, the Iranian norms should be followed, and this means India [should follow the Iranian norms].[878]

Moreover, there are notable sections dedicated to Iranian history. The tone of the Zoroastrian authors is different from that of the Muslims. The most revealing example is that the birth of Muhammad is presented as a world disaster and the cause of the ruin of Iran and Zoroastrianism.

> The reign of Nushiravan son of Qubad, who was called Kasra, lasted for 48 years and in Mada'in he had constructed an immense arch, which was 60 *gaz* long and 60 *gaz* wide, and on the night when the Arab prophet was born from his mother that arch crumbled and fell and that night Nushiravan dreamt that a person gave him a roll of paper and said read, and he read that when the era of Alexander

reaches the year 900 a prophet will rise from the Arabic peninsula and claim to be a prophet, and his deeds will have repercussions in the seven lands (all over the world), and he will subdue everybody, and will take away kingship from your family, and will make naught of the royal creed and religion, and the world will be defiled, spoiled and corrupted, and he will pile badness upon badness, and lies, crookedness, and betrayal will increase, and the population of Zoroastrians will become subjugated by that people and will have a very hard life, and the Zoroastrian religion will be rendered weak, and the majority of the *Behdins* (Zoroastrians) will become heretics due to oppression and violence. And as Nushiravan woke up, he started trembling and for an hour lost consciousness, and they threw rose water and musk on him till he woke up and became very wistful.[879]

During the reign of Yazdgird, war broke out between Arabs and Persians over the issue of the conversion of the Persians to the religion of the Arabs, and Yazdgird refused this demand and stood by his own religion, and Umar b. Khattab wrote a letter to Yazdgird demanding his conversion, but the latter refused. Therefore Sa'ad Vaqqas was sent with an important and crowded army, they went towards Mada'in and plundered the treasury of Yazdgird, and all the fruit of Greek wisdom was taken to Umar b. Khattab, and he said to burn them all and said 'the Quran is sufficient for us', and Yazdgird took flight from the Arabs and fled to Central Iran and from there to Khurasan and was killed at Merv, and the Arab army appropriated all the Iranian kingdoms and propagated the *Hashimite* religion and the world remained filled with badness and foulness and will remain so until the day of resurrection when the world will be cleansed from badness and foulness.[880]

This study of the *rivayats* should be closed with the citation of an extract on the Afghans' invasion of Kirman. This is an interesting passage, as the poet mentions a historical fact. The author of this text reviles the Mongols; however, there are sources in which it is mentioned that the Zoroastrians supported the Afghans.[881] We infer from this poem that there were a number of Zoroastrians who remained loyal to the Persians.

On Mahmud Afghan's invasion of Kirman, his looting of the city and his injustice:

So Kirman was plundered during this time,
Calamity hit the body of the people, as if they were the target of archers;
An army from *Nimruz* (Sistan),
Took the direction of Kirman full of grudge.

When this news came to the inhabitants of Kirman;
The commander surrendered in front of the gate;
He piled on his head the dust of shame,
Accepted to flee without waging war.
The army fled like the commander,
All the nobility fled;
None of the nobility remained in Kirman,
There was no solution for Kirmanis;
Out of desperation they shed tears,
One by one they fled.
A group took the path of the mountains,
A group took the path of the desert.
A group hid their wealth in wells,
A group remained petrified on their feet;
All were bewildered in this situation,
Looking for a remedy for this agony;
Then came the commander of plunderers,
The world conqueror, Mahmud, the lawless.
He was the son of *Vays*, a renowned warrior,
The successful Afghan commander.
An army was ready to attack in each area of Kirman,
And they were all ready to plunder Kirman.
Everywhere his men like leopards,
Were ready to give up their lives and wash their clutches with blood.
The horsemen, full of hatred, fully armed
All were proud warriors armed with spears.
All with ugly creeds and malicious,
All of bad race and bad kind;
All blood-thirsty and vicious,
All cruel and ruthless.
One more harmful than the other,
Each more eager than the other to torture the people.
Everywhere like looting *deavs* (demons),
Led as they were by a mighty general.[882]

It is noteworthy that interest in Iran among the Parsis was ignited after the Mongols had given an impetus to Persian culture. Moreover, by the 16th century the Mughals had made Persian the language of their court, thereby enhancing its status in the Indian subcontinent. The rule of more tolerant monarchs in India made it a haven for the Iranian poets and artists of the time, who could not express their ideas freely in Safavid Iran.[883] The most famous Mughal monarch, Akbar (1556-1605), was a great patron of art and literature and encouraged translations and other literary activities. He invited Parsi priests to his court, and it is believed that he adopted some of the Zoroastrian beliefs.[884] Iranian Zoroastrians seized the new opportunity offered in India, and Zoroastrian high priests such as Dastur Ardashir Nushirvan, Azar Kayvan and Khusraw b. Isfandiyar travelled to Akbar Shah's court. In 1597 Dastur Ardashir Nushirvan of Kirman wrote to Dastur Kamdin Padam of Broach that he had just returned from India 'where he had been invited by the Mughal Emperor Akbar to help compile a Persian dictionary'.[885] The Mubid Azar Kayvan (1529-1614 or 1533-1618) was another Zoroastrian high priest who went to India in the 1570's, drawn by the 'symposiac environment' created by Akbar Shah. The fact that he was a native of Fars is interesting as after the 11th century there are not many references to Zoroastrians in that province. According to Tavakoli-Targhi, he lived in Istakhr. However, we know that in the first half of the 11th century a certain amir Qutlmesh demolished Istakhr, which remained in ruins ever since.[886] It is more likely that, as reported by Bausani, he was from Shiraz.[887]

Putting the debate about his birthplace aside, Azar Kayvan was a very charismatic figure. He founded the *Ishraqi* School. It was the first time since the fall of the last Zoroastrian leaders in the 9th century that a socio-cultural movement at such a level had been launched under the auspices of a Zoroastrian. He owed his success partly to the Safavids, who by striving to create a 'national' identity had legitimated an interest in Ancient Iran. Thus, Azar Kayvan's initiative had echoes among Muslims. The *mujtahid* Baha'uddin Amili, one of the masters of Mulla Sadra (Sadr al-Din Shirazi d. 1640), and Mulla Sadra himself were Azar Kayvan's disciples. This is a rare example of a movement generated by a non-Muslim and followed by Muslim adepts. Azar Kayvan combined mystical ideas from Iranian Islam with spiritual thoughts revealed by the sages of Ancient Iran. He was inspired by Shaykh al-Ishraq Shahab al-Din Yahya Suhravardi (d. 1191), who had explored the Philosophy of Light introduced by the ancient wise men of Iran.[888]

Azar Kayvan began his early scholarly activities in Iran, where he spent thirty years disseminating his ideas. His intellectual movement, however, was not acceptable to the Safavid establishment. The Zoroastrian priest had won a considerable number of disciples, and the Safavids, who had striven to consolidate Shi'ism in Iran, were suspicious of any new religious movement. As a result, Azar Kayvan moved to India with a number of his disciples. Ultimately he chose to settle in Patna, which had become one of the flourishing centres of Persian culture in India. The amount of literature written by his disciples attests to the wide and favourable reception of his ideas in his second home. One of his most renowned Muslim disciples is Mir Abu al-Qasim Fendereski (a figure of the School of Isfahan), who translated texts from Sanskrit to

Persian. He also had an influential follower, Fazlallah Shirazi (d. 1588), who was an advisor to Akbar Shah.[889] Unfortunately, many of the treatises written by his followers are no longer extant, but at least the titles of their works are mentioned in *Sharestan* and *Dabistan-i Mazhab*. *Sharestan* itself was written by another Zoroastrian *mubid* called Farzana Bahram b. Farhad b. Isfandiyar. The Iranian Zoroastrian authors cited are Mubid Sorush b. Kayvan b. Kamgar who wrote *Zar-i Dast Afshar*, Mubid Kushi, who produced the *Zayanda Rud*, and Mubid Hush, who wrote *Kesh Tab*. The three works mentioned here, along with a short tractate entitled *Zawra-ye Bastan*, were gathered in a volume called *Ayin-i Hushang*. According to the author of the *Dabistan-i Mazhab*, Mubid Farzana Bahram b. Farshad (referred to as Bahram-e *Kucak*) translated the Arabic works of Suhravardi into Persian and wrote a book called *Arzhang-i Mani* (Mani's picture). Finally, Mubid Khudajuy produced the *Jam-i Kay Khusraw*. It is interesting that Khodajuy was from Herat, as this demonstrates that there were still Zoroastrians in the eastern provinces of Iran in the 16th century. There were certainly non-Zoroastrian authors from Azar Kayvan's circle who also wrote notable volumes. We are told that besides Zoroastrians and Muslims, his disciples included Jews, Christians and Hindus, but little is known of their intellectual endeavours.[890]

Although the majority of the texts were written in India, their authors were all Iranians who had deemed it better to continue their activities in Mughal India. Tavakoli-Targhi asserts that this was a neo-Mazdean renaissance, and indeed Mughal India enabled them to reconstruct Mazdaism. Although the 'Illuminationist philosophy' (or Philosophy of Light) that they adopted was Islamic in 'style', reflecting the Muslim environment, its aspirations were Zoroastrian. According to Tavakoli-Targhi, although the neo-Mazdeanist writers of these texts claimed to be simple translators of precepts written by pre-Islamic Persian sages, their aim was to 'reverse the Islamification of pre-Islamic Persian historical memory and to fashion a glorified Iran-centred past.' The *dasatir* they produced were devoid of Arabic words and ethnocentric. They inspired generations of intellectuals who followed, such as Muhammad Husayn Khalaf Tabrizi, who compiled a popular Persian dictionary in 1651. These *dasatir* enjoyed further interest among the Iranian nationalists in the 20th century, as they exalted the Iranian people. Indeed, Bahram b. Farhad concluded in the *Sharestan*: 'it was proved by reason and tradition that (...) Persians are the most righteous of all people and excel over all other nations.'[891]

The cultural collaboration between Zoroastrians and Muslims was not confined to Azar Kayvan's circle. Cases are attested in which Muslim authors referred to non-Muslim scholars as they regarded the latter as authorities in certain fields, especially in religion. For example, there were elements in Judaism or Zoroastrianism which were relevant to Islam and were of interest to the Muslim scholars. It appears that Muhammad Baqir al-Majlisi (1628-1700) was among such scholars. He is known as one of the greatest Persian scholars of the Safavid period, and produced an encyclopaedic collection of Shi'ite tradition, the *Bihar al-Anwar* (The Seas of Light). In this work he treats topics including *nawruz* and the Persian calendar. Majlisi quotes from Mu'alla b. Khunays who apparently said to Ja'far al-Sadiq that *nawruz* is a holy day which the Persians retained after converting to Islam, and became a holy day for Shi'ites, although the Arabs tried to suppress it.[892] Although the author tries to give to the celebration an Islamic apparel, it is likely that he also turned to Zoroastrians for clarification. Walbridge suggests that there are traces of direct borrowing.[893] Majlisi's works reflects the religious changes implemented by the Safavids, who encouraged a reformulation of the Iranian traditions. As we saw, this cultural policy had repercussions on the Zoroastrians and the Jews.

Conclusion

The decline of the Safavid dynasty, like that of the Sassanians was wrought by a foreign invasion, during the reigns of incompetent monarchs. Whilst we know almost nothing about the situation of religious minorities on the eve of the Arab invasion, we have substantial information about their situation prior to the Afghan invasion.

The social and political order immediately before and after the coming of the Afghans summarizes well the history of the religious communities in Iran. Whereas, on one hand, the religious majority has always been vulnerable and owed its superior position to the ruling classes, the religious minorities were independent, and had to rely on their own resources without help from the powerful.

The last phases of Safavid rule proved to be very difficult for the Zoroastrians, Jews and Christians living in Iran. Shah Sulayman, who acceded to the throne in 1666, was a weak monarch, un-interested in the social and political affairs of his country. He neglected governmental institutions such as the *divan* (council of state) and the *majlis* (court assembly), retreating to the *harem*, allowing the eunuchs and the clergy to interfere more and more in the decisions of state. The weakening of bureaucrats or military figures enabled the religious establishment gradually to increase its influence and change the religious policy of the country. By the end of the 17th century, all the non-Shi'ite elements of the country were under strong pressure to convert.[894] After Shah Sulayman, Shah Sultan Husayn (1694-1722) showed the same indifference towards the affairs of the state. He let the financial situation of Iran deteriorate and did not look after the army. As a consequence, the country headed towards catastrophe. Unrest in the remoter provinces of the kingdom, along with the inability of central government to quell it, alerted the powerful neighbouring Empires that the Safavid state was on the verge of collapse.

At this time, the power of the Shi'ite clergy had increased to the extent that a post of *mulla bashi* (head of mullas) was established.[895] At the political level, the influence of the *mulla bashi* was strong enough to topple a Grand Vizier such as Fath Ali Khan in 1720.[896] Not only was the intervention of the clergy detrimental to the king and his kingdom, but their involvement in politics had a serious impact on the religious minorities, including Sunnite Muslims who were mainly living in the peripheral provinces of the country. The Zoroastrians in Isfahan had been compelled to become Muslim.[897] The privileges of the Armenians of Julfa had been abolished. The Jews had to bear financial extortions in a number of towns in the regions of Kashan and Isfahan,[898] and like the two other minority communities were now subject to the caprice of the Muslim ecclesiastics.

If the non-Muslims on the Iranian Plateau had no chance to defy the Shi'ite establishment, the Sunnite Afghans living on the fringes of eastern Iran had the opportunity to do so. In attacking the Safavids, however, they relied heavily on one non-Muslim community in particular: the Zoroastrians. Sultan Husayn was too detached from reality to perceive the political developments in the region. Blinded by the clergy and his *harem*, he paid no heed to his generals and viziers and alienated the ablest figures of his kingdom.[899] Once again the throne of Iran was destined to fall to an 'outsider'. After Alexander and Umar b. al-Khattab, it was the turn of the Afghan Mir Mahmud to conquer Iran.[900]

The hardship suffered by Sunnites and the non-Muslim population at the hand of the Shi'ites becomes manifest in the Afghans' treatment of the Iranian majority and in the collaboration of the Zoroastrians with the Afghan invaders upon their arrival. The

Zoroastrians played a key role in the Afghans' overthrow of the Safavids. Qandahar itself had a Zoroastrian community which took an active part in the military campaigns of Mir Mahmud. Mir Mahmud's ablest general was a Zoroastrian of Qandahar.[901] His presence in the Afghan army was so crucial that he was called Nasrullah, literally 'help sent by God'. The number of Zoroastrians in Mahmud's army was significant enough to make him give a separate speech just for them, saying 'that the hour was now come, which would free them from the yoke of their tyrants; that liberty was now in their own hands, if they would prove themselves, on this occasion, worthy heirs of the valour of their ancestors.'[902] This was the first time since the 9th century that Zoroastrians were mentioned fighting in Iran. The presence of the Zoroastrian contingents in the army helped the Afghans obtain the support of the local Zoroastrians in Kirman, Yazd and Isfahan.[903] Many Zoroastrians lost their lives in Yazd because of their support for the Afghans.[904]

Neither the Jews nor the Armenians assisted the Afghans like the Zoroastrians. They had no co-religionists in the Afghan army and they had not been mistreated by the Safavids as much as the Zoroastrians, who had been compelled to accept Islam under Shah Sulayman.[905] Despite the fact that the Afghans' fury was directed towards the Shi'ite Iranians, the Jews and the Armenians were overawed by the coming of the Afghans. Upon their arrival, the Afghans took the Armenians' wealth for spoils of war and plundered New Julfa.[906] The Jews of Isfahan, like their Muslim neighbours, suffered from starvation during the Afghans' siege of their town. But neither the Jews nor the Armenians were put to the sword like the Shi'ites.[907]

The benevolence of the Afghans towards the non-Muslims and their mistreatment of the Shi'ites had won them the sympathy of the Jews who hoped that Afghan rule would last.[908] The Armenians on the other hand displayed a more ambiguous attitude, as they had suffered from the Afghans' heavy financial extortion. They had even provided the Safavid court with intelligence despite the fact that the Shi'ite rulers had disarmed New Julfa and abandoned the Armenians to the Afghans.[909]

The attitude of the various non-Muslim groups was different towards the invader, but overall none of them suffered as much as the Iranian majority. There were many reasons for their better situation. While the non-Muslims had neither numerical superiority and had no organized army to rely on like the majority, they had the advantage of being self-reliant and experienced in negotiating their status with stronger groups belonging to another faith. As they did not identify with the masters of their country, they appeared reliable to invaders. Their marginalization in times of religious persecutions conducted by rulers was compensated by their ascendancy over the majority after takeovers by invaders. This is clearly manifest at the end of the Safavid period: prior to the arrival of the Afghans, the Shi'ite clergy pushed the Safavid government and the local governors against non-Muslims, and after the arrival of the Afghans, the Sunnite Afghans ranked the non-Muslims in an official edict at Isfahan socially above the Shi'ite majority.[910]

This was not the first time in history that religious minorities in Iran received precedence over the Iranian majority. The Mongol and Arab invaders, as we saw earlier, had already showed them special favour.

Conclusion

Although since the 6th century B.C. people of various creeds have been living among the Persians who dominated Iran politically, the history of religious minorities in that country becomes interesting after the 3rd century of the Christian era, when the Sassanians established Zoroastrianism as a state religion.[911] With the advent of the Sassanians, Zoroastrianism was legally enforced in Iran, and non-Zoroastrian communities had to adapt to the new socio-political setting in which they had become minorities and needed state recognition.

The Arab invasion of Iran in the 7th century introduced Islam to the country and in the first centuries of Islamic rule, the Jews and Christians found themselves in a much better position than the Zoroastrians. Indeed, Zoroastrianism did not enjoy the same level of tolerance granted to the Jews and Christians within the realm of Islam.[912] In addition, Zoroastrianism had lost the state support on which it had heavily relied under the Sassanians. As a consequence, the power of the Zoroastrian nobility and clerical class had waned dramatically, and the cohesion of the Zoroastrian community had been damaged. Nonetheless, until the 9th century the Zoroastrians composed the majority of the population and the fall of the Zoroastrian state and the imposition of Islam as the official religion was not acceptable to them. The diplomatic negotiations between Muslim Arabs and Zoroastrian Iranians were not longlasting, and ultimately tension between both communities led to armed conflicts and the complete destruction of the Zoroastrian forces. After the 9th century the Zoroastrian population was left with the options of apostasy, migration, martyrdom or marginalization. With the patience of history they learned to accept their fate and acquired the social and political skills that were vital for their survival as a religious minority.

On the other hand, the Jews and Christians who had the experience of living as minorities in Iran, were not so overwhelmed by the changes wrought by the Arab invaders and accepted the new reality and its conditions more easily. Already they had had to negotiate their status prior to the advent of Islam, from the time the Sassanians had established Zoroastrianism as a state religion. They had been subject to sporadic persecutions, but, generally, their close contacts with the court enabled them to defend the interests of their community. Culturally they had flourished under the Sassanians and had established important intellectual centres in towns such as Sura, Pumbedita, Nehardia, Nisibis, Gundishapur and even Merv on the eastern frontier of Iran. The multicultural characteristic of western Iran and the Zoroastrians' 'liberal' approach towards proselytization, being harsh only on apostates, enabled Christians to remain numerically dominant in provinces like Asuristan (Iraq) and Armenia. The intellectual, political and demographic rise of Jews and Christians enabled them to secure for themselves high positions right after the fall of the Sassanian Empire. They continued to act as physicians and administrators as in the past, and assisted the Muslim Arabs in their cultural ambition of building a new civilization. At times the Christians were held under suspicion for sharing the same religion as the Byzantine enemies of the Arabs, but by and large the Christian population enjoyed a high prestige in the caliphate, and suffered much less from the pressure born by Zoroastrian bureaucrats and prominent scholars who were compelled to embrace Islam.

As the Muslims acquired the subtle skills of governing empires and perfected their knowledge in arts, medicine and other sciences, the Jews and Christians were left with fewer opportunities at the court and in government. Nonetheless, they were never completely eliminated from the administration of the Muslim state. The perseverance of Jews and Christians in remaining active in the public life of Islamic Iran helped them avoid marginalization, as had happened to the Zoroastrians, and afforded them, as we saw, even an unexpected chance to rise above the Muslims after the Mongols had invaded Iran. Although the Iranian Jewry produced two of the most efficient grand viziers in Iranian history and the Christians dominated the government at this time, the Jews' and Christians' political talents were not the sole reason for their exalted status. Political circumstances favoured them as the Mongols could not trust the Muslim majority, just as Arabs had mistrusted the Zoroastrians five centuries earlier. The Mongols' desire to establish political and commercial relations with European Christian powers enhanced even more the influence of Christians, who were selected as Mongol envoys. A further effect of the Mongols' arrival was to raise the status of Persian so that it replaced Arabic as the dominant learned language, thereby reintegrating the non-Muslim population into the sphere of the Classical Persian culture. The Iranian Jewry produced the most accomplished of the non-Muslim Iranian poets at this period, and the Zoroastrians abandoned the Pahlavi script and along with the Christians began writing their literature in Persian.[913] McChesney talks about a Persian literary imperialism that encompassed the borders of Iran, affecting the non-Arab Muslim world.[914]

With the conversion of the Mongol rulers to Islam, the Iranian Christians' association with Persian culture and their domination of Iranian politics came to a sudden end. Contrary to the Afghans in the 18th century, the Mongols had sensed that their reliance on the religious minorities to consolidate their power was doomed to failure and by accepting Islam they were certain to obtain the allegiance of the majority of the Iranians. The Jews' and Christians' loss of authority and support from the rulers made them vulnerable to the vindictive action of Muslims. Iranian Christianity suffered immensely as most of the dioceses in Iran disappeared from the records after the 14th century. Timur Lang's horrific passage, along with natural catastrophes and nomadic raids damaged the ancient Church of Iran (or Nestorian Church) in such a way that it was not able to recover. Its members lost their vitality and ambition, and retired to remote and isolated places, as the Zoroastrians had done a few centuries earlier. The 're-Islamification' of Iran had such a traumatising effect on these Christians that they felt estranged from the dominating Persian culture. They maintained a separate language and gradually developed a separate identity, which encouraged missionaries in the 19th century to call them Assyrians.[915]

For more than a thousand years the Christians had been active in Iran. The Sassanian king Hormizd considered them as one of the pillars of his Empire.[916] Their cultural divorce and their political disengagement certainly impoverished Iranian society. Nonetheless, Iran was not destined to continue the course of history without a vibrant Christian community. The Safavids were resolved to reintroduce another Christian community, the Armenians, who not only took over the role of Nestorian Christians in diplomacy, but also led the commercial activities of Iran. The economic prosperity of the country in the 17th century along with the expansion of political and cultural contacts benefited also the Jews and Zoroastrians, who were also motivated to remain active culturally. It is true, however, that the majority of the non-Muslims were not wealthy, but neither were the majority of the Muslims. In times of social peace, the poor among them shared the same fate.

At present, the anti-Iranian attitude in the world generated after the Islamic revolution in 1979 has caused many to demonize the Iranians and those who tackled the topic of non-Muslim Iranians have portrayed them as oppressed, culturally static, and materially and spiritually impoverished communities. Up to now, most authors writing on non-

Muslims in the land of Islam have been obsessed with anecdotes of persecution. Their importance, however, does not rely on their having endured persecutions. It is their political input, their economic dynamism and cultural activities that distinguish non-Muslims in Iranian history. Even after the first centuries of Islamic rule, they continued to play a special role in Iran as political circumstances and their distinctive skills made them ideal ambassadors and successful tradesmen. The Safavid period offers the best examples of the non-Muslims' involvement in trade and diplomacy. As we saw, even in the late medieval period, under Muslim Shi'ite rule, the Armenians, as well as dominating the foreign trade, were selected as envoys to European courts; and the Zoroastrians and Jews controlled the finest wool trade and the market of the finest precious stones respectively.

Apart from ignoring the successes of religious minorities, some authors have treated non-Muslims as foreign entities. How could Zoroastrians be considered aliens in the land of their ancestors, or Jews who as Walter Fischel says, 'have been living on Iran's soil from the dawn of the first Persian Empire,'[917] be regarded as foreigners? Even Armenians, who arrived only under the Safavids, had developed a sense of belonging to Iran.[918] This is evinced in their attitude towards European Christians in the 17th century, whom they regarded as intruders and rivals rather than co-religionists, and corroborated by their loyalty to the leaders of their own community and rulers of Iran. Moreover, their cultural activities demonstrate that they were fully integrated into the Iranian society. This is manifest in the architecture of the Armenians' churches in Isfahan, and the literature left by Jews and Zoroastrians, which apart from reflecting their intellectual and artistic talents, shows their knowledge and appreciation of Classical Persian masterpieces.

The partisan approach towards the study of non-Muslims has undermined the distinct role and potentials of Iranian Zoroastrians, Jews and Christians. An important part of Iranian history cannot be grasped without a survey of the non-Muslims' participation in the country's economic and political development. The political ascendancy of non-Muslims under the Mongols was exceptional, and perhaps best explained by the fact that the Mongols were not initially Muslim themselves; however, we saw that throughout Iranian history, non-Muslims, despite their delicate position, were skilled at finding strategies to overcome their social handicaps thanks to their great achievement in trade and diplomacy. Even the Zoroastrians who appeared as debilitated and neutralized demonstrated during the Afghan invasion that they too had not lost their vigour and tenacity.

As John Joseph says, 'the lot of a minority, especially a religious minority, is a hard one anywhere and at any time.'[919] However, the experience of those minorities, who still exist, could not be confined to hardships, otherwise these minorities would not have survived. Their spiritual strength and their ability to adapt without assimilating afforded them a unique position in the society. As minorities, they not only inherited the traditions of their ancestors, but also acquired the culture of the majority among whom they lived. Their cultural sensitivity made them both more open to foreign people and useful as bridges between civilizations. Indubitably, religious minorities have enriched their societies and in the case of Iran have left a deep trace in its history.

Notes on the Text

1. Sunil Sharma, *Persian Poetry at the Indian Frontier*, New Delhi, Orient Longman, 2000, p. XI.
2. Peter Christensen, *The Decline of Iranshahr: Irrigation and Environments in the History of the Middle East, 500 B.C. to A.D. 1500*, tr. Steve Sampson, Copenhagen, 1993, p.146: cf. Moses Khorenats'i; *Shahrihā i Erān (The Provincial Capitals of Eranshahr)*, tr. from Pahlavi by J. Markwart, Rome, Pontifico Istituto Biblico, 1931, p. 21 fn 53.
3. Menachem Ben-Sasson, "Varieties of Inter-Communal Relations in the Geonic Period", *The Jews of Medieval Islam*, ed. Daniel Frank, Leiden, Brill, 1995, p. 18.
4. Moshe Gil, "The Exilarchate", *The Jews of Medieval Islam*, Leiden, Brill, 1995, p. 34; Bernard Lewis, *The Jews of Islam*, Princeton, 1984, p. 106.
5. S. N. Nasr, "Life Sciences, Alchemy and Medicine", *The Cambridge History of Iran*, Cambridge, 1975, p. 398.
6. Gholam H. Sadighi, *Les Mouvements Religieux Iraniens au 2e et au 3e siècle de l'Hégire*, Paris, Les Presses Modernes, 1938, p. 93 fn.
7. J. M. Fiey, *Chrétiens syriaques sous les Abbassides surtout à Baghdad (749-1258)*, Louvain, 1980, p. 268; Bar Hebraeus, *The Chronography of Bar Hebraeus*, ed. & tr. E. A. W. Budge, Oxford, 1932, vol. 1 pp. 391-392 [457].
8. Nasr, 1975, p. 398: Arabic was adopted in the 8th century 'as the scientific and philosophical language of discourse.'
9. Lewis, 1984, p. 40.
10. W. J. Fischel, "Persia", *Encyclopaedia Judaica*, 1971, vol. XIII cols. 313-314.
11. *A Chronicle of the Carmelites in Persia: and the Papal Mission of the 17th and 18th Centuries*, London, Eyre and Spottiswoode, 1939, I p. 153: 'To this inclination and propensity of favouring Christians is to be added the fact that the Muhammadan creed of the Persians according to the interpretation given to it by Ali, thinks well of Christians out of charity, whereas the Turkish creed according to the interpretation of Uthman looks on them quite to the contrary.'
12. Arthur Christensen, *L'Iran sous les Sassanides*, Copenhagen, Munksgaard, 1944, p.88; J. Wiesehöfer, "Ardašir", *Encyclopædia Iranica*, London, Routledge, 1987, p. 376.
13. Mario Grignaschi, "Quelques spécimens de la littérature Sassanide conservés dans la bibliothèque d'Istanbul (Le *Kārnāmag d'Anushirwān* pp. 16-45)", *Journal Asiatique*, 1966, t. 254, p. 20: Khusraw Anushiravan ordered the construction of fire temples in regions inhabited by Turks, and ordered the Zoroastrian priests to teach young Turks the Zoroastrian precepts.
14. J. Labourt, *Le Christianisme dans l'Empire Perse sous la Dynastie Sassanide (224-632)*, Paris, Librairies Victor Lecoffre, 1904, p.105.
15. Fischel, 1971, col. 308.
16. *Shahrihā i Erān*, 1931, p. 11 fn 10.

17. J. Newman, *The Agricultural Life of the Jews in Babylonia*, London, 1932, pp. 1-2.
18. *The New Jerusalem Bible*, London, Darton, 1985, Second Book of Kings 17.6; Fischel, 1971, col. 306: 'Traditions and legends connect the origin of the Jewish Diaspora in Persia with various events. The starting points being regarded as the deportation of Israelites in the time of Tiglath-Pileser III (d. 727 B.C.) from Samaria to the cities of Media and Persia, the forced migration in the time of Sargon II of Assyria (d. 705) and of his son Sennacherib (d. 681).'
19. Abd al-Husain Zarrinkub, "The Arab Conquest of Iran", *The Cambridge History of Iran*, 1975 (reprint. 1999), vol. 4 p. 30; Lewis, 1984, p. 19; Jacob Neusner, *A History of the Jews of Babylonia*, Leiden, Brill, 1970, vol. 5 p. 132.
20. Jacob Neusner, "Jews in Iran", *The Cambridge History of Iran*, Cambridge, 1983, vol. 3 p. 913.
21. *Babylonian Talmud*, Baba Batra 54b; Newman, 1932, p. 191.
22. *Babylonian Talmud*, ed. I. Epstein, Baba Kamma 117a; Newman, 1932, p. 53: 'The Jews in Babylonia [under the Sassanians] enjoyed an almost autonomous life and lived in conformity with the laws and traditions of their forefathers.'
23. Mshiha-zkha, *Sources Syriaques*, ed. A. Mingana, Leipzig, 1908, vol. I p. 108.
24. Newman, 1932, p. 10.
25. Geo Widengren, "The Status of the Jews in the Sassanian Empire", *Iranica Antiqua*, Leiden, Brill,1961, vol. I, p. 128; *The Babylonian Talmud*, Mo'ed Qatan 26a.
26. Labourt, 1904, p. 8; Dudley Wright, *The Talmud*, London, Williams and Norgate, 1932, pp. 82, 84.
27. *Babylonian Talmud*, Aboda Zara 76a.
28. *Chronique de Séert (Histoire Nestorienne Inédite)*, ed. Mgr Sddai Scher & Abbé Périer, Paris, 1907, Part 1 (Patrologia Orientalis 4), p. 297.
29. *Babylonian Talmud*, Ta'anit 24b.
30. *Shahrihā i Erān*, 1931, p. 19 fn 47.
31. *Ibid.*, p. 29.
32. Louis H. Gray, "The Jews in Pahlavi Literature", *Actes du XIVe Congrès International des Orientalistes 1905*, Paris, Leroux, 1906, section I pp.190-192.
33. *Babylonian Talmud*, Ketubot 61 a & b, Zebahim 19 a; Gray, 1906, p. 191; Felix Lazarus, "Die Häupter der Vertriebenen; Beiträge zu einer Geschichte des Exilsfürsten in Babylonien unter der Arsakiden und Sassaniden", *Jahrbücher für judische Geschichte und Literatur*, ed. N. Brüll, Frankfurt-am-Main, 1890, vol. X pp. 135-138.
34. Newman, 1932, pp. 15-16.
35. *Ibid.*, pp. 2-6: on the importance of the Jewish population in the Western provinces of the Sassanian Empire.
36. Widengren, 1961, p. 145 cf. *Chronique de Michel le Syrien*, ed. J. B. Chabot, Paris, 1901, II p. 191, IV p. 279.
37. Widengren, 1961, p. 156.
38. *Babylonian Talmud*, Sanhedrin 25b, Bekorot 31a; Newman, 1932, pp. 176-177.
39. *Babylonian Talmud*, Nedarim 62b.

40. *Babylonian Talmud*, Yebamot 46a; Newman, 1932, p. 33: The majority of the Jews, like the majority of the Iranians, were poor and worked as ploughmen or cultivators; Grignaschi, *Le Kārnāmag d'Anushirwān*, 1966, p. 18.
41. Newman, 1932, p. 168.
42. *Babylonian Talmud*, Keritot 6a, Shabbath 12a, 32b, 33a, 112a,109a, Hullin 58b, Ketubot 65a, Ta'anit 26a; Newman, 1932, pp. 27-28.
43. Newman, 1932, p. 34; *Babylonian Talmud*, Ketubot 67a.
44. *Babylonian Talmud*, Pesah 113a.
45. *Babylonian Talmud*, Gittin 31b; Newman, 1932, p. 29.
46. *Babylonian Talmud*, Gittin 14a & 14b.
47. *Babylonian Talmud*, Mo'ed Katan 17a & 17b; Newman, 1932, p. 30.
48. *Babylonian Talmud*, Ta'anit 20b.
49. *Babylonian Talmud*, Baba Batra 8b, Ketubot 49b, Baba Mezi'a 77b.
50. Newman, 1932, p. 67; *Babylonian Talmud*, Gittin 86a, Bezah 14b, Pesah 40b.
51. Widengren, 1961, pp.146, 158.
52. Christensen, 1941, p. 38; Neusner, 1983, vol. 3 p. 921; Newman, 1932, p. 1.
53. Newman, 1932, p. 12.
54. Moshe Beer, "Pumbedita", *Encyclopaedia Judaica*, 1971, vol. XIII col.1384: *Babylonian Talmud*, Hor. 14a; BM 38b; Neusner, 1983, vol. 3 pp. 919-920; Wright, 1932, p. 84.
55. Eliezer Bashan, "Sura", *Encyclopaedia Judaica*, 1971, vol. XV col. 523.
56. Wright, 1932, pp. 40, 85.
57. *Ibid.*, p. 83.
58. *Babylonian Talmud*, Yoma 10a.
59. Laurence E. Browne, *The Eclipse of Christianity in Asia*, Cambridge, 1933, p. 50.
60. Christensen, 1944, p.267.
61. Labourt, 1904, p. 89.
62. *Synodicon Orientale (Recueil des Synodes Nestoriennes)*, ed. J. B. Chabot, Paris, Imprimerie Nationale, 1902, p. 366 no 3: A physician from Nisibis appealed to Khusraw I on behalf of the Christians against the authority of the Catholicos.
63. *Ibid.*, pp. 272, 276; Christensen, 1944, p. 269.
64. Labourt, 1904, p. 125, 135; A. Mingana, "The Early Spread of Christianity in Central Asia and the Far East: A New Document", *Bulletin of the John Rylands Library*, Manchester, 1925, IX p. 371, ll. 8ff; Nestorius asserted the independence of both natures, the divine as well as the human, in the person of Christ. He considered that Mary could not be called the mother of God, but merely the mother of Christ.
65. J. P. Asmussen, "Christians in Iran", *Cambridge History of Iran*, Cambridge, 1983, vol. 3 pp. 942-943.
66. D. Khaleghi-Motlagh, "Anōšazād", *Encyclopaedia Iranica*, 1987, vol. II pp. 99-100; *Histoire de Saint Mar Ahoudemmeh 6th c. (Histoire d'Ahoudemmeh et de Marouta)*, ed. F. Nau, Paris, 1905, pp. 33-35 (fols. 215-216): on the conversion of one of the sons of Khusraw baptised by Ahoudemmeh; Labourt, 1904, p. 189.
67. Labourt, 1904, p. 163.
68. *Ibid.*, pp. 190-191.

69. *Synodicon Orientale*, 1902, pp, 353-354.
70. Labourt, pp. 195-196.
71. Widengren, 1961, pp. 154-155.
72. Tabari, *The History of al-Tabari*, New York, 1999, vol. 5, tr. C. E. Bosworth, p. 298.
73. Mshiha-zkha, 1908, pp, 146-147: The School of Nisibis was founded by Narsai, at the end of Yazdgird II's reign (438-457); Labourt, 1904, pp. 144, 164, 290, 291-293.
74. Labourt, 1904, pp. 298-299.
75. The *Mafrian* was the head of the Jacobite Church.
76. Mar Denha, *Histoire des Divines Actions de Saint Mar Marouta l'Ancien (7th c.)* (*Histoire d'Ahoudemmeh et de Marouta*), ed. F. Nau, Paris, 1905, pp. 65-66 (fol.199).
77. The doctrine of the Jacobite Church is Monophysite. It holds that Christ is not 'in two natures' (human and divine), but is 'one nature out of two natures.'
78. F. Nau, *Histoire d'Ahoudemmeh et de Marouta*, Paris, 1905, p. 12: cf. *History of John Bishop of Ephesus*, Oxford, 1853, 1.VI chap. 20.
79. Mar Denha, 1905, p. 75 (fol. 202); I. Guidi (ed.), "Un nuovo testo siriaco sulla storia degli ultimi Sassanidi", *Actes du VIIIe Congrès International des Orientalistes 1889*, Leiden, 1891, section sémitique (B) p. 18.
80. *Un nuovo testo siriaco*, 1891, p. 16; Tabari, 1999, vol. 5 pp. 305, 312 fnte 729, 379.
81. *Un nuovo testo siriaco*, 1891, pp. 19-20; Labourt, 1904, pp. 223-224, 229.
82. *Un nuovo testo siriaco*, 1891, pp. 4, 23.
83. *Chronique de Séert*, 1919, Part 1 (Patrologia Orientalis 13), p. 55.
84. Thomas of Marga, *The Historia Monastica of Thomas Bishop of Marga AD 840* (*The Book of Governors*), ed. & tr. E. A. W. Budge, London, Kegan Paul, 1893, pp. 112-114.
85. Afraat, "Les 22 premières Démonstrations", *Patrologia Syriaca*, Paris, Parisot, 1894, t. I p. LXV cf. Théodoret, *Histoire religieuse*, chap. 1; *Acta Sanctorum Martyrum*, ed. Evode Assemani, Rome, 1748, t. I pp. 144-145, 165-166.
86. *Un nuovo testo siriaco*, 1891, p. 25; Labourt, 1904, pp. 235-236.
87. Tabari, 1999, vol. 5 pp. 398-399.
88. Thomas of Marga, 1893, p. 89; S. Gerö, "Only a Change of Masters? The Christians of Iran and the Muslim Conquest", *Transition Periods in Iranian History*, 1985, p. 48.
89. Thomas of Marga, 1893, pp. 124-125; *Chronique de Séert*, 1919, Part II (Patrologia Orientalis 13), p. 557; Tabari, 1999, vol. 5 pp. 404-405; Labourt, 1904, pp. 242-243.
90. Labourt, 1904, p. 245.
91. *Un nuovo testo siriaco*, 1891, p. 26.
92. Gerö, 1985, p. 45: cf. *Chronica minora I, Corpus Scriptorum Christianorum Orientalium*, ed. I. Guidi, Paris, 1903, p. 37 lines 1 ff.
93. Moshe Gil & Shaul Shaked, Book Review of Michael Morony's "Iraq after the Muslim Conquest", *Journal of the American Oriental Society*, Oct-Dec 1986, vol. 106 no 4 p. 821: cf. *Tarbiz* 48 [1979], pp. 35ff.
94. Tabari, 1990, XV, tr. R. Stephen Humphreys, p. 89.

95. Gerö, 1985, p. 43.
96. Aubry R. Vine, *The Nestorian Churches*, London, Independent Press, 1937, p. 70.
97. Robert G. Hoyland, *Seeing Islam as Others Saw It: A Survey and Evaluation of Christian, Jewish and Zoroastrian Writings on Early Islam*, Princeton (N.J.), The Darwin Press, 1997, pp. 15, 18; Lewis, 1984, p. 19; Neusner, 1970, V p. 132; Nau, 1905, p. 55.
98. Baladhuri, *Futūh al-Buldān* (*The Origins of the Islamic State*), tr. Philip Khuri Hitti, 1916, I p. 442, II pp. 105-109; Tabari, 1989, XIII, tr. G. Juynboll, p.143: on different army leaders and regiments joining the Arabs before the death of Yazdgird III.
99. Raghib al-Isfahani, *Muhādarāt al-Udabā'*, Cairo, Matba al-Amira, 1908, vol. 1 p. 73.
100. Tabari, 1990, XV, tr. S. Humphreys, pp. 8-9; Baladhuri, 1916, I p. 489; II pp. 3-7.
101. Hoyland, 1997, pp. 15-17.
102. John bar Penkaye, *Sources Syriaques*, ed. Alphonse Mingana, Leipzig, Otto Harrassowitz, 1907, vol. 1 p. 171 (p. 151 in Syriac).
103. Gerö, 1985, p. 47.
104. Baladhuri, 1916, I pp. 120-124.
105. Baladhuri, 1916, I p. 419: Regarding the amount of taxes imposed on Iranian towns; A. S. Tritton, *The Caliphs and their non-Muslim Subjects*, London, 1930, pp. 2, 10: on the Muslims' exemption from paying taxes.
106. Tabari, 1994, XIV, tr. G. Rex Smith, p. 9.
107. Tabari, XIV p. 142; Tabari, XV pp. 6-7.
108. Jahiz, *Kitāb al-Akhbār wa Kayfa Tasihh* (Al-Ġahiz: Les Nations Civilisées et leurs Croyances Religieuses), ed. Charles Pellat, *Journal Asiatique*, Paris, 1967, t. 255, p. 86.
109. W. Barthold, *Iran*, tr. G. K. Nariman & ed. M. E. Dadrawala, Bombay, 1935, p. 136; Ian Gillman & Hans-Joachim Klimkeit, *Christians in Asia before 1500*, Richmond (Surrey), Curzon, 1999, p. 130.
110. Baladhuri, 1916, I pp. 465-466; Tabari, 1996, XXII, tr. Fishbein, p. 179 fn 648.
111. Zarrinkub, 1975, p. 46.
112. Baladhuri, 1916, I p. 466.
113. F. Gabrieli, "Ibn al-Mukaffa'", *Encyclopaedia of Islam*, 1971, vol. III p. 883.
114. Tabari, 1989, XXVI, tr. Carole Hillenbrand, pp. 56-57.
115. Tabari, 1989, XXV, tr. Khalid Yahya Blankship, p. 61: During the reign of al-Hisham in 724, an Arab was sent to Rayy, where he claimed to be the new tax collector. He was presented as such: 'This is only a crazy bedouin Arab, for the governor never sent an Arab to supervise taxation before. He is only in charge of the military supplies.'
116. Tabari, XIV p. 142; XXV p. 183; XXVI p.8.
117. Janet Kestenberg Amighi, *The Zoroastrians of Iran: Conversion, Assimilation, or Persistence*, New York, AMS Press, 1990, p.64.
118. Ibn Qutayba, *'Uyūn al-Akhbār*, tr. J. Horovitz, *Islamic Culture*, 1930, IV p. 497; Gabrieli, 1971, III p. 803.

119. Gholam Hossein Sadighi, *Les Mouvements Religieux Iraniens au IIe et au IIIe siècle de l'hégire*, Paris, Les Presses Modernes, 1938, p. 32: cf. Muhammad Jahchiyari, *Kitāb al-Wuzarā' wa' l-Kuttāb*, ed. Max Jaffé, Leipzig, 1930.
120. Ibn Rustah, *Kitāb al-A'lak un Nafisa*, ed. M. J. de Goeje, Leiden, Brill, 1892, pp. 196-197.
121. Hoyland, 1997, pp. 203-204.
122. For the pattern of Arab settlement in Iran see Parvaneh Pourshariati, "Local Histories of Khurasan and the Pattern of Arab Settlement", *Studia Iranica*, Paris, 1998, 27 pp. 53-79.
123. Wilferd Madelung, *Religious Trends in Islamic Iran*, Albany (N.Y.), Bibliotheca Persica, 1988, pp. 2-6.
124. R.W. Bulliet, "Conversion to Islam and the Emergence of a Muslim Society in Iran", *Conversion to Islam*, Holmes and Meier Publishers, New York, 1979, pp. 31, 35; Bénédicte Landron, *Chrétiens et Musulmans en Irak: Attitudes Nestoriennes vis-à-vis de l'Islam*, Paris, Cariscript, 1994, p. 57; This appears to be true at least until the 9th century when the *Mubid-i Mubidan* was still convoked along with the Catholicos to assemblies at the court. After the 9th century, no Zoroastrian high priest is mentioned in such gatherings; Mas'udi, *Kitāb al-Tanbīh wa' l-Ishrāf* (*Le livre de l'Avertissement et de la Révision*), tr. B. Carra de Vaux, Paris, 1896, p. 153: 'Les Perses espèrent et croient que, dans l'avenir, le pouvoir leur reviendra et que leur empire sera rétabli.'
125. Narshakhi, *The History of Bukhara*, tr. Richard N. Frye, Cambridge (Ma.), Mediaeval Academy of America, 1954, pp. 30-31, 48, 53, 60-62.
126. Jamsheed K. Choksy, *Conflict and Cooperation: Zoroastrian Subalterns and Muslim Elites in Medieval Iranian Society*, New York, Columbia University Press, 1997, p.40; Sadighi, 1938, p.68.
127. Tabari, XXVI, pp.66-68; XXVII pp.109, 138; Tabari, 1995, XXVIII, tr. Jane Dammen McAuliffe, p.33 fnte 158; Sadighi, 1938, p.41.
128. Robert Brody, "Zoroastrian Themes in Geonic Responsa", *Irano-Judaica IV*, Jerusalem, 1999, p. 181: On the feigned conversion of Iranians to Islam in the 8th century, "many Zoroastrians who lived at that time and converted to Islam...their heart was not free of Zoroastrianism...And even the second and third generations were equivocal."
129. Tabari, XXVIII, pp. 44-46.
130. Ya'qubi, *Al-Buldan (Les Pays)*, tr. Gaston Wiet, Cairo, 1937, p. 129.
131. The Sassanians had converted an important number of Turks to Zoroastrianism cf. Grignaschi, *Le Kārnāmag d'Anushirwān*, 1966, p. 19-20; V. Altman, "Ancient Khorezmian Civilization in the Light of the Latest Archaeological Discoveries (1937-1945)", *Journal of the American Oriental Society*, 1947, 67 p. 83: on religion in Khwarazm.
132. Ibn al-Nadim, *Kitāb al-Fihrist* (The Fihrist of Ibn al-Nadim), tr. Bayard Dodge, New York, Columbia University Press, 1970, II pp. 823-824.
133. B.S. Amoretti, "Sects and Heresies", *The Cambridge History of Iran*, Cambridge, 1975, vol.4 p. 497; Sadighi, 1938, pp. 151-152, 157.
134. Tabari, 1990, XXIX, pp. 44, 47-48; Ya'qubi, *Tarikh*, ed. Th. Houtsma, Leiden,1883, vol. II p. 457; Concerning other authors see Amoretti, 1975, p. 497.
135. Bar Hebraeus, 1932, I p. 114; Elias of Nisibis, 1910, p. 110.

136. Bar Hebraeus, 1932, I p. 114; Elias of Nisibis, 1910, p. 110; Tabari, 1990, XXIX, p. 48.
137. Narshakhi, 1954, p. 75.
138. Ya'qubi, 1937, p. 111.
139. Narshakhi, 1954, pp. 8-10, 65-74.
140. Amoretti, 1975, p. 504-505.
141. Masu'di, 1873, VII p. 130.
142. Tabari, XXXII pp.64-65; Tabari, 1991, XXXIII, tr. C.E. Bosworth, pp. 2-3, 14-15, 18-19, 47, 75.
143. Ya'qubi, *Kitāb al-Buldān*, ed. Juynboll, Leiden, Brill, 1861, pp. 48, 51.
144. Mas'udi, 1871, VI pp. 187-188; Tabari, 1995, XXVIII p. 44; Madelung, 1997, pp. 874-875; Hoyland, 1997, p. 29 fn 63.
145. Tabari, 1987, XXXII p. 182.
146. Tabari, 1991, XXXIII pp. 80-82.
147. Tabari, 1991, XXXIII p. 188.
148. Sadighi, 1938, p. 276.
149. S. M. Stern, "Ya'qub the Coppersmith and Persian National Sentiment", *Iran and Islam*, ed. C. E. Bosworth, Edinburgh, 1971, p. 537: 'The last Persian revolts conducted in the name of the old national religion were put down by the end of the third decade of the 9th c. A. D.'
150. Tabari, XXVIII pp80-82; Tabari, 1990, XXIX, tr. Hugh Kennedy, pp.4-5: In 760, al-Mansur continued his assaults in Tabaristan and invaded the territory of Daylam, where apparently Muslims were being killed.
151. Tabari, XXXIII, p. 157.
152. Tabari, XXXIII pp 92, 95,119, 135, 138, 139, 149, 150, 157, 172, 180-193, 199, 200; Baladhuri, 1916, II pp.45-48.
153. C. L. Cahen, "Dhimma", *Encyclopaedia of Islam*, 1965, vol. II p. 227: 'The term used to designate the sort of indefinitely renewed contract through which the Muslim community accords hospitality and protection to members of other revealed religions, on condition of their acknowledging the domination of Islam. The beneficiaries of the *dhimma* are called *dhimmi*s.' Bat Ye'or, *Islam and Dhimmitude, where Civilizations Collide*, Lancaster, Dickinson University Press, 2002, p. 51: Emanating from a context of war, the *dhimma* consituties 'a protection pact granted by the conquerors, assuring the vanquished an institutional legal framework which would guarantee their religious freedom, rights and duties. For the victors, it assured a political and economic supremacy.'
154. See A. Tritton, *The Caliphs and their non- Muslim Subjects*.
155. Antoine Fattal, *Le Statut Légal des Non-Musulmans en Pays d'Islam*, Beirut, Imprimerie Catholique,1958, p. 117.
156. *Dinkard*, ed. & tr. Dastur Behramjee Sanjana, Bombay, Duftur Ashkara Press, 1888, vol. 5 pp. 291-294; Martan Farrux-i Ohrmazddatan, *Škand Gumānik Vīčār* (*La Solution Décisive des Doutes*), ed. Jean de Menasce, Fribourg (Switz.), 1945, pp. 127-171 (XI 1-18, XII); *Bundahishn (Zand-ākāsīh, Iranian or Greater Bundahishn)*, ed. B. T. Anklesaria, Bombay, 1956, p. 3 (Preface), pp. 277-279 (XXXIII.20): 'And when the sovereignty came to Yazdkart, he ruled for twenty years; then the Tajis [Arabs] came to Iranshahr in large numbers (...); they promulgated their own code of irreligion, and eradicated many usages of faith of the ancients, enfeebled the revelation of Mazda-worship (...) And from the

beginning of creation to this day, no calamity greater than this has befallen; for owing to their misdeeds, vile law and bad creed, pestilence, want and other evils have made their abode in Iran.'

157. *Psalm Daniel (Geschichte Daniels), Ein Apokryph*, ed. & tr. Herman Zotenberg, *Archiv für Wissenschaftliche Erforschung des alten Testaments*, ed. A. Merx, Halle, 1867, vol. 1-4 p. 407, English translation taken from Hoyland, 1997, p. 329.

158. Hoyland, 1997, pp.343, 346, 385 cf. *Chronicle of Zuqnin, Incerti auctoris chronicon anonymum pseudo-Dionysianum vulgo dictum II*, ed. J. B. Chabot, Paris, CSCO, 1933, p. 385.

159. Tabari, 1989, XXXIV, tr.by Joel L. Kraemer, pp.89-94, 128; Bar Hebraeus, 1932, I p.141: The author notes al-Mutawakkil's hatred for Christians, but relates to the Caliph's hostility towards the Shi'ites with his levelling the tomb of Husayn b. Ali.

160. Richard W. Bulliet, *Conversion to Islam in the Medieval Period*, Cambridge (Ma.), Harvard University Press, 1979, pp. 19, 47.

161. Tabari, 1987, XXXII, tr. C. E. Bosworth, p. 52 fn, pp. 9-10; Tabari, 1992, XXXI, tr. Michael Fishbein, p. 237; Tabari, XXX, p. 294.

162. *Tārīkh-i Sīstān*, ed. Malik Shu'ara Bahar, Tehran, Khavar, 1935, pp. 328-329.

163. Roy Mottahedeh, "The Abbasid Caliphate in Iran", *The Cambridge History of Iran*, Cambridge, 1975, vol. IV pp. 107-108; C. E. Bosworth, "The Tahirids and the Saffarids", *idem*, p. 111.

164. Ibn Qutayba, 1930, p. 497: The Barmakids were suspected of being fake Muslims and practising an Iranian religion.

165. F. Daftary, "Sectarian and national movements in Iran, Khurasan and Transoxania during Umayyad and early Abbasid times", *History of Civilizations of Central Asia*, Paris, UNESCO Publishing, 1998, p. 125.

166. Stein, 1971, pp. 541-543.

167. N. N. Negmatov, "The Samanid State", *History of Civilizations of Central Asia*, Paris, UNESCO, 1998, pp. 77-79.

168. Mas'udi, 1896, p. 149; A. Tafazzoli, "Ādurbād Emedān", *Encyclopaedia Iranica*, 1985, vol. I p. 477: Tafazzoli asserts that Isfandiyar was the son of Adurbad-i Emedan, the high priest who had compiled the third Dinkard; Choksy, 1997, p. 37.

169. Ya'qubi, 1861, p. 9; L. Massignon, "Nawbakht", *Encyclopaedia of Islam*, 1991, vol. VII, p. 1043; J. C. Kraemer, "Nawbakhti", *Encyclopaedia of Islam*, 1991, vol. VII, p. 1044.

170. Mottahedeh, 1975, p. 104.

171. *Ibid.*, p. 105.

172. David Morgan, *Medieval Persia 1040-1797*, London, Longman, 1988, pp. 2-3. Cyril Elgood, *A Medical History of Persia*, Cambridge, 1951, pp. VII-VIII.

173. *Tārīkh-i Sīstān*, 1935, p. 209.

174. Bulliet argues that in the early phase of Islam in Iran, those who converted to Islam chose Arabic names for themselves and their sons: see note 160.

175. *Tārīkh-i Sīstān*, 1935, p. 195.

176. Daftary, 1998, p. 132; Stern 1971, pp. 544-545: Ya'qub, who established the Saffarid dynasty, was already eulogized as a descendant of Sassanians and legitimate heir to the throne of Iran by the poet Ibrahim b. Mamshadh.

177. A. Tafazzoli, "Ādurfarnbag i Farroxzādān", *Encyclopaedia Iranica*, 1985, vol. I pp. 477-478.
178. G. Kreyenbroeck, "The Zoroastrian Priesthood after the Fall of the Sasanian Empire", *Transition Periods in Iranian History*, Actes du Symposium de Fribourg-en-Brisgau, Cahiers de Studia Iranica 5, Leuven, Peeters, 1987, p. 155.
179. *Pahlavi Texts*, ed. Jamasp Jamasp-Asana, Tehran, National Library of Iran, 1992, p. 28; Martan Farrux-i Ohrmazddatan, *Škand Gumānik Vičār*, ed. J. De Menasce, Fribourg, 1945, p. 8; Jean de Menasce, "Zoroastrian Literature after the Muslim Conquest", *The Cambridge History of Iran*, Cambridge, 1975, vol. IV pp. 551-553.
180. Ibn al-Nadim,1970, p. 589.
181. C. Huart, "Ibn al-Mukaffa'", *Encyclopaedia of Islam*, 1927, vol. II pp. 404-405.
182. C. Van Arendonk, "Ibn Khordādhbeh", *Encyclopaedia of Islam*, 1927, vol. III p. 398; C. E. Bosworth, "Ebn Khordādbeh", *Encyclopaedia Iranica*, 1998, vol. VIII pp. 37-38.
183. Julie Meisami, *Persian Historigraphy*, Edinburgh University Press, 1999, p. 40; Cf. Krasnawolska, 1978: pp. 174-174; De Blois, 1992 pp. 171-176. G. Lazard, Pahlavi, "Parsi, Dari: les langues de l'Iran d'après Ibn al-Muqaffa", *Iran and Islam in Memory of the late Vladimir Minorsky*, Edinburgh University Press, 1971, p. 365: Lazard tells us that the *Zartusht-nāma* is translated by the Zoroastrian author in 978 AD as the Pahlavi scripture was no longer intelligible even to the majority of the Zoroastrians; cf. *Mélanges Massé*, Tehran, 1963, pp. 337-342.
184. *Tārīkh-i Sīstān*, 1935, pp. 16-17, 34, 37, 375; Charles Melville, "Ebn Esfandīār", *Encyclopaedia Iranica*, 1998, vol. VIII p. 21: Ebn Esfandiar, a historian of the 13th c. also used the Zoroastrian (or Solar Persian) calendar in his *Tārikh-i Tabaristān*.
185. C. De Fouchécour, "Le Testament moral de Chosroes dans la littérature persane", *Mémorial Jean de Menasce*, ed. A. Tafazzoli, Louvain, Imprimerie Orientaliste, 1974, p. 419.
186. Kay Kavus b. Eskandar, *Qābus Nāmeh*, ed. Said Naficy, Tehran, 1933, Introd. pp. y, ya, yaj; C. E. Bosworth, "Kay Kā'ūs b. Iskandar", *Encyclopaedia of Islam*, 1978, vol. IV p. 815.
187. Mottahedeh, 1975, pp. 107-108; Richard N. Frye, *The Golden Age of Persia: The Arabs in the East*, London, Weidenfeld and Nicolson, 1975, p. 196.
188. Amir H. Siddiqi, *Caliphate and Kingship in Medieval Persia*, 1937, reprinted Philadelphia, Porcupine Press, 1977 - no page numbering.
189. Meisami, 1999, p. 52.
190. Mez, 1937, p. 35.
191. Regarding non-Muslim leaders at the court cf. Annemarie Schimmel, "The Ornament of the Saints: The Religious Situation in Iran in Pre-Safavid Times", *Iranian Studies (Studies on Isfahan)*, 1974, no 1-2 p. 95-96.
192. Elias of Nisibis, 1910, p. 95.
193. Bar Hebraeus, *Chronicon Ecclesiasticum*, ed. & tr. T. J. Lamy & J. B. Abbeloos, Leuven, Peeters, 1872, vol. I cols. 368-372: Although this section refers to the early Abbasid period, it reflects the situation of Jacobites and Nestorians under the Umayyads.
194. Mez, 1937, p. 35.

195. Bulliet, 1979, pp. 81-83.
196. Landron, 1994, p.31.
197. Fiey, 1980, pp. 14-15.
198. Ibn Abi Usaybi'a, *'Uyūn al-Anbā' fi Tabaqāt al-Atibbā*, ed. A. Müller, Cairo, 1882, I pp. 123-125; Ibn al-Nadim, 1970, p. 697; Elias of Nisibis, 1910, p. 109.
199. Ibn Abi Usaybi'a, 1882, pp. 133-134.
200. Elgood, 1951, p. 76; Fiey, 1980, pp. 20-26; Habib Levy, *Tārīkh-i Yahūd-i Īrān*, Tehran, Broukhim, 1960, vol. 2 pp. 355-356.
201. Thomas of Marga, 1893, pp. 283-284; *Synodicon Orientale*, 1902, p. 515 fn 4; Elias of Nisibis, 1910, pp. 44-45; Fiey, 1980, p. 12.
202. *Synodicon Orientale*, 1902, p. 516: He was from Kashgar and became patriarch thanks to the Caliph al-Mahdi's support.
203. Landron, 1994, p. 45.
204. Thomas of Marga, 1896, pp. 447-448, 467-468, 490, 505: on the number of bishoprics created by Timothy all over Iran from Elam to Gilan; *Synodicon Orientale*, 1902, p. 603 fn 5; Gillman, 1999, pp. 130-131.
205. Thomas of Marga, 1893, p. 384 fn 1, pp. 385-386, 391; *Synodicon Orientale*, 1902, p. 603 fn 5; Fiey, 1980, p. 35.
206. Robin E. Waterfield, *Christians in Persia: Assyrians, Armenians, Roman Catholics and Protestants*, London, George Allen and Unwin Ltd, 1973, pp. 39-40; Landron, 1994, p. 48 cf. Timothée Ier, *Les Canons Ecclesiastiques*, trans. J. Labourt, Paris, 1907.
207. Mari b. Sulayman, *Akhbār Batārikat Kursīy al-Mashriq* (*Maris, Amri et Slibae de Patriarchis Nestorianorum Commentaria*), ed. E. Gismondi, Rome, 1896, I p. 73: Regarding the conversion of Khaqan of Kashgar; Gillman, 1999, pp. 150, 218 cf. Thomas of Marga, *Book of Genesis* (Liber Superiorum), ed. A. Mingana, 1925, p. 307; Waterfield, 1973, pp. 39-40.
208. Mas'udi, *Murūj al-Dhahab wa Ma'ādin al-Jawhar* (*Prairies d'or*), tr. G. Barbier de Meynard & Pavet de Courtelle, Paris, 1875, VIII pp. 292-293; Mahbub (Agapius) of Manbij, *Kitāb al-'Unvan* (*Histoire Universelle*), ed. & tr. A. Vasiliev, 1909 (Patrologia Orientalis), VIII p. 547.
209. Nuwayri, *Nihāyat al-Arab fi Funūn al-Adab*, Cairo, Dar al-Kutub al-Masriya, 1933, IX, p. 145.
210. Fiey, 1980, p. 42.
211. Ibn Abi Usaybi'a, 1882, I pp. 126, 134: Despite the fact that he had been presented a mule's urine as that of a beautiful slave girl, Bokhtisho was not duped and allegedly exclaimed: 'In that case the girl was bewitched, for only a mule could pass such a urine.'
212. Bar Hebraeus, 1932, I pp. 122-123 [133-134].
213. Bar Hebraeus, *Chronicon Ecclesiasticum*, 1874, II cols. 170-172.
214. Jean Maurice Fiey, *Les Communautés syriaques en Iran et Irak des origines à 1552*, London, Variorum Reprints, 1979, II p. 190, III pp. 256-257, V p. 340.
215. Waterfield, 1973, p. 41.
216. Steven M. Wasserstrom, *Between Muslim and Jew, The Problem of Symbiosis under Early Islam*, Princeton, 1995, p. 22.
217. Wasserstrom, 1995, pp. 71, 88.

218. Shahrastani, *Kitāb al-Milal wa al-Nihal* (*Livre des Religions et des Sectes*), tr. Jean Jolivet and Guy Monnot, Paris, Peeters, 1986, vol. I pp. 604-605; Moses Maimonides, "Iggeret Teiman", tr. Boaz Cohen, *A Maimonides Reader*, ed. Isadore Twersky, New York, 1972, pp. 458-459. Qirqisani, *Ya'qub al-Qirqisani on Jewish Sects and Christianity*, ed. Bruno Chiesa & tr. Wilfrid Lockwood, Frankfurt, Peter Lang, 1984, p. 103.

219. After the Arab invasion the head of the Academies of Sura or Pumbedita was called Gaon (pl. Geonim).

220. The Karaites rejected rabbinic Judaism and accepted only Scripture as authoritative (cf. *Encyclopaedia Judaica*).

221. Ibn al-Hiti, *Ibn al-Hiti's Arabic Chronicle of Karaite Doctors*, tr. G. Margoliouth, London, Reprinted from the *Jewish Quarterly Review*, 1897, p. 9.

222. Wasserstrom, 1995, pp. 30-31; Moshe Gil, *A History of Palestine (634-1099)*, tr. Ethel Broido, Cambridge, 1992, p. 783: on the success of early Karaism in Iran.

223. Their presence in Khazaria has convinced a few scholars that they were at the source of the Khazars' conversion to Judaism in the 8th century. See Omeljian Pritsak, "The Khazar Kingdom's Conversion to Judaism", *Harvard Ukranian Studies*, 1980, 3.2 pp. 280-281; Altman, 1947, p. 82; D. M. Dunlop, *The History of Jewish Khazars*, Princeton, Princeton University Press, 1954, p. 135: on Iranian Jews and trade.

224. Wasserstrom, 1995, pp. 18-19; Levy, 1960, vol. II p. 350, 359-362.

225. Abraham David, "David ben Judah", *Encyclopaedia Judaica*, 1971, vol. V col. 1351.

226. Bar Hebraeus, *Chronicon Ecclesiasticum*, 1872, I. cols. 368-372; Denys of Tell-Mahre, *Chronique de Denys de Tell-Mahré*, ed. J. B. Chabot, Paris, 1895, p. XX: The edict favoured schism, but according to the Christian sources, al-Ma'mun was prompted to proclaim the edict by the Jews who disapproved of their Exilarch.

227. Ibn al-Nadim, 1970, p. 805.

228. Bar Hebraeus, 1932, I p. 133 [145].

229. Landron, 1994, p. 57: cf. Michel le Syrien, *Chronique de Majdal*, ed. L. Chabot, p. 94.

230. Ibn Abi Usaybi'a, 1882, I p. 164; Tabari, XXXIII, pp. 29-31: With regards to Fadl b. Marwan's power and influence; D. Sourdel, *Le vizirat abbaside de 749 à 936*, Damascus, PIFD, 1959, vol . I pp. 246-247.

231. Bar Hebraeus, 1932, I p. 138 [151]: Bar Hebraeus was a Jacobite, and therefore had no reason to lie about Ali b. Sahl b. Rabban al-Tabari's being a Nestorian.

232. Ibn al-Qifti, *Tārīkh al-Hukamā'-i Qiftī*, tr. (to Persian) Behin Darai, Tehran, 1968, pp. 320-321. Levy, 1960, vol. II pp. 358-359; Sassoon, 1949, p. 40; Fiey, 1980, p. 96; A. Mingana, "The Book of Religion and Empire", *The Early Christian-Muslim Dialogue: A Collection of Documents from the First Three Islamic Centuries (632-900 A.D.)*, ed. N. A. Newman, Hatfield (Pa.), Interdisciplinary Biblical Research Institute, 1993, pp. 559-561; Nasr, 1975, IV p. 416.

233. Fattal, 1958, p. 159.

234. E.g. N. Levtzion, "Conversion to Islam in Syria and Palestine" *Conversion and Continuity*, ed. Michael Gervus; Bernard Lewis, *Jews of Islam*; Bat Ye'or, *The Decline of Eastern Christianity under Islam*; H. Goddard, *A History of Christian-Muslim Relations*.

Notes

235. Bar Hebraeus, 1932, I p. 143 [157]; Ibn Abi Usaybi'a, 1882, I pp. 138-144.
236. Ibn Abi Usaybi'a, 1882, I pp. 153-158.
237. Jahiz, *Kitab al-Bukhala'* (*The Book of Misers*), tr. R. B. Sergeant, Reading, 1997, pp. 86-87; Charles Pellat, "Jahiz à Bagdad", *Rivista degli studi orientali*, 1952, XXVII p. 54.
238. Tabari, 1985, XXXV, tr. George Saliba, p. 11; Bosworth, 1975, IV p. 103.
239. Tabari, 1985, XXXVIII, tr. Franz Rosethal, pp. 42-43.
240. Mari b. Sulayman, 1899, I p. 84; tr. of the passage:

ما وليت نصرانياً سوى عمر بن يوسف للأنبار و الجهابذة يهود و مجوس واعتهدت عليهم لثقتهم لا ميلاً اليهم لكن لثقتي بهم فقال المعتضد اذا وجدت نصرانيا يصلح لك فاستخدمه فهو آمن من اليهود يتوقعون عود الملك اليهم و آمن من المسلم لأنه بموافقته لك في الدين يروم الاحتيال على منزلتك و موضعك و آمن من المجوس لأن المملكة كانت فيهم و وصاه بالإحسان إليهم و خرج مروراً.

241. Fiey, 1979, III b p.147; IV pp. 372, 376-377.
242. David Solomon Sassoon, *A History of the Jews in Baghdad*, Letchworth, 1949, pp. 17-18.
243. *Ibid.*, pp. 36-37.
244. David E. Sklare, *Samuel ben Hofni Gaon and his Cultural World*, Leiden, Brill, 1996, p.3.
245. *Ibid.*, pp. 4-7.
246. Wasserstrom, 1995, p. 44; Sklare, 1996, p. 127; Qirqisani, *Kitab al-Anwar wa'l Maraqib*, ed. L. Nemoy, New York, 1939, vol. 1 pp. 4, 74: According to Qirqisani, most of the Jewry of Tustar adhered to *Karaism*.
247. Fiey, 1980, p. 139.
248. Sourdel, 1959, p. 418 cf. Hilal, pp. 95-96.
249. Ibn Naqqash, *Fetwa relatif à la condition des dhimmis et patriculièrement des Chrétiens en pays musulmans*, tr. C. Belin, Journal Asiatique, 4e série, 1851, t. 18 p. 456.
250. Landron, 1994, p. 92; Mez, 1937, p. 52 cf. Ibn al-Hajja, *Diwan* p. 18, Ibn al-Athir VIII p. 518.
251. Ibn Abi Usaybi'a, 1882, pp. 144, 310.
252. Elgood, 1951, p. 158: he was called Ali b. al-Abbas al-Majusi (Haly Abbas).
253. Walter J. Fischel, "Persia", *Encyclopaedia Judaica*, col. 13:310-311; Fiey, 1980, pp. 215-216.
254. Ibn al-Athir, *Al-Kamil fi' l-Tarikh* (*The Annals of the Saljuk Turks*), tr. D. S. Richards, London, Routledge, 2002, p. 248.
255. Fiey, 1980, pp. 213-214.
256. Ibn al-Athir, 2002, p. 248.
257. Ibn al-Qifti, 1968, pp. 463-466, 468-472.
258. Levy, 1960, II pp. 385-391, 393-395: the Caliph al-Muttaqi (940-944) had abolished the seat of the Exilarch, and under the reign of the Caliph al-Muti (946-974) the *gavanim* had been abolished too.
259. Benjamin of Tudela, *The Itinerary of Benjamin of Tudela*, ed. & tr. Marcus N. Adler, New York, Philipp Feldheim, 1907, pp. 38-39, 42, 58.
260. Elgood, 1951, p. 227.
261. Poll-tax meant for non-Muslim.
262. Fiey, 1980, p. 262 cf. Sliwa p. 115.

263. Bar Hebraeus, 1932, I pp. 391-392 [457-458].
264. Walter J. Fischel, "Israel in Iran (A Survey of Judeo-Persian Literature)", *The Jews, Their History, Culture, and Religion*, Philadelphia, The Jewish Publication Society of America, 1949, pp. 823-824.
265. J. Samso, "Māshā'allah", *Encyclopaedia of Islam*,1991, vol. VI pp. 710-711.
266. D. Gimaret, "Mu'tazila", *Encyclopaedia of Islam*, 1993, vol. VII, pp. 782, 787: 'The name of a religious movement founded at Basra, in the first half of the 8th century by Wasil b. Ata (d. 748). The origin of the term is defined as 'those who separate themselves, who stand aside.' According to some, the movement appeared as a result of the position of neutrality taken by a group during the fight between Umar and Ali.' The mu'tazilis' approach towards God and Religion are based on philosophical reasoning; Madelung, 1988, p. 28: Madelung says that the movement had a great echo in Iran and Iraq.
267. S. Enderwitz, "Shu'ubiyya", *Encyclopaedia of Islam*, 1997, vol. IX pp. 513-514: 'A movement within the early Muslim society which denied any privileged position of the Arabs. The *Shu'ubiyya* movement, which appeared in the 8th c. and reached its peak in the 9th c., called for equality between non-Arabs and Arabs, to the claim of non-Arab supremacy which denied any significance, past or present, of the Arabs. Most of the Shu'ubis were Persians, although references to Arameans, Copts and Berbers, among others, are also found in the literature.'
268. Fischel, 1949, pp. 817-820: One of the famous forerunners of *Shu'ubism* was Abu Ubayda Amr b. al-Muthanna (d. 825) whose grandfather was allegedly a Jew from Iran.
269. Qirqisani, 1984, pp. 102-103; Leon Nemoy, "Anan ben David", *Encyclopaedia Judaica*, 1971, vol. II col. 920.
270. Leon Nemoy, "Karaites", *Encyclopaedia Judaica*, 1971, vol. X cols. 764-766.
271. Qirqisani, 1984, pp. 94, 104; Nemoy, "Karaites", 1971, cols. 767-768; Gil, 1992, pp. 783-784.
272. Sklare, 1996, p. 127.
273. *Ibid.*, p. 49.
274. Mas'udi, 1896, p. 160; Abraham S. Halkin, "Saadiah Gaon", *Encyclopaedia Judaica*, 1971, vol. XIV cols. 543-547.
275. Sklare, 1996, p. 11.
276. Fischel, 1949, pp. 820-822.
277. Bar Hebraeus, 1932, I pp. 115-116 [125].
278. Ibn al-Nadim, 1970, I p. 697; Ibn Abi Usaybi'a, 1882, I pp. 123-125.
279. Landron, 1994, pp. 49-50; *Timothy's Apology*, ed. & tr. A. Mingana, *Woodbrooke Studies*), Cambridge, 1928, pp. 15-90.
280. *Synodicon Orientale*, 1902, p. 615.
281. Landron, 1994, p. 60: cf Ali b. Rabban al-Tabari, *Paradis de la Sagesse sur la Médecine*, German tr. A. Siggel, Akademie des Wissenschaften und der Literature, p. 361.
282. Elgood, 1951, pp. 103-104.
283. Bar Hebraeus, 1932, I pp. 147-148 [162-163]; Ibn al-Nadim, 1970, pp. 585, 588, 592-593, 599, 603, 604, 614, 640; Elgood, 1951, pp. 107, 109, 115; Landron, 1994, p. 66.
284. Ibn Abi Usaybi'a, 1882, I pp. 138-144.

285. Ibn al-Nadim, 1970, p. 589.
286. Ibn Abi Usaybi'a, 1882, I pp. 175-183.
287. Elgood, 1951, p. 89.
288. Ibn Abi Usaybi'a, 1882, I p. 282; Ibn al-Nadim, 1970, pp. 46, 59.
289. Mas'udi, 1896, pp. 160-161.
290. Elgood, 1951, p. 161; Suhayl Qasa, "La medecine sous les Abbassides", *al-Masarra*, 1974, 60 pp. 754-763, 818-823.
291. Fiey, 1980, p. 73 cf. Salim Taha, *Traduction et traducteurs célèbres en Islam, dans Sumer*, 1976, XXXII, pp. 339-390; Hugh Goddard, *A History of Christian Muslim Relations*, Edinburgh University Press, 1980, pp. 54-55 cf. I. R. Netton, *Al-Farabi and his School*, London, Routledge, 1992, pp. 1-11; J. L. Kraemer, *Humanism in the Renaissance of Islam*, Leiden, Brill, 1992, 2nd ed. pp. 75-77, 104-107.
292. Fiey, 1980, p. 249; Landron, 1994, p. 126.
293. Meisami, 1999, p. 225; Bat Ye'or, *The Decline of Eastern Christianity under Islam*, London, Associated University Press, 1996, pp. 234-235.
294. Edward G. Browne, *A Literary History of Persia*, Cambridge, University Press, 1964, vol. II pp. 432-433: 'The Arab invasion of Persia no doubt wrought much devastation and caused much suffering, but the Arabs were in the phrase of their Spanish foes, "knights (...) and gentlemen (...)" The Mongols, on the other hand (...) surpassed in cruelty the most barbarous people.' However, such opinion should be accepted with scepticism, as there is no serious proof that the Arab and the Greek invaders were less brutal than the Mongols.
295. J. M. Fiey, *Chrétiens Syriaques sous les Mongols (Il-Khanat de Perse XIIIe-XIVe s.)*, Louvain, CSCO, 1975, p. 4 cf: *Anonymi Auctoris Chronicon ad A. C. 1234 Pertinens*, trad. Albert Abouna, CSCO, 1974, vol. 354, S. 154, p.175; Bar Hebraeus, 1932, vol. I p. 397 [464].
296. Hoyland, 1997, p. 25 fnte 51: Isho'yahb Patriarch III, *Liber Epistularum Mar Isho'yahb*, ed. & tr. Rubens Duval, Paris, CSCO, 1905, 64 pp. 171-172 (Syriac pp. 237-238) 'There are hints [in the words of the Nestorian patriarch Isho'yahb III (649-659)] that there was regret among some at the passing of Sassanian rule. Isho'yahb had to rebuke sharply one bishop who had been mourning for the "dead kingdom".' For the Jews' resentment of Arab rule see fn 159.
297. Tabari, 1999, V p. 298: Khusraw II (590-628) had two Christian wives, and Hormizd IV (579-590) allegedly replied to the complaints of the Zoroastrian priests: 'Just as our royal throne cannot stand on its two front legs without the two back ones, our kingdom cannot stand or endure firmly if we cause the Christians and adherents of other faiths, who differ in belief from ourselves, to become hostile to us.' Hoyland, 1997, p.17; Asmussen, 1983, p. 929.
298. Kirakos of Gantzak, "Les Mongols d'après les historiens arméniens", tr. E. Dulaurier, *Journal Asiatique*, Paris, 1858, XI p. 492.
299. Rashid al-Din, *Jāmi' al-Tawārīkh*, ed. Muhammad Rawshan & Mustafa Musavi, Tehran, Nashr-i Alburz, 1994, I p. 842: on Muslims in the administration.
300. Bar Hebraeus, 1932, vol. I, pp. XLV, 354 [411]: The Mongols sent an envoy to their opponents before fighting them and say: 'If ye will submit yourselves obediently ye shall find good treatment and rest, but if ye resist, as for us what do we know... Let [the Mongols] magnify and pay honour to the modest... and the scribes, and wise men, to whatsoever people they may belong, and let them hate the wicked.'

301. Morgan, 1988, pp. 43, 47-48; Charles Pellat, "Khwarazm-Shahs", *Encyclopaedia of Islam*, 1978, vol. IV pp. 1067-1068.
302. Johannes de Plano Carpini, "The Voyage of Johannes de Plano Carpini (1246)", *The Texts and Versions of John de Plano Carpini and William de Rubruquis*, ed. C. R. Beazley, London, Hakluyt Society, 1903, pp. 114-115: Carpini mentions the surrender of the Naimans, the Karekitays and the Huyris (Uighurs) to the Mongols; William de Rubruquis, "The Journal of Frier William de Rubruquis (1253)", *The Texts and Versions of John de Plano Carpini and William de Rubruquis*, ed. C. R. Beazley, London, Hakluyt Society, 1903, p. 214: He mentions that the Naimans were Nestorian; Fiey, 1975, p.1: The tribes in question are the Uighurs of Turfan and Tarim, the Naimans, and the Keraits of the Baikal Lake; Bertold Spuler, *The Muslim World, A Historical Survey*, tr. R. Bagley, Leiden, Brill, 1969, part 2 p. 5; Devin DeWeese, *Islamization and native religion in the Golden Horde : Baba Tükles and conversion to Islam in historical and epic tradition*, University Park (Pa), Pennsylvania State University Press, 1994, p. 308: The Nestorians of Iran were active proselytizers in Central and eastern Asia. Mar Abd Ishu, the Nestorian Metropolitan of Merv had recorded the conversion of some Turkic tribes to Nestorian Christianity in 1007.
303. William de Rubruquis, 1903, p. 232: He says that the administration of the Mongol Empire had been in the hands of Nestorians since Gengis Khan.
304. Juwayni, *Tārīkh-i Jāhān Gushā* (*The History of the World Conqueror*), tr. from the text of M. M. Qazwini by J. A. Boyle, 1958, p. 25; Bar Hebraeus, 1932, I p. 354 [411]: on the adoption of the Uighur script; Johannes de Plano Carpini, 1903, p. 115: Mentions that the Uighurs were Nestorian and that the Mongols adopted their script; Sh. Bira, "The Mongols and their State in the 12th to the 13th century", *History of Civilizations of Central Asia*, Paris, UNESCO, 1998, IV p. 251; David Morgan, "The Great *Yasa* of Gengis Khan and Mongol Law in the Il-Khanate", *BSOAS*, London, 1986, vol. 49, pp. 166-168: It is certain that the Mongols had a written legal code. Whether there was an actual *Great Yasa* (Mongol decree) promulgated by Gengis Khan or not as Morgan disputes, is not important in this study.
305. Juwayni, 1958, p.162.
306. Spuler, 1969, part 2 p.16; cf. *The Mission of Friar William of Rubruck*, tr. P. Jackson, London, Hakluyt Society, 1990, ser II no. 173 p. 178.
307. Bar Hebraeus, 1932, I p.490 [575].
308. *Ibid.*, p.356 [413].
309. C. Lemercier-Quelquejay, *La paix mongole*, Paris, Flammarion, 1970, Questions d'Histoire no13, pp. 76-77; Fiey, 1975, p. 3; Juwayni, 1958, p. 26: Refers to Gengis Khan's religious tolerance.
310. Rashid al-Din, 1994, I pp. 465-466; Bar Hebraeus, 1932, I p. 376 [438].
311. Juwayni,1958, pp. 65-67.
312. Juwayni,1958, pp. 103-104, 120-122; Bar Hebraeus, 1932, I pp. 376, 381-382 [438, 445]: According to Bar Hebraeus, the Mongols did not plunder Bukhara but set fire to it because soldiers were hidden in the town. In Samarqand they spared just the young people under the age 20.
313. Mary Boyce, *Zoroastrianism, Its Antiquity and Constant Vigour*, Costa Mesa (Ca.), Mazda Publishers, 1992, p.156: cf. K. Schippmann, *Die iranischen Feuerheiligtümer*, Berlin, 1971, pp. 38-39.

Notes

314. Bar Hebraeus, 1932, I p. 433-434 [507].
315. David Bundy, "The Syriac and Armenian Christian Responses to the Islamification of the Mongols", *Medieval Christian Perception of Islam, A Book of Essays*, New York, 1996, p. 43: cf. *Chronicon ad AC 1234 pertinens* (CSCO 109, Syr. 56 [text], CSCO 354, Syr. 154 [trans.], 236 [text], 179 [trans.]); Fiey, 1975, p. 5: *Anonymi auctoris chronicon ad. A. C. 1234 pertinens*, pp. 175-178.
316. Rashid al-Din, 1994, I p. 499.
317. *Genuinae Relationes inter Sedem Apostolicam et Assyriorum Orientalium seu Chaldaeorum Ecclesiam*, ed. Samuel Giamil, Rome, 1902, pp. 1-3.
318. Kirakos of Gantzak, 1858, pp. 253-255.
319. Thomas T. Allsen, *Culture and Conquest in Mongol Eurasia*, Cambridge, 2001, p. 148.
320. Rashid al-Din, 1994, I pp. 685-686; Juwayni, 1958, p 45 on the same story.
321. Johannes de Plano Carpini, 1903, pp. 137-139, 141: Like most Christians the author says that Guyuk was bound to become Christians, but this time the author seems to be objective as Guyuk's predilection is confirmed by Juzjani and Rashid al-Din. Carpini also refers to Qadaq and Chinqay.
322. C. Lemercier Quelquejay, 1970, p. 88.
323. Juzjani, *Tabaqāt-i-Nāsirī*, ed. Abdulah Habibi, Kabul, Historical Society of Afghanistan, 1963, pp. 171-175.
324. Rashid al-Din, 1994, II p.809.
325. Fiey, 1975, p. 13.
326. Juzjani, 1963, p. 182.
327. Juwayni, 1958, p. 599; Bar Hebraeus, 1932, I p. 417-418 [489] (based on Juwayni); Rashid al-Din, 1994, II pp. 844-845: Rashid al-Din makes no reference to Jews.
328. Juwayni, 1958, p. 589.
329. Rashid al-Din, 1994, II p. 845.
330. Bar Hebraeus, 1932, I pp. 417-418 [489]: on the exemption of the clergy from taxes; Fiey, 1975, pp. 15-16.
331. Rashid al-Din, 1994, II pp. 920-921.
332. Rashid al-Din, 1994, II p. 922; Bar Hebraeus, 1932, I p. 418: He mentions that the Jews did not benefit from the edicts of the Great Khan at this time.
333. Rashid al-Din, 1994, II pp. 880, 886, 891.
334. Juzjani, 1963, p. 217; De Weese, 1994, p. 82 fnte 21: on Sartaq's conversion to Christianity; Bar Hebraeus, 1932, I p. 398 [465]: 'This man [Sartaq] loved the Christian religion, and was baptized.'; William de Rubruquis, 1903, pp. 211, 214: on Sartaq being a Nestorian and like the Armenians, disapproving of images.
335. Juzjani, 1963, p. 215; Marco Polo, *The Book of Ser Marco Polo*, ed. Henri Cordier, London, John Murray (3rd ed.), 1921, I pp. 183-186: He alluded to the event, but based on hearsay he propounds that the church was not destroyed. He says, however, that Samarqand, like Kashgar had an important Nestorian community.
336. David Christian, *A History of Russia, Central Asia and Mongolia*, Oxford, 1998, I pp. 311, 356: on the missionaries sent by the Catholicos Timothy to Central Asia in the 8th and 9th c..

337. Bar Hebraeus, 1932, I pp. 422-424 [495-497]: on the destruction of the Ismailis; J.A. Boyle, "Dynastic and Political History of the Il-Khans", *The Cambridge History of Iran,* Cambridge, 1968, vol 5 pp. 340-342; Peter Thorau, *The Lion of Egypt*, tr. P. Holt, New York, Longman, 1992, p.77; Fiey, 1975, p. 21.

338. Bar Hebraeus, 1932, I pp. 398, 416 [465, 488]: on Sarghaghtani Beki's governing predispositions; John C. England, *The Hidden History of Christianity in Asia, The Churches of the East before the year 1500*, Delhi, ISPCK, 1998, p.83: '[Doquz Khatun was] lauded by John of Plano Carpini, Rashid al-Din and Bar Hebraeus for her intelligence, integrity and administrative skills' (cf. Morris Rossabi, *Khubilai Khan: His Life and Times*, Berkeley, University of California,1988, pp.11-14).

339. Bar Hebraeus, 1932, I pp. 429-431 [504-505]: on the fall of Baghdad and the Caliph into Mongol hands.

340. Spuler, 1969, pp. 22, 24.

341. Bar Hebraeus, 1932, I p. 431 [505]; Kirakos of Gantzak, 1858, p. 491.

342. Juwayni, *Tarikh-i Jahan Gusha*, ed. Mirza M. Qazwini, Leiden, Brill, 1916, II p. 164; Rashid al-Din, 1994, I p. 553.

343. W. E. D. Allen, *A History of the Georgian People*, London, Kegan Paul, 1932, p. 116: The Georgian expedition in Baghdad was led by Ulu David, a Georgian prince from Tiflis.

344. Kirakos of Gantzak, 1858, p. 491.

345. Juzjani, 1963, pp. 190-192; A. Bausani, "Religion under the Mongols", *The Cambridge History of Iran*, Cambridge, 1968, p. 539; Browne, 1928, vol II pp.464-465; Spuler, 1969, part 2 p. 19; Boyle, 1968, p. 348.

346. S. H. Nasr, "Ithna 'Ashariyya", *Encyclopaedia of Islam*, Leiden, 1978, vol. III p. 277: [Twelver or] '*Ithna 'Ashariyya*, is the name of that branch of [Shi'ite] Islam that believes in twelve Imams beginning with Ali and ending with Muhammad al-Mahdi.'

347. Grigor of Akanc', "History of the Nation of the Archers", tr. R. P. Blake and R. N. Frye, *Harvard Journal of Asiatic Studies*, 1949, vol. 12 p. 341; Vartan, "Histoire Universelle", ed. E. Dulaurier, *Journal Asiatique*, 1860, V-XVI p. 290.

348. Maqrizi, *Kitab al-Suluk li Ma'rifat Duwal al-Muluk* (Histoire *des Sultans Mamlouks de l'Egypte*), tr. M. Quatremère, Paris, 1837, I p. 98.

349. Henry H. Howorth, *History of the Mongols*, London, Longman, 1888, III p. 150

350. Franco Ometto, "Khatun Abadi, the Ayatollah who translated the Gospels", *Islamochristiana*, 2002, 28 pp. 55-56: on Izzidin Muhammad b. Muzaffar.

351. Sa'di, *Gulestan-i Sa'di*, ed. Iranparast, Tehran, Fanous, 1977, p.3; translation of the verse: 'O bountiful One, who from thy invisible treasury, You provide subsistence for the Gabr and the Christian, How could'st thou deprive your friends, Whilst having regard for enemies?'

352. See "Gabr", *A Persian Dictionary*, ed. Mo'in, Tehran, Amir Kabir Publishing House, 1983, vol 3 p. 3193: defined as *mulhid* (heretic)*, but parast* (idolater); Juwayni, 1912, I pp. 53-54: The author refers to the Mongol Kuchlug as *gabr*; Juzjani, 1963, p. 79: The Hindu leader Malka is called *gabr*; Amnon Netzer, *Poem of the Jews of Persia and Bukhara*, Jerusalem, 1971, p. 1: The word *gabr* is even used by Iranian Jews. The poet Shahin uses it to refer to Egyptians:

چه آن گبران ز فرعون آن شنیدند چه آتش جمله از پا در رمیدند

353. *Nakus*: is defined by Tritton (1930, p. 5) as a board beaten with a stick or hammer taking the place of bells in eastern churches.

Notes
181

354. Bar Hebraeus, 1932, I p. 431 [506]; Fiey, 1975, pp. 13, 24 (cf. *Al-Hawādith al-Jāmi'a*, ed. Mustafa Jawad, Baghdad, 1351 H., p. 333), p. 25 ; Mari b. Sulayman, *Akhbār Batārika Kursī al-Mashriq* (*De Patriarchis Nestrorianorum Commentaria*), ed. H. Gismondi, Rome, 1899, t. II pp. 120-121.
355. Bar Hebraeus, 1932, I pp. 444, 446 [520-521, 524]; Fiey, 1975, pp. 30-31.
356. Marco Polo, 1921, I pp. 60, 69, 75: Marco Polo who visited Iran about two decades after the conquest of Hulagu, confirms that Christians were numerically important at Baghdad, Northern Mesopotamia and Azerbaijan.
357. Bar Hebraeus, 1932, I p. 418 [490]: King Hethum at the service of Mongke Khan; Fiey, 1975, p. 7; Boyle, 1968, pp. 350, 352; Bundy, 1996 p. 39: In fact the Armenians of Cilicia had not much choice but to collaborate, or else they would have suffered more Mongol incursions in their country.
358. Bar Hebraeus, 1932, I pp. XVII, XLIII; Paul Pelliot, *Les Mongols et la Papauté*, Paris, Librairie August Picard, 1923, vol. 2 pp. 29-66.
359. Morgan, 1988, p. 62.
360. Bar Hebraeus, 1932, I pp. 506-507 [595-596]; Rashid al-Din, 1994, II pp. 1335, 1356-1357.
361. Amnon Netzer, "Rashid al-Din and his Jewish Background", *Irano-Judaica III*, Jerusalem, Ben Zvi Institute, 1994, pp.118,124: Rashid al-Din's date of conversion has been thoroughly discussed by Amnon Netzer based on Nasir al-Din al-Kirmani's *Nasā'im al-Ashār min Latā'im al-Akhbār*, and Sayf al-Din Uqayli's *Dastūr al-Wuzarā'*; Browne, 1928, pp. 69; Rashid al-Din, 1994, II p.1383: Rashid al-Din mentions that he was a physician by profession.
362. Rashid al-Din, 1994, II p. 1254, 1332: on the construction of Shamanist and Buddhist temples and the importation of Buddhist and Shamanist priests from India, Tibet and Khitai.
363. Bar Hebraeus, 1932, I p. 447 [524-525]; Fiey, 1975, p. 35.
364. Thorau, 1991, p. 187.
365. Bar Hebraeus, 1932, I pp. 443, 445 [520, 522]; Fiey, 1975, pp. 30, 33, 35.
366. Bar Hebraeus, 1932, I p. 449 [526].
367. *Ibid.*, pp. 451, 456 [529, 535].
368. *Ibid.*, pp. 440-443 [515-519]: In 1260, Muslim troops broke into Mosul and persecuted Christians forcing many to convert, but the Mongol army led by the Nestorian Samdaghu took back the city and restored the order in favour of the Christians; p. 483, 487 [567, 572]: But later in 1289 Christian villages, such as Pishabur, were subject to plundering, and active Christian missionaries were killed without the Mongol authorities intervening.
369. *The Monks of Kublai Khan*, tr. E. A. W. Budge, London, Religious Tract Society, 1928, p. 152-154; Spuler, 1969, pp. 30-31; Gillman, 1999, p. 140; James D. Ryan, "Christian Wives of Mongol Khans: Tartar Queens and Missionary Expectations in Asia", *Journal of Royal Asiatic Society*, Cambridge, 1998, vol. 8 p. 415.
370. Bar Hebraeus, 1932, I p. 466 [548].
371. Marco Polo, 1921, I p. 467; Fiey, 1975, p. 41.
372. *Monks of Kublai Khan*, 1928, p. 158; *Histoire de Mar Jabalaha III Patriarche des Nestoriens (1281-1317) et du Moine Rabban Çauma, Ambassadeur du Roi Argoun en Occident (1287)*, tr. J. B. Chabot, Paris, Ernest Leroux, 1895, pp. 146-149.

373. Gillman, 1999, p. 142.
374. Bar Hebraeus, *Chronicon Ecclesiasticum*, 1877, III col. 476: describing the ruin of Jacobite centres.
375. Also known as Hethum of Korykos.
376. Jean Hayton, "La flor des estoires de la terre d'Orient", *Recueil des Historiens des Croisades, Documents Arméniens*, Paris, 1906, II pp.185-186; Marco Polo, 1921, II p. 473: Ahmad Teguder sought refuge with the sultan of Egypt.
377. Bar Hebraeus, 1932, I p. 474 [556].
378. *Ibid.*, pp. 477-478 [560-561]; Morgan, 1988, p. 66.
379. Bar Hebraeus, 1932, I pp. 456 [535], 472 [554].
380. *Ibid.*, pp. 484-485 [569].
381. François Tournebize, *Histoire Politique et Religieuse de l'Arménie jusqu'à l'an 1393*, Paris, 1910, pp. 289, 292-293, 300: In 1243 the Catholicos Constantine I proclaimed that the Pope was the head of all Churches, but in 1254 he turned against Rome, while he had accepted the condition of union formulated by Pope Innocent III, p. 301 The Catholicos Constantine II was presumably deposed because he had submitted to Rome.
382. Bar Hebraeus, 1932, I p. 478 [560].
383. *Ibid.*, pp. 479-481 [562-565], 484-485 [568-569].
384. *Ibid.*, pp. 478-479 [561-562], 484-485 [569].
385. *Ibid.*, pp. 484 [569], 488 [573], 490 [575]: 'The man (of high rank) was never seen at the Gate of the Kingdom, unless perchance [he was] a Jew. And through this state of affairs many of the Jews who were on the fringes of the world gathered together to him.'
386. Morgan, 1988, p. 69.
387. Bar Hebraeus, 1932, I p. 490 [575].
388. *Ibid.*, p. 479 [562]: 'And behold, at the present day there is a Jewish governor and general director on the throne of the House of Abbas. Observe how Islam hath been brought low! And [the Muslims] neither cease nor rest from their wickedness and their tyranny.' p. 488 [572].
389. *Ibid.*, pp. 485-486 [570]: There were Christian Mongols living in the mountains called Kāshāye, and who fought the Muslims.
390. *Ibid.*, p. 489 [574].
391. Bar Hebraeus, 1932, I p. 490 [575]; Morgan, 1988, p. 69; Spuler, 1969, p. 34; Boyle, 1968, p. 355.
392. Bar Hebraeus, 1932, I p. 491 [576]; Fiey, 1975, p. 57
393. Netzer, 1994, p. 123; Bar Hebraeus, 1932, I p. 496 [582]; Allsen, 2001, p. 127: Points to the fact that Rashid al-Din entered the service of Gaikhatu first as a cook, which was the preliminary step for reaching high positions at the court. This element is corroborated by Mamluk sources studied by Reuven Amitai-Preiss, "New Material from Mamluk Sources for the Biography of Rashid al-Din", *Oxford Studies in Islamic Art*, 1996, vol. 12 p. 25.
394. Bar Hebraeus, 1932, I pp. 494-500 [579-587]; *Monks of Kublai Khan*, 1928, pp. 201-202, 208-209.
395. Jean Hayton, "Relation", *L'Extrême Orient au Moyen Age*, ed. Louis de Backer, Paris, 1877, p. 199; Marco Polo, 1921, II p. 476.
396. Bar Hebraeus, 1932, I p. 505 [593].

397. Fra Ricoldo de Monte Croce, "Itinéraire", *L'Extrême Orient au Moyen Age*, ed. Louis de Backer, Paris, 1877, p. 297.
398. Rashid al-Din, 1940, pp. 68: on Baydu's disapproval of Nawruz, p. 78: on the construction of Buddhist temples; Boyle, 1968, p. 378.
399. Bar Hebraeus, 1932, I p. 505 [593]: 'To the Christians Baydu used to say, "I am a Christian", and he hung a cross on his neck. To the Muslims he showed that he was a Muslim, but he was never able to learn the ablutions and the fasts. And he never went to pray with them.' Rashid al-Din, 1940, p. 87: Ghazan did not truly respect Islamic rules, and remained attached to Mongol traditions. He married his stepmother according to the Mongol custom, although this was unacceptable in Islam; Boyle, 1968, p. 379; Charles Melville, "Pādshāh-i Islām: The Conversion of Sultān Mahmūd Ghāzān Khān", *Pembroke Papers 1*, Cambridge, 1990, p. 171: Ghazan needed 'the backing of those Mongol leaders and their troops who had already embraced Islam.' Reuven Amitai- Preiss, "Ghazan, Islam and Mongol Tradition: A View from the Mamluk Sultanate", *Bulletin of SOAS*, 1996, LIX pp. 1-3.
400. Spuler, 1969, pp. 36-37.
401. Browne, 1928, vol. 1 pp. 44, 444.
402. Christensen, 1993, p. 43.
403. Howorth, 1888, III p. 421.
404. Rashid al-Din, 1994, II pp. 1259.
405. *Monks of Kublai Khan,* 1928, pp. 210-222.
406. Rashid al-Din, 1994, II pp.1356-1357: (Based on Bausani's tr., 1968, p. 542) '(...) Ghazan commanded (...) that all the community of Buddhists should be converted to Islam (...) but (they) were Muslims outwardly (...) and (Ghazan) said to them: 'Let those among you who wish to return to India, to Kashmir, to Tibet (...) and let those who remain here cease to be hypocrites.' But some persevered in their hypocrisy (...) and Ghazan said: 'My father was an idolater (...) and built for himself a temple which he made *waqf* for the community (of Buddhists). That temple I have destroyed; go ye there and live on alms.''; Howorth, 1888, III p. 422 cf. *Histoire de la Géorgie*, pp. 616-617 & Stephen Orphelian, *Histoire de la Siounie*, pp. 261-262; Bar Hebraeus, 1932, I p. 507 [596]: They persecuted the Christians and the Jews but their attitude 'was twice as fierce (...) against the priests who were worshippers of idols. And a very large number of the pagan priests, because of the way in which they were persecuted, became Muslims.'
407. E. Blochet, *Introduction à l'histoire des Mongols de Fadl Allah Rashid ed-din*, Leiden, Brill, 1910, p. 30.
408. *Ibid.*, pp. 20-28.
409. Rashid al-Din, 1994, II p. 1135; *Monks of Kublai Khan,* 1928, p. 221.
410. *Monks of Kublai Khan,* 1928, pp. 222, 225, 229-230; Fiey, 1975, pp. 68-69.
411. *Monks of Kublai Khan,* 1928, pp. 237, 239, 242-243, 250-251; Fiey, 1975, pp. 69-71; Boyle, 1968, p. 380.
412. Spuler, 1969, p. 35.
413. *Monks of Kublai Khan*, 1928, pp. 255-257; *Histoire de Mar Jabalaha III*, 1895, pp. 146-149.
414. Blochet, 1910, p. 19.
415. *Ibid.*, pp. 26-27.

416. *Ibid.*, pp. 20-22.
417. Hafiz Abru, *Zayl-i Jāmi' al-Tawārīkh-i Rashīdī (703-781 H.)*, ed. Khanbaba Bayani, Tehran, 1977, p. 100: Quoted from Abu al-Qasim al-Kashani, Paris, 1787; Netzer, 1994, pp. 123-124; Walter J. Fischel, "Über Raschid ad-Daulas jüdische Ursprung, Ein Beitrag zur Geschichte des Judenfrage in Persien unter den Mongolen", *Monatsschrift für Geschichte und Wissenschaft des Judentums*, Breslau, Stefan Munz, 1937, 81 p.150.
418. Blochet, 1910, p.20; Jean Aubin, "Le patronage culturel en Iran sous les Ilkhans, Une grande famille de Yazd", *Le Monde Iranien et l'Islam*, Paris, Société d'histoire de l'Orient, 1976, p. 108: Jean Aubin says that Sa'd al-Din Savaji surrounded himself by Persians and was favourable to Shi'ism. He did not surround himself with Jews like Rashid al-Din.
419. *Monks of Kublai Khan*, 1928, pp. 257-260; *Histoire de Mar Jabalaha III*, 1895, pp. 149-152.
420. Hafiz Abru, 1977, p. 101 fn 1; Spuler, 1969, p. 39; Boyle, 1968, p. 401; Bausani, 1968, p. 543: He had also been a Buddhist.
421. *Monks of Kublai Khan*, 1928, pp. 303-305; *Histoire de Mar Jabalaha III*, 1895, pp. 177-179.
422. Gillman, 1999, p. 142.
423. Hafiz Abru, 1977, pp. 128-129.
424. Blochet, 1910, p. 52.
425. Fiey, 1975, pp. 80-81.
426. *Histoire de Mar Jabalaha III*, 1895, p. 167 no 2.
427. Spuler, 1969, p. 39.
428. *Monks of Kublai Khan*, 1928, p. 287; *Histoire de Mar Jabalaha III*, 1895, p. 168: Eulogy of Amir Chupan; Fiey, 1975, pp. 80-82.
429. Walter J. Fischel, "Neue Beitrage zur Geschichte der Juden Baghdads im islamischen Mittelalter", *Monatsschrift für Geschichte unde Wissenschaft des Judentums*, Breslau, Stefan Munz, 1937, 81 p. 419.
430. Rashid al-Din, 1994, pp. 1035-1038; Kirakos of Gantzak, 1858, p. 496; Grigor of Akanc', 1949, p. 335.
431. Morgan, 1986, p. 60.
432. Vartan, 1860, pp. 300-305.
433. J. Richard, "Le Début des Relations entre la Papauté et les Mongols de Perse", *Journal Asiatique*, Paris, 1949, tome 237 pp. 291-297; David Morgan, *The Mongols*, Oxford, Basil Blackwell, 1987, p. 185.
434. Spuler, 1969, pp. 28-29.
435. Ryan, 1988, p. 414: cf. Setton, *The Papacy and the Levant*, i, p. 118; Fiey, 1975, pp. 35-36.
436. Luciano Petech, "Les Marchands Italiens dans l'Empire Mongol", *Journal Asiatique*, Paris, Imprimerie Nationale, 1962, tome 250 pp. 550-551, 553, 557, 560-564.
437. Odoric de Pordenone, *Les Voyages en Asie au XIV e siècle du bienheureux frère Odoric de Pordenone*, Paris, Ernest Leroux, 1891, pp. 70-72: He mentions four monks, Thomas of Dolentin, Jack of Pade, Peter of Seins and Demetrius of Tiflis, staying with a local Nestorian inhabitant.

438. Bar Hebraeus, 1932, I p. 492 [578]; Ryan, 1988, p. 415: cf. J. Chabot, "Notes sur les relations du roi Argun avec l'Occident", *Revue de l'Orient Latin*, 1894, ser. II, X pp. 566-638; Boyle, 1968, pp. 370-371: cf. Moule, *Christians in China*, p. 106.

439. *Monks of Kublai Khan,* 1928, pp. 171, 174; Antoine Mostaert and F. W. Cleaves, *Les Lettres de 1289 et 1305 des Ilkhans Arghun et Oljeitu à Philippe le Bel*, Cambridge (MA), 1962, p.18: on letters of Arghun to Philippe le Bel.

440. Fra Ricoldo de Monte Croce, 1877, pp. 322-324.

441. J. Richard, "An Account of the Battle of Hattin, referring to Frankish Mercenaries in Oriental Moslem States", *Speculum*, 1952, XXVII, pp. 168-177.

442. Spuler, 1969, p. 37.

443. *Monks of Kublai Khan*, 1928, pp. 241-242; *Histoire de Mar Jabalaha III*, 1895, pp. 132; J. Richard, "Mongols and Franks", *Journal of Asian History*, Indiana University, 1969, III, 1 p. 55.

444. Fiey, 1975, p. 93: cf: Antonio Hayek, *Le relazioni della Chiesa Siro-Giacobita colla Santa Sede dal 1143 al 1656*, typed thesis, Rome, 1936, pp. 40-41.

445. Boyle, 1968, p. 392.

446. *Histoire de Mar Jabalaha III*, 1895, 249-256.

447. Fiey, 1975, p. 93: cf. Hayek, 1936, pp. 40-44.

448. Bar Hebraeus, *Chronicon Ecclesiasticum*, 1877, III col. 476.

449. Spuler, 1969, p. 39; Boyle, 1968, p. 399; Mostaert & Cleaves, 1962, pp. 56-57, pp. 402-403: Howorth, 1888, III pp. 576-589.

450. Fiey, 1979, I pp. 292-293; Odoric de Pordenone, 1891, pp. XIX.

451. Boyle, 1968, p. 413.

452. Fiey, 1975, pp. 80-81: cf. R. Loernetz, "Les Missions Dominicaines en Orient au XIVe siècle et la Société des Frères Pérégrinants pour le Christ", *Archivum Fratrum Praedicatorum*, 1932, II pp.1-83; 1933, III pp.1-55; 1934, IV pp. 1-47 & cf. "La Société des Frères Pérégrinants", Rome, 1937, pp. 135-198: "La Mission de Perse"; Spuler, 1969, p. 39.

453. Gillman, 1999, p. 143.

454. Browne, 1928, p. 443; see also chapter 2, section 4 on the emergence of New Persian.

455. Thorau, 1991, p.221.

456. *Ardā Viraz Nāmag* (*Le Livre d'Arda Viraz*), ed. & tr. Philippe Gignoux, Paris, Bibliothèque Iranienne, 1984, cahier no 14 p. 15: on the date of the latest Pahlavi texts.

457. . Amuzgar, "Bahrām (-e) Pa du", *Encyclopaedia Iranica*, 1989, vol. III pp. 524-525.

458. R. Afifi (ed.), *Ardā virāf nāma ye manzum e Zartosht Bahram e Pazhdo*, Mashhad, 1964, pp. 15-17; C. Rempis, "Qui est l'auteur de Zartusht-Nameh?", *Mélanges d'orientalisme offerts à Henry Massé à l'occasion de son 75e anniversaire*, Tehran, 1963, pp. 341-342; Olga Yastrebova, "The Manuscripts of Čangranghāče-nāme and Ardā Virāf Nāme by Zartošt e Bahram e Pa dū", *Studia Orientalia*, Helsinki, 2003, vol. 95 p. 251.

459. Zartusht-i Bahram b. Pajdu, *Zartusht-nāma* (*Le Livre de Zoroastre*), ed. Frederic Rosenberg, St. Petersbourg, Commissionnaires de l'Académie Impériale des Sciences, 1904, p. 2.

460. *Ibid.*, p.72 verse 58.1401-1403:

ترکان و بیکند و ختلان و چین   بر آید سپاهی به ایران زمین
چو برگردد از مهتران تخت و بخت   ابا بندگان افتد تاج و تخت
بسی نعمت و مال گرد آورند   مر آنرا بزیر زمین گسترند

461. Zartusht-i Bahram (ed. Afifi), *Arda viraf nama*, 1964, p. 17 verses 11-14:

که در دوران دروندی هزاره   گزند دیو بی کناره
کردن خداوند اگرچه ما بدین در   بسی تقصیر داریم از همه در
بدینگونه شده عاجز ز دیوان   ز دست ترک دروندان غریوان
جهان گشته ز سر تا پا نسادان   نسا آمیخته با خان و با مان

462. Boyce, 1992, p.156.

463. Yastrebova, 2003, p. 257.

464. Shapurji Kavasji Hodivala, *Parsis of Ancient India*, Bombay, 1920, p. 55; Mary Boyce, *Zoroastrians, Their Religious Beliefs and Practices*, London, Routledge and Kegan Paul, 1979, p. 170.

465. Gordon Johnson, *Cultural Atlas of India*, Oxford, Andromad, 1996, p. 81.

466. Ludwig Paul, "Early Judeo-Persian between Middle and New Persian", *Irano-Judaica V*, Jerusalem, 2003, p. 97.

467. Fischel, 1949, pp. 823-824.

468. See Ludwig Paul above.

469. Jacob Katz, "Religion as a Uniting and Dividing Force in Modern Jewish History", *The Role of Religion in Modern Jewish History*, Cambridge (MA), 1975, p. 6: says that such apostates still belong to Jewish History.

470. Blochet, 1910, p. 80.

471. Juwayni, 1958, p. XXVII.

472. *Ibid.*, p. 599: 'Those who were exempt from the taxes were by the ordinance of Gengis Khan and Qa'an (Ugeday), i.e. of the Moslems the great *sayyids* and the excellent *imams*, of the Christians, whom they call *erke'un*... and of the idolaters the priests whom they call *toyin*...The Jews heard of this ordinance and not being included in that category they became exceedingly vexed and annoyed.' Spuler, 1939, p. 249.

473. Blochet, 1910, pp. 26, 29-30; Fischel, 1937, pp. 149-150.

474. Qutbi al-Ahri, *Tarikh-i Shaykh Uwais*, ed. & tr. J. B. Van Loon, The Hague, Excelsor, 1954, p. 146 (tr. p. 48).

475. Ibn al-Ukhuwwa, *Ma'alim al-Qurba fi Ahkam al-Hisba*, ed. Reuben Levy, Cambridge, 1938, p. 56: 'No Muslim occupies himself with it: everyone repairs to the study of Law and more particularly that portion of it which is given over to disputes and litigiousness.' cf. also Ibn Hadjar; Rashid al-Din, 1994, II p. 1383: Rashid al-Din himself says that he was a physician; Blochet, 1910, p. 30: He says that he was a pharmacist and a physician.

476. Elgood, 1951, pp. 312-315.

477. Allsen, 2001, p. 144.

478. Boyle, 1969, p. 417; Allsen, 2001, pp. 144-145: on the collaboration of Chinese translators and physicians.

479. Fischel, 1949, pp. 827-828.

480. J. P. Asmussen, *Studies in Judeo-Persian Literature*, Leiden, Brill, 1973, p. 9.

481.	Vera B. Moreen, *In Queen Esther's Garden, An Anthology of Judeo-Persian*, New Haven, Yale University Press, 2000, pp. 26-30.
482.	Fischel, 1949, pp. 829-834.
483.	Moreen, 2000, p. 290.
484.	Fiey, 1975, p. 59.
485.	*Monks of Kublai Khan*, 1928, pp. 5, 197.
486.	Bar Hebraeus, *Chronicon Ecclesiasticum*, 1877, III cols. 452-454; *Monks of Kublai Khan*, 1928, p. 153.
487.	*Monks of Kublai Khan,* 1928, p. 92; Aubry R.Vine, *The Nestorian Churches*, London, Independant Press, 1937, p.156.
488.	Fiey, 1979, VII p. 426; Fiey, 1975, p. 94: Bar Hebraeus, 1877, II col. 484.
489.	Bar Hebraeus, 1932, I p. 508 [596]: The author mentions three splendid churches destroyed in Arbela during the rule of Nawruz; Rashid al-Din, 1994, II p. 1285; Fiey, 1975, pp. 85-86.
490.	Boyle, 1968, p. 34.
491.	Mari b. Sulayman, 1899, II p. 84: on the trust of Abbasid caliphs in Christian officials.
492.	Ibn Fazlallah al-Umari, *Masālik al-Absār fi Mamālik al-Amsār* (*Das Mongolische Weltreich*), ed. Klaus Lech, Wiesbaden, Otto Harrassowitz, 1968, p. 119: on the last wave of Islamization conducted by Tarmashirin in Central Asia about 1325.
493.	Marco Polo, 1921, I pp. 183-186; William of Rubruquis, 1903, p. 228: Nestorians were accordingly dispersed in the Central Asian territories under Mongol rule at the borders of Persia.
494.	Hamdallah Mustawfi Qazwini, *Nuzhat al-Qulūb*, ed. G. Le Strange, Leiden, Brill, 1913, p. 152; J. M. Fiey, "Chrétientés Syriaques du Horasan et du Ségestan", *Le Muséon*, Louvain, 1973, LXXXVI, 1-2 pp. 89, 92; Fiey, 1979, II, pp. 177-178, 189-193; IV pp. 372, 376, 377.
495.	Morgan, 1988, pp. 83-84, 88-89.
496.	Morgan, 1988, p. 93; H. R. Roemer, "Timur in Iran", *The Cambridge History of Iran*, Cambridge, 1986, pp. 56, 89.
497.	Beatrice Forbes Manz, *The Rise and Rule of Tamerlane*, Cambridge, 1989, pp. 83, 107. Morgan, 1988, pp. 92-93; Roemer, "Timur in Iran", pp. 55, 58.
498.	Sharaf al-Din Ali Yazdi, *Zafar Nāma* (*Histoire de Timurbec*), tr. Petis de la Croix, Paris, Robert Marc d'Espilly, 1722, I pp. 392-395, II pp. 317, 329, 368, 374, 378, 384, III pp. 223, 242-252, 359, 409, IV pp. 88, 98, 102, 116; Roemer, "Timur in Iran", pp. 59, 75; Allen, 1932, pp. 123-125.
499.	Yazdi, 1722, II pp. 392-393.
500.	Jonas Hanway, *A Historical Account of the British Trade over the Caspian Sea with the Revolutions of Persia*, London, 1753, I p. 186.
501.	Bar Hebraeus, 1932, vol. II p. XXX; Yazdi, 1722, II pp. 241, 253-254, 259: Regarding Takrit; Roemer, "Timur in Iran", p.71.
502.	Bar Hebraeus, 1932, II pp. XXX-XXXI.
503.	Dawlatshah Samarqandi, *Tadhkirāt al-Shu'arā'*, ed. E. G. Browne, London, Luzac, 1901, p. 330.
504.	Yazdi, 1722, III p. 268.
505.	John E. Woods, *The Aqquyunlu, Clan, Confederation, Empire*, Minneapolis, Bibliotheca Islamica, 1976, p. 55.

506. Bar Hebraeus, 1932, II p. XXXIII.
507. Roemer, "Timur in Iran", pp. 51-53: Timur Lang spared the religious communities in Transoxania as they acted as spies for him.
508. Roemer, "Timur in Iran", p. 89.
509. Bar Hebraeus, 1932, II pp. XXXIII-XXXVII.
510. Yazdi, 1722, IV p. 221.
511. Bar Hebraeus, 1932, II pp. XXXVII-LII.
512. Ibn Fazlallah al-Umari, 1968, p. 119; E. Blochet, "La conquête des états nestoriens de l'Asie Centrale par les Schiites: les influences chrétiennes et bouddhiques dans le dogme islamique", *Revue de l'Orient Chrétien*, Paris, 1925/6, XXV pp. 54-55.
513. *Documents Inédits pour servir à l' histoire du Christianisme en Orient*, ed. Antoine Rabbath, Paris, A. Picard et Fils, 1907, I p. 95: From excerpts of the French consulate in Aleppo dating from 1683 and a letter of the French consul Ferriol to a French minister dated 1704, we know that the Nestorian Patriarch (Isaac) was still residing in Mosul; Sharaf al-Din Bidlisi, *Sharafnāma (Fastes de la Nation Kourde)*, ed. & tr. François B. Charnoy, St. Petersbourg, 1868, p. 439: Charnoy, who edited Bidlisi's work in 1868, refers to the residence of the Nestorian Patriarch (Simeon), who was then located in the Hakkari mountains (in a village called Erkoush).
514. J. M. Fiey, "Adharbayjan chrétien", *Le Muséon*, Louvain, 1973, LXXXVI, 1-2 pp. 397-435; C. E. Bonin, "Notes sur les commnuautés nestoriennes de l'Asie Centrale", *Journal Asiatique*, 1900, XV pp. 584-592; Sa'id Naficy, *Masīhiyat dar Īrān*, Tehran, 1964, pp. 340-359.
515. *Genuinae Relationes*, 1902, pp. 64-65: In the list of the ecclesiastical dioceses of Persia sent by the Patriarch Awdisho IV Marun to Pope Pius IV in 1562, not a single diocese from southern Iran appears, although they were mentioned in the lists of the early 13th century. Austen Henry Layard, *Nineveh and its Remains, with an Account of a Visit to the Chaldean Christians of Kurdistan and the Yezidis*, London, John Murray, 1849, vol. 1 p. 257; Aziz S. Atiya, *A History of Eastern Christianity*, London, 1968, p. 284; John Joseph, *The Nestorians and their Muslim Neighbors*, Princeton (N. J.), 1961, pp. 23, 33, 36: on the Nestorian population being concentrated in the Hakkari mountains (Julamerik).
516. Laurence Lockhart, "European Contacts with Persia, 1350-1736", *The Cambridge History of Iran*, Cambridge, 1986, p. 375; Roemer, "Timur in Iran", p. 78.
517. Woods, 1976, pp. 68, 99, 118-119, 128: cf. Muhyi Gülşeni (d. 1617), *Menākib-i Şerif-i Hazret-i Sultan Gülşeni*, MS British Library Or 12958 ff. 5a - 6b & Abu Bakr Tihrani Isfahani, *Kitāb-i Diyār-Bakriye*, eds. N. Lugal and F. Sümer, Ankara, 1962, p. 136; H. R. Roemer, "The Türkmen Dynasties", *The Cambridge History of Iran*, Cambridge, 1986, pp. 175-176, 178-179, 182; Browne, 1920, pp. 407-408; H. R. Roemer, "The Successors of Timur", *The Cambridge History of Iran*, Cambridge, 1986, pp. 115-116.
518. *I Viaggi in Persia degli Ambasciatori Veneti Barbaro e Contarini*, ed. L. Lockhart, R. Morozzo delle Rocca, M. F. Tiepolo, Rome, Libreria dello Stato, 1973, pp. XI, 16; Lockhart, 1986, pp. 377-378.
519. Lockhart, 1986, p. 378.
520. *I Viaggi in Persia*, 1973, p. 147.

521. Browne, 1920, pp. 397-398: cf. Abd al-Razzaq, *Matla'al-Sa'dayn*, from Quatremère, *Notice et Extraits des Manuscrits de la Bibliothèque du Roi*, vol. XIV pp. 1-473; Denys Lombard & Chen Dasheng, "Le rôle des étrangers dans le commerce maritime de Quanzhou (Zeitun)", *Marchands et hommes d'affaires asiatiques dans l'Océan Indien et la Mer de Chine 13e-20e siècles*, Paris, 1988, p. 28: on the presence of a Chinese amiral Zheng He at Hormuz in 1417.
522. Lockhart, 1986, p. 380.
523. "Indian Subcontinent", *Encyclopaedia Britannica (Macropaedia)*, 1975, vol. 9 pp. 365, 367.
524. Mario Vitalone, *The Persian Revāyats: A Bibliographic Reconnaissance*, Napoli, Istituto Universitario Orientale, 1987, pp. 6-7.
525. Hossein Nasr, "Religion in Safavid Persia", *Iranian Studies (Studies on Isfahan)*, 1974, no. 1-2, p. 271.
526. Roger M. Savory, "Is There an Ultimate Use for Historians? Reflections on Safavid History and Historiography", *The Annual Noruz Lecture Series*, Washington DC, Foundation for Iranian Studies, 1995 - unpublished conference.
527. Fattal, 1958, pp. 116-118: cf. Michel le Syrien, II 488; *Chronicum Anonymum*, I 293; Denys, 18; Isfahani, XV 13; Ibn Abi Usaybi'a; I 116; Ibn Qutayba, *'Uyūn*, I 76.
528. Browne, 1920, p. 407: Marta was the daughter of Despina Khatun, the Byzantine princess referred to earlier.
529. Jean Chardin, *Voyages du Chevalier Chardin en Perse*, ed. L. Langlès, Paris, Le Normant, 1811, IX pp. 29-37: on the divergences between Sunnites and Shi'ites, one of the causes of antagonism between Safavids and Ottomans.
530. Khurshah b. Qubad al-Husayni, *Tārīkh-i Ilchī -i Nizām Shāh (History of the Safavid Dynasty until 972 H (1565 A.D.))*, ed. M.R. Nasiri and Koichi Haneda, Tehran, 2000, p. 8. H. R. Roemer, "The Safavid Period", *The Cambridge History of Iran*, Cambridge, 1986, vol. 6 pp. 211-212.
531. Hasan Rumlu, *A Chronicle of the Early Safawis: The Ahsan al-Tawārīkh*, tr. C. Seddon, Baroda, Oriental Institute, 1934, vol. I pp. 135, 143, 159, 160, 168, 169, p. 270, p. 274, p.280; Roemer, 1986, p. 245.
532. *Chronicle of the Carmelites in Persia*, London, Eyre & Spottiswoode, 1939, vol. I p. 43.
533. Chardin, 1811, V pp. 226-228.
534. Kathryn Babayan, "The Safavid Synthesis: From Qizilbash Islam to Imamite Shi'ism", *Iranian Studies*, 1994, vol. 27, II 1-4, p.137: on the Safavid's breakaway from the Qizilbash and the adoption of the slave system for consolidating their power; Roemer, "The Safavid Period", p. 246.
535. Hasan Rumlu, 1934, pp. 135, 143, 159.
536. Madelung, 1988, p. 1: 'Unlike Judaism and Christianity whose prophetic origins were acknowledged by Islam, Zoroastrianism, even though it gained a similar legal status as the "book religions" tolerated by the Quran, was unequivocally condemned as a false religion.'
537. Nicolas Sanson, *The Present State of Persia* (tr.), London, M. Gilliflower, 1695, p. 189: Father Sanson, who visited Iran between 1683 and 1691, said that they were treated worse than the Jews; Babai b. Farhad, *Iranian Jewry during the Afghan Invasion: The Kitab-i Sar Guzasht-i Kashan of Babai b. Farhad*, ed. & tr. Vera Moreen, Stuttgart, Franz Steiner Verlag, 1990, pp. 63-64.

538. *Mīno Khirad or Vasf-i Khirad, and Noshīravān and his "Marqūzan" (Dakhma)*, transcribed in 1251 Anno Yazdgirdi (1883) from a manuscript written by Anushiravan Pur Marzban in 1620, Dastur Meherjirana Library, Navsari (India), fols. 253-254.
539. *Ibid.*, fol. 257.
540. *Ibid.*, fol. 273.
541. *Ibid.*, fols. 274-275.
542. *Good Religion* is a synonym of Zoroastrianism.
543. The author uses Arabic words such as *nabi* and *rasul* in order to allude to Muhammad, saving the Persian synonyms of the word for Zarathushtra.
544. *Mīno Khirad*, 1883, fol. 286.
545. Arthur comte de Gobineau, *Trois en Asie de 1855 à 1858*, Paris, 1905, p. 375.
546. Cornelius Le Bruyn, *Travels into Muscovy, Persia and Part of the East Indies*, tr. from French), London, A. Bettesworth, 1737, I p. 221: 'When a Christian or any other person who is not of the Persian [Muslim] religion, embraces their faith, he inherits all his father's fortune, and the fortunes of all his relations.'
547. *Ibid.*, II p. 145: 'The Guebres (Zoroastrians) are dispersed in several cities of Persia in which places they enjoy more liberty than is allowed them at Isfahan.'
548. Vitalone, 1987, p. 8.
549. Raphaël du Mans, *Raphaël du Mans Missionnaire en Perse au XVIIIe s.*, ed. Francis Richard, Paris, 1995, II pp. 7-8; Chardin, 1811, IV pp. 154, 162 fnte; Willem Floor, "The Dutch and the Persian Silk Trade", *Safavid Persia, The History and Politics of an Islamic Society*, London, I.B. Tauris, 1996, p. 329; Jean Aubin, "Témoignage et oui-dire de Josefa Barbaro sur la Perse (1487)", *Middle East and Indian Ocean XVIe-XIXe s.*, Paris, 1985, 2.I p. 78.
550. Vitalone, 1987, pp. 8-9.
551. Jean de Thévenot, *Voyages de Monsieur de Thévenot*, Paris, Charles Angot, 1689, V p. 170.
552. Arakel of Tabriz, "Livre d'Histoires", *Collection d'Historiens Arméniens*, ed. M. Brosset, St. Petersbourg, 1874, p. 489. Chardin, 1811, VIII pp. 100-101, 112, 355, 356.
553. Pietro della Valle, *I Viaggi di Pietro della Valle*, ed. F. Gaeta & L. Lockhart, Rome, 1972, I p. 77; Chardin, 1811, VIII pp. 358-359, X p. 22.
554. Nora Kathleen Firby, *European Travellers and their Perceptions of Zoroastrians in the 17th and 18th Centuries*, Belin, Dietrich Reimer, 1988, p. 28-29: Nicola Hemmis visited Isfahan between 1623-1624.
555. Chardin, 1811, III pp. 356-357.
556. *Ibid.*, p. 292.
557. André Daulier-Deslandes, *The Beauties of Persia*, tr. from French, London, The Persia Society, 1926 (reedition of 1673) p. 7, 27-28: He visted Persia about 1665 and said that the law was the same for Christians and Muslims under Shah Abbas and that the Armenians has their own magistrates; Chardin, 1811, III p. 409: Eulogizes the Iranian Muslims for their tolerance, saying that even the apostates were allowed to return to their initial religion; VIII p. 360: Zoroastrians had their own magistrates.
558. Chardin, 1811, VIII p. 362.

559.	Le Bruyn, 1737, II pp. 215, 226.; Chardin, 1811, IV p. 260: Visited Isfahan about 1650, and says that the Zoroastrians of the town referred him to the priests of Yazd for questions with regards to the Avesta and the ancient languages, VIII pp. 361-362: The Zoroastrians of the town knew nothing of their own religion apart from a number of superstitions; Du Mans, 1995, II p. 307: Wrote on Zoroastrians of Isfahan in 1684, and says that they were ignorant plebeians; Daulier-Deslandes, 1926, p. 26: The Zoroastrians were reluctant to speak about their religion; Sanson, 1695, pp. 183-184: Their priest withheld information.; Pietro della Valle, 1972, p. 79: He could not learn much from the Zoroastrians of Isfahan, but he would go another place where they were more numerous, more wealthy and more knowledgeable; Firby, 1988, p. 70: on forced conversions.
560.	Firby, 1988, p. 29: Nicola Hemmis said that the Zoroastrians had industrious merchants.
561.	*Story of Kāwūs and Afsad*, transcribed in 1252 Anno Yazdgirdi (1884) from a manuscript written and completed between the 16th and 18th century, Dastur Meherjirana Library, Navsari (India), Catalogue F. 62, fol. 3: 'My country was the land of Iran, Inside Yazd was thus my home; Commerce was my vocation and profession, Every kingdom was my trading place.'; Floor, 1996, p. 339; Charles Melville, "Shah Abbas and the Pilgrimage to Mashhad in 1601", *Safavid Persia*, London, Tauris, p. 213: The importance of the *jizya* received from the Zoroastrians of Yazd demonstrates that they were not so poor a community.
562.	Jean-Baptiste Tavernier, *Voyages en Perse*, Paris, Editions du Carrefour, 1930, p. 79: Visited Isfahan in 1647; Chardin, 1811, VIII p. 356: Estimated the entire population of Iran and India to be about 80,000; Mary Boyce, "The Fire-Temples of Kirman", *Acta Orientalia*, 1966, I p. 30.
563.	E. G. Browne, *A Year Amongst the Persians*, London, Adam & Charles Black, 1893, p. 471.
564.	Mary Boyce, "The Zoroastrian Houses of Yazd", *Iran and Islam*, Edinburgh, 1971, p. 126; Nile Green, "The Survival of Zoroastrianism in Yazd", *Iran*, London, 2000, vol. 38 p. 115.
565.	John Fryer, *A New Account of East-India and Persia (1672-1681)*, London, R. Chriswell, 1698, pp. 392-393: They were the off-scum of the earth in Isfahan, a state in which were neither the Jews nor the Christians, p. 267: Their women acted as 'comedians and whores' at the court. Sanson, 1695, pp. 183-184: Their poverty and cruel slavery to which they were reduced; Le Bruyn, 1737, II p. 145.
566.	Walter J. Fischel, "The Jews in Mediaeval Iran from the Sixteenth to the Eighteenth Centuries: Political, Economic and Communal Aspects", *Irano-Judaica*, Jerusalem, Ben-Zvi Institute, 1982, p. 266: cf. Tomé Pires, *Suma Oriental* (1512-1515), London, Hakluyt Society Publications, 1944, vol. I p. 27.
567.	Fischel, 1982, p. 268.
568.	Iskandar Beg Munshi, *Zayl-i Tārikh-i Ālam ārā-yi Abbāsī*, ed. S. Khwansari, Tehran, 1938, p.881; Arakel of Tabriz, 1874, p. 488; Pietro della Valle, 1972, p. 177; Matthee, 1999, p. 76.
569.	Vera B. Moreen, *Iranian Jewry's Hour of Peril and Heroism: A Study of Babai ibn Lutf's Chronicle (1616-1662)*, Columbia University Press, 1987, pp. 81-85.
570.	Thévenot, Paris, 1689, p. 411: Despite the efforts of the vizier, the Jews maintained their religion, but were forced to wear a special patch on their stomach.; Fryer, 1698, p. 249: Visited Lar in 1676, and wrote that the dress code was only in force in that town as the governor was a *Haji*.

571. Moreen, 1987, pp. 86-87, 90, 92-94, 130; Chardin, 1811, III p. 409: Eulogizes the Muslim Iranians for their tolerance as they allowed apostates to return to their initial religion.
572. Du Mans, 1995, II p. 34: In 1660, he wrote that the Jews were officially converted to Islam, but still practised Judaism in private; *Chronicle of the Carmelites*, 1939, pp. 364-365: The edict concerned also the Mandeans (an age-old non-Muslim community) who were forced to convert in large numbers; Arakel of Tabriz, 1874, pp. 489-496; Wahid Qazwini, 'Ābbās-nāma, ed. I. Dehqan, Arak, 1951, pp. 218-219.
573. Arakel of Tabriz, 1874, pp. 494-495: Provides us with a long list of Iranian towns and provinces, where the Jews were not compelled to convert. These were, Gulpaygan, Khunsar, Bandar (Abbas), Shushtar, Hamadan, Yazd, Damavand, Astarabad, Farahabad, and the provinces of Kirman, Khurasan, and Gilan; *Documents Inédits*, 1907, I p. 86: In the letter sent by a Jesuit from Isfahan in 1659, it is mentioned that the Shah had converted the Jews to Islam and was planning to do the same with the Armenians.
574. Moreen, 1987, pp. 95, 102-103, 105; Vera B.Moreen, "The Status of Religious Minorities in Safavid Iran between 1617-1661", *Journal of Near Eastern Studies*, 1981, vol.40, pp. 123-125, 146-148, 223-232 cf. *Kitāb-i Anūsī*, pp. 69-70, 96-98, 118-123, 134-135, 148-149,151-162, 204-206, 213-218; Fischel, 1982, pp. 275-276, 279.
575. Rudi Matthee, "The Career of Muhammad Beg, Grand Vizier of Shah Abbas II (r. 1642-1666)", *Iranian Studies*, 1991, vol. XXIV no 1-4 pp. 27-28: The Grand Vizier preceding Muhmmad Beg, Khalifa Sultan, had already decreed the forceful conversion of Jews in 1645; Chardin, 1811, VI pp. 135-136: Informs us that the messianic movement of Shabbatai Tzvi took place in 1666, and after its failure, the Jews paid the due taxes expected by the Muslim authorities.
576. *Documents Inédits*, 1910, II p. 311; Daulier-Deslandes, 1926, p. 40: Says that this messiah was an impostor and was converted to Islam in Constantinople about 1665-1666; Du Mans, 1995, II pp. 236-237: on the Jews expecting the messiah.
577. Du Mans, 1995, II p.237.
578. Fryer, 1698, p. 346; Daulier-Deslandes, 1926, p. 14: In 1665 Isfahan had many Jews and few Indians. This demonstrates that by this date they had been allowed to return to their original faith; Chardin, 1811, VIII p. 446: Visited Shiraz in 1673 and wrote that the Jews and the Armenians of the town practised their religion without any hindrance.
579. *Chronicle of the Carmelites*, 1939, p. 364; *Documents Inédits*, 1910, II p. 311: Father Alexander of Rhodes who visited Iran in 1659 was surprised by the size of the Jewish community in Iran: '(...) les juifs qui restent répandus par toute la Perse en une multitude incroyable.'; Fryer, 1698, p. 249: He visited Iran between and expressed his amazement at the large number of Jews living in Iran.
580. Moreen, 2000, pp. 232-238.
581. Fischel, 1982, pp. 268, 287-288.
582. Babai b. Farhad, 1990, pp. 16, 39-40.
583. Moreen, 1987, pp. 108-109.
584. Pietro della Valle, 1972, p. 437: In 1618 he said that Farahabad had 40,000 Armenian houses, 12,000 Georgian and 7,000 Jewish. Farahabad was then the major town on the Caspian coast; Arakel of Tabriz, 1874, p. 333: In 1610 he

said that Georgians, Armenians, Muslims and Jews were settled at Farahabad, and all were given houses, vineyards and gardens.

585. Arakel of Tabriz, 1874, p. 495.
586. Moreen, 1987, pp. 108-114: cf. Iskandar Beg Munshi, 1938, vol. 2 pp. 850, 881, 900-901, 1111.
587. Sussan Babaie et al., *Slaves of the Shah: New Elites of Safavid Iran*, London, I. B. Tauris, 2004, p. 63; Charles Melville, "New Light on the reign of Shah Abbas: Volume III of the Afzal al-Tawārīkh", *Society and Culture in the Early Modern Middle East, Studies on Iran in the Safavid Period*, ed. Andrew J. Newman, Leiden, 2003, p. 79: Khuzani Isfahani, *Afzal al-Tavārikh*, fols 409 a-b fol 410 a; Matthee, 1999, pp. 44, 102: cf. *Bronnen tot de geschiedenis der Ost indische Compagnie in Perzie 1611-1638*, ed. H. Dunlop, The Hague, 1930, p. 357; Pietro della Valle, 1972, p. 177, 179, 214: He wrote in 1618 that Farahabad was built by Shah Abbas for the settlement of deportees from Georgia, which included Georgians, Armenians, Jews and Muslims, the latter being just a minority there.
588. Adam Olearius, *Voyages and Travells of the Ambassadors sent by Frederich Dutch of Holstein to the Great Duke of Moscovy and the King of Persia*, London, J. Starky, 1669, p. 165.
589. Franz Caspar Schillinger, *Persianische und Ost-Indianische Reise*, Nuremberg, 1707, p. 266.
590. Tavernier, 1930, p. 319.
591. A. Tenreiro, *Itinerarios da India a Portugal por Terra*, ed. A. Baiao, Coimbra, 1923, p. 360; J. Aubin, "Références pour Lar médiévale", *Journal Asiatique*, Paris, 1955, p. 452.
592. Pietro della Valle, 1973, p.148.
593. Thévenot, 1689, IV p. 462: Accordingly, the town had a large Jewish community; Thomas Herbert, *Travels in Persia*, ed. E. Denison Ross and E. Powers, London, Routledge, 1928, pp. 29-30: He says that the composition of the town was a mixture of Jews and Muslims; Tenreiro, 1923, p. 360.
594. Fischel, 1982, p. 271: cf. Hans Dernschwam's *Tagebuch* (1553-1554), extracts, published in *MGWJ*, vol. 68, 1924, pp. 241-248.
595. Fischel, 1982, p. 271: cf. *The Responsa of Moshe Alshaikh*, ed. Venetia, 1605, paragr. 118.
596. Fischel, 1982, pp. 272-273: cf. G. Schurhammer, *Archivum Historicum Societatis Iesu*, 1933, pp. 291-309 & Moses Pereyra de Paiva, *Notisias dos Judeos de Coching*, Amsterdam, 1687 (new pub. by M. B. Amzalak, Lisbon, 1923).
597. Pietro della Valle, *The Travels of Pietro della Valle in India (1622)*, ed. E. Grey, London, Hakluyt Society Publications,1891, vol. II, p. 401.
598. Pedro Teixeira, *The Travels of Pedro Teixeira with his chronicle of the Kings of Ormuz and the Kings of Persia*, tr. & ed. by W. F. Sinclair, London, Hakluyt Society Publications, 1901, pp. 39, 44, 168.
599. Garcia de Silva Figueroa, *L'Ambassade de Don Garcia de Silva Figueroa en Perse*, tr. A. de Wicquefort, Paris, 1667, pp. 465-468.
600. *Chronicle of the Carmelites*, 1939, I p. 26.

601. Antonio de Gouvea, *Relation des grandes guerres et victoires obtenues par le roy de Perse Chah Abbas contre les empereurs de Turquie*, Rouen, Nicholas Loyelet, 1646, pp. 56-58.
602. Pietro della Valle, 1972, p.144: Regarding Mulla Massih; Chardin, 1811, III p. 464; Moreen, 1987, pp. 92-94.
603. Moreen, 2000, pp. 255-256.
604. Chardin, 1811, VI pp. 26-27, 133: on the profession of Jewish women.
605. Moreen, 1987, pp. 150-151.
606. Abbé Carré, *Travels of Abbé Carré in India and the Near East 1672-1674*, tr. Lady Fawcett & ed. C. L. Fawcett, Hakluyt Series, London 1947, p. 828; Chardin, 1811, VIII p. 508: In addition he says that 1/3 of the inhabitants were Indian.
607. Tavernier, 1930, p. 304; Le Bruyn, 1737, II p. 46.
608. Olearius, 1669, p. 165; Le Bruyn, 1737, II p. 46.
609. Fischel, 1982, p. 282: cf. Chardin, II p. 307; Babai b. Farhad, 1990, pp. 41, 65; Moreen, 2000, pp. 255-256.
610. Babai b. Farhad, 1990, pp. 69-70; Bruce Masters, "The Treaties of Erzurum (1823 & 1848) and the Changing Status of Iranians in the Ottoman Empire", *Iranian Studies*, 1991, vol. XXIV, 1-4, p. 5: Iranian Muslims, Jews and Armenians, were sold in the slave market of Aleppo after the 1730 Ottoman occupation of Hamadan.
611. Moreen, 1987, p. 12.
612. Tavernier, 1930, p. 15; Fischel, 1982, p. 270.
613. Moreen, 1987, pp. 102-103.
614. Tavernier, 1930, pp. 68-69.
615. Moreen, 1987, p. 190 (Appendix C).
616. Tavernier, 1930, p. 239.
617. K. Bayani, *Les Relations de l'Iran avec l'Europe Occidentale à l'époque Safavide*, Paris, Librairie d'Amérique et d'Orient,1937, p. 196: cf. A.E. Perse, no 6 fol. 202-203.
618. Chardin, 1811, VI pp. 122, 134; Fryer, 1698, p. 384: He says that the Jews and Baniyans were involved in this business in 1677; Du Mans, 1995, II p. 251: He confirms that they acted as moneylenders.
619. Moreen, 1987, p. 203 (Appendix E); Moreen, 2000, pp. 223-229.
620. Moreen, 2000, pp. 232-238.
621. Babai b. Farhad, 1990, pp. 45-46.
622. Moreen, 1987, pp. 150-151.
623. Fryer, 1698, p. 263.
624. Ina Baghdiantz McCabe, *The Shah's Silk for Europe's Silver, The Eurasian Trade of the Julfa Armenians in Safavid Iran and India (1530-1750)*, Atlanta, Scholars Press, 1999, p.6
625. Vazken S. Ghougassian, *The Emergence of the Armenian Diocese of New Julfa in the Seventeenth Century*, Atlanta, Scholars Press, 1998, p. 18 cf. Armenian sources cited by this author.
626. Pietro della Valle, 1973, p. 169.
627. Baghdiantz,1999, p. 42.

Notes 195

628. *Chronicle of the Carmelites*, 1939, I p. 45.
629. Ruy Gonzalez de Clavijo, *Embassy to Tamerlane*, tr. Guy Le Strange, London, 1928, pp. 285, 288-289; Josefa Barbaro & Ambrogio Contarini, *Travels to Tana and Persia*, tr. Williams Thomas & ed. Lord Stanley of Aderley, London, Hakluyt Society, 1873, p. 79.
630. Anthony Jenkinson, *Early Voyages and Travels to Russia and Persia*, ed. E. Delmar Morgan & C. H. Cook, London, Hakluyt Society, 1886, II pp. 397, 409-410.
631. Jenkinson, 1886, II p. 420.
632. Baghdiantz, 1999, p.6.
633. Arakel of Tabriz, 1874, pp. 287-288.
634. *Ibid.*, p. 278.
635. Arakel of Tabriz, 1874, p. 288; Mirza Junabadi, *Rawzat al-Safaviyya*, ed. Ghulamreza Tabatabai Majid, Tehran, 2001, pp. 771-772.
636. Chardin, 1811, II p. 299, VIII p.111; Junabadi, 2001, pp. 771-772; Edmund M. Herzig, "The Rise of Julfa Merchants in the Late Sixteenth Century", *Safavid Persia, The History and Politics of an Islamic Society*, London, I.B. Tauris, 1996, pp. 314; Matthee, 1999, p. 85.
637. Du Mans, 1995, II p. 139: There were Armenians from various towns deported to Isfahan; Arakel of Tabriz, 1874, pp. 289-290, 488: Mentions that the Armenians were carried to Iran in different waves.
638. Tavernier, 1930, p. 7; Du Mans, 1995, II p. 139: Says that there were 30,000 Armenian families transported to the region; Arakel of Tabriz, 1874, pp. 333, 441: on the deportation of Armenians from Nakhchevan to Farahabad.
639. Edmund Herzig, "The Deportation of the Armenians in 1604-1605 and Europe's Myth of Shah Abbas I", *Pembroke Papers I*, Cambridge, 1990, p. 68.
640. Pietro della Valle, 1972, p. 30: States that the Ottoman threat was the reason for the Armenians' deportation; Chardin, 1811, VIII p. 112: The account of the European travellers like Chardin can lead the reader to regard Shah Abbas as a charitable protector of Armenians; Ronald Ferrier, "Trade from the mid-14th Century to the End of the Safavid Period", *The Cambridge History of Iran*, Cambridge, 1986, p. 454.
641. Arakel of Tabriz, 1874, p. 291; *Chronicle of the Carmelites*, 1939, I pp. 99-100; Nasrallah Falsafi, *Zindigānī-yi Shāh 'Abbās-i Awwal*, Tehran, Chap-i Kayhan, 1959, vol. 3 p. 232; Matthee, 1999, p. 76; Chardin, 1811, III p. 291: Chardin is mistaken when he says that the Armenians had nothing when they arrived in Isfahan.
642. In order to avoid any confusion, the Julfa neighbourhood near Isfahan would henceforth be referred to as New Julfa.
643. Arakel of Tabriz, 1874, p. 300; Baghdiantz, 1999, pp. 79, 129.
644. Matthee, 1999, p. 74.
645. Arakel of Tabriz, 1874, p. 592: on the deportation of 1500 Muslim families by Shah Abbas II in 1660.
646. *Documents Inédits*, 1907, I p. 441: Father Alexander of Saint-Sylvester, who wrote in 1653, estimated the population of New Julfa to be 60,000, nearly all of them Armenians; Tavernier, 1930, p. 70; *Chronicle of the Carmelites*, 1939, pp. 157-158: About 1608, there were apparently 400,000 families in Iran, fn 1: Father John Thaddeus says that they composed by far the greatest number of

Christians in Iran.
647. Baghdiantz, 1999, pp. 24, 30.
648. Herzig, 1996, p. 310; Jenkinson, 1886, II pp. 406, 410.
649. Lockhart, 1986, pp. 374, 376.
650. Herzig, 1996, pp. 307-308, 313.
651. Arakel of Tabriz, 1874, p. 280.
652. Baghdiantz, 1999, p. 2.
653. Arakel of Tabriz, 1874, pp. 275-276, 278, 280, 282, 292: Shah Abbas duped these ecclesiastics, and Arakel says that they deserved all the hardships they experienced as they were the cause of Armenia's sufferings.
654. Floor, 1996, p. 351; Mesrovb Jacob Seth, *Armenians in India*, Calcutta, 1937, pp. 15, 227.
655. Baghdiantz, 1999, p. 10.
656. *Chronicle of the Carmelites*, 1939, p. 47; Pietro della Valle, 1972, p.30: on New Julfa in 1617, exclusively inhabited by rich Armenian merchants; Baghdiantz, 1999, p. 45.
657. Baghdiantz, 1999, p.33, p. 83 with translation of the decree, p. 87; Thévenot, 1689, III pp. 390-391: The Armenians paid for their privileges 500 *tumans* per year; Du Mans, 1995, II pp. 141-142: Shah Abbas' support to Armenians.
658. Du Mans, 1995, II pp. 138-139: on the Armenians' control over the silk trade and their providing the country with silver; Baghdiantz, 1999, pp. 3-4, 6.
659. Tavernier, 1930, pp. 62-67; Chardin, 1811, VII p. 260: Regarding the ceremonies of Armenians and their Muslim spectators; Daulier-Deslandes, 1926, p. 26: Muslims were forbidden to settle in New Julfa; Zakaria the Diacre, "Mémoires historiques sur les Sofis", *Collection d'Historiens Arméniens*, ed. M. Brosset, St. Petersbourg, 1876, II p. 80: on Shah Safi's appreciation of Armenians and his visit to their homes; Le Bruyn, 1737, vol. I p.185: With regards to their ceremonies.
660. Hanway, 1753, III p. 115; Thévenot, 1689, III p. 269: Each deported community had been granted a neighbourhood named after their original town, such as Erivan or Nakhchevan, but none of them had been granted the privileges of Julfan Armenians.
661. *Chronicle of the Carmelites*, 1939, I p. 157.
662. Pietro della Valle, 1972, pp. 160-161, 175, 177: Farahabad was chosen as the main centre of the Caspian provinces.
663. Baghdiantz, 1999, p. 2.
664. Tavernier, 1930, pp. 56-62; Ferrier, 1986, pp. 454-456.
665. Tavernier, 1930, pp. 62-67; Baghdiantz, 1999, pp. 20-21; Ferrier,1986, pp. 454-456.
666. Baghdiantz, 1999, pp. 44-45.
667. Tavernier, 1930, pp. 56-62.
668. Baghdiantz, 1999, pp.6, 33, 50-51: Georgians as commander-in-chief, p.129.
669. Matthee, 1999, pp. 20, 22: Comments on the role of Azeris in trade, p. 87.
670. Fryer, 1698, p. 263: Eulogizes the Armenians' business skills and knowledge of trade.
671. Ferrier, 1986, pp. 457-459; Matthee, 1999, p. 123.

Notes

672. François Martin, *Mémoires de François Martin, Fondateur de Pondichéry (1665-1696)*, ed. A. Martineau, Paris, 1931, vol. 1 pp. 219-220.
673. Tavernier, 1930, pp. 21, 240, 242; Daulier-Deslandes, 1926, p. 9.
674. Chardin, 1811, III pp. 102, 107, 221, 385, 451-452, IV p. 5; Fryer, 1698, p. 332: on the commerce of semi-precious stones.
675. Pietro della Valle, 1972, p. 40: Armenians controlled the trade between Iran and the Ottoman Empire; Chardin, 1811, IV p. 161; Sanson, 1695, pp. 138-139: Along with the Indians, there were a number of Armenians acting as moneylenders; Ferrier, 1986, p. 472.
676. Chardin, 1927, pp. 280-282; Baghdiantz, 1999, pp. 29, 138-139, 151; Ferrier, 1986, pp. 465-466.
677. Le Bruyn, 1737, I pp. 78-79, 82, 90: Le Bruyn travelled with a number of Armenian merchants in Russia on his way to Astrakhan. He says that about 40 Armenian families had settled in the town.
678. Mathee, 1999, p. 201.
679. Ferrier, 1986, pp. 473-475: cf. Purchas, IV pp. 272-273; Ghougassian, 1998, p. 65.
680. Thévenot, 1689, IV pp. 485-487: He visited Gombroon and says that the Armenians had vessels of their own, IV p. 636, He adds that some vessels belonging to other nations were mainly booked by Armenian passengers.
681. None of the following authors mention the Armenians: Guy de Boe, *Exchange and Trade in Medieval Europe*, Zellik, 1997; E.B. Fryde, *Studies in Medieval Trade and Finance*, London, 1983; David Jacoby, *Trade, Commodities and Shipping in the Medieval Mediterranean*, Aldershot, 1997; R.S. Lopez, *Medieval Trade in the Mediterranean World*, London, 1955; M.M. Postan, *Medieval Trade and Finance*, Cambridge, 1973; Immanuel Wallerstein, *The Politics of the World-Economy: The States, the Movements, and the Civilizations*, Cambridge, 1984.
682. Herzig, 1996, p. 318: Raphael du Mans, *Estat de la Perse en 1660*, ed. C. Schéfer, (Paris, 1890; reprint Fanborough 1969), p.192 & J. de Thévenot, *Voyages de M. de Thévenot*, 3 parts (Paris, 1664-84), II p. 146.
683. *Chronicle of the Carmelites*, 1939, I pp. 192, 295.
684. Louis Bergasse, *Histoire du Commerce de Marseille de 1599 à 1660*, ed. Gaston Rambert, Paris, Plon, 1954, IV pp. 64-70; Robert Paris, *Histoire du Commerce de Marseille de 1660 à 1789*, ed. Gaston Rambert, Paris, Plon, 1957, V pp. 9-16.
685. Ferrier, 1986, pp. 454-456.
686. Ferrier, 1986, pp. 459-460; Seth, 1937, pp. 233-239: They were, however, lured by the concessions given to them by the English, and established their business in the English trade ports in India.
687. Ferrier, 1986, pp. 468-469.
688. François Bernier, *Travels in the Mogul Empire (1656-1668)*, tr. A. Constable & ed. V. Smith, Oxford, 1914, p. 292; Chardin, 1811, IX pp. 214-215.
689. Bergasse, 1954, IV p. 500; Paris, 1957, V pp. 16, 424-425.
690. Baghdiantz, 1999, pp. 293-300, 309: cf. Bibliothèque Nationale, Manuscript fr. 8972, fol. 192 r; *loc. cit.*, p. 309.
691. Du Mans, 1995, II p. 150; Herzig, 1996, p. 318: cf. Thévenot, *Voyages*, 1664-84, II p.146; Martin, 1931, I pp. 219-220; Baghdiantz, 1999, p. 166.

692. Le Bruyn, 1737, I p. 244.
693. Baghdiantz, 1999, pp. 3-4.
694. Chardin, 1811, III pp. 144-145, 291, VIII p. 106 Adds that at the time of his visit, the Armenians were losing their wealth, VIII p. 178, X p. 9 V: Mentions a few other wealthy Armenians, such as the Farhat brothers, and Zakariya, whose family name is not provided; Pietro della Valle, 1972, p. 438: Cites Khwaja Abedik; Du Mans, 1995, I p. 157: Here, the Catholic Shahrimanian family and the famous Shafraz family are mentioned; Francis Richard, *Raphaël du Mans Missionnaire en Perse au XVIII* s.*, Paris, 1995, I p. 87: According to ambassador Nointel, Agha Piri was the richest Armenian in 1671; Baghdiantz, 1999, 3-5, 68, 103, 171.
695. Ghougassian, 1998, p. 93: cf. Appendix I, doc. # 11 of the cited book; Arakel of Tabriz, 1874, p. 476: Arakel says that the seat of the *katholikos* was transferred back to Echmiazin during the reign of Shah Safi by the *katholikos* Philippos in 1633.
696. Thévenot, 1689, V p. 46: on Armenians in Surat; Ghougassian, 1998, p. 2.
697. Baghdiantz, 1999, p. XIX.
698. Herzig, 1996, p.313.
699. Arakel of Tabriz, 1874, pp. 300-301: Shah Abbas I had reduced their taxes, and in case of discord between them and the Muslims punished the Muslims, and allowed them to construct churches.
700. Arakel of Tabriz, 1874, p. 300.
701. Pietro della Valle, 1972, p. 437: Armenians paid the Shah and gave him numerous gifts; Baghdiantz, 1999, p. 166.
702. Baghdiantz, 1999, p. 141: cf. Appendix A of the book, 143.
703. Pietro della Valle, 1972, p. 334: on the Armenian background of Allahverdi Khan (sold as a slave in Georgia), p. 354: Imam Quli Khan governor of Shiraz, and Yussuf Khan governor of Shirvan, were also Armenian apostates; Baghdiantz, 1999, pp. 50-51, 139, 178.
704. Matthee, 1999, p. 20.
705. Iskandar Beg Munshi, 1938, p. 281; *Tadhkirat al-Mulūk: A Manual of Safavid Administration*, ed. & tr. V. Minorsky, London, 1940, pp. 65-66: Muhammad Beg was born into an Armenian family of Tailors in Tabriz.
706. Tavernier, 1930, p. 224; Du Mans, 1995, II pp. 216-217, 234: Yakobian appealed to the court against the Catholics settled in New Julfa.
707. Tavernier, 1930, p. 225; Le Bruyn, 1737, I p. 226: on the *naqqashbashi* and his authority over the Armenians of Isfahan.
708. Tavernier, 1930, pp. 62-67; Le Bruyn, 1737, p. 233: The European monarchs commonly selected Armenians as their envoys to the Persian court. Le Bruyn, however, deplores their choice.
709. Herzig, 1996, p. 315.
710. *Chronicle of the Carmelites*, 1939, I p. 26.
711. Jenkinson, 1886, I pp. 150-156: This happened in 1562.
712. Chardin, 1811, III pp. 118-119: The envoy of the French company was sent to the court along with the Prevost of New Julfa and the principal Armenian merchants of the town; Daulier-Deslandes, 1926, p. 257: They spoke up to five languages including Italian and French; Seth, 1937, p. 88: They even functioned as interpreters at Akbar's court in India, p. 282: The English East India

Company had an Armenian interpreter at the Safavid court.
713. Tavernier, 1930, pp. 91-92, 95, 106.
714. *Chronicle of the Carmelites*, 1939, I pp. 70-91.
715. L. B. Zekiyan, "Xoja Safar, ambasciatore di Shah Abbas a Venezia", *Oriente Moderno*, 1978, 58 p. 361; Matthee, 1999, p. 87.
716. *Chronicle of the Carmelites*, 1939, I p. 192.
717. Pietro della Valle, 1972, p. 418.
718. Zygmunt Pucko, "The Activity of Polish Jesuits in Persia and Neighbouring Countries in the 17th and 18th Centuries", *Proceedings of the Third European Conference of Iranian Studies*, Wiesbaden, Dr. Ludwig Reichert Verlag, 1999, part 2 p. 309; Maria Szuppe, "Un marchand du Roi de Pologne en Perse 1601-1602", *Moyen Orient & Océan Indien*, 1986, no 3 pp. 81-110.
719. Ferrier, 1986, pp. 473-475: cf. Purchas, IV pp. 272-273; Ghougassian, 1998, p. 65.
720. Vahan Bayburdyan, *Naqsh-i Arāmana-ye Irānī dar Tijārat-i Bayn al-Milali tā Pāyān-i Sada-ye 17 Mīlādi*, tr. Adik Baghdasariyan, Tehran, 1996, pp. 97-98; Matthee, 1999, p. 194.
721. Matthee, 1999, p. 194.
722. Bayani, 1937, pp. 173-174.
723. Father Krusinski, *The History of the Revolution of Persia*, London, J. Pemberton, 1728, I pp. 173-177: Israel Orie presented himself as the ambassador of the Czar at the Safavid court, but carried also his business in Isfahan selling his merchandise.
724. Bayani, 1937, pp. 117-118.
725. Ferrier, 1986, pp. 459-460.
726. Bayani, 1937, pp. 180, 186, 188, 189, 189, 192, 193: cf. A. E. Perse, no 2 fol. 34-40; *loc. cit.*, pp. 351-352.
727. Paris, 1957, vol.5 p.16.
728. *Chronicle of the Carmelites*, 1939, p. 102.
729. Baghdiantz, 1999, p. 151; Floor, 1996, p. 347.
730. Baghdiantz, 1999, p. 169.
731. *Ibid.*, p. 261.
732. Du Mans, 1995, II pp. 33-34.
733. Chardin, 1811, II p. 185: on the Armenians' resistance to Islam and Catholicism and their cursing the Pope.
734. M. Le Baron Henrion, *Histoire Générale des Missions Catholiques depuis le 3e siècle jusqu'à nos jours*, Paris, Gaume et Frères, 1847, II.2 p. 242: cf. R. P. Philippe de la Très-Sainte Trinité, *Carme-Déchaussée Voyages d'Orient*, p. 143; R. P. Louis de Sainte-Thérèse Carme-Déchaussée visiteur général, *Annales des Carmes Déchaussez de France*, t. 1 p. 332.
735. Arakel of Tabriz, 1874, pp. 355-361.
736. *Chronicle of the Carmelites*, 1939, I pp. 73, 96, 100-101.
737. *Chronicle of the Carmelites*, 1939, I p. 150, 208 fn 1; *Documents Inédits*, 1907, I pp. 442-443: It is interesting that while the missionaries could not get the approval of the Shah for converting Armenians, they were given a free hand for converting Mandeans, reported Father Alexander in 1653.

738. Du Mans, 1995, I pp. 309-312: on the perseverance of the Capucins and the Carmelites in 1693.
739. Tavernier, 1930, pp. 67-68; Chardin, 1811, VIII p. 110: on Armenians preventing the Jesuits from teaching Armenian children; Baghdiantz, 1999, p.147.
740. *Chronicle of the Carmelites*, 1939, I p. 377.
741. *Documents Inédits*, 1907, I p. 442: Father Alexander of Saint-Sylvester says that the Armenians had made them leave New Julfa; Du Mans, 1995, I pp. 146-7, 157: In 1665, Raphaël du Mans wrote that he did not dare settle in New Julfa, as he did not wish to be humiliated like the Jesuit Gabriel de Chinon, expelled from there 10 years earlier, he also mentions that they were forbidden from teaching in New Julfa; Baghdiantz, 1999, pp. 180-181.
742. Chardin, 1811, II pp. 300-301, XIX p. 238.
743. Baghdiantz, 1999, pp. 186-188: cf. Ter Yovhaneanc (1980), vol. 2 pp. 260-263; Chardin, 1811, III pp. 143-144.
744. *Chronicle of the Carmelites*, 1939, vol. I p. 456.
745. Chardin, 1811, III p. 147, VII p. 436: The missionaries were not coming to Iran for spiritual purposes but 'qu'ils n'entretiennent ces missions en Orient principalement que pour l'aggrandissement et pour la réputation de leur ordre.'
746. Ghougassian, 1998, p. 117; Joseph Pitton de Tournefort, *Relation d'un voyage du Levant*, Lyon, 1727, III, p. 173: on bishop Napet and his bribing the court for obtaining the seat of *katholikos*.
747. *Chronicle of the Carmelites*, 1939, I p. 457 fn 3, I p. 521; Sanson, 1695, p. 119: Believes that there was no hope in converting Armenians; Du Mans, 1995, I p. 189.
748. *Chronicle of the Carmelites*, 1939, I p. 460, II p. 861.
749. *Ibid.*, I p. 465.
750. *Chronicle of the Carmelites*, 1939, I p. 453; Chardin, 1811, VI p. 158: The Catholic missionaries had less difficulty converting Christians other than Armenians.
751. *Chronicle of the Carmelites*, 1939, I p. 494.
752. Gregorio Pereira Fidalgo, *L'Ambassade de Gregorio Pereira Fidalgo à la cour de Chah Soltan-Hosseyn 1696-1697*, ed. Jean Aubin, Lisbonne, 1971, pp. 73-74; Chardin, 1811, VII p. 315, VIII p. 114: The tax revenues of New Julfa belonged to the Queen mother, thus, there was a bond between her and the dignitaries of New Julfa; Fryer, 1698, p. 268: on the protection given by the Queen mother.
753. Ghougassian, 1998, p. 153: taken from Y. Ter Yovhaneanc's paper.
754. *Ibid.*, pp. 154-155.
755. *Chronicle of the Carmelites*, 1939, I p. 523.
756. Moreen, 1987, pp. 138-139.
757. Ferrier, 1986, pp. 465-466.
758. Chardin, 1811, III p. 146.
759. *Chronicle of the Carmelites*, 1939, I pp. 364-367.
760. Chardin, 1811, XIX p. 342; Matthee, 1991, p. 20 cf. Tavernier, *Six Voyages*, I p. 616.
761. Arakel of Tabriz, 1874, pp. 341, 347; *Chronicle of the Carmelites*, 1939, I pp. 197-199; Du Mans,1995, II p.144.

Notes 201

762. Bayani, 1937, pp. 186-193: cf. A. E. Perse, no 2 fol. 34-40, 351, 352; *loc. cit.*, pp. 138-140: cf. H. Dunlop, *L'Histoire de la Compagnie des Indes Orientales en Perse*, t. 72 pp. 679-680.
763. Matthee, 1999, p. 5: Agrees that the Armenians do not owe much to Europeans.
764. *Chronicle of the Carmelites*, 1939, I pp. 255-257; Chardin, 1811, III p. 146.
765. *Documents Inédits*, 1907, I pp. 440-441: Father Alexander of Saint-Sylvester wrote about this incident in 1656.
766. *Chronicle of the Carmelites*, 1939, I p. 288; Arakel of Tabriz, 1874, p. 302; Du Mans, 1995, II pp. 20, 35, 144; Falsafi, 1959, III pp. 232, 235.
767. Matthee, 1999, p. 83; Thévenot, 1689, III pp. 361-362: There were ways to bribe the Muslim judges and thus, the Armenians' wealth was saved; Du Mans, 1995, II p. 329: on wealthy Armenians bribing Muslim judges.
768. Chardin, 1811, X p. 14: Until then the Julfan Armenians paid 400 *tumans* per year to the Shah and were exempted from any other taxes; X pp. 15-20: The vizier Ali Quli Khan extorted money from them; Sanson, 1695, p. 8: Says that Shah Sulayman returned to the poor Armenians the money taken by Ali Quli Khan.
769. Baghdiantz, 1999, pp. 186-188: cf. Ter Yovhaneanc (1980), vol. 2 pp. 260-263; Chardin, 1811, III p. 119, VIII p. 103: New Julfa had 11 churches; Daulier-Deslandes, 1926, p. 26: New Julfa had more than twenty well built churches.
770. *Chronicle of the Carmelites*, 1939, I pp. 406-412; Baghdiantz, 1999, pp. 193-194.
771. Baghdiantz, 1999, p.166; Krusinski, 1728, p. 62: on the departure of Armenians; Jenkinson, 1886, I p. 58 fnte 1: Already in 1667 the Russians were striving to lure the Armenian merchants into their country.
772. Baghdiantz, 1999, pp. 186-188.
773. *Chronicle of the Carmelites*, 1939, I pp. 406-412; Bergasse, 1954, IV pp. 498, 500, 503: on the Armenians' migration and settlement in France; Seth, 1937, pp. 108, 120, 122-133: on the individual migration of Armenians to India, and on their settlement in India as evinced in the Armenian cemetery of Agra; p. 126 The author exclaims that there were no Armenian women buried in the cemetery before 1777, therefore the Armenians must not have migrated with their families until the beginning of the 18th century.
774. Baghdiantz, 1999, p. 186.
775. Krusinski, 1728, pp. 180-181: Father Krusinski, who was in Iran from 1705 to 1725, says however, that the Armenians of Julfa were still very wealthy.
776. Du Mans, 1995, II p. 143.
777. Chardin, 1811, VIII p. 106, X p. 21: In 1675 the poorer Armenians and the Zoroastrians had already been moved to New Julfa; Arakel of Tabriz, 1874, pp. 486-489: Shah Abbas II moved them from the centre of Isfahan; Daulier-Deslandes, 1926, p. 25; *Documents Inédits*, 1910, II p. 311: The Jesuit Alexander of Rhodes wrote in 1659 that the non-Julfan Armenians feared that the Shah would compel them to become Muslims like the Jews, but instead he forced them out of Isfahan; Baghdiantz, 1999, p. 86: Tavernier, 1981, vol. 2 p. 152; Ghougassian, 1998, p. 34: cf. Fryer, 1698, vol. II pp. 252-253.
778. Hanway, 1753, p. 116; Krusinski, 1728, II p. 44: Confirms Hanway's statement.

779. Ghougassian, 1998, p. 70; Du Mans, 1995, II p. 291: Gives relatively more information on Armenians deported from Erivan and Nakhchevan than the other European authors.
780. Chardin, 1811, V pp. 226-228, 235, 283, 306, 308, 333; Matthee, 1999, p. 63: on Shah Isma'il's import of Georgian and Circassian slaves.
781. Baghdiantz, 1999, pp. 50-51.
782. *Chronicle of the Carmelites*, 1939, II pp. 812-813; Fryer, 1698, p. 284: '...[Georgians] being a martial people bred up to the wars, and now serve the Emperor as his best infantry; of these, forty thousand are at present in arms under military pay, in and about Spahan.'
783. Le Bruyn, 1737, pp. 211, 233.
784. *Chronicle of the Carmelites*, 1939, II p. 813.
785. Anthony Sherley, *Sir Anthony Sherley and his Persian Adventure*, ed. E. Denison Ross, London, Routledge, 1933, p. 158: on Armenian and Georgian renegades at the court of Shah Abbas I; Pietro della Valle, 1972, pp. 239, 258; Du Mans, 1995, II pp. 19, 116.
786. *Chronicle of the Carmelites*, 1939, I pp. 48, 161; R. M. Savory, "The Safavid Administrative System", *The Cambridge History of Iran*, Cambridge, 1986, vol. 6 p. 363.
787. *Chronicle of the Carmelites*, 1939, I pp. 87-88, 153.
788. Tavernier, 1930, p. 148.
789. Tavernier, 1930, p. 154 fnte 2; Chardin, 1811, XIX p. 408; Krusinski, 1728, p. 122.
790. Sanson, 1695, p. 62: on Georgian and Circassian women in the *harem*.
791. Maria Szuppe, "La participation des femmes de la famille royale à l'exercice du pouvoir en Iran safavide au XVIe siècle", *Studia Iranica*, L'Association pour l'Avancement des Etudes Iraniennes, 1994, XXIII.2 p. 236 fnte 112; Fryer, 1698, p. 284: on the Queen mother's Georgian origins and royal descent.
792. Chardin, 1811, II p. 43.
793. Bayani, 1937, pp. 19-21.
794. Chardin, 1811, II p. 63, V p. 334, VII p. 319, X p. 29; Matthee, 1991, p. 31; Jenkinson, 1886, I p. 146; Arakel of Tabriz, 1874, pp. 275, 318-319.
795. Savory, 1986, p. 364; Roemer, "The Safavid Period", 1986, p. 272; Chardin, 1811, III pp. 403-404; Chardin, 1811, VI p. 152; Pietro della Valle, 1972, p. 349; Fryer, 1698, p. 256; Arakel of Tabriz, 1874, p. 334; Le Bruyn, 1737, I pp. 232-233.
796. *Chronicle of the Carmelites*, 1939, I pp. 322-323.
797. *Ibid.*, II pp. 898-899: In 1634, Father Ignatius of Jesus sought to reach the surviving Circassians transplanted by Shah Abbas I in Shiraz. They had requested spiritual help, but had no priests.
798. Joseph, 1961, pp. 30-31; see the difference with the account in *The Monks of Kublai Khan*, 1928, Introduction - pp. 92-94.
799. *Genuinae Relationes*, 1902, pp. 102-103: Based on letters gathered in the Vatican; p. 121: A letter from 1587 mentions the division of the community between those who adopted Catholicism (and were called afterwards Chaldeans) and those who remained Nestorian (called henceforth Assyrians).
800. *Chronicle of the Carmelites*, 1939, I pp. 382-383, 385, 388-389.

Notes

801. Tavernier, 1930, p. 59; Pietro della Valle, 1972, p. 40.
802. Joseph, 1961, pp. 30-31.
803. *Chronicle of the Carmelites*, 1939, I pp. 255-257; Moreen, 1981, pp. 131-132.
804. *Chronicle of the Carmelites*, 1939, I pp. 197-199.
805. *Ibid.*, p. 377.
806. *Ibid.*, pp. 382-383.
807. *Ibid.*, pp. 364-367.
808. Joseph, 1961, pp. 30-31.
809. Daulier-Deslandes, 1926, pp. 18-19, 26: Mentions that Armenians had brought an organ and paintings from Europe. Many of the paintings in the Churches were also brought from Europe.
810. Ghougassian, 1998, pp. 170-171, 174.
811. Le Bruyn, 1737, pp. 226-227.
812. Chardin, 1811, VIII p. 104.
813. Ghougassian, 1998, p. 60: cf. Tavernier, 1930, p. 225.
814. Ghougassian, 1998, pp. 182-183.
815. Ghougassian, 1998, pp. 182-183; *Documents Inédits*, 1907, I p. 447: The Carmelite Father Philippe, who was in Iran 1629-1640, witnessed the splendour of the houses owned by rich Julfan merchants.
816. Ghougassian, 1998, pp. 170-171, 174.
817. Seth, 1937, pp. 4-5.
818. Seth, 1937, p. 168; Asmussen, 1973, p. 111.
819. Amnon Netzer, *Manuscripts of the Jews of Persia in the Ben Zvi Institute*, Jerusalem, Ben Zvi Institute, 1985, p. 234.
820. Fischel, 1982, p. 290; Fischel, 1949, vol. III p. 836; Ugo Tucci, "Una relazione di Giovan Battista Vecchietti sulla Persia e sul Regno di Hormuz (1587)", *Oriente Moderno*, Roma, April 1955, XXXV-4 p. 150 fn 4: Giambattista Vecchietti (1552-1619) brought many manuscripts from the Orient, especially from Persia and India.
821. Fischel, 1949, pp. 826, 828, 830-831.
822. Moreen, 2000, pp. 30, 121-122.
823. Fischel, 1949, pp. 826, 828, 830-831.
824. Fischel, 1949, p. 835.
825. Moreen, 2000, pp. 119-122.
826. Mattatiah was a Jewish leader.
827. Moreen, 2000, pp. 159, 161-162, 171.
828. Moreen, 2000, pp. 184-185, 190-192.
829. He was active 80-110 A.D. cf Moreen, 2000, p. 342 fnte 4.
830. Netzer,1971, p. 101; Moreen, 2000, pp. 185, 188-189: The translation of the verses are from Moreen, except the ones in bracket which are my own; For another version of the translation see David Yeroushalmi, *The Judeo-Persian Poet 'Emrāni and his 'Book of Treasure'*, Leiden, Brill, 1995, pp. 269-275.
831. Yeroushalmi, 1995, pp. 269 fn 5, 275 fn 23.
832. *Ibid.*, p. 17: It is 1848 of the Seleucid era equivalent to 1536 AD.
833. For the original Persian text see Netzer, 1971, p. 112.

834.	For the original Persian text see Netzer, 1971, pp. 113-116.
835.	Moreen, 2000, p. 176; Fischel, 1949, p. 835.
836.	Moreen, 2000, p. 179.
837.	*Ibid.*, p. 143.
838.	*Ibid.*, p. 146.
839.	A type of narrated poem in rhymed couplets.
840.	Moreen, 1987, pp. 27, 43-44.
841.	Netzer, 1971, p. 154; Moreen, 2000, p. 284: This is her translation of the excerpt, but I have maintained Babai's form of the names; Ishaq (*Isaac*), Harun (*Aaron*), Moshe (*Moses*), Yahushu' (*Joshua*), and Yormia (*Tobiah*).
842.	Babai b. Farhad, 1990, p. 7: cf. v.144.
843.	Babai b. Farhad, 1990, p. 29.
844.	Moreen, 2000, p. 255.
845.	Zohar (or the Book of Splendour) is a mystical commentary on the Pentateuch. This book has an important place in the Jewish mystical literature.
846.	Kabbalists wrote on Jewish mystical tradition.
847.	Moses Maimonides is the most notable figure of Judaism in the post-talmudic era. He was a philosopher and an authority in rabbinic studies. He was born in Cordoba (Spain).
848.	El'azar was interested in Messer Leon's work as he was an adept of Maimonides cf. Yehoshua Horowitz, "Leon, Messer David ben Judah", *Encyclopaedia Judaica*, 1971, vol. XI cols. 27-28.
849.	Moreen, 2000, pp. 255-256.
850.	Fischel, 1949, p. 844.
851.	Moreen, 2000, p. 289.
852.	Babai b. Farhad, 1990, p. 44 fnte 238.
853.	Moreen, 2000, pp. 289-290; Babai b. Farhad, 1990, p. 16.
854.	Moreen, 2000, pp. 292-293.
855.	Moreen, 2000, pp. 146-148.
856.	For the original Persian text see Netzer, 1971, p.139.
857.	Fischel, 1949, p. 843; Moreen, 2000, p. 269.
858.	For the original Persian text see Netzer, 1971, p. 203.
859.	Moreen, 2000, p. 147 fnte. 4 cf. Muhammad Badi' b. Mawlana Muhammad Sharif Samarqandi (Maliha), *Muzakkir al-Ashab*, ms. 610, Fond Vostochnykh Rukopisei Akademiia Nauk, Dushanbe (Tajikestan), circa end of 17th c., pp. 197-198.
860.	A religious man vowed to poverty and austerity.
861.	Asmussen, 1973, pp. 110, 113-114; Niccolao Manucci, *Storia do Mogor, or Mogul India 1653-1708*, tr. William Irvine, London, J. Murray, 1907, I p. 223: Sarmad was according to him an atheist.
862.	Asmussen, 1973, p. 112.
863.	Seth, 1937, p. 174: شاه شاها نیم زاهد چونتو عریان نیستم، شوق و ذوق شورشم لیکن پریشان نیستم، بت پرستم کافرم از اهل ایمان نیستم، سوی مسجد میروم اما مسلمان نیستم.
864.	Asmussen, 1973, p. 111.

865. Fischel, 1982, p. 286: cf. Moses Pereyra de Paiva, *Notisias dos Judeos de Coching*, Amsterdam, 1687 (new pub. M.B. Amzalak, Lisbon, 1923).
866. Seth, 1937, pp. VII, IX.
867. Lord Henry, *Discoveries of the Sect of the Banians and Persees*, London, 1630, p. 4.
868. *A Collection of Letters from Iran written to the Mobeds and Behdins of India*, "Letter to Dastur Barzo Kamdin brought by Shariar Rustam Sandal in AnnoYazdgirdi 1019", Manuscript from the Dastur Meherjirana Library, Navsari (India), Catalogue F. 45 - VIII.9, pp. 269-270; Vitalone, 1987, p. 16.
869. *Rivayat-i Dastur Darab Hormazdyar*, transcribed in 1235 Anno Yazdgirdi (1867) from a manuscript completed in 1049 Anno Yazdgirdi (1681), Dastur Meherjirana Library, Navsari (India), I fol. 144:

کبوتر با کبوتر باز با باز   کند همجنس با همجنس پرواز

870. Frédéric Rosenberg, "Notices de Littérature Parsie", *Tracts of Pahlawi, Parsi and Persian Literature*, St. Petersbourg, 1909, p. 5 fn 2
871. *Rivayat-i Dastur Darab Hormazdyar*, 1867, I fol. 200.
872. *Koshti* is the sacred girdle wore by Zoroastrians.
873. *Rivayat-i Dastur Darab Hormazdyar*, 1867, I fol. 277-278.
874. *Ibid.*, fol. 384.
875. *Ibid.*, fol. 510.
876. *Ibid.*, fol. 519-521.
877. *Ibid.*, fol. 527.
878. *Rivayat of Kavus Kamdin, V. A letter from Iran in reply to a letter from Surat*, transcribed from a manuscript completed in 1254 Anno Yazdgirdi (1886), Dastur Meherjirana Library, Navsari (India), fol. 200.
879. *Vajarkard Dini or Dinkard*, from a manuscript transcribed in 1156 Anno Yazdgirdi (1788), Dastur Meherjirana Library, Navsari (India), fols. 213-215.
880. *Ibid.*, fol. 217.
881. These sources are mentioned at the end of the chapter.
882. *Mino Khirad*, 1883, fol. 139.
883. Jean Chardin, *Travels in Persia*, tr. Sir Percy Sykes, London, Argonaut Press, 1927, p. 130: Chardin confirms that there was more freedom in the Mughal Empire than in Iran.
884. Firby, 1988, p. 89: cf. Ahmad, p. 178; Sharma, p. 59.
885. Vitalone, 1987, p. 14.
886. A. D. H. Bivar, "Estakr", *Encyclopædia Iranica*, Costa Mesa (Ca.), Mazda Publishers, 1998, vol. VIII pp. 643-644.
887. Alessandro Bausani, *Persia Religiosa da Zaratustra a Baha'ullah*, Milano, Il Saggiatore, 1959, p. 387: cf Modi, "A Parsee High Priest, Dastur Azar Kaiwan with his Zoroastrian Disciples in Patna", *Journal of the K. R. Cama Oriental Institue*, 1932, XX, pp. 1-85.
888. Henri Corbin, "Azar Kayvan", *Encyclopædia Iranica*, 1989, pp. 183-187.
889. Mohamad Tavakoli-Targhi, "Contested Memories of Pre-Islamic Iran", *Medieval History*, 1999, Journal 3 pp. 245-275 - Journal still unpublished.
890. Corbin, 1989, pp. 183-187.
891. Tavakoli-Targhi, 1999, pp. 245-275.

892. John Walbridge, "A Persian Gulf in the Seas of Lights: The Chapter on Nawruz in the *Biḥār al-Anwār*", *Iran*, 1997, vol. XXXV p. 83: cf. *Biḥār al-Anwār*, Tehran, vol. LIX p. 92.
893. Walbridge, 1997, p. 90.
894. Morgan, 1988, p. 149; Roemer, "The Safavid Period", 1986, pp. 307, 313-314.
895. J. Calmard, "Mollā", *Encyclopaedia of Islam*, 1993, vol. VII p. 222; Morgan, 1988, p. 149.
896. Roemer, "The Safavid Period", 1986, p. 319.
897. Krusinski, 1728, II pp. 197-198: The decree was passed under Shah Sulayman and reinforced under Sultan Husayn.
898. Babai b. Farhad, 1990, pp. 27-29.
899. The people in question were the military figures such as Gurgin Khan, Prince Vakhtanga, Lutf Ali Khan, and the Grand Vizier Fath Ali Khan: Krusinski, 1728, I pp. 225, 229, 253, 268-269, II p. 367; Hanway, 1753, III pp. 73-83.
900. Gurgin Khan, the Georgian commander in chief, had warned Sultan Husayn about the rise of the ambitious Afghan leader Mir Vays, who despite being captured in 1704 was sent back by Sultan Husayn in 1709 to Qandahar, where he took full power. After his death, his son Mir Mahmud usurped the power in 1717 and led the army to the Iranian Plateau: Krusinski, 1728, I pp. 151-155, 164-165, 182-183, 189, 196, 201-202, 207-208; Hanway, 1753, III pp. 31, 42, 50, 56-57, 58.
901. Krusinski, 1728, II p. 113.
902. Hanway, 1753, III pp. 105, 248.
903. Krusinski, 1728, I pp. 220-221, II pp. 11-13, 47-49, 120; Hanway, 1753, III pp. 99, 104, 117-118, 166; Jean Aubin, "Les Sunnites du Lārestān et la Chute des Safavides", *Revue des Études Islamiques*, Paris, 1965, XXXIII pp. 93, 153, 159 : 'Sous le choc de l'invasion afghane les défections ont été moins nombreuses que les fidélités. Seuls les minoritaires, Sunnites et Zoroastriens, qui n'avaient rien à perdre se sont engagés (les Arméniens beaucoup moins).'
904. Krusinski, 1728, II p. 146; Hanway, 1753, III p. 203.
905. Krusinski, 1728, II pp. 197-198; *Chronicle of the Carmelites*, 1939, I p. 474: Gives 1697-98 as a date for their forced conversion; Babai b. Farhad, 1990, p. 64: The hardships bore by the Zoroastrians is manifest in the declaration proclaimed by Mahmud's successor Shah Ashraf at Kashan: 'And whoever is not Muslim will not be oppressed even if he belongs to the Zoroastrian faith.' Willem Floor, *The Afghan Occupation of Safavid Persia 1721-1729*, Paris , Cahiers de Studia Iranica 9, 1998, pp. 50, 57: Information gathered from the Colonial Archives in the Netherlands.
906. Krusinski, 1728, II pp. 46, 61-62; Hanway, 1753, III p. 120.
907. Babai b. Farhad, 1990, pp. 30-31; Floor, 1998, p. 93: Zoroastrians and Armenians were not molested.
908. Babai b. Farhad, 1990, pp. 45, 48-49; Moreen, 2001, pp. 289, 292-293.
909. Krusinski, 1728, II p. 46.
910. Krusinski, 1728, II pp. 197-198: Edict of Shah Ashraf.
911. Before the Sassanians, the Iranian state did not identify itself with a specific religion despite the preponderance of Zoroastrianism in that country.

912.	Fattal, 1958, p. 117-118, 268: The case of Zoroastrians was always uncertain; *Chronique de Séert*, 1919, part II (Orientalis 13) p. 628: 'The Arabs destroyed fire temples but honoured Christians.'
913.	The Nestorian Christians have not left any material written in Persian from this period; however, in some works of translations written in Syriac the translator has testified that the original text was written in Persian. This shows that the Nestorians had begun writing in Persian under the Mongols: cf. Anecdotes related to the lives of Rabban Bar Sauma and Mar Yahballaha III in *The Monks of Kublai Khan*, 1928, p. XIV.
914.	R. D. McChesney, *Central Asia, Foundations of Change*, Princeton, 1996, p. 236.
915.	R. Macuch, "Assyrians in Iran", *Encyclopaedia Iranica*, 1987, II p. 818.
916.	Tabari, 1999, V p. 298.
917.	Fischel, 1949, p. 817: He says that 'Jews are an inseparable part of Iran's national destiny.'
918.	Baghdiantz, 1999, p. 5.
919.	Joseph, 1961, p. 25.

Appendix

Chapter 5 - Section 1

Excerpts from *Mino Khirad or Vasf-i Khirad, and Nushirvan and his "Marquzan"*, copied in 1251 Anno Yazdgirdi (1883) from a manuscript written by Anushirvan Pur Marzban in 1620, Dastur Meherijirana Library, Navsari (India).

fol. 253-254

از آن پس یکی نامه آورد پیش   بخط زراتشت پاکیزه کیش
که بُد یکسر آن نامه ای معنوی   نوشته بر او به خط پهلوی
چو آن نامه را رامش آرام خواند   در او درج معنی بر ایشان فشاد
هر آنچه که آید بگیتی پدید   همیخواند و در گوش ایشان شنید
نشانهای عهد محمد تمام   بیان کرد از نامه با نظام
که از مکه آید چگونه پدید   بر او یار گردد سیاه و سپید
....

چو موبد مران داستانها بخواند علی چونکه بشنید خیره بماند

Appendix

fol. 257

به آتشگه فارس خواندم چنین   که نوشیروان آن شه بآفرین

به کوه مداءن یکی دخمه ساخت   سرش را بگردون گردان فراخت

بدان کوه خواهم کنون یافت راه   که لختی کنم دخمه اش را نگاه

مگر از ره داد او بر خورم   چو بر رسم و آیین او بنگرم

fol. 273

بنزدیک مرغوزن بی نظیر   چنین گفت با نامداران امیر

که نزدیک این دخمه نامدار   نباید که باشیم برزین سوار

fols. 274-275

روان شد علی بر سوی شاه داد   چو چشمش منوشیروان بر افتاد

چون آن فّرو آن یال آگنده دید   لب خویشتن را بدندان گذید...

بنزدیک تختش ستایش نمود   ستایش همی بر ترایش نمود

[بگفتا]

چرا من بر او کینه ای خواستم   بناهای وی را تبه خواستم

از آن کارها پشیمان منم   ببخشا ای یارب که پیچان منم...

نوشته بدینان شه دادگر   که زین جهان چونکه سازم گذر

پس از من گذشته بسی سالیان   یکی پادشه باشد از تازیان

بمرغوزن آید بدیدار من   چو بیند هنرها و کردار من

به من پر ز نیکوی بنگرد   برین دخمه پر وقفها گسترد

fols. 286-287

سه روزش بد اندر مداءن مقام   چهارم سوی کعبه برداشت گام

سوی خانه اعظم آورد روی   بر آنجا زیارت نمود ز آرزوی

بهر جا که رو کرد شیر خدای   همی بر نهان بود نیکی فزای

سخن داشت از داد نوشیروان   همی بود به یاد نوشیروان

یکی عهد بنوشت با دین و داد   زدین بهی کرد هر گونه یاد

که از اهل بهدین ستم دور باد   جفاجوی آن قوم رنجور بآد

رساند کسی گر بران قوم بیم   او را جای باشد به قعر جحیم

بران قوم هر کس بود خوش منش   نبیند ز آل نبی سرزنش

بهر دو سرا باشدش خوشدلی   به قول رسول و به عهد علی

دگر باره دین بهی را علم   فرازید و برکند بیخ ستم

Appendix

Chapter 5 - Section 2

Excerpts from Amnon Netzer, *Poems of the Jews of Persia and Bukhara*, Jerusalem, 1971.

Ganj-nama (Mulana Imrani)

ربی یوسی هکهن فرماید:

باشی بمیان سروران تاج	خواهی نشوی بخلق محتاج
هرگز نکنی جوی خیانت	باید که ترا بود امانت
پیش تو امانتی که دارد	یاری که امانتی سپارد
زانگونه که امر کرده تورا .	باید که نگاه داری او را
قایم دل آنکسی که دایم	عالم بامانت است قایم
کاری ننهد نگردن کس	یک جونبرد زخرمن کس
از مدعیان چه باک دارد	شخصی که حساب پاک دارد
در خواندن علم بود مدارا	این پند ز بنده گیر یارا
فرزند پدر بحق رساند	زنهار مگو پسر بخواند
از علم مراست کام حاصل	یا خود پدرم که هست فاضل
نیکو سخنی است گر بدانی	خوش گفت حکیم این معانی
از فضل پدر ترا چه حاصل	"گیرم پدر تو بود فاضل

Ganj-nama (Mulana Imrani)

در سال اتتمج٠ از هدایت   حق کرده به بنده این عنایت
یارب که همیشه در جهان باد   زو باد دل جهانیان شاد
بر جمله خجسته باد و پیروز   آراسته باد همچو نوروز
یارب پی این رسد کءولا٠   بر خسته دلان بود رفوا٠
صد رحمت کردگار یزدان   بروح روان ابن عمران

p.113-116 - Story of the Seven Brothers (Mulana Imrani)

یکی بشنو که بر اولاد یعقوب   چها آمد از آن گبران مقلوب
ببین تا آن سرافرازان دیندار   چها دیدند از آن گبران کفار
چه محنتها و زحمتها کشیدند   بهر بابی ازین دنیا چه دیدند
ز بابل و ز ادومی٠ ستمکار   چها آمد بدان قومان دیندار
سر خود یک بیک بر کف نهادند   عنان دین حق از دست ندادند
نخستین بخت نصر آن گبر عارل٠   چو آمد بار اول او ز بابل
بسوزانید میقداش٠ خدا را   پس آنکه ملک خاص حق تعالی
زاسرائیل توراه٠ را بر انداخت   جهان را جملگی زیر و زبر ساخت
بیک روز آن ستمکار نگونسار   بکشت از اهل دین بیرون ز اشمار
...

چو شد هفتاد سال آخر دگر بار   کریم پر کرم دانای اسرار
دگر ره رحمت خود را عیان کرد   نظر بر حال آن بیچارگان کرد
...

بدست لشکر پاراس و مادی٠   در آورد آن سگان را جمله از پی

Appendix

شـه پاراس و مادی. آن نکو رای
جهانبان داد الهام تمامش
جهان را چون مسخر کرد یکسر
منادی کرد در هر ملک و کشور
روان گردند بشهر خود دگربار
دگر میقداش. حق آباد سازند
فرستاد آنگهی آن مرد هشیار
که میباید که بر اولاد عبّر

...

از این تاریخ چون شد چارصد سال
بحکم اینکه عاوون. کار گشتیم
چو شد این عهد را تقصیر بسیار
همه چون بخت نصر گبرخونخواه
دگر ره ملک خاص حق گرفتند
چو پای آن عارلیم و طمییم.
دگر میقداش. را کردند ویران
پس آنگاهی ستم بنیاد کردند

که کورش خواند او را مرد دانای
جهان بگرفت و حاصل گشت کامش
جهانبان بر دلش انداخت دیگر
که باشد اندر آنجا نسل عبّر.
کنند آباد ملک خاص جبار
ز غمهای جهان آزاد گردند
بسرداران آن موضع دگر بار
نگردد کس مزاحم بار دیگر

دگر باره ز ما برگشت اقبال
همه از راه میصواه. دور گشتیم
ز روم آمد سپاه و خیل بسیار
سرهنگانش همه خونریز بد خواه
از آنجانب سوی میقداش. رفتند
رسید آنجا در آنجا کرد تصمیم
که صد لعنت بر ایشان باد گبران
ابا یعقوبیان بیداد کردند

Daniyal-nama (Khwaja Bukhara'i)

سزاوول فرستادن بلشاصر با طراف دیار خود بسبب جمع کردن لشکر و
سوار شدن بجنگ داریوش عراقی و کورش پارسی

ملک بسیار از این معنی بر آشفت	زیانگیر این سخن چون پیش شه گفت
بفرق تاج زرین شاه پر زد	بمردی دامن خود بر کمر زد
که راند خلق را از امر شاهی	بهر جانب سزاوول کرد راهی
ز سرپا ساخته وویش دویدند	سپاه شه چو این فرمان شنیدند

...

چه سهراب جوان و رستم زال	ببازوی قوی و یال و کوپال
که یکتا بود در ایام ماضی	چه بیژن هر یکی در ترک تازی
بسان بهمن وسام نریمان	دلاور هر یکی در روز میدان
زبرزو و فرامرز ی فریدون	بمردی هر یکی بودند افزون
بهیجا هر یکی افراسیابی	نه عاری هیچیک در هیچ بابی

Appendix

Kitab-i Anusi: (Babai b. Lutf)

مقدمه کتاب انوسی.

الهی حق بینیان درگاه بمهر و مشتری و زهره و ماه
بحق رفعت عرش عظیم بحق جمله خاصان قدیمت
بحق جملی ملّاخ. مقدم بحق عرش و فروش و نسل آدم
بحق نوح و ابراهیم سرور باسحق و بیعقوب پیامبر
بحق یوسف صدیق و مسکین که بودی داءماً شمع دل و دین
بحق موشه. و هارون. و پینحاس. که شد در درگه تو خاص و اخلاص
بداود و بدرگاه سلیمون. بحق گرد یهوشوع بن نون.
بحق یرمیا. آن پیر با فر بیاد آور خدا آن جور قیصر

Antiukus-nama (Yusuf b. Ishaq b. Musa)

صفت شرح آنطیوکوس را گوید

همی خواهم ز مطلب سازم اظهار اگر گردد مدد از لطف جبار
ز آنطیوکوس اکنون داستانی همی خواهم کنم اکنون بیانی
شجاعی بود آن شاه ستمکار که بودی لشکرش بیرون ز اشمار
کشید لشکر بسوی هند ناگاه مسخر کرد و برگردید آن شاه
بسوی روم لشکر برد فراوان گرفت او روم را برگشت شادان
بزیر حکم چندین شهرها کرد پس آنگه رو بشهر خویش آورد
بتخت سلطنت بنشست خرم بشادی روز و شب بود فارغ از غم
خراجش را ز هر اطراف عالم بدادندی شهان از بیش و از کم

Excerpt from *Rivayat-i Dastur Darab Hormazdyar*, copied in 1235 Anno Yazdgirdi (1867) from a manuscript completed in 1049 Anno Yazgird (1681), Dastur Meherijirana Library, Navsari (India) I.

fol. 200 *Rivayat-i Kamdin Shapur*

چنین بوقت سیاوسیوش ببندست آن دیو پی رأی هوش

و زآنپس چو از بند گردد رها شود کشته بردست سام اژدها

بدینسان فریدون بدانش پژوه ببسته بردماوند کوه

ازآن پس خردمندان راد مرد بپرسد دیگر ز مینو خرد

fol. 277

زراتشت زایشان بدید آنزمان که بودند کستی همه بر میان

انیران و ایران ندانی اکثر بگویم که یابی از ایشان خبر

چو زراتشت اسپیمان در جهان آمد پدید مردم ایران زمین را کشتی بسته دید

فرق آنست ایران و انیران میان بند کشتی دارند بر میان ایرانیان

fol. 384 *Rivayat-i Kamdin Bahra*

از روایات کامدین بهره

پرسش آنکه استودان کهنه بر زمین انیران باشد و چو آب در زمین میکنند استخوان مردگان در آب می ایستد و انیران نمیفروشد و نمی گذارد که پرامن آن استودان دیوار کنند و بیم آن هست که آن استودان در کشت و برز آورند. آن استخوان در زیر خاک شود واوستان چون – پاسخ اینکه: دست در دامن پادشاه باید زدن و بخواهش بسی تا آن استخوانها از آب

Appendix 217

بپرهیزید و پرسنده گفت که این نیز کردیم و یکچندی از شرم مردمان و از ترس پادشاه دست از آن پاره جای بداشتیم و لیکن از امید ایمنی نیست. گزراند. گفت که زمانه دورانی است و جهد خویش باید کرد و بر امید بهی میباید بود که مگر روزی آید که آنزمین از دست انیران بیرون توان کرد و چون جهد خویشتن کرده باشی و آن کار برود کرفه عظیم و بزرگوار باشد اگر بنه رود تو کم گناه باشی.

fol. 510 *Rivayat-i Nariman Hoshang*

از روایات نریمان هوشنگ

پرسش: میوه هر بابت که مسلمانان می آورند بدست ایشان خوردن و نخوردن و با جددینان وانیرانیان نشستن و با ایشان خوردن یا نه.

پاسخ اینکه: هر بابت از دست ایشان که ترامیدن دارد و یعنی که تخمه رویندگی می باشد چون بشویند شاید خوردن وگر چون تخمه رویندگی ندارد در دین بهدین نمیباشد و با ایشان نشستن و طعام خوردن بهیچ نوع و بهیچ وچیزی نمی شاید گناه باشد.

fols. 519-521 *Rivayat-i Kamdin Bahra*

از روایات کامدین بهره

پرسش اینکه: انیری که دل بدین به دارد و بنسا رمین شد و از ترس دیگران برشنوم نتواند کردن - دادستان چون پاسخ اینکه در هشتم فرگرد وندیوداد گوید که هر کس که شصت فرسنگ از برشنوم کرد و باشد رمین، کسی را ندای باید گرفت پادیاب کرد و خشک کرد و هم ا ندای گاو پادیاب بگرفت و هم با ندای بر سر وی میریخت تا همه جای تر شود و پس بخاک خویشتن را از آن نم پادیاب خشک کند تا سی بار پادیاب می شوید و با خاک خشک میکند و پس یکبار با آب بشوید ... و انیری که دل به دین دارد و رمین شود همچنین باید شست.

fol. 527 *Rivayat-i Kawus Kaman*

از روایت کاووس کامان

در باب اینکه ایزد هر درد را داروءی داده است همه حقیقت آن

ترا باید دانستن که زدار اهرمن دیندارانند و از دار او خرند خشم؛ بسیار دانش باید تا او را بتوانند زدن چه کین آنست که چون در تن راه دهند، راه دین بسته شود...

در میان مسلمانان چو کین در افتاد آسپس (ز آن پس) بهفتاد و سه گروه شدند و هیچ آن نام نمی برند که در مذهب سخن می گویند و همه کین کشتن حسن و حسین بود و ایشان رفتند و کین در جهان مانده است پس به آن باشد که کین در تن راه ندهد زیرا پرهیز کردن را به از دارو خردن است و مقصود آنکه ز دار هر بدی نیکی است و ز دار گرسنگی نانست و ز دار تشنگی آبست و ز دار برهنگی جامه است.

Appendix

Rivayat-i Kawus Kamdin, V. A letter from Iran in reply to a letter from Surat, copied from a manuscript completed in 1254 Anno Yazdgirdi (1886), Dastur Meherijirana Library, Navsari (India).

fols. 114-116

از اجتهام و کثرت دستوران و موبدان و فاضلان و کاملان این طایفه که از آدم تا بعالم شاهد حال و گواه این حقیقتند... اینچنین گفته گوئی در نزد مردمان اهل تمیز بسیار بعید و غریب می نماید و هرگاه ایشان بر آنند که چون از سبب حادثه ها قطع دولت و غالب گشتن اهل عرب شاید اشتباه بظهور رسیده باشد. درست فرموده اند تا ما بعد از انتقال دولت ما مردم حقیقت ایران بملوک طوایف مبدل و منتهی گشت و تا به مدتها که مقاتل و مجادله عظیم واقع بود تا عنقریب چهار صد سال از مرور مدت مذکور بتدریج ملک ایران بدخل عرب بر آمد قایم الملوک گشتند، چنانکه حقیقت روی داد این مقال در کتبها و تواریخها نظم و نثر مفصل مذکور و مسطور است لیکن در این باب شاید بمطالعه مردمان اهل آنجانب نرسیده باشد و دیگر آنکه اعلام فرموده بودند که چون بعضی مردمان از مره موندان و حلقه بهدینان از سبب یکماهه اختلافی که فیما بین اینجانب و آن جانب واقعه بود بسبب اختلاف مذکور رخنه و شک در خاطر اکثر مردمان راه یافته که امور و مهمات دینی از جمع اسباب در عالم اختلاف و مبدل گذران است. بنابرین تفاوت آنرا تبدیل نموده به روش ایران مقرر و منظور داشته هند (باید روش ایران را دنبال کند).

Vajarkard Dini or Dinkard, from a manuscript copied in 1156 Anno Yazgirdi (1788), Dastur Meherijirana Library, Navsari (India).

fols. 213-215

پادشاهی نوشیروان بن قباد، که او را کسری خوانند چهل و هشت سال بود و در مداءن طاقی عظیم بساخت که مقدار شصت گز طول و شصت گز عرض داشت و شبی که پیغمبر عربی از مادر متولد شد آن طاق بر هم شکست و بیفتاد و همان شب نوشیروان در خواب دید که شخصی رقعت بدو داد و گفت بخوان. چون بخواند نوشته بود که چون تاریخ اسکندر به نهصد سال رسد پیغمبری از جزیره عرب برخیزد و دعوای پیغمبری کند و برهان او بهفت کشور برسد، همه عالم مسخر گرداند و پادشاهی از این خاندان شما ببرد و دین و آیین کیان ناچیز کند و جهان به آلودگی و ناپاکی و فسخ و فساد ببالاید و بدی بر بدی افزون کرد و دروغ و کژی و خیانت در جهان روا گردد وجماعت بهدینان تابع آن قوم باشند و زندگانی بسختی گذرانند ودین زراتشتی ضعیف گردد و اکثر بهدینان از ظلم و تعدی بدین دروند شوند و چون نوشیروان از خواب برجست در لرزه افتاد و ساعتی بیهوش گشت و کلاب و شک بر وی پاشیدند تا بهوش آمد و بسیار اندیشناک شد.

Appendix

fol. 217

زمان پادشاهی یزدگرد فتنه در میان عرب وعجم واقع شده بود
که ملوک عجم بدین عرب در آید و یزدگرد از این سخن
پذیرفته نشد و بر دین خود قایم بود و عمر بن خطاب نامه به
یزدگرد نوشت که بر دین ایشان گراید و نپذیرفت. پس آنگاه
سعد و قاص باسپاه گران روی به مداءن نهادند و خزانه یزدگرد
بتاراج بردند و آنچه حکمت یونان بود بنزد عمر خطاب بردند،
بفرمود که همه را بسوزانید و گفت که ما را قران بس است و
یزدگرد از نسیب تازیان روی بهزیمت نهاد و بگریخت و
بجانب عراقین رفت و از آنجا بخراسان رفت و در مرو کشته
شد و لشکر عرب تمام ممالک ایران را بتصرف خود گرفتند و
دین هاشمی رواج کردند و جهان بر بدی و آلودگی بماند تا
آنوقتی که رستاخیز شود و جهان از بدی و آلودگی پاک گردد.

Excerpts from *Mino Khirad or Vasf-i Khirad, and Nushirvan and his "Marquzan"*, copied in 1251 Anno Yazdgirdi (1883) from a manuscript written by Anushirvan Pur Marzban in 1620, Dastur Meherijirana Library, Navsari (India).

fols. 139-140 On the Invasion of Mahmud the Afghan

لشکر کشیدن محمود افغان بکرمان و در غارت و بیدادی او گوید

بلا را خلق اماج شد	که کرمان در این وقت تاراج شد
روانشد بکرمان زمین کینه توز	یکی لشکر از جانب نیم روز
سپهدار گردید اسیر سر بر	چو بر اهل کرمان رسید این خبر

هزیمت پذیرفت ناکرده جنگ	پراکنده بر فرق خود خاک ننگ
بزرگان نهادند سر در گریز	سپه جمله رفت و سپهدار نیز
بکرمانیان راه درمان نماند	کسی از بزرگان بکرمان نماند
یکایک بسویی گریزان شدند	به بیچارگی اشک ریزان شدند
گروهی به وادی شده راه جوی	گروهی بکهسار کردند روی
گروهی فرومانده بر جای خویش	گروهی به چه کرده مهوای خویش
برین درد جویای درمان شده	سراسر درین کار حیران شده
جهانجوی محمود بیدادگر	که آمد سپهدار تاراجگر
سپهدار افغان گسترده کام	که بودش پدر ویس جنگی بنام
بتاراج کرمان سرافراخته	ز هر سو کران لشکری ساخته
زجان شسته دست و بخون شسته	سپاهش سراسر بسان پلنگ چنگ
همه گرد گردنکش نیزه دار	سواران کین جوی با گبر ودار
همه بد نژاد و همه بد گهر	همه زشت کیش و همه کینه ور
سراسر جفاجوی و بی زینهار	همه خون مردم خور و ناپکار
پی قصد مردم ستمکار تر	همه یک ز دیگر پر آزارتر
سپه کش بر ایشان یکی مرد گرد	سراسر چو دیوان با دستبرد

Selected Bibliography

Primary Sources

Medieval Sources

ABU YUSUF (d. 798). *Kitab al-Kharaj (Taxation in Islam)*, tr. A. Ben Shemesh, Leiden, Brill, 1969, 3 vols.

'AHARI, Abu Bakr al-Qutbi (14th c.). *Tarikh-i Shaykh Uwais*, ed. & tr. J. B. Van Loon, The Hague, Excelsor, 1954.

APHRAATES (4th c.). *Aphraatis Sapientis Persae, Demonstrationes (The (22) Homilies of Aphraates the Persian Sage), Patrologia Syriaca*, ed. D. I. Parisol, Paris, Firman-Didot, 1894, t. I.

ARAKEL OF TABRIZ (17th c.). "Livres d'Histoires", *Collection d'Historiens Arméniens*, ed. & tr. M. Brosset, St. Petersbourg, 1874, I pp. 267-608.

BABAI B. FARHAD (18th c). *Iranian Jewry during the Afghan Invasion: The Kitab-i Sar Guzasht-i Kashan of Babai ibn Farhad*, ed. Vera B. Moreen, Stuttgart, Franz Steiner, 1990.

BALADHURI (d. 892). *Futuh al-Buldan (The Origins of the Islamic State)*, tr. P.K. Hitti and F.C. Murgotten, New York, 1916.

BAR HEBRAEUS (d. 1286). *Chronicon Ecclesiasticum*, ed. & tr. T. J. Lamy & J. B. Abbeloos, Leuven, Peeters, 1872, 2 vols.

BAR HEBRAEUS (d. 1286). *Chronography*, ed. & tr. E. A. Wallis Budge, London 1932, 2 vols.

BIDLISI, Sharaf al-Din (16th c.). *Sharaf-nama (Fastes de la Nation Kourde)*, ed. & tr. François B. Charnoy, St. Petersbourg, 1868.

DENYS OF TELL-MAHRE (d. 845). *Chronique de Denys de Tell-Mahré*, ed. J. B. Chabot, Paris, 1895.

ELIAS OF NISIBIS (d. 1190). *Chronography (Chronographie de Mar Elie Bar Šinaya Métropolitain de Nisibe)*, tr. L. J. Delaporte, Bibliothèques de l'École des Hautes Études, Paris 1910.

GRIGOR OF AKANC' (13th c.). "History of the Nation of the Archers", tr. R. P. Blake and R. N. Frye, *Harvard Journal of Asiatic Studies*, 1949, XII pp. 269-399.

HAFIZ ABRU (d. 1430). *Zayl-i-Jami' al-Tawarik-i Rashidi (703-781 H.)*, ed. Khanbaba Bayani, Tehran, 1977.

HASAN RUMLU (16th c.). *A Chronicle of the Early Safawis: The Ahsan al-Tawarikh*, tr. C. Seddon, Baroda, Oriental Institute, 1934.

HAYTON, Jean (d. 1308). "La flor des estoires de la terre d'Orient", *Recueil des Historiens des Croisades, Documents Arméniens*, ed. E. Dulaurier, Comte Riant, C. Schefer, Louis de Mas Latrie, Paris, Imprimerie Nationale, 1906, II pp. 113-253.

HAYTON, Jean (d. 1308). "Relation", *L'Extrême Orient au Moyen Age*, ed. Louis de Backer, Paris, 1877, pp. 125-255.

IBN ABI USAYBI'A (d. 1279). *Uyun al-Anba' fi Tabaqat al-Atibba*, ed. A. Müller, Cairo, 1882, 2 vols.

IBN AL-ATHIR (d. 1233). *Al-Kamil fi 'l-Tarikh (The Annals of the Saljuk Turks)*, tr. D. S. Richards, London, Routledge, 2000.

IBN FADLALLAH AL-'UMARI (d. 1349). *Masalik al-Absar fi Mamalik al-Amar (Das Mongolische Weltreich)*, ed. Klaus Lech, Wiesbaden, Otto Harrassowitz, 1968.

IBN AL-HITI (15th c.). *Ibn al-Hiti's Arabic Chronicle of Karaite Doctors*, tr. G. Margoliouth, London, Reprinted from the *Jewish Quarterly Review*, 1897.

IBN ISFANDIYAR (13th c.). *Tarikh-i Tabaristan (613 H., 1216 A.D.)*, ed. 'Abbas Eqbal, Tehran, Khavar, 1988.

IBN KHALLIKAN (d. 1282). *Wafayat al-'Ayan wa-Anba' al-Zaman*, ed. Ihsan Abbas, Beirut, 1968-72.

IBN AL-NADIM (d. 995). *Kitab al-Fihrist (The Fihrist of Ibn al-Nadim)*, tr. Bayard Dodge, New York, Columbia University Press, 1970.

IBN AL-QIFTI (13th c.). *Tarikh al-Hukama'-i Qifti*, tr. (to Persian) Behin Darai, Tehran, 1968.

IBN QUTAYBA (d. 889). *'Uyun al-Akhbar*, tr. J. Horovitz, *Islamic Culture*, 1930, IV.

IBN RUSTAH (9th - 10th c.). *Kitab al-A'lak un Nafisa*, ed. M. J. De Goeje, Leiden, Brill, 1892.

IBN AL-UKHUWWA (1329). *Ma'alim al-Qurba fi Ahkam al-Hisba*, ed. Reuben Levy, Cambridge, 1938.

ISKANDAR BEG MUNSHI (d. 1628). *Zayl-e Tarikh-i Alam Aray-yi Abbasi*, ed. S. Khwansari, Tehran, 1938.

ISHO'YAHB PATRIARCH III (d. 659). *Liber Epistularum Mar Isho yahb*, ed. & tr. Rubens Duval, Paris, CSCO, 1905.

ISTAKHRI (d. 958). *Kitab Masalik wa Mamalik*, ed. Iraj Afshar, Tehran, Intisharat-i Ilm va Farhang, 1990.

JAHIZ (d. 869), *Kitab al-Akhbar wa Kayfa Tasihh* (Al-Gahiz: Les Nations Civilisées et leurs Croyances Religieuses), ed. Charles Pellat, *Journal Asiatique*, Paris, 1967, t. 255, pp. 65-105.

JAHIZ (d. 869). *Kitab al-Bukhala' (The Book of Misers)*, tr. R. B. Sergeant, Reading, 1997.

JOHN CATHOLICOS (17th c.). *Histoire d'Arménie par le patriarche Jean VI dit Jean Catholicos (Littérature Historique de l'Arménie)*, tr. M. J. Saint-Martin & ed. F. Nève, Paris, 1841.

JOHN BAR PENKAYE (7th c.). *Sources Syriaques*, ed. A. Mingana, Leipzig, 1907, I pp. 172-197 (Syriac pp. 143-171).

JUNABADI, Mirza Qasim (16th c.). *Rawzat al-Safaviyya*, ed. Ghulamreza Tabatabai Majed, Tehran, 2001.

JUWAYNI. *Tarikh-i Jahan Gusha*, ed. Mirza M. Qazwini, Leiden, Brill, 1912-1916, 2 vols.

JUWAYNI (d. 1283). *Tarikh-i Jahan Gusha (The History of the World Conqueror)*, tr. from the text of M. M. Qazwini by J. A. Boyle, Manchester, Manchester University Press, 1958, 2 vols.

JUJZANI (d. 1260). *Tabaqat-i Nasiri*, ed. Abdulah Habibi, Kabul, Historical Society of Afghanistan, 1963.

KEYKAVUS B. ISKANDAR (d. 1089). *Qabus Namah*, ed. Said Naficy, Tehran, 1933.

KHURSHAH B. QUBAD AL-HUSAYNI (d. 1565). *Tarikh-i Ilchi-i Nizam Shah (History of the Safavid Dynasty until 972 H (1565 A.D.)*, ed. M.R. Nasiri and Koichi Haneda, Tehran, 2000.

KIRAKOS OF GANTZAK (d. 1271). "Les Mongols d'après les historiens arméniens", tr. E. Dulaurier, *Journal Asiatique*, Paris, 1858, XI.

MAHBUB (AGAPIUS) OF MANBIJ (10th c.). *Kitab al-Unvan (Histoire Universelle)*, ed. & tr. A. Vasiliev, 1909 (Patrologia Orientalis), VIII.

MAIMONIDES, Moses (d. 1204). *Iggeret Teiman*, tr. Boaz Cohen, *A Maimonides Reader*, ed. Isadore Twersky, New York, 1972, pp. 437-463.

MAQRIZI (d. 1442). *Suluk li Ma'rifa al-Duwal al-Muluk (Histoire des Sultans Mamlouks de l'Egypte)*, tr. M. Quatremère, Paris, 1837, 2 vols.

MAR DENHA (7th c.). *Histoire des Divines Actions de Saint Mar Marouta l'Ancien (7th c.) (Histoire d'Ahoudemmeh et de Marouta)*, ed. F. Nau, Paris, 1905, pp. 52-96.

MARI B. SULAYMAN (13th c.). *Akhbar Batarikat Kurs y al-Mashriq (Maris, Amri et Slibae de Patriarchis Nestorianorum Commentaria)*, ed. E. Gismondi, Rome, 1896, 2 vols.

MARTAN FARRUX-I OHRMAZDDATAN (10th c.). *Skand Gumarik Vicar (La solution décisive des doutes)*, ed. J. De Menasce, Fribourg (Switz.), 1945.

MARTIN, François (17th c.). *Mémoires de François, Fondateur de Pondichéry (1665-1696)*, ed. A. eau, Paris, 1931, 3 vols.

MAS'UDI (d. 956). *Kitab al-Tanbih wa' l-Ishraf (Le livre de l'Avertissement et de la Révision)*, tr. B. Carra de Vaux, Paris, 1896.

MAS'UDI (d. 956). *Muruj al-Dhahab wa Ma'adin al-Jawhar (Prairies d'or)*, tr. G. Barbier de Meynard & Pavet de Courtelle, Paris, 1875, 7 vols.

MICHAEL LE SYRIEN (12th c.). *Chronique de Michel le Syrien Patriarche Jacobite d'Antioche 1166-1199*, ed. & tr. J. B. Chabot as *Chronique de Michel le Syrien,* Paris 1905.

MSHIHA-ZHKA (6th c.). *Sources Syriaques*, ed. A. Mingana, Leipzig, 1908, I pp. 76-158 (Syriac pp. 1-75).

MUSTAWFI QAZWINI, Hamdallah (14th c.). *Nuzhat al-Qulub*, ed. G. Le Strange, Leiden, Brill, 1913.

NARSHAKHI (10th c.). *History of Bukhara*, tr. R. N. Frye, Cambridge Ma., 1954.

NIZAMI, Aruzi Samarqandi (12th c.). *Chahar Maqala*, ed. Muhammad Mu'in, Tehran, Kitabfurushi-i Zawar, 1952.

NUWAYRI (d. 1323). *Nihayat al-Arab fi Funun al-Adab*, Cairo, Dar al-Kutub al-Masriya, 1933, 23 vols.

QAZWINI, Yahya ibn Abd al-Latif (d. 1555). *Lubb al-Tawarikh*, Tehran, Mu'assasah-i Khavar, 1935.

QIRQISANI (10th c.). *Kitab al-Anwar wa'l Maraqib*, ed. L. Nemoy, New York, 1939, 5 vols.

QIRQISANI (10th c.). *Ya' qub al-Qirqisani on Jewish Sects and Christianity*, ed. Bruno Chiesa & tr. Wilfrid Lockwood, Frankfurt am Main, Peter Lang, 1984.

RABBAN HORMIZD (7th c.). *The Histories of Rabban Hormizd the Persian and Rabban Bar-Idta*, ed. E. A. W. Budge, London, Luzac, 1902, 2 vols.

RAGHIB AL-ISFAHANI (d. 1108). *Muhadarat al-Udaba wa-Muhawarat al-Shu'ara wa al-Bulagha'*, Cairo, Matba' al-Amira, 1908, 2 vols.

RASHID AL-DIN (d. 1318). *Jami al-Tawarikh*, ed. Muhammad Rushan & Mustafa Musavi, Tehran, Nashr-i Alburz, 1994, 4 vols.

RASHID AL-DIN (d. 1318). *Jami al-Tawarikh, Tarikh-i Mubarak-i Ghazani (Histoire générale du monde jusqu'a 704 H.)*, ed. E. Blochet, Leiden, 1911, 2 vols.

RASHID AL-DIN (d. 1318). *Jami al-Tawarikh, Tarikh-i Mubarak-i Ghazani (Geschichte Gazan Khan's aus dem Tarikh-I Mubarak-i Ghazani)*, in Persian, ed. Karl Jahn, London, Luzac & Co, 1940.

RASHID AL-DIN (d. 1318). *Jami al-Tawarikh (The Successors of Gengis Khan from Mongke Khan (1251-1259) to Temur Oljeitu (1294-1307)*, tr. J. A. Boyle, New York, Columbia University Press, 1971.

RUMLU, Hasan (16th c.). *A Chronicle of the Early Safawis: The Ahsan al-Tawarikh*, tr. C. Seddon, Baroda, Oriental Institute, 1934, 2 vols.

RUMLU, Hasan (16th c.). *Ahsan al-Tawar1kh*, ed. A. Nava'i, Tehran, Chapkhaniy-i Haydari, 1979.

SA'DI (d. 1291). *Golestan-i Sa'di*, ed. Iranparast, Tehran, Fanous, 1977.

SAMARQANDI, Dawlatshah (d. 1494). *Tazkirat al-Shu'ara'*, ed. E. G. Browne, London, Luzac, 1901.

SHAHRASTANI (d. 1153). *Kitab al-Milal wa'l-Nihal (Livre des Religions et des Sectes)*, tr. Jean Jolivet and Guy Monnot, Paris, Peeters, 1986, 2 vols.

SHARAF AL-DIN SHAMI (d. 1455). *Zafar-nama (Histoire des conquêtes de Tamerlane intitulée Zafarnama par Nizamuddin Shami)*, ed. F. Tauer, Prague, 2 vols, 1937-1956.

TABARI, Abu Ja'far Muhammad (d. 923). *Tarikh al-Rusul wa'l-Muluk* (*The History of al-Tabari*), various translators, ed. Ehsan Yarshater, Albany N.Y., State University of N.Y. Press.

TABARI, 'Ali b. Sahl Rabban (9th c.). *The Book of Religion and Empire*, ed. A Mingana, Manchester, 1922.

THOMAS OF MARGA (9th c.). *The Historia Monastica of Thomas Bishop of Marga AD 840* (*The Book of Governors*), ed. & tr. E. A. W. Budge, London, Kegan Paul, 1893.

VARTAN (d. 1271). "Histoire Universelle", ed. E. Dulaurier, *Journal Asiatique*, Paris, 1860, XVI pp. 273-322.

WAHID QAZWINI (1694). *Abbas-nama*, ed. I. Dehqan, Arak, 1951.

YA'QUBI (d. 897). *Al-Buldan (Les Pays)*, tr. Gaston Wiet, Cairo, 1937.

YA'QUBI (d. 897). *Kitab al-Buldan*, ed. Juynboll, Leiden, Brill, 1861.

YA'QUBI (d. 897). *Tarikh*, ed. Th. Houtsma, Leiden, 1883, 2 vols.

YAZDI, Sharaf al-Din 'Ali (d. 1454). *Zafar Nama* (*Histoire de Timurbec*), tr. Petis de la Croix, Paris, Robert Marc d'Espilly, 1722, 4 vols.

ZAKARIA THE DIACRE (d. 1699). "Mémoires historiques sur les Sofis", *Collection d'Historiens Arméniens*, ed. M. Brosset, St. Petersbourg, 1876, II pp. 1-154.

ZARTUSHT-I BAHRAM B. PAJDU (13th c.). *Zartusht-nama (Le Livre de Zoroastre)*, ed. Frederic Rosenberg, St. Petersbourg, Commissionnaires de l'Académie Impériale des Sciences, 1904.

Arda Viraz Namag (Le Livre d'Arda Viraz), ed. & tr. Philippe Gignoux, Paris, Bibliothèque Iranienne, 1984, cahier no. 14.

Babylonian Talmud, ed. I. Epstein, London, Soncino, 1935-1948.

Bundahishn (Zand-akasih, Iranian or Greater Bundahishn), ed. B. T. Anklesaria, Bombay, 1956.

Chronique de Séert (*Histoire Nestorienne Inédite*), ed. Mgr Sddai Scher & Abbé Périer, Paris, 1907, Part 1 (Patrologia Orientalis 4).

A Collection of Letters from Iran written to the Mobeds and Behdins of India, "Letter to Dastur Barzo Kamdin brought by Shariar Rustam Sandal in AnnoYazdgirdi 1019", Manuscript from the Dastur Meherjirana Library, Navsari (India), Catalogue F. 45 - VIII.9.

Dinkard, ed. & tr. Dastur Behramjee Sanjana, Bombay, Duftur Ashkara Press, 1888.

Histoire de Mar Jabalaha III Patriarche des Nestoriens (1281-1317) et du Moine Rabban Çauma, Ambassadeur du Roi Argoun en Occident (1287), tr. J. B. Chabot, Paris, Ernest Leroux, 1895.

Histoire de Saint Mar Ahoudemmeh 6ᵉ siècle (*Histoire d'Ahoudemmeh et de Marouta*), ed. F. Nau, Paris, 1905, pp. 5-51.

Mino Khirad or Vasf-i Khirad, and Noshiravan and his "Marquzan" (Dakhma), transcribed in 1251 Anno Yazdgirdi (1883) from a manuscript written by Anushiravan Pur Marzban in 1620, Dastur Meherjirana Library, Navsari (India), Catalogue F. 62.

The Monks of Kublai Khan, tr. E. A. W. Budge, London, Religious Tract Society, 1928.

New Jerusalem Bible, London, Darton, 1985.

Psalm Daniel (Geschichte Daniels), Ein Apokryph, ed. & tr. Herman Zotenberg, *Archiv für Wissenschaftliche Erforschung des alten Testaments*, ed. A. Merx, Halle, 1867, I-IV pp. 385-427.

Rivayat-i Dastur Darab Hormazdyar, transcribed in 1235 Anno Yazdgirdi (1867) from a manuscript completed in 1049 Anno Yazdgirdi (1681), Dastur Meherjirana Library, Navsari (India), Catalogue F. 59, I.

Rivayat of Kawus Kamdin, V. A letter from Iran in reply to a letter from Surat, transcribed from a manuscript completed in 1254 Anno Yazdgirdi (1886), Dastur Meherjirana Library, Navsari (India), Catalogue F. 60, V.

Shahriha I Eran (The Provincial Capitals of Eranshahr), tr. J. Markwart, Rome, Pontificio Istituto Biblico, 1931.

Story of Kavus and Afsad, transcribed in 1252 Anno Yazdgirdi (1884) from a manuscript written completed between the 16th and 18th century, Dastur Meherjirana Library, Navsari (India), Catalogue F. 62.

Synodicon Orientale (Synodicon Orientale ou Recueil de Synodes Nestoriennes), ed. & tr. J. B. Chabot, Paris, Imprimerie Nationale, 1902.

Tadhkirat al-Muluk: A Manual of Safavid Administration, ed. & tr. V. Minorsky, London, 1940.

Tarikh-i Sistan, (Anonymous writers 1062 & 1325) ed. M Bahar, Tehran, Khavar, 1935.

Timothy's Apology, ed. & tr. A. Mingana, *Woodbrooke Studies*, Cambridge, 1928.

Vajarkard Dini or Dinkard, from a manuscript transcribed in 1156 Anno Yazdgirdi (1788), Dastur Meherjirana Library, Navsari (India), Catalogue F 61.

Records of Medieval European Travellers

BARBARO, Josefa & CONTARINI, Ambrogio (15th c.). *Travels to Tana and Persia*, tr. Williams Thomas & ed. Lord Stanley of Aderley, London, Hakluyt Society, 1873.

BENJAMIN OF TUDELA (12th c.). *The Itinerary of Benjamin of Tudela*, ed. & tr. Marcus N. Adler, New York, Philipp Feldheim, 1907.

BERNIER, François (d. 1688). *Travels in the Mogul Empire (1656-1668)*, tr. A. Constable & ed. V. Smith, Oxford, 1914.

CARRÉ, Abbé (17th c.). *Travels of Abbé Carré in India and the Near East 1672-1674*, tr. Lady Fawcett & ed. C. L. Fawcett, Hakluyt Series, London, 1947.

CHARDIN, Jean (d. 1713). *Travels in Persia*, ed. Sir Percy Sykes, London, Argonaut Press, 1927.

Selected Bibliography

CHARDIN, Jean (d. 1713). *Voyages du Chevalier Chardin en Perse*, ed. L. Langlès, Paris, Le Normant, 1811, 10 vols.

DE CLAVIJO, Don Ruy Gonzalez (d. 1412). *Embassy to Tamerlane 1403-1406*, tr. G. Le Strange, London, 1928.

DE GOUVEA, Antonio (17th c.). *Relation des grandes guerres et victoires obtenues par le roy de Perse Chah Abbas contre les empereurs de Turquie*, Rouen, Nicholas Loyelet, 1646.

DE SILVA FIGUEROA, Garcia D. (17th c.). *L'Ambassade de D. Garcia de Silva Figueroa en Perse*, tr. A. de Wicquefort, Paris, 1667.

DU MANS, Raphaël (d. 1696). *Estat de la Perse en 1660*, Paris, E. Leroux, 1890, Reprint: Franborough, Gregg, 1969.

DU MANS, Raphaël (d. 1696). *Raphaël du Mans Missionnaire en Perse au XVIIIe s.*, ed. Francis Richard, Paris, 1995, 2 vols.

FRA RICOLDO DE MONTE CROCE (d. 1309). "Itinéraire", *L'Extrême Orient au Moyen Age*, ed. Louis de Backer, Paris, 1877, pp. 272-356.

FRYER, John (d. 1733). *A New Account of East-India and Persia (1672-1681)*, London, R. Chriswell, 1698.

GAUDEREAU, Abbé (17th c.). *Relation de la mort de Schah Soliman, roy de Perse, et du couronnement du Sultan Ussain, son fils*, Paris, 1696.

HANWAY, Jonas (d. 1786). *A Historical Account of the British Trade over the Caspian Sea with the Revolutions of Persia*, London, 1753, 3 vols.

HENRY, Lord (16th c.). *Discoveries of the Sect of the Banians and Persees*, London, 1630.

HERBERT, Thomas (d. 1682). *Travels in Persia*, ed. E. Denison Ross and E. Powers, London, Routledge, 1928.

JENKINSON, Anthony (d. 1609). *Early Voyages and Travels to Russia and Persia*, ed. E. Delmar Morgan & C. H. Cook, London, Hakluyt Society, 1886, 2 vols.

JOHANNES DE PLANO CARPINI (d. 1252). "The Voyage of Johannes de Plano Carpini (1246)", *The Texts and Versions of John de Plano Carpini and William de Rubruquis*, ed. C. R. Beazley, London, Hakluyt Society, 1903 pp. 43-144.

KRUSINSKI, Father T. J. (d. 1756). *The History of the Revolution of Persia*, London, J. Pemberton, 1728, 2 vols.

LE BRUYN, Cornelius (d. 1722). *Travels into Muscovy, Persia and Part of the East Indies*, tr. from French, London, A. Bettesworth, 1737, 2 vols.

MANUCCI, Niccolao (17th c.). *Storia do Mogor, or Mogul India 1653-1708*, tr. William Irvine, London, J. Murray, 1907, 4 vols.

MARCO POLO (d. 1323). *The Books of Sir Marco Polo*, H. Cordier, London, John Murray (3rd ed.), 1921, 2 vols.

ODORIC DA PORDENONE (14th c.). *Les Voyages en Asie au XIV e siecle du bienheureux frere Odoric de Pordenone*, ed. Henri Cordier, Paris, Ernest Leroux, 1891.

OLEARIUS, A. (1671). *Voyages and Travells of the Ambassadors sent by Frederick Dutch of Holstein to the Great Duke of Moscovy and the King of Persia*, London, J. Starky, 1669.

PEREIRO FIDALGO, Gregorio (end 17th c. - early 18th c.). *L'Ambassade de Gregorio Pereira Fidalgo à la cour de Chah Soltan-Hosseyn 1696-1697*, ed. Jean Aubin, Lisbonne, 1971.

PIETRO DELLA VALLE (d. 1652). *I Viaggi di Pietro della Valle*, ed. F. Gaeta & L. Lockhart, Rome, 1972, 2 vols.

PIETRO DELLA VALLE (d. 1652). *The Travels of Pietro della Valle in India (1622)*, ed. E. Grey, London, Hakluyt Society Publications, 1891, 2 vols.

SANSON, Nicolas (d. 1667). *The Present State of Persia*, tr. from French, London, M. Gilliflower, 1695.

SCHILLINGER, Franz Caspar (18th c.). *Persianische und Ost-Indianische Reise*, Nuremberg, 1707.

SHERLEY, Sir Anthony (17th c.). *Sir Anthony Sherley and his Persian Adventure*, ed. E. Denison Ross, London, Routledge, 1933.

STODARD, R. (17th c.). *The Journal of Robert Stodard - An account of Sir Dodmore Cotton's mission in Persia in 1628-1629*, ed. Sir Denison Ross, London, 1935.

TAVERNIER, J. B. (d. 1689). *Voyage en Perse et description de ce royaume*, ed. P. Pascal, Paris, Editions du Carrefour, 1930.

TEIXEIRA, Pedro B. (end 16th c. - mid 17th c.). *The Travels of Pedro Teixeira with his chronicle of the Kings of Ormuz and the Kings of Persia*, tr. & ed. by W. F. Sinclair, London, Hakluyt Society Publications, 1901.

TENREIRO, A. (16th c.). "Itinerario de Antonio Tenrreyro", *Itinerarios da India a Portugal por Terra*, ed. A. Baiao, Coimbra, 1923, pp. 1-130.

THEVENOT, J. (17th c.). *Voyages de Monsieur de Thévenot*, Paris, Charles Angot, 1689, 5 vols.

WILLIAM DE RUBRUQUIS (d. 1270). "The Journal of Frier William de Rubruquis (1253)", *The Texts and Versions of John de Plano Carpini and William de Rubruquis*, ed. C. R. Beazley, London, Hakluyt Society, 1903, pp. 144-183.

A Chronicle of the Carmelites in Persia and the Papal Mission of the XVIIth and XVIIIth centuries, London, Eyre & Spottiswoode, 1939, 2 vols.

Documents Inédits pour servir à l' histoire du Christianisme en Orient, ed. Antoine Rabbath, Paris, A. Picard et Fils, 1907-1910, 2 vols.

Genuinae Relationes inter Sedem Apostolicam et Assyriorum Orientalium seu Chaldaeorum Ecclesiam, ed. Samuel Giamil, Rome, 1902.

I Viaggi in Persia degli Ambasciatori Veneti Barbaro e Contarini, ed. L. Lockhart, R. Morozzo delle Rocca, M. F. Tiepolo, Rome, Libreria di Stato, 1973.

Secondary Sources

Books

ALLEN, W. E. D. *A History of the Georgian People*, London, Kegan Paul, 1932.

ALLSEN, Thomas T. *Culture and Conquest in Mongol Eurasia*, Cambridge, Cambridge University Press, 2001.

ARBERRY, A. J. (ed.). *Religion in the Middle East*, London, Cambridge University Press, 1969.

ASIMOV, M. S. & BOSWORTH, C. E. *History of Civilizations of Central Asia*, IV, Paris, UNESCO Publishing, 1998.

ASMUSSEN, J. P. *Studies in Judeo-Persian Literature*, Leiden, Brill, 1973.

ATIYA, Aziz S. *A History of Eastern Christianity*, London, Methuen, 1968.

BABAIE, Sussan et al. *Slaves of the Shah: New Elites of Safavid Iran*, London, I.B.Tauris, 2004.

BAGHDIANTZ McCABE, Ina. *The Shah's Silk for Europe's Silver, The Eurasian Trade of the Julfa Armenians in Safavid Iran and India (1530-1750)*, Atlanta, Scholars Press, 1999.

BAGOT, Sir John. *The Great Arab Conquests*, London, Hoddler and Stoughton, 1963.

BARTHOLD, W. *Iran*, tr. G. K. Nariman & ed. M. E. Dadrawala, Bombay, 1935.

BATRA, Raveendra N. *Muslim Civilization and the Crisis in Iran*, Dallas, Venus Books, 1980.

BAT YE'OR. *The Decline of Eastern Christianity under Islam: From Jihad to Dhimmitude*, London, Associated University Presses, 1996.

BAT YE'OR. *Islam and Dhimmitude, where Civilizations Collide*, Lancaster, Dickinson University Press, 2002.

BAUSANI, A. *Persia Religiosa: da Zaratustra a Baha'ullah*, Milan, Il Saggiatore, 1959.

BAYANI, K. *Les Relations de l'Iran avec l'Europe Occidentale à l'époque Safavide*, Paris, Librairie d'Amérique et d'Orient, 1937.

BAYBURDYAN, Vahan. *Naqsh-i Aramana-yi Irani dar Tijarat-i Bayn al-Milaliya Payan-I Sada-yi 17 Miladi*, tr. Adik Baghdasariyan, Tehran, 1996.

BEAL, S. *The Life of Hiuen-Tsiang*, London, 1911 (On Buddhism in Iran).

BELLAN, Lucien-Louis. *Chah Abbas I*, Paris, Librairie Orientaliste Paul Geuthner, 1932.

BLOCHET, E. *Introduction à l'Histoire des Mongols de Fadl-Allah Rashid ed-din*, Leiden, Brill, 1910.

BOSWORTH, C. E. *The History of the Saffarids of Sistan and the Maliks of Nimruz (861-1543)*, Costa Mesa (Calif.), Mazda Publishers, 1994.

BOSWORTH, C. E. (ed.). *History of the Saljuq Turks, The Saljuq-Nama of Zahir al-Din Nishapuri*, Richmond, Curzon Press, 2000.

BOSWORTH, C. E. *The Arabs, Byzantium and Iran: Studies in early Islamic history and culture*, Brookfield Vt, Variorum, 1996.

BOSWORTH, C. E. *Islamic Dynasties: A chronological and genealogical handbook*, Edinburgh, University Press, 1967.

BOSWORTH, C. E. *Medieval Islamic Underworld*, Leiden, E.J. Brill, 1976.

BOSWORTH, C. E. *Sistan under the Arabs*, Rome, ISMEO, 1968.

BOYCE, Mary. *A Persian Stronghold of Zoroastrianism*, Oxford, Clarendon Press, 1977.

BOYCE. Mary. *Zoroastrianism, Its Antiquity and Constant Vigour*, Costa Mesa (Ca.), Mazda Publishers, 1992.

BOYCE, Mary. *Zoroastrians: Their Religious Beliefs and Practices*, London, Routledge and Kegan Paul, 1979.

BRAUER, Erich. *The Jews of Kurdistan*, Detroit, Wayne State University Press, 1993.

BROWNE, E. G. *A Literary History of Persia*, Cambridge, Cambridge University Press, 1964, 4 vols.

BROWNE, E. G. *A Year Amongst the Persians*, London, Adam & Charles Black, 1893.

BROWNE, L. E. *The Eclipse of Christianity in Asia from the Time of Muhammad till the 14th c.*, (1933) reprint New York, 1967.

BULLIET, Richard W. *Conversion to Islam in the Medieval Period*, Cambridge Ma., Harvard University Press, 1979.

BULLIET, Richard W. *Islam: The View from the Edge*, New York, Columbia University Press, 1994.

BULLIET, Richard W. *Patricians of Nishapur: A Study in Medieval Islamic Social History*, Cambridge (Ma.), Harvard University Press, 1972.

CHAQUERI, Cosroe (ed.). *The Armenians of Iran*, Cambridge (Ma.), Harvard University Press, 1998.

CHOKR, Melhem. *Zandaqa et Zindiqis en Islam au Second Siècle de l'Hégire*, Damas, L'Institut Francais d'Etudes Arabes de Damas, 1993.

CHOKSY, Jamsheed K. *Conflict and Cooperation: Zoroastrian Subalterns and Muslim Elites in Medieval Iranian Society*, New York, Columbia University Press, 1997.

CHRISTENSEN, A. *L'Iran sous les Sassanides*, Copenhagen, Ejnar Munksgaard, 1944.

CHRISTENSEN, Peter. *The Decline of Iranshahr: Irrigation and Environments in the History of the Middle East, 500 B.C. to A.D. 1500*, Copenhagen, 1993.

CHRISTIAN, David. *A History of Russia, Central Asia and Mongolia*, Oxford, 1998, I.

CRONE, Patricia. *God's Caliph: Religious Authority in the First Centuries of Islam*, Cambridge, Cambridge University Press, 1986.

DANIEL, Elton L. *The Political and Social History of Khurasan under Abbasid Rule 747-820*, Minneapolis, Bibliotheca ca, 1979.

DARMO, Mar Thoma (ed.). *Letters of Patriarch Timothy I (778-820 A.D.)*, Trichur (Kerala), Mar Narsai Press, 1982.

DAULIER-DESLANDES, André. *The Beauties of Persia*, tr. from French, London, The Persia Society, 1926 (reedition of 1673).

DAVAR, Firoze C. *Iran and India through the Ages*, London, Asia Publishing House, 1962.

DENNETT, D. C. *Conversion and the Poll Tax in Early Islam*, Cambridge (Ma.), Harvard University Press, 1950.

DE WEESE, Devin. *Islamization and native religion in the Golden Horde: Baba Tükles and conversion to Islam in historical and epic tradition*, University Park (Pa), Pennsylvania State University Press, 1994.

DONALDSON, Dwight M. *The Shi'ite Religion: A History of Islam in Persia and Iraq*, London, 1933.

DUNLOP, D. M. *The History of Jewish Khazars*, Princeton, Princeton University Press, 1954.

ELGOOD, Cyril. *A Medical History of Persia and the Eastern Caliphate from the Earliest Times until the Year 1932 A.D.*, Cambridge, University Press, 1951.

ENGLAND, John C. *The Hidden History of Christianity in Asia, The Churches of the East before the year 1500*, Delhi, ISPCK, 1998.

FATTAL, Antoine. *Le statut légal des non-musulmans en pays d'Islam*, Beirut, Imprimerie Catholique, 1958.

FIEY, J. M. *Chrétiens syriaques sous les Abbassides surtout à Baghdad (749-1258)*, Louvain, CSCO, 1980.

FIEY, J. M. *Chrétiens Syriaques sous les Mongols (Il-Khanat de Perse XIIIe-XIVe s.)*, Louvain, CSCO, 1975.

FIEY, J. M. *Communautés syriaques en Iran et Irak des origines à 1552*, London, Variorum Reprints, 1979.

FIRBY, Nora Kathleen. *European Travelers and their Perception of Zoroastrians in the 17th and 18th Century*, Berlin, Verlag von Dietrich Reiner, 1988.

FISCHEL, Walter J. *Jews in the Economic and Political Life of Mediaeval Islam*, London, The Royal Asiatic Society monographs 22, 1968.

FLOOR, Willem. *The Afghan Occupation of Safavid Persia (1721-1729)*, Paris, Cahiers de Studia Iranica 9, 1998.

FORBES MANZ, Beatrice. *The Rise and Rule of Tamerlane*, Cambridge, Cambridge University Press, 1989.

RICHARD, Francis. *Raphaël du Mans Missionnaire en Perse au XVIIIe siècle*, Paris, 1995, I.

FRYE, Richard N. *The Golden Age of Persia: The Arabs in the East*, London, Weidenfeld and Nicolson, 1975.

FRYE, Richard N. *The Heritage of Central Asia: From Antiquity to the Turkish Expansion*, Princeton, Markus Wiener Publishers, 1996.

FRYE, Richard N. *Islamic Iran and Central Asia 7-12th c.*, London, Variorum Reprints, 1979.

GERVERS, M. & JIBRAN BIKHAZI, Ramzi (ed.). *Conversion and Continuity: Indigenous Christian Communities in Islamic Lands Eigth to Eighteenth Centuries*, Toronto, Pontifical Institute of Mediaeval Studies, 1990.

GHOUGASSIAN, Vazken S. *The Emergence of the Armenian Diocese of New Julfa in the Seventeenth Century*, Atlanta, Scholars Press, 1998.

GIL, Moshe. *A History of Palestine (634-1099)*, tr. Ethel Broido, Cambridge, Cambridge University Press, 1992.

GILLMAN, Ian & KLIMKEIT, Hans-Joachim. *Christians in Asia before 1500*, Richmond, Curzon, 1999.

GLUBB, Sir John Bagot. *The Great Arab Conquests*, London, Hodder and Stoughton, 1963.

GOBINEAU, Arthur comte de. *Trois en Asie de 1855 à 1858*, Paris, 1905.

GODDARD, Hugh. *A History of Christian-Muslim Relations*, Edinburgh, Edinburgh University Press, 2000.

GOLDZIHER, Ignaz. *Muslim Studies*, ed. C. R. Barber & S. M. Stern, London, George Allen and Unwin Ltd, 1967.

GRAY, Louis Herbert. *The Foundations of the Iranian Religions being a Series of the Ratanbai Katrak Lectures delivered at Oxford*, Bombay, D. B. Taraporevala, 1930.

GUTAS, Dimitri. *Greek Thought, Arabic Culture: The Graeco-Arabic Translation Movement in Baghdad and Early Abbasid Society 8th - 10th centuries*, London, Routledge, 1998.

HENRION, M. Le Baron. *Histoire Générale des Missions Catholiques depuis le 3e siècle jusqu'à nos jours*, Paris, Gaume et Frères, 1847, 2 vols.

HINDS, Martin. *Studies in Early Islamic History*, Princeton, Darwin Press, 1996.

HODGSON, Marshall G. S. *The Venture of Islam*, Chicago, Chicago University Press, 1974, 3 vols.

HODIVALA, Shapurji Kavasji. *Parsis of Ancient India*, Bombay, 1920.

HOUTUM-SCHINDLER, A. *Eastern Persian Irak*, London, John Murray, 1898.

HOWORTH, Henry H. *History of the Mongols*, London, Longman, 1888, 3 vols.

HOYLAND, Robert G. *Seeing Islam as Others Saw It: A Survey and Evaluation of Christian, Jewish and Zoroastrian Writings on Early Islam*, Princeton (N.J.), The Darwin Press, 1997.

JOHNSON, Gordon. *Cultural Atlas of India*, Oxford, Andromad, 1996.

JOSEPH, John. *The Nestorians and their Muslim Neighbors*, Princeton (N. J.), 1961.

JUYNBOLL, G. H. (ed.). *Studies on the First Century of Islamic Society*, Illinois, Southern Illinois University Press, 1982.

KOLBAS, J. G. *The Mongols in Iran: Chingiz Khan to Uljaytu 1220-1309*, Richmond, Curzon Press, 2000.

KESTENBERG-AMIGHI, Janet. *The Zoroastrians of Iran: Conversion, Assimilation and Persistence*, New York, AMS Press, 1990.

KHANIKOFF, Nicolas de. *Mémoire sur la Partie Méridionale de l'Asie Centrale*, Paris, Imprimerie de La Martinet, 1861.

LABOURT, J. *Le Christianisme dans l'Empire Perse*, Paris, Librairie Victor Lecoffre, 1904.

LAMBTON, Ann K. S. *Continuity and Change in Medieval Persia*, New York, Bibliotheca Persica, 1988.

LANDRON, Bénédicte. *Chrétiens et Musulmans en Irak: Attitudes Nestoriennes vis-à-vis de l'Islam*, Paris, Cariscript, 1994.

LAYARD, Austen Henry. *Nineveh and its Remains, with an Account of a Visit to the Chaldean Christians of Kurdistan and the Yezidis*, London, John Murray, 1849, 2 vols.

LEMERCIER-QUELQUEJAY, C. *La paix mongole*, Paris, Flammarion, Questions d'Histoire 13, 1970.

LE STRANGE, G. *Baghdad during the Abbasid Caliphate from Contemporary Arabic and Persian Sources*, Oxford, Clarendon Press, 1900.

LE STRANGE, G. *The Lands of Eastern Caliphate*, Cambridge, Cambridge University Press, 1905.

LEVI, Habib. *Comprehensive History of the Jews of Iran: the Outset of the Diaspora*, tr. George W. Maschke, Costa Mesa (Ca.), Mazda Publishers, 1999.

LEVI, Habib. *Tarikh-I Yahud-i Iran*, Tehran, Broukhim, 1960, 3 vols.

LEWIS, Bernard. *The Jews of Islam*, Princeton, Princeton University Press, 1984.

MADELUNG, Wilferd. *Religious Trends in Early Islamic Iran*, Albany (N.Y.), Bibliotheca Persica, 1988.

MARGOLIOUTH, D. S. *The Eclipse of the Abbasid Caliphate*, Oxford, 1921, 3 vols.

MATTHEE, Rudolph. *The Politics of Trade in Safavid Iran: Silk for Silver 1600-1730*, Cambridge, Cambridge University Press, 1999.

MAZZAOUI, Michel M. *The Origins of the Safawids: Shi'ism, Sufism and the Gulat*, Wiesbaden, Franz Steiner Verlag, Steiner Verlag, 1972.

McCHESNEY, R. D. *Central Asia, Foundations of Change*, Princeton, 1996.

MEISAMI, Julie. *Persian Historiography*, Edinburgh, Edinburgh University Press, 1999.

MELVILLE, Charles (ed.). *Pembroke Papers*, Cambridge, Centre of Middle Eastern Studies, 1990.

MELVILLE, Charles (ed.). *Safavid Persia: The History and Politics of an Islamic Society*, London, I.B.Tauris, 1996.

MELVILLE, Charles. *The Fall of Amir Chupan and the Decline of the Ilkhanate, 1327-37: A decade of discord in Mongol Iran*, Bloomington (Indiana), Research Institute for Inner Asian Studies, 1999.

MEZ, Adam. *The Renaissance of Islam* (transl. Salahuddin Khuda Bukhsh & D. S. Margoliouth), London, Luzac & Co. 1937.

MONNOT, G. *"Penseurs musulmans et religions iraniennes" Abd al-Jabbar et ses devanciers*, Paris, Librairie Philosophique, 1974.

MORGAN, David. *Medieval Persia 1040-1797*, London, Longman, 1988.

MORGAN, David. *The Mongols*, Oxford, Basil Blackwell, 1987.

MOREEN, Vera B. *Iranian Jewry's Hour of Peril and Heroism: A Study of Babai ibn Lutf's Chronicle (1616-1662)*, Columbia University Press, 1987.

MOREEN, Vera B. *In Queen Esther's Garden, An Anthology of Judeo-Persian*, New Haven, Yale University Press, 2000.

MORONY, Michael G. *Iraq after the Muslim Conquest*, Princeton, Princeton University Press, 1984.

MOSTAERT, Antoine & CLEAVES, F. W. *Les Lettres de 1289 et 1305 des Ilkhans Arghun et Oljeitu à Philippe le Bel*, Cambridge (MA), 1962.

MOTTAHEDEH, Roy P. *The Shu'ubiyah Controversy and the Social History of Early Islamic Iran*, Princeton, 1980.

NAIPAUL, V. S. *Beyond Belief: Islamic Excursions among the Converted Peoples*, New Delhi, Viking, 1998.

NETZER, Amnon. *Manuscripts of the Jews of Persia in the Ben Zvi Institute*, Jerusalem, Ben Zvi Institute, 1985.

NETZER, Amnon (ed). *Paydavand* (Judeo-Iranian and Jewish Studies Series, no 1), Costa Mesa (Ca.), Mazda Publishers, 1996.

NETZER, Amnon (ed.). *Poem of the Jews of Persia and Bukhara*, Jerusalem, 1971.

NEUSNER, J. *Aprahat and Judaism: The Christian-Jewish Argument in 4th Islamic Iran*, Leiden, Brill, 1971.

NEUSNER, J. *A History of the Jews in Babylonia*, Leiden, Brill, 1970, 5 vols.

NEWMAN, J. *The Agricultural Life of the Jews in Babylonia*, London, Oxford University Press, 1932.

OHSSON, Baron d'. *Histoire des Mongols depuis Tchinguis-Khan jusqu'à Timour Bey ou Tamerlan*, 1st ed. 1824, 2nd ed. 1835.

PELLIOT, Paul. *Les Mongols et la Papauté*, Paris, Librairie August Picard, 1923, 2 vols.

RAMBERT, Gaston. *Histoire du Commerce de Marseille de 1599 à 1660*, ed. Gaston Rambert, Paris, Plon, 1949-1966, 7 vols.

RYPKA, J., & al. *History of Iranian Literature*, Dordrecht, D. Reidel, 1968.

SADIGHI, Gholam Hossein. *Les Mouvements Religieux Iraniens au IIe et au IIe siècle de l'hégire*, Paris, Les Presses Modernes, 1938.

SALEMANN, Carl. *List of Oriental Manuscripts Presented to the Asiatic Museum*, Petersburg, 1898.

SASSOON, David Solomon. *A History of the Jews in Baghdad*, Letchworth, 1949.

SAVORY, Roger Mervyn. *Iran under the Safavids*, Cambridge, Cambridge University Press, 1980.

SETH, Mesrovb Jacob. *Armenians in India*, Calcutta, 1937.

SHAKED, Shaul (ed.). *From Zoroastrian Iran to Islam: Studies in Religious History and Intercultural Contacts*, Aldershot (U.S.A.), Variorum, 1995.

SHAKED, Shaul & NETZER, Amnon (ed.). *Irano-Judaica II*, Jerusalem, Ben-zvi institute, 1990.

SHARON, M. (ed.). *Studies in Islamic History and Civilization*, Jerusalem, Leiden, 1986.

SHBOUL, Ahmad M. *Al-Mas'udi and His World*, London, Ithaca Press, 1979.

SIDDIQI, Amir H. *Caliphate and Kingship in Medieval Persia*, 1937, reprinted Philadelphia, Porcupine Press, 1977.

SKLARE, David E. *Samuel ben Hofni Gaon and his Cultural World*, Leiden, Brill, 1996.

SOURDEL, D. *Le vizirat abbaside de 749 a 936*, Damascus, PIFD, 1959, 2 vols.

SPULER, B. *Iran in Früh-Islamischer Zeit*, Wiesbaden, Akademie der Wissenschaften, 1952.

SPULER, Bertold. *The Mongol Period*, tr. F. Bagley, Leiden, Brill, 1969.

SPULER, Bertold. *The Muslim World, A Historical Survey*, tr. F. R. C. Bagley, Leiden, Brill, 1969.

STILLMAN, N. A. *The Jews of Arab Lands*, Philadelphia, 1979.

TAJBAKSH, Ahmad. *Iran dar Zaman-i Safaviyeh*, Tabriz, Kitabfurushi-i Chihr, 1961.

THORAU, Thorau. *The Lion of Egypt*, tr. P. Holt, New York, Longman, 1992.

TOURNEBIZE, François. *Histoire Politique et Religieuse de l'Arménie jusque'à l'an 1393*, Paris, 1910.

TOURNEFORT, Joseph Pitton de. *Relation d'un voyage du Levant*, Lyon, 1727, 3 vols.

TRITTON, Arthur S. *The Caliphs and their Non-Muslim Subjects: A critical study of the covenant of Umar*, London, F. Cass., 1930.

VINE, Aubry R. *The Nestorian Churches (A Concise History of Nestorian Christianity in Asia from the Persian Schism to the Modern Assyrians*, London, Independent Press, 1937.

VITALONE, Mario. *The Persian Revayats: A Bibliographic Reconnaissance*, Napoli, Istituto Universitario Orientale, 1987.

WASSERSTROM, Steven M. *Between Muslim and Jew, The Problem of Symbiosis under Early Islam*, Princeton, 1995.

WATERFIELD, Robin E. *Christians in Persia: Assyrians, Armenians, Roman Catholics and Protestants*, London, George Allen and Unwin Ltd, 1973.

WIGRAM, W. A. *An Introduction to the History of the Assyrian Church or the Church of the Sassanid Persian Empire 100-640 A. D.*, London, 1910.

WILLIAMS, John Alden. *Themes of Islamic Civilization*, Berkeley, University of California Press, 1971.

WOODS, John E. *The Aqquyunlu, Clan, Confederation, Empire*, Minneapolis, Bibliotheca Islamica, 1976.

WRIGHT, Dudley. *The Talmud*, London, Williams and Norgate, 1932.

YEROUSHALMI, David. *The Judeo-Persian Poet 'Emrani and his 'Book of Treasure'*, Leiden, Brill, 1995.

YOUNG, W. G. *Patriarch, Shah and Caliph. A Study of the Relationships of the Church of the East with the Sassanid Empire and the Early Caliphates with Special Reference to Available Translated Syriac Sources*, Rawalpindi, 1974.

ZAKERI, Mohsen. *Sasanid Soldiers in Early Muslim Society*, Wiesbaden, Harrassowitz Verlag, 1995.

ZARRINKUB, Abd al-Husayn. *Tarikh-i Iran ba'd az Islam*, Tehran, Vizarat Amuzesh va Parvaresh, 1965.

Au carrefour des religions: mélanges offerts a Philippe Gignoux, Bures-sur-Yvette, Groupe pour l'étude de la civilisation du Moyen Orient, 1995.

Papers in Honour of Mary Boyce, Leiden, Brill, 1985.

Articles

ADHAMI, Siamak. "Some Remarks on 'Ulama-ye': A Zoroastrian Polemic", *Studia Iranica*, Paris, Association pour l'Avancement des Etudes Iraniennes, 1999, tome 28.2, pp. 205-214.

ALTMAN, V. "Ancient Khorezmian Civilization in the Light of the Latest Archeological Discoveries (1937-1945)", *Journal of the American Oriental Society*, 67 pp. 81-85.

AMITAI-PREISS, Reuven. "Ghazan, Islam and Mongol Tradition: A View from the Mamluk Sultanate", *Bulletin of School of Oriental and African Studies*, 1996, LIX pp. 1-10.

AMITAI-PREISS, Reuven. "New Material from Mamluk Sources for the Biography of Rashid al-Din", *Oxford Studies in Islamic Art*, 1996, XII pp. 23-37.

AMORETTI, B. S. "Sects and Heresies", *The Cambridge History of Iran*, Cambridge, Cambridge University Press, IV pp. 481-519.

ASHRAFYAN, K. Z. "Central Asia under Timur from 1370 to the early fifteenth century", *History of Civilizations of Central Asia*, ed. M. S. Asimov & C. E. Bosworth, Paris, UNESCO Publishing, 1998, IV pp. 319-347.

ASMUSSEN, J. P. "Christians in Iran", *The Cambridge History of Iran*, Cambridge, Cambridge University Press, 1983, III pp. 924-948.

AUBIN, Jean. "Chroniques persanes et relations italiennes. Notes sur les sources narratives du regne de Shah Esma'il Ier", *Studia Iranica*, Paris, 1995, tome 24 pp. 247-260.

AUBIN, Jean. "Le patronage culturel en Iran sous les Ilkhans, Une grande famille de Yazd", *Le Monde Iranien et l'Islam*, Paris, Société d'histoire de l'Orient, 1976, III pp. 107-118.

AUBIN, Jean. "Références pour Lar Médiévale", *Journal Asiatique*, Paris, 1955, IV pp. 491-506.

AUBIN, Jean. "Les Sunnites du Larestan et la Chute des Safavides", *Revue des Études ques*, Paris, 1965, XXXIII, pp. 151-171.

AUBIN, Jean. "Témoignage et oui-dire de Josefa Barbaro sur la Perse (1487)", *Middle East and Indian Ocean XVIe-XIXe s.*, Paris, 1985, 2.I pp. 71-84.

BABAYAN, Kathryn. "The Safavid Synthesis: From Qizilbash Islam to Imamite Shi'ism", *Iranian Studies*, 1994, XXVII, II 1-4, pp. 135-161.

BACHER, W. "Les Juifs de Perse au XVIIe et au XVIIIe siecle (tr. of a Jewish chronicle)", *Revue des Etudes Juives*, Paris, LIII pp.77-97.

BAUSANI, A. "Religion under the Mongols", *The Cambridge History of Iran*, Cambridge University Press, 1968, V pp. 538-549.

BEN-SASSON, Menachem. "Varieties of Inter-Communal Relations in the Geonic Period", *The Jews of Medieval Islam*, ed. Daniel Frank, Leiden, Brill, 1995, pp. 17-32.

BIRA, Sh. "The Mongols and their state in the 12th to the 13th century", *History of Civilizations of Central Asia*, ed. M. S. Asimov & C. E. Bosworth, Paris, UNESCO Publishing, 1998, IV pp. 243-261.

BLOCHET, E. "La conquête des états nestoriens de l'Asie Centrale par les Schietes: les influences chrétiennes et bouddhiques dans le dogme que", *Revue de l'Orient Chrétien*, Paris, 1925-1926, 3e serie t. XXV, no 1-2 pp. 3-131.

BONIN, C. E. "Notes sur les commnuautés nestoriennes de l'Asie Centrale", *Journal Asiatique*, 1900, XV.1 pp. 584-592.

BOSWORTH, C. E. "Al-Khwarazmi on Various Faiths and Sects (Chiefly Iranian)", *Iranica Varia*, Leiden, Brill, 1990, pp. 10-19.

BOSWORTH, C. E. & CLAUSON, Gerard Sir. *Al-Xwarazmi on the Peoples of Central Asia*, The Journal of Royal Asiatic Studies, London, 1965, pp. 2-12.

BOSWORTH, C. E. "The Ghaznavids", *History of Civilizations of Central Asia*, ed. M. S. Asimov & C. E. Bosworth, Paris, UNESCO Publishing, 1998, pp. 95-117.

BOSWORTH, C. E. "The Political and Dynastic History of the Iranian World (A. D. 1000-1217)", *The Cambridge History of Iran*, Cambridge, 1968, V pp. 1-202.

BOSWORTH, C. E. "The Tahirids and the Saffarids", *The Cambridge History of Iran*, Cambridge, 1975, IV pp. 90-135.

BOYCE, Mary. "The Fire-Temples of Kirman", *Acta Orientalia*, 1966, I pp. 50-72.

BOYCE, Mary. "The Zoroastrian Houses of Yazd", *Iran and Islam*, Edinburgh, 1971, pp. 125-148.

BOYLE, J. A. "Dynastic and Political History of the Il-Khans", *The Cambridge History of Iran*, Cambridge University Press, 1968, V pp. 303-421.

BOYLE, J. A. "Kirakos of Ganjak on the Mongols", *Central Asiatic Journal*, 1963, VIII, 3.1 pp. 199-214.

BRODY, Robert. "Zoroastrian Themes in Geonic Responsa", *Irano-Judaica IV*, Jerusalem, 1999, pp. 179-186.

BROWNE, L. E. "The Patriarch Timothy and the Caliph al-Mahdi", *Moslem World*, 1931, XXI pp. 38-45.

BULLIET, R. W. "Conversion to Islam and the Emergence of a Muslim Society in Iran", *Conversion to Islam*, ed. N. Levtzion, Holmes and Meier Publishers, New York, 1979, pp. 30-51.

BUNDY, David. "The Syriac and Armenian Christian Responses to the fication of the Mongols", *Medieval Christian Perception of Islam, A Book of Essays*, New York, 1996, pp. 33-53.

CHAUMONT, M.-L. "Recherches sur le clergé zoroastrian: Le herbad", *Revue de l'Histoire des Religions*, 1960, CLVIII pp. 55-80, 161-179.

CHOKSY, Jamshid. "Conflict, Coexistence, and Cooperation: Muslims and Zoroastrians in Eastern Iran during the Medieval Period", *Muslim World*, 1990, 80 III-IV, pp. 213-223.

CHOKSY, J. K. "Zoroastrians in Muslim Iran: selected problems of co-existence and interaction during the early medieval period", *Iranian Studies*, 1990, XX pp. 17-30.

CRONE, Patricia. "Kavad's Heresy and Mazdak's Revolt", *Iran*, London, 1991, XXIX pp. 21-42.

DAFTARY, F. "Sectarian and national movements in Iran, Khurasan and Transoxania during Umayyad and early Abbasid times", *History of Civilizations of Central Asia*, ed. M. S. Asimov & C. E. Bosworth, Paris, UNESCO Publishing, 1998, IV pp. 41-59.

DE BLOIS, François. "A Persian Poem Lamenting the Arab Conquest", *Studies in Honour of Clifford Edmund Bosworth*, Leiden, Brill, 2000, II, pp. 82-95.

DE FOUCHECOUR, C. "Le Testament moral de Chosroes dans la littérature persane", *Mémorial Jean de Menasce*, ed. A. Tafazzoli, Louvain, Imprimerie Orientaliste, 1974, pp. 419-432.

DESOUZA, A. "Minorities in the Historical Context of Islam", *Al Mushir*, 1998, 40 ii pp. 72-81.

DULAURIER, E. "Les Mongols d'après les historiens arméniens", *Journal Asiatique*, 1858, XI pp. 192-255.

EPHRAT, Daphna & ELMAN, Yaakov. "Orality and the Institutionalization of Tradition: The Growth of the Geonic Yeshiva and the Islamic Madrasa", *Transmitting Jewish Traditions: Orality, Textuality, and Cultural Diffusion*, New Haven, Yale University Press, 2000, pp. 107-137.

FATTAL, Antoine. "Comment les dhimmis étaient jugés en terre d'Islam", *Cahier Histoire Eg.*, 1951, III pp. 321-341.

FERRIER, Ronald. "Trade from the mid-14th Century to the End of the Safavid Period", *The Cambridge History of Iran*, Cambridge, 1986, VI pp. 412-490.

FIEY, J. M. "Adharbayjan chrétien", *Le Muséon*, Louvain, 1973, LXXXVI, 1-2 pp. 397-435.

FIEY, J. M. "Chrétientés Syriaques du Horasan et du Ségestan", *Le Muséon*, Louvain, 1973, LXXXVI, 1-2 pp. 75-104.

FISCHEL, Walter J. "The Rediscovery of the Medieval Jewish Community at Firuzkuh in Central Afghanistan", *Journal of the American Oriental Society*, April-June 1965, LXXXV, no. 2 pp. 148-153.

FISCHEL, Walter J. "Israel in Iran", *The Jews, Their History, Culture and Religion*, ed. Louis Finkelstein, New York, The Jewish Publication Society of America, 1949, pp. 817-857.

FISCHEL, Walter J. "Neue Beitrage zur Geschichte der Juden Baghdads im schen Mittelalter", *Monatsschrift für Geschichte unde Wissenschaft des Judentums*, Breslau, Stefan Munz, 1937, LXXXI pp. 416-422.

FISCHEL, Walter J. "Über Raschid ad-Daulas jüdische Ursprung, Ein Beitrag zur Geschichte des Judenfrage in Persien unter den Mongolen", *Monatsschrift für Geschichte und Wissenschaft des Judentums*, Breslau, Stefan Munz, 1937, LXXXI pp. 145-153.

FISCHEL, Walter J. "The Jews in Mediaeval Iran from the 16th to the 18th Centuries; Political, Economic and Communal Aspects", *Irano-Judaica*, Jerusalem, Ben Zvi Institute, 1982, pp. 265-291.

FISCHEL, Walter J. "Azarbaijan in Jewish History", *Proceedings of the American Academy for Jewish Research*, 1953, XXII, pp. 1-21.

FLOOR, Willem. "The Dutch and the Persian Silk Trade", *Safavid Persia*, ed. C. Melville, London, I.B.Tauris, 1996, pp. 323-368.

FRYE, Richard N. "Pre-Islamic and Early Islamic Cultures in Central Asia", *Turko-Persia in Historical Perspective*, Cambridge, Cambridge University Press, 1991, pp. 35-52.

GARSOIAN, Nina. "The Two Voices of Armenian Mediaeval Historiography: The Iranian Index", *Studia Iranica*, Paris, 1996, t. XXV pp. 7-44.

GERO, S. "Only a Change of Masters? The Christians of Iran and the Muslim Conquest", *Transition Periods in Iranian History*, Leuven, Association pour l'avancement des études iraniennes, 1987, pp. 43-48.

GIGNOUX, Philippe. "L'inscription de Kartir à Sar Mashhad", *Journal Asiatique*, Paris, 1968, t. CCLVI, pp. 387-418.

GIGNOUX, Philippe. "Sur quelques relations entre chrétiens et mazdéens d'après des sources syriaques", *Studia Iranica*, 1999, t. XXVIII pp. 83-94.

GREEN, Nile. "The Survival of Zoroastrianism in Yazd", *Iran*, London, 2000, XXXVIII pp. 115-122.

GUIDI, I. (ed.). "Un nuovo testo siriaco sulla storia degli ultimi Sassanidi", *Actes du VIIIe Congrès International des Orientalistes 1889*, Leiden, 1891, section sémitique (B), pp. 3-36.

GIL, Moshe. "The Exilarchate", *The Jews of Medieval Islam*, ed. Daniel Frank, Leiden, Brill, 1995, pp. 33-66.

GUILLAUME, Alfred. "The Meaning of Amaniya in Surah 2:73", *The World of Islam*, London, Macmillan and Co. Ltd, 1959, pp. 41-46.

GOITEIN, S. D. "Minority Selfrule and Government Control in Islam", *Studia ca*, 1970, XXXI pp. 101-116.

GRAY, Louis H. "The Jews in Pahlavi Literature", *Actes du XIVe Congrès International des Orientalistes 1905*, Paris, 1906, section 1, pp. 172-192.

HERZIG, Edmund. "The Deportation of the Armenians in 1604-1605 and Europe's Myth of Shah 'Abbas I", *Pembroke Papers I*, Cambridge, 1990, pp. 59-71.

HERZIG, Edmund. "The Rise of Julfa Merchants in the Late Sixteenth Century", *Safavid Persia*, ed. C. Melville, London, I.B.Tauris, 1996, pp. 305-322.

HINDS, Martin. "The First Arab Conquests in Fars", *Iran*, London, 1984, XXII pp. 39-54.

HODGSON, M. G. S. "The Isma'ili State", *The Cambridge History of Iran*, Cambridge University Press, 1968, V pp. 422-482.

JONES, A. H. M. "Were Ancient Heresies National or Social Movements in Disguise?" *Journal of Theological Studies*, 1959, X pp. 280-298.

KASAI, N. & NATSAGDORJ, S. "Socio-economic development: food and clothing in eastern Iran and Central Asia", *History of Civilizations of Central Asia*, ed. M. S. Asimov & C. E. Bosworth, Paris, UNESCO, 1998, IV pp. 381-390.

KATZ, Jacob. "Religion as a Uniting and Dividing Force in Modern Jewish History", *The Role of Religion in Modern Jewish History*, ed. Jacob Katz, Cambridge (MA), 1975, pp. 1-19.

KENNEDY, Hugh. "The Barmakid Revolution in Islamic Government", *Pembroke Papers 1*, ed. C. Melville, 1990, pp. 89-98.

KREYENBROEK, G. "The Zoroastrian Priesthood after the Fall of the Sasanian Empire", *Transition Periods in Iranian History*, Leuven, Association pour l'avancement des études iraniennes, 1987, pp. 151-166.

LAZARD, G. Pahlavi, "Parsi, Dari: les langues de l'Iran d'après Ibn al-Muqaffa'", *Iran and Islam in Memory of the late Vladimir Minorsky*, Edinburgh University Press, 1971, pp. 361-392.

LAZARUS, Felix. "Die Häupter der Vertriebenen; Beiträge zu einer Geschichte des Exilsfürsten in Babylonien unter der Arsakiden und Sassaniden", *Jahrbücher für judische Geschichte und Literatur*, ed. N. Brüll, Frankfurt-am-Main, 1890, X pp. 1-183.

LOCKHART, Laurence. "European Contacts with Persia, 1350-1736", *The Cambridge History of Iran*, Cambridge, Cambridge University Press, 1986, VI pp. 373-411.

LOEB, L. D. "Dhimmi Statuts and Jewish Roles in Iranian Society", *Ethnic Groups*, 1976, I pp. 89-105.

LOMBARD, Denys & DASHENG, Chen. "Le rôle des étrangers dans le commerce maritime de Quanzhou (Zeitun)", *Marchands et hommes d'affaires asiatiques dans l'Océan Indien et la Mer de Chine 13e-20e siècles*, ed. Denys Lombard & Jean Aubin, Paris, 1988, pp. 21-29.

MASTERS, Bruce. "The Treaties of Erzurum (1823 & 1848) and the Changing Status of Iranians in the Ottoman Empire", *Iranian Studies*, 1991, XXIV, no 1-4, pp. 3-15.

MATTHEE, Rudi. "The Career of Muhammad Beg, Grand Vizier of Shah 'Abbas II (r. 1642-1666)", *Iranian Studies*, 1991, XXIV, no 1-4 pp. 17- 36.

MAZUMDAR, Sanjoy & MAZUMDAR, Shampa. "Intergroup Social Relations and Architecture: Vernacular Architecture and Issues of Status, Power, and Conflict", *Environment and Behaviour*, 1999, XXIX, iii pp. 374-421.

MELVILLE, Charles. "New Light on the reign of Shah 'Abbas: Volume III of the Afzal al-Tawarikh", *Society and Culture in the Early Modern Middle East, Studies on Iran in the Safavid Period*, ed. Andrew J. Newman, Leiden, 2003, pp. 63-96.

MELVILLE, Charles. "Padshah-i Islam: The Conversion of Sultan Mahmud Ghazan Khan", *Pembroke Papers 1*, ed. C. Melville, Cambridge, Cambridge University Press, 1990, pp. 159-177.

MELVILLE, Charles. "Shah 'Abbas and the Pilgrimage to Mashhad in 1601", *Safavid Persia*, ed. C. Melville, London, I.B.Tauris, pp. 191-229.

MENASCE, Jean de. "Problème des Mazdéens dans l'Iran musulman", *Festschrift für Wilhelm Eilers*, Wiesbaden, 1967, pp. 220-230.

MENASCE, Jean de Menasce. "Zoroastrian Literature after the Muslim Conquest", *The Cambridge History of Iran*, Cambridge, 1975, IV pp. 543-565.

MINGANA, A. "The Early Spread of Christianity in Central Asia and the Far East: A New Document", *Bulletin of the John Rylands Library*, Manchester, 1925, XIX pp. 297-367.

MINORSKY, Vladimir. "Early Hebrew Persian Documents", *Journal of the Royal Asiatic Society*, London, 1942, pp. 181-194.

MINORSKY, Vladimir. "The Middle East in Western Politics in the 13th, 15th and 16th centuries", *Journal of the Royal Central Asian Society*, London, Oct 1940, pp. 427-461.

MOREEN, Vera B. "A Shi'i-Jewish 'Debate' (*Munazara*) in the Eighteenth Century", *Journal of the American Oriental Society*, Ann Arbor (Michigan), Oct-Dec 1999, CXIX, 4, pp. 570-589.

MOREEN, Vera B. "The Status of Religious Minorities in Safavid Iran between 1617-1661", *Journal of Near Eastern Studies*, 1981, XL pp. 119-134.

MORGAN, David. "The Great *Yasa* of Gengis Khan and Mongol Law in the Il-Khanate", *Bulletin of the School of Oriental and African Studies*, London, 1986, XLIX pp. 163-176.

MORONY, M. G. "Conquerors and Conquered: Iran", *Studies on the First Century of Islamic Society*, ed. G. H. Juynboll, Alton, Southern Illinois University Press, 1982, pp. 73-87.

MORONY, M. G. "The Effects of the Muslim Conquest on the Persian Population of Iraq", *Iran*, 1976, XIV pp. 41-59.

MOTTAHEDEH, Roy. "The Abbasid Caliphate in Iran", *The Cambridge History of Iran*, Cambridge, 1975, IV pp. 57-89.

NASR, H. "Religion in Safavid Persia", *Iranian Studies (Studies on Isfahan)*, 1974, no. 1-2, pp. 271-281.

NASR, S. N. "Life Sciences, Alchemy and Medicine", *The Cambridge History of Iran*, Cambridge, 1975, IV pp. 396-441.

NEGMATOV, N. N. "The Samanid State", *History of Civilizations of Central Asia*, ed. M. S. Asimov & C. E. Bosworth, Paris, UNESCO, 1998, IV pp. 77-94.

NETZER, Amnon. "Rashid al-Din and his Jewish Background", *Irano-Judaica III*, Jerusalem, Ben Zvi Institute, 1994, pp. 118-126.

NEUSNER, J. "Jews in Iran", *The Cambridge History of Iran*, Cambridge, Cambridge University Press, 1993, III pp. 909-923.

NIZAMI, K. A. "Popular movements, religious trends and Sufi influence on the masses in the post-Abbasid period", *History of Civilizations of Central Asia*, M. S. Asimov & C. E. Bosworth, Paris, UNESCO Publishing, 1998, IV pp. 365-380.

NYBERG, H. S. "Sassanid Mazdeism according to Moslem Sources", *Journal of the K.R. Cama Oriental Institute*, 1958, XXXIX pp. 3-63.

OMETTO, Franco. "Khatun Abadi, the Ayatollah who translated the Gospels", *Islamochristiana*, 2002, 28 pp. 55-72.

PAUL, Ludwig. "Early Judeo-Persian between Middle and New Persian", *Irano-Judaica V*, ed. Shaul Shaked & Amnon Netzer, Jerusalem, 2003, pp. 96-104.

PELLAT, Charles. "Jahiz à Bagdad", *Rivista degli studi orientali*, 1952, XXVII pp. 47-67.

PETECH, Luciano. "Les Marchands Italiens dans l'Empire Mongol", *Journal Asiatique*, Paris, Imprimerie Nationale, 1962, t. CCL pp. 549-574.

POURSHARIATI, Parvaneh. "Local Histories of Khurasan and the Pattern of Arab Settlement", *Studia Iranica*, Paris, 1998, t. XXVII pp. 41-82.

PUCKO, Zygmunt. "The Activity of Polish Jesuits in Persia and Neighbouring Countries in the 17th and 18th Centuries", *Proceedings of the Third European Conference of Iranian Studies*, ed. C. Melville, Wiesbaden, Dr. Ludwig Reichert Verlag, 1999, part 2 pp. 309-316.

PRITSAK, Omeljan. "Khazar Kingdom's Conversion", *Harvard Ukranian Studies*, 1980, II pp. 261-281.

REKAYA, M. "La place des provinces sudcaspiennes dans l'histoire de l'Iran de la conquête Arabe à l'avènement des Zaydites (637-864 ap. J.C.): particularisme régional ou rôle national?", *Revista degli Studi Orientali*, 1973-4, XLVIII pp. 117-152.

REKAYA, M. "L'intégration de l'ex-empire Sassanide dans l'aire culturelle que au Haut Moyen Age (VII-XIe siècles): A propos des travaux recents", *L'Arabisant*, 1987, XXVI pp. 59-68.

REKAYA, M. "Mazyar: Résistance ou intégration d'une province iranienne au monde musulman au milieu du IXe siècle ap. J.C.", *Studia Iranica*, 1973, t. II pp. 143-192.

RICHARD, J. "An Account of the Battle of Hattin, referring to Frankish Mercenaries in Oriental Moslem States", *Speculum*, 1952, XXVII, pp. 168-177.

RICHARD, J. "Le Début des Relations entre la Papauté et les Mongols de Perse", *Journal Asiatique*, Paris, 1939, t. CCXXXVII pp. 291-297.

RICHARD, J. "The Mongols and Franks", *Journal of Asian History*, Indiana University, 1969, III pp. 45-58.

RICHARD, Yann. "Minorités Religieuses en Iran: Note de Lecture sur deux Publications Récentes", *Studia Iranica*, 2002, t. XXXI / 2, pp. 267-272.

ROEMER, H. R. "The Safavid Period", *The Cambridge History of Iran*, Cambridge, 1986, VI pp. 189-350.

ROEMER, H. R. "The Successors of Timur", *The Cambridge History of Iran*, Cambridge, 1986, VI pp. 98-146.

ROEMER, H. R. "Timur in Iran", *The Cambridge History of Iran*, Cambridge, 1986, VI pp. 42-97.

ROEMER, H. R. "The Türkmen Dynasties", *The Cambridge History of Iran*, Cambridge, 1986, VI pp. 147-188.

ROSENBERG, Frédéric. "Notices de Littérature Parsie", *Tracts of Pahlawi, Parsi and Persian Literature*, St. Petersbourg, 1909, pp. 1-74.

ROTH, Norman. "Dhimma: Jews and Muslims in the Early Medieval Period", *Studies in Honour of Clifford Edmund Bosworth*, Leiden, Brill, I pp. 238-266.

RYAN, James D. "Christian Wives of Mongol Khans: Tartar Queens and Missionary Expectations in Asia", *Journal of Royal Asiatic Society*, Cambridge, 1998, VIII pp. 411-442.

SAVORY, R. M. "The Safavid Administrative System", *The Cambridge History of Iran*, Cambridge, 1986, VI pp. 351-372.

SELIGSOHN, Max. "The Hebrew-Persian Manuscripts of the British Museum", *Jewish Quarterly Review*, London, 1903, XV pp. 278-301.

SHABAN, M. A. "Khurasan at the Time of the Arab Conquest", *Iran and Islam in Memory of V. Minorsky*, Edinburgh, 1971, pp. 479-490.

SHAH, Nasim Hasan. "The Concept of al-Dhimmah and the Rights and Duties of Dhimmis in an Islamic State", *Journal of Muslim Minority Affairs*, Institute of Muslim Minority Affairs, 1988, IX pp. 217-222.

SINOR, D. "The Kitan and the Kara Khitay", *History of Civilizations of Central Asia*, M .S. Asimov & C. E. Bosworth, Paris, UNESCO Publishing, 1998, IV pp. 227-242.

SOURDEL, D. "La politique religieuse du calife abbaside al-Ma'mun", *Revue des Etudes ques*, 1962, XXX pp. 27-48.

SPULER, Bertold. "La situation de l'Iran à l'époque de Marco Polo", *Oriente Poliano*, Rome, Instituto Italiano per il Medio ed Estremo Oriente, 1957, pp. 121-132.

SPULER, Bertold. "Le Christianisme chez les Mongols aux XIIIe et XIVe siècles", *Tracta Altaica Denis Sinor*, Wiesbaden, 1976, pp. 621-631.

SPULER, Bertold. "Les Iraniens et le gouvernement des Arabes au début de la domination de l'Islam", *Orientalia Suecana*, 1984-1986, XXXIII-XXXV pp. 395-400.

SPULER, Bertold. "L'Islam et les Minorités", *Festschrift H. R. Roemer*, Beirut, 1979, pp. 609-619.

STERN, S. M. "Ya'qub the Coppersmith and Persian National Sentiment", *Iran and Islam*, ed. C. E. Bosworth, Edinburgh, 1971, pp. 535-556.

SZUPPE, Maria. "La participation des femmes de la famille royale à l'exercice du pouvoir en irna safavide au XVIe siècle", *Studia Iranica*, L'Association pour l'Avancement des Etudes Iraniennes, 1994, XXIII.2 pp. 211-258.

SZUPPE, Maria. "Un marchand du Roi de Pologne en Perse 1601-1602", *Moyen Orient & Océan Indien*, 1986, III pp. 81-110.

TAVAKOLI-TARGHI, Mohamad. "Contested Memories of Pre-Islamic Iran", *Medieval History*, 1999, Journal 3 pp. 245-275 - Journal still unpublished.

TIRMIDHI, B. M. "Zoroastrians and their fire temples in Iran and adjoining countries from the 9th to the 14th centuries as gleaned from the Arabic geographical works", *Islamic Culture*, 1950, XXIV pp. 271-284.

TUCCI, Ugo. "Una relazione di Giovan Battista Vecchietti sulla Persia e sul Regno di Hormuz (1587)", *Oriente Moderno*, Roma, April 1955, XXXV-4 pp. 149-160.

WALBRIDGE, John. "A Persian Gulf in the Sea of Lights: The Chapter on Naw-ruz in the Bihar al-Anwar", *Iran*, British Institute of Persian Studies, 1997, XXXV, pp. 83-92.

WIDENGREN, Geo. "The Status of the Jews in the Sassanian Empire", *Iranica Antiqua*, Leiden, Brill, 1961, I pp. 117-162.

YASTREBOVA, Olga. "The Manuscripts of Cangranghace-name and Arda Viraf Name by Zartost e Bahram e Pazdu", *Studia Orientalia*, Helsinki, 2003, 95 pp. 251-261.

ZARRINKUB, Abd al-Husayn. "The Arab Conquest of Iran and its Aftermath", *The Cambridge History of Iran*, Cambridge, Cambridge University Press, 1975, IV pp. 1-56.

ZEKIYAN, L. B. "Xoja Safar, ambasciatore di Shah Abbas a Venezia", *Oriente Moderno*, 1978, LVIII pp. 357-367.

Reviews

GIL, Moshe & SHAKED, Shaul. Book Review of Michael Morony's "Iraq after the Muslim Conquest", *Journal of the American Oriental Society*, Oct-Dec 1986, vol. 106 no 4 pp. 819-823.

Other Sources

Encyclopaedia references appear in detail in the footnotes and have not been repeated here.

Index

A'sam, Hubaysh al- 48
aarlims 140
Aaron 141
    Bar Hebraeus' father 63
aavun 140
Aban 35
Abaqa 58, 64, 65, 75, 80
Abbas I, Shah 101, 103, 104, 107,
    111, 112, 114-117, 120,
    122-124, 127, 130-132, 141,
    147
Abbas II, Shah 102, 104, 113, 120,
    123, 125, 128-130, 132, 135,
    141
Abbasid
    administrative system 42
    caliph 42
    Caliphate 32
    caliphs 27, 53, 87
    capital 41, 44
    court 39
    divan 41
    dynasty 16
    Empire 41
    government 22, 31, 34
    revolution 20, 21
    rule 25
Abbasids 3, 16, 19, 20, 22, 24, 28, 33,
    37, 45, 47, 50
Abbé Carré 109
Abd al-Rahman, Salih b. 18
Abd al-Razzaq 92
Abd Isho b. Bahriz 49
Abdiso bar Berikka 85
Abi al-Aron, Mansur b. 73
Abi Salih, Fayd b. 35
ablution 69, 149
Aboda Zara 8
Abraham 141
    bishop of Haditha 39
    Catholicos 42
Abu Galib 44
Abu Muslim 20, 21, 23

Abu Sa'id 73, 78, 82-84, 88
Abu Salama 28
Abu Salem 86
Abu Yahya of Merv 49
academic
    centres 9, 15, 47
    institutions 2, 136
    school 10
academic institutions 136
academies 14
academies, Jewish 3, 9, 10, 37, 42, 44,
    45
accession
    of Ahmad Teguder 65
    of al-Mahdi 48
    of Arghun 66
    of Berke 59
    of Ghazan 69
    of the Umayyads 17
    of Uljaytu 71
Achaemenid period 111
Adam, William 78
Adam's offspring 141
administration 3, 4, 17-20, 25, 29, 30,
    33, 40-43, 49, 50, 53, 54, 63,
    82, 160
administrative
    abilities 46
    chaos 69
    cooperation 50
    language 18
    positions 16, 53, 63, 89, 121
    skills 60, 67, 86
    staff 91
    tools 2
administrator
    Ali Rabban al-Tabari 39
    the Uighur monk Ashmut 66
administrators
    Christian 66
    Jewish and Christian 17, 34, 160
    Muslim 40
    non-Muslim 45, 89

Index

Zoroastrian 33
Adonites 139
Adud al-Dawla Fana 42
Adurbad-i Emedan 25, 28
Afghan
   army 157
   commander 152
   invasion 1, 3, 134, 142, 155, 163
   leader 156
   monarch 142
   occupation 89
   rule 157
Afghans 151, 155-157, 161
Afrasiyab 144
Afshin 24, 25
Afzal al-Tawarikh 107
agents 63, 70, 118, 122
Agha Piri 119, 120, 125, 128
Agra 129
agricultural
   skills 103
   soil 107
ahd-nama 100
Ahmad
   Saffarid ruler 30
   Teguder 65, 66, 69
Ahoudemmeh 11
Ahriman 149
Ahwazi, Abu Ya'qub al- 49
Akbar, Shah 121, 152, 154
Al-Adab al-Saghir 31
Aleksander, katholikos 126
Aleppo 63, 91, 110
Alexander 84, 150, 156
Alexander IV, Pope 74
Alexander, Mirza Zul-Qarnai 135
Ali 5, 26, 46, 97, 99, 100
Ali Quli Khan, vizier 128
Ali Shah, Grand Vizier 73
Allah 73
Allahverdi Khan (Armenian) 120, 121
Allahverdi Khan (Georgian) 104, 130
allegiance 24, 25, 33, 161
Almagest 48
alms 9, 70
Alvand 95
ambassador
   Byzantine 77

Gregorio Pereira Fidalgo 126
Israel Orie 122
Jewish 108
Nointel 120
sieur Michel 123
Thomas Baker 122
Uighur monk 66
ambassadors
   Armenian 121, 122
   Christian 162
   European 127
   Italian 78, 92
   Nestorian 4, 57, 76
   Nestorian & other Christians 74
ambergis 149
Ambrogio Contarini 92
Amid 73, 89
Amin al-Dawla 43, 137
Amin, al- 34
Amina 142
amir
   Ali 98
   Qutlmesh 153
Amir Chupan 72, 73, 78
Amir Matta 67
Amoraim 9
Amram
   Aaron b. 41
   Bishr 41
Ananda, Emperor of China 82
Anatolia 90
Anbari, Ahmad b. Isra'il al- 39
andarz 32
Andronicus II 77
angels 141
Anna Baet, Church 135
Annals, Jewish chronology 47
anti-Abbasid 45
anti-Arab 21
anti-ascetic 11
anti-Christian 8, 71
anti-Iranian 161
anti-Islamic 21
anti-Muslim 65
anti-Nestorianism 85
anti-Talmudic 46
Antioch 64, 74
Antiochus 144

antiquity 111
Antonio de Gouvea 108
Anushazad 11
Anushiravan, Khusraw 6, 11, 32, 98, 99
anusim 74, 106
apologetics 49
apostate 3
   Christian 65
   Jewish 106
   Sunbad 22
   Zoroastrian 11, 31
apostates
   Armenian 121
   Jewish 82, 86
   non-Muslims in general 101, 104
   Zoroastrian 160
apostle, Thomas 36
Apostolic, Church 120, 124, 126
Aq Qoyunlu 91, 95, 97
Arab
   academic world 47
   accent 40
   army 151
   authorities 19
   circles 26
   civilization 29
   conquest 1, 2, 25, 150
   delegation 48
   domination 32
   dynasties 33
   empire 50
   establishment 3, 27, 37
   govenor 19
   governor 27
   governors 19
   invaders 52, 158, 159
   invasion 2, 10, 14-17, 30, 35, 37, 45, 52, 71, 75, 86, 91, 93, 155, 159
   Islamic world 87
   king Zahak 147
   military men 18
   opponents 27
   prophet 150
   rule 2, 15, 17, 46, 52, 66
   rulers 2, 21, 28, 29
   settlement 20
   speaking world 31
   tax collector 19
Arab-speaking 29
Arabian genealogies 27
Arabic 2, 4, 18, 19, 24, 29-32, 37, 47-49, 62, 65, 73, 79, 81, 82, 85, 99, 136, 142, 146, 151, 154, 160
Arabicized 33
Arabs 1-3, 6, 13, 15, 17-20, 24-27, 29, 33, 37, 45, 46, 50, 52, 68, 72, 90, 93, 95, 99, 150, 151, 155, 159, 160
Arakel of Tabriz 104, 107, 112, 114, 124
Aramaic 142
Arameans 46
Araxes 96, 113
Arbela 63, 65, 66, 69, 71-73, 86
Archbishop
   of Echmiazin 120
   of Merv 14
   of New Julfa 120, 124
archbishop of Sultaniya 91
archers 151
archiduke Ferdinand 122
architects 85
architecture 162
Arda Viraz Nama 79, 80
Ardashir
   Papakan 7
   son of Isfandiyar 83
Ardashir-nama 83
arel 139
Arghun 66, 67, 76
Aristotle 48
Armenia 6, 111-114, 117, 120, 129, 160
Armenian
   cemetry of Agra 129
Armenian
   apostates 121
   artisans 121
   Catholics 125
   children 125
   churches 112, 120, 124, 128, 135
   clergy 66, 124
   cleric 128

Index

colonies 120
communities 84
community 111, 125, 128
converts 120
dignitaries 121
ecclesiastics 125
envoys 122
families 113, 117, 119
family of Tabriz 121
governor of Mush 67
houses 107
interpreter 121
Jew 145
merchant 112, 122, 128, 135
merchants 115, 117, 118, 120-122, 128, 129
messenger 121
monks 78
paintings 135
passengers 118
patriarch 125
physician 63
population 112, 113, 117
priests 122
renegades 130
settlements 120
sources 112
subjects 124
suburbs 128
village 112
women 121, 129
Armenians 2, 4, 59, 63, 76, 78, 92, 94, 101, 105, 107, 108, 110-135, 145, 156, 157, 161, 162
Arok 66
Arrajan 37
artisans 54, 121, 129
artists 83, 135, 152
Arzhang-i Mani 154
Asad 40
Ashmut, Uighur monk 66
Ashqar, family al- 44
Ashraf, Shah 142, 143, 157, 158
Asia 43, 76, 81, 92, 118, 132
Assassins 64
Assyrians 132, 161
Astarabad 105
Astrakhan 117

astrologer 45, 48, 79
astronomer 48, 60
astronomy 142
Asuristan 6, 8, 9, 160
Ata, Wasil b. 46
atabeg 56
Atatmah, Year 139
Athari, Masha'allah b. 45
Athens 12
Attar 81, 137
Aturfarnbag i Farrukhzatan 30
Aturpat-i Emetan 30
Augustin
    Fathers 124
    missionaries 125
Augustins 124, 125, 127
Aurangzeb 145
autonomy 120
Avadick 135
Avanchinz, Marvara 119
Avesta 101
Awdisho IV Marun 91
Awdisho of Nisibis 87
Ayin-i Hushang 154
Ayn Jalut 59, 61
Azadmard, Shapur b. 30
Azerbaijan 24, 60, 63, 65-67, 77, 88, 89, 116, 131-133
Azeri merchants 114
Azeris 116
Baba Batra 7, 9
Baba Kamma 7
Baba Mezi'a 9
Babai b. Farhad 97, 106, 109, 142, 143
Babai b. Lutf 83, 103, 107, 110, 141
Babak 24
Babylon 45, 71, 139
Babylonians 139
Badr al-Din Lu Lu 62
Baghdad 28, 34, 36, 37, 41-46, 48, 49, 52, 53, 59, 60, 62-64, 66, 67, 70, 73, 74, 77, 81, 90, 126, 131
Baghdiantz 114, 116, 119, 120
Bagrat V 89
Baha'uddin Amili 153
Bahadur, Abu Sa'id 83, 84
Bahariyyat 79

Bahman 144
Bahrain 18
Bahram Chubin 9, 28
Bahram Gur 8
Bahram Pajdu 79
Bahram-e Kucak 154
Bahramis 19
Baikal Lake 54
Baikand 80
Baker, Thomas 122
Baladhuri 18
Balkh 28
Balkhi, Hiwi al- 41, 47
Balshasar 143
Banan, Salmawayh b. 39
Bandar Abbas 105, 109, 118, 122
Bandar Kung 109
Baniyan tradesmen 119
Baniyans 108, 110, 123, 127
banker
    from Tabriz 70
    Netira 41
bankers 41, 43, 110, 119
Bar Hebraeus 13, 22, 36, 39, 44, 54, 55, 60, 63-68, 85, 89
Bar Kochba 37
Bar Sauma 70, 76, 77, 85, 160
Barakat, Hibatallah Abu al- 43
barashnom 149
Baraz 22
Barmaki, Yahya al- 48
Barmakid 28, 34, 48
Barthelemy of Bologna 78
Barzaeus, Gaspar 108
Barzou 144
Basra 35, 45, 46
battle 24, 32, 54, 59, 144, 150
Batu 63
Bausani, Alessandro 153
Baydu 68, 69
Bayt al-Hikma 48
Behdin Asa Jamshid 147
Behdins 150, 151
Behnam Shabhti 90
Bekorot 9
Benedict XI, Pope 78
Benjamin of Tudela 43, 44
Berbers 46

Bereshit-nama 83
Berke 59, 60, 69
Beth Abishai 90
Beth Ishak 90
Beth Kudsh 90
Beth Risha 90
Beth Sebhiryana 90
Bezah 9
Bible 83, 85, 139
Bihafrid Mahfravardan 21, 22
Bihar al-Anwar 155
Birtis, fort of 96
Biruni 47
bishoprics 3, 11, 13, 35, 40, 78, 129
bishops 11, 36, 65, 77
Biur Milot Ha-Torah 83
Bizhan 144
blasphemy 40
Bokhtisho 34-36, 39, 42, 47, 49
Bologna 125
Boniface IX, Pope 91
Boqa 66
Bourandokht 13
brewery 9
bribe 19, 114, 117, 128, 142
British Library 83
Brother David 74
Buddhism 64
Buddhist
    majority of Mongols 86
    Mongols 62
    priests 58
    temples 64, 68, 69
Buddhists 70
Bukhara 23, 55, 81, 142, 144, 145
Bulliet, Richard 21, 27, 30
Bunyat 23
bureaucracy 19, 53, 62, 89
butcher 104
Buyid
    amir Adud al-Dawla 42
    amirs 42
Buyid
    court 42
    rule 42
Buyids 28, 42
Byzantine
    borders 27

Index 253

Emperor 12, 64, 77
enemies 160
general 8
princess 91, 95
Byzantine Empire 3, 10, 12
Byzantines 10, 13, 24, 26, 33-35
Byzantium 11, 13, 24, 33, 36, 48, 49
Caesar 141
caliphate 22, 24, 25, 33, 35, 38-42, 160
caliphs 16, 20, 27, 34, 38, 43, 49-51, 53, 69, 86, 87
Callendars 119
Callinicum 26
campaign 7, 88, 89, 96, 120, 130, 157
Capucins 124, 125
caravan services 110
caravanserai 110
Carmelite missionaries 104
Carmelites 5, 112, 115, 121, 124-126, 128, 130, 132
carpenters 121
Carpini, John of Plano 60
Caspian
    area 103
    coast 103, 107, 113
    provinces 32, 115
    sea 114
Caterino Zeno 92
Catholic
    Armenians 129
    bishop 78, 91, 126
    bishoprics 78
    Church 124, 126
    community 75
    countries 123, 124
    emissaries 126
    faith 127
    family 120
    mission 124
    missionaries 75, 124-126, 131, 132
    monarchs 125, 126
    priests 124
    sovereigns 118, 124
    theology 77
catholicate 35
Catholicism 75, 122, 124, 125, 127, 129, 132

Catholicos 10-13, 15, 21, 33, 35, 36, 38, 42, 43, 48, 50, 59, 62, 64-66, 68, 70-73, 76, 77, 85
Caucasian
    Christian 130
    population 114
    women 130
Caucasus 56, 60, 94, 95, 113, 114, 120, 130
Central Asia 21, 54, 59, 87
Central Asian 63, 87
ceremony 44, 65, 115, 149
Chaghatai, Khanate of 87
Chaldeans 132
Chancellery 43
Chardin 101, 109, 110, 113, 119, 120, 125, 127, 135
Charles II of Naples 76
chieftain 54, 141
China 77, 78, 80, 82, 90, 114, 143
Chinese
    amiral 92
    art and science 87
    Qara Khitais 54
    translators 82
Chinqay 56
Christ 12, 126
Christianity 6, 10, 14, 31, 35, 40, 51, 54, 56, 59, 63, 64, 68, 74, 76, 77, 87, 97, 105, 113, 131, 161
Christians 1-8, 10-18, 20, 21, 25-27, 31, 33-40, 42-46, 48-79, 82, 84-86, 89-91, 93, 94, 101-103, 112, 113, 115, 121, 123-128, 130, 132, 133, 155, 159-162
Chronicle of the Carmelites 96, 108, 118
churches 35, 60, 64, 69-71, 74, 86, 102, 112, 120, 124, 126, 128, 131, 134, 135, 162
Circassians 94, 130, 131
circumcise 58, 130
civilization 1, 5, 15, 29, 31, 32, 45, 48, 50, 51, 92, 160
Clement XI, Pope 126
Cochin 108
Colbert 119
Colonial Archives 157

comedians 102
commander-in-chief 116, 120, 130
commerce 94, 100, 102, 109, 111,
    116, 117, 142
concessions 118, 123, 131
conflict 37, 47, 124, 159
conqueror 4, 21, 25, 152
Constantine I, Catholicos 66
Constantine II, Catholicos 66
Constantine, Emperor 10
Constantinople 91, 105
conversion 1, 3, 6, 11, 16, 20, 21, 25,
    35, 37, 43, 51, 54, 57, 59, 64,
    69-71, 75, 77, 82, 87, 89, 93,
    97, 101, 102, 104-106, 110,
    124, 125, 133, 142, 145, 149,
    151, 157, 161
Copts 46
Cordoba 142
Council of Lyon 66, 75
councils 9
counsels 32
court 2, 3, 7-11, 13-15, 21, 25, 29,
    33-36, 38, 41-44, 46, 47, 56-58,
    63, 64, 67, 68, 71, 72, 75, 76,
    78, 81, 85, 86, 92, 94, 96, 102,
    105, 106, 108, 110, 116, 117,
    119-122, 125-128, 130, 131,
    134, 135, 152, 155, 157, 159,
    160, 162
cow 149
craftsmanship 86, 132
craftsmen 88
Ctesiphon 11, 12, 73
culture 4, 20, 21, 32, 47, 50, 51, 79,
    86, 92, 102, 103, 152, 153, 160,
    161, 163
customs 122
Cyrus 83, 140
Czar 122
Dabistan-i Mazhab 145, 154
Dadestan 149
Dadisho 11
Dadistan-i Denig 30
Dadoye 19
dakhma 98, 99
Damascene Christians 61
Damascus 61, 90

Damavand 105, 147
Damghan 46
Daniel (Prophet) 26
Daniyal-nama 143
Dara 26
Dari 79
Dariush 143
dasatir 154
Dastur Ardashir 147
Dastur Ardashir Nushirvan 153
Dastur Bahram 147
Dastur Kamdin Padam 147, 153
dasturs 92, 150
David
    Abraham 38
    Anan b. 46
    Yehudah b. 140
David and Solomon 141
David of Abarquh 109
Dawlatshah 29
Daylam 20, 24, 28, 37
dayyan 142
deav 147, 152
Dehkhwarqan 78
Delhi 145
Demetrius 76
demons 80
Denha I, Catholicos 64, 70
Denha, Jacobite Mafrian 12
Denys 38, 77, 78
Despina Khatun 64, 95
Deuteronomy 82
dhimma 25
dhimmi 25, 36, 42, 44, 45, 82
Diaspora 7
Diatessaron of Tatien 84
dictionary 83, 153, 154
dinar 18, 30
Dinawar 40
Dinkard 28, 30
diocese 6, 78, 87, 91, 120, 161
diplomacy 4, 63, 85, 95, 161, 162
diplomats 74, 76, 121
dirham 18
discriminatory laws 19, 36, 39, 43, 51,
    100
diwan al-mawali 44
Diyarbakir 67, 89

Index

Doghuz Khatun 60, 63
Dominican 75, 125
Doquz Khatun 59, 60
druggists 111
Dutch 118, 123, 127
Dutch company 117
Dutch sources 107
East India companies 114, 118, 119
Easter ceremony 65
Eastern Asia 54
Eastern Syriac Church 73
Echmiazin 120
economy 95, 107, 110, 117, 119, 122, 129, 130, 132
Edesaci, Nahapet 125
Edessa 26, 89
Edessa, School of 12
Edward I of England 76
Edward II 78
Edwards, Arthur 112
Egypt 45, 46, 66, 71-73, 78, 90, 143
Egyptians 62
El'azar
    Refu'ah b. 142
    Yehudah b. 109, 142
Elias of Nisibis 22
Elie III 50
Eliyahu 110
emasculate 57
emigration 129
emissaries 46, 74, 126, 131
England 118
English
    company 117
    East India Company 118, 121
    merchant 112, 129
    merchants 118
    trade 118
    vessels 123
epic 83, 137
epidemics 91
Erivan 115, 129
erke'un 82
Erkoush 91
Esther 83
Ethiopia 78
eunuch 40, 156
Euphrates 17, 89

Europe 4, 56, 74, 76, 78, 85, 88, 91, 94, 105, 108, 114, 117, 118, 121, 123, 124, 129, 134, 136
Europeans 74, 92, 123, 128
Ewen Namag 30
excommunication 124
Exilarch 7-9, 15, 37, 38, 40-44, 46
Exodus 82
Ezekiel, Judah b. 9
Ezra-nama 83
factory 119
Falashan 113
Farabi, al- 49
Farahabad 104-107, 113, 115
Faramarz 144
Fargard 149
Farhat brothers 120
Faridun 84
Farrukhanshah, Isa b. 39
Fars 19, 25, 28, 30, 36, 42, 48, 91, 101, 104, 153
Fath Ali Khan 156
Fath-nama 137
Father Alexander
    of Rhodes 105, 106, 124, 129
    of Saint-Sylevester 125
    of Saint-Sylvester 113, 128
Father Ambroise 125
Father Ignatius 131
Father John Thaddeus 130
Father Krusinski 122
Fattal, Antoine 25
fatwa 104
Fayyum 46
Fendereski, Mir Abu al-Qasim 153
Fereidun 144, 147
Firdaws al-Hakim 48
Firdawsi 32, 33, 83, 137, 141, 143, 147
fire temple 6, 55, 69, 80, 87, 98, 102, 147, 159
Fischel, Walter 5
food 58, 71, 141
fortress 59, 71
fortune-tellers 109
Fra Ricoldo de Monte 77
Fra Ricoldo of Monte Croce 68
France 118, 119, 123, 129

Francis of Perugia 78
Franciscan 75, 78
Frankish rule 64
Franks 74, 77
French
  ambassador 123
  company 121
  consulate 91
  East India Company 119
  factory 119
  government 119, 123
  merchant 121
  merchants 118, 119, 123, 125
  missionaries 125
Fryer, John 104, 105, 111
Fugger family 119
gabr 62, 96
Gabriel Bokhtisho 49
Gabriel de Chinon 125
Gabriel II Abidallah Bokhtish 42
Gabriel II Bokhtisho 34, 36, 49
Gabriel III Bokhtisho 49
Gabriel of Shiggar 12
Gabriol, Salomon b. 83
Gaikhatu 68, 84
Ganj-nama 137-139
Gaon 37, 40, 41, 106
Garcia de Silva Figueroa 108
Gazarta of Beth Sharwaye 89
Gemara 46
Gengis Khan 54-56, 82, 88
Genoa 114
Genoese manufacturers 114
Geometry 48
geonim 37, 38, 42, 46, 47
Georges b. Gabriel Bokhtish 47
Georges, a convert to Nest 12
Georges, Catholicos 35
Georgia 89, 96, 103, 107, 121, 131
Georgian
  communities 131
  houses 107
  Jews 107, 113
  king 89
  kings 121
  nobles 96
  prince 60
  princes 131

princesses 130, 131
prisoners 131
renegades 130
slaves 130
soldiers 130
territories 96
throne 131
wives 130
women 96, 130
Georgians 60, 89, 94, 96, 107, 116, 130, 131
Germany 119
Ghazan 64, 68-71, 77, 82, 89
Ghaznavid 33
gifts 8, 120
Gilan 35, 37, 105, 107, 113, 114
Gilgal 112
Giosafat Barbaro 92, 107, 112
girdle 107, 148
Gittin 9
Gobineau, count de 100
gold 20, 58, 114, 128
Golden Age 16, 50, 66
Golden Horde 58, 63, 75, 79
Gombroon 109, 118, 122
Grand Vizier 4, 43, 64-67, 71, 72, 78, 86, 104-106, 127, 156
Gregory XIII, Pope 108
Grigor of Akanc 60
Gudarz 89
Gundishapur 12, 15, 34, 35, 40, 45, 47, 48, 51, 73, 85, 160
Gundishapur, Academy of 48
Gurgan 23
Gurgani, Isa Abu Sahl al- 49
Gurgin Khan 156
Guyuk 56
Guzia 90
Ha-Levi, Judah 83
Hafiz 4, 83, 136, 143
Haft Baradaran 144
Haji 104
Hajjaj b. Yusuf 19, 33
Hakim Da'ud al-Tabib 51
Hakim Davud 109
Hakkari mountains 91
Halakha, Babylonian 42
Haly Abbas 42

Index 257

Hamadan 37, 65, 70, 71, 82, 105, 106, 108-110
Hamid al-Din 58
Hanbali 25
Hanon Isho 63, 64
Hanukka 106
Hanukkah-nama 137
Hanway, Jonas 129
harem 62, 94, 96, 109, 121, 128, 130, 156
Harran 26
Harun al-Rashid 34, 36, 48
Hasan and Husayn 150
Hashimite religion 151
Hasnun 44
Hayawayh (Hiwi al-Balkhi) 41
Haylan, Yuhanna b. 49
Hayton, Jean 66, 68
Hebrew 44, 45, 47, 82, 108, 139, 142
Hebrews 140
Hemmis, Nicola 101
Henry III of Castile 91
Herat 84, 87, 88, 154
Herbert, Thomas 108
heresies 18, 36
heterodox movements 42
Hethum I 63, 70, 77
Hethum of Korykos 66
Hezekiah 42
Hibatallah
    Abu al-Hasan 43
Hifz al-Sihha 48
High Commissioners 77
high priest 25, 28, 31, 101, 149, 152
high priest 21
Hindu 62, 149, 154
Hira 48
Hisda 9
Hisham, al- 19
Hnanisho II 35
Hobot Yehudah 142
Hofni, Samuel b. 47
Homer 48
Hormizd IV 11, 52, 161
Hormuz 92, 108, 110, 112, 123, 124
hospital 34, 42, 47, 48, 82
Hulagu 58-61, 63, 65, 74, 79, 84
Hullin 9

Hulvan 12
Hungary 74
Husayn, son of Ali 26
Husayni, Khurshah al- 96
Iberian kings 108
Ibn Abd al-Rahman, Sahlih 18
Ibn Abdallah, Ala 18
Ibn Abi Usaybi'a 39
Ibn Adi, Abu Zakariya 49
Ibn al-Alqami 60
Ibn al-Athir 43
Ibn al-Furat, Muhassin 41, 42
Ibn al-Layth, Amr 28, 29
Ibn al-Layth, Yaqub 28
Ibn al-Nadim 31, 49
Ibn al-Qifti 39
Ibn al-Rumi 29
Ibn al-Salt, Abu Nuh al-Anb 35, 48
Ibn al-Tilmiz 43
Ibn al-Ukhuwwa 82
Ibn Fadlan, Abu Abdallah 44
Ibn Khallikan 39
Ibn Khurdadbih 31
Ibn Mashiah, Aharon 141
Ibn Muqaffa 19, 20, 31
Ibn Safiya 44
Ibn Samha, Abu Sa'd 43
Ibraniyya, Pinhas b. Bata al- 47
idolater 25, 62, 70, 82, 145
idols 70
Ifra Hormizd 8
Il-Khan 63, 65, 67, 68, 73, 75, 87
Il-Khanate 60, 63, 67, 75
Imam Quli Khan 121
imams 55, 82
Imrani 136, 138, 139, 141, 142
India 37, 64, 70, 78, 81, 88, 92, 100, 102, 108, 118, 119, 121, 129, 132, 135, 136, 143-147, 149, 150, 152, 154
Indian
    attack 130
    co-religionists 81
    coastlines 100
    coasts 114
    medicine 48
    Ocean 92
    subcontinent 152

trade 117, 119
tradesmen 123
Indians 105, 108, 117
Indo-Iranian trade 119
industry 107, 117
infidel 95, 97, 137, 139, 145, 148
Innocent III, Pope 66
insurrection 3, 22, 25
Iranahindkastani 120
Irano-Babylonian 47
Irano-Byzantine 6
Irano-Roman 6
Iranophile 27
Iranshahr 25
Iraq 6, 19, 27, 46, 53, 57, 67, 91, 160
Isa, Ali b. 41
Isaac, Christian secretary 64
Isaac, Nestorian Patriarch 91
Isaac, tax collector 108
Isawiyya 37
Isfahan 2, 8, 19, 23, 37, 44, 100-105, 107, 110, 111, 113-115, 117, 120-122, 127-129, 131, 132, 134, 136, 141, 153, 156, 157, 162
Isfahani, al-
  Abu Isaac b. Jacob 37
  Hamza 47
  Zadwayh b. Shahwayh 31
Isfahanians 37
Isfandiyar 28
Isfandiyar, Khusraw b. 153
Isfandiyar-i Aturpat 28
Ishaq, Hunayn b. 48, 49
Ishaq, Prophet 141
Ishaq, the Turk 22
Isho Bokht 48
Isho'yahb 13
Isho'yahb III 52
Ishraqi School 153
Iskandar, Kaykavus b. 32
Islam 1, 2, 6, 16-21, 24, 25, 27, 29, 31, 35, 37-39, 42, 43, 45, 47, 51-53, 57, 59, 60, 64, 65, 68-71, 73, 79, 82, 89, 93-96, 104-106, 109, 113, 121, 125, 127, 128, 131, 132, 142, 145, 153, 155, 157, 159, 160, 162

Isma'il I, Shah 93, 95, 97, 102
Ismailis 57, 59, 60, 65
Ispahbad 22, 25
Israel 139
Israel of Kashgar 49
Israelites 7, 26, 137
Istakhr 153
Istanbul 112, 122
Istanbul, Academy of 136
Italian merchants 75, 78, 114
Italians 116
Italy 119, 125, 135
Iwanis (John) of Tabriz 84
Izad 149
Izz al-Dawla 42
Jacobites 13, 33, 38, 48, 65, 78, 88, 89, 132
jahbadh 40, 41
Jahiz, al- 39
Jahm, Ali b. 29
Jalal Abdallah 42
Jalayirids 88
Jam-i Kay Khusraw 154
Jamasp-nama 31
James II of Aragon 76
Jami 136, 141
Jami' al-Tawarikh 56, 72
Jamshid 84
Jawhari 72
Jedivdad 149
Jerusalem 13, 46, 76
Jesuits 125, 128
Jesus 11
jeweller 105, 110
jewels 110, 116
Jewess 7
Jewry 7-9, 14, 37, 41, 42, 44, 45, 103, 105, 106, 108, 110, 111, 127, 136, 139, 141, 142, 160
Jews 1-4, 6-10, 12-18, 21, 25-27, 31, 33-35, 37-42, 44-47, 49-55, 57, 58, 62, 64, 66, 67, 70-74, 81-83, 86, 89, 90, 94, 97, 102-113, 115, 116, 121, 127-129, 133, 136, 138, 139, 141-143, 145-147, 155-157, 159-162
Jibrail of Bartelli 86
jizya 44, 69, 71, 72, 86, 102

Index

Job of Edessa 49
Johannes de Galonifontibus 91
Johary 70
John bar Nagore, convent 86
John bar Penkaye 18
John of Daylam 20
John the Baptist, convent of 72, 73, 85
John XXII, Pope 78
Johudak 70, 72
Joseph of Arbela 73
Joseph, Jewish ambassador 108
Joseph, Kohen Zedeq b. 41
Joseph, Metropolitan of Mer 35
Joseph, physician 11
Joseph, Saadia b. 46
Judah, David b. 38
Judaism 6, 14, 31, 37, 38, 47, 51, 64, 82, 97, 104-106, 142, 145, 155
Judeo-Arabic 47, 138
Judeo-Persian 4, 72, 81, 83, 136, 137, 139, 143, 145, 149
Julamerik 91
Julayechi, Khachatur 135
Julayechi, Simeon 135
Julfa 113, 114
Jupiter 141
Juwayni 54, 55, 57, 58, 65, 67, 82
Juzjani 56, 57
Kabbalists 142
Kafir 145
Kahana, Mubashshir 41
kalantar 117, 119, 121, 125, 128
Kalila wa Dimna 31
Kama, Kavus 149
kamar 8
Kamdin Bahreh 148
Kaphar Shama 90
Kara'im 46
Karaism 37, 42, 46, 47
Karaites 37, 38, 40, 46
Karamlaiss 67
Karbala 71
Karekitays 54
Karkuye 81
Kartamin, Monastery of 90
Karts 88
Kashan 106, 109, 110, 121, 136, 137, 142, 156, 157
Kashani, Abu al-Qasim al- 72
Kashani, Benyamin Mishael 142
Kashani, Mir Abu al-Qasim 72
Kashgar 35, 59
Kashkaraya, Abu al-Husayn b. 49
Kashmir 70
kashrut 104
Kasra 150
katholikos, seat of the 120, 125
Katib al-Insha 43
Kavad I 8
Kaykavus, author of Zartus 80
Kaykhusraw, Kaykavus 32
Kaykhusraw, Mihraban 81
Kelemchi, Isa 76
Keprath 90
Keraits 54
Keritot 9
Kesarachi, Khachatur 134
Kesh tab 154
Ketubot 8, 9
Khalifa Sultan 105
Khalil Khan 105
Khan Baliq 78
Khan Khalil 110
Khanate of Persia 72, 73, 77, 78
kharaj 51
Khayzarun, al- 36
Khazaria 38
Khazars 38
Khirad-nama 32
Khitai 58, 64
Khizanat al-Hikma 48
Khotan 55
Khudai-nama 31
Khujandi, Jalal al-Din 58
Khunays, Mu'alla b. 155
Khunkar, Aharon 110
Khunsar 105
Khurasan 19, 21-25, 27, 28, 32, 38, 41, 49, 68, 71, 84, 88, 101, 105, 151
Khurramabad 104
Khurramdins 23, 24
Khurshid, Ispahbad 22
Khusraw II 10, 12, 52
Khusraw Khan 120

Khutlan 80
Khuzistan 11, 41, 45
Khwaja Awet 125
Khwaja Balazar Yahud 107
Khwaja Bukhara'i 143, 145
Khwaja Khacik 114
Khwaja Minas 118
Khwaja Mirak 112
Khwaja Safar Azaria 118
Khwarazmshah, Jala al-Din 60
Khwarazmshahs 54
kings 9, 26, 33, 78, 83, 98, 108, 121, 144, 147, 151
Kirakos of Gantzak 52, 56
kirfeh 148
Kirkuk 91
Kirman 30, 100-102, 105, 152, 153, 157
Kirmani, Nasir al-Din al- 47, 64
Kitab al-Anwar wa'l-Maraqib 46
Kitab al-Burhan 49
Kitab al-Masalik 31
Kitab-i Anusi 103, 104, 141
Kitab-i Sar Guzasht 142
Kitbuqa 59, 61
koshti 148
Kostand 135
kraga 9
Kuchlug 55, 62
Kurds 59, 71, 72, 90
Kurosh 143
Kutlu Beg 65
Ladino 138
Lake Urumia 91
Lar 104, 107, 109-111, 136, 140
Latin
　language 12, 82
　powers 75, 77
　states 73, 77, 78
Lawasun Shir Mazan Ughali 96
Le Bruyn, Cornelius 101, 102, 117, 121, 130, 134
legate, Jacobite 74
legends 7, 32
Leon, David Messer 142
letter 18, 41, 56, 72, 74, 76-79, 82, 90, 91, 97, 100, 105, 108, 118, 122, 125, 126, 132, 147, 151

Levi, Meir 110
Leviticus 82
Lewis, Bernard 4
Library of Wisdom 48
Life of Marouta 12
literature
　apocalyptic 16, 25
　Armenian 135
　Christian 26
　didactic 140
　didactic and religious 30
　Jewish 82, 136
　Jewish mystical 142
　Judeo-Persian 4, 143, 149
　Ladino 138
　Muslim 49
　Pahlavi 32, 81
　Persian 4, 135, 136
　rabbinic 83
　Zoroastrian 30
Livorno 122
livres tournois 120
Lord Henry 146
Lord of Arbela 65
Lord of Mosul 62
Louis IX 57, 74
Louis XIV 127, 129
Lutf Ali Khan 156
Ma'ara 90
Ma'mun, al- 3, 26, 27, 30, 38, 40, 48, 49
Mada'in 35, 98, 99, 150, 151
Madelung, Wilferd 21, 24
madrasa 74
Magians 18, 40
magic 104
magistrates 101
Mahdi, al- 35, 36, 48
mahdi, Messiah 142
Mahmud Afghan 151, 156, 157
Mahmud Ghaznavid 33, 42
Mahoze 13
Maimonides, Moses 138, 142
Maipherqat 10
majlis 155
Majlisi, Muhammad Baqir al- 155
Majusi, Ali b. al-Abbas al- 42
Makhzan al-pand 140

Makkikha II 62, 70
Maliki 25
Malikshah II 43
Malka 62
mallakh 141
Mamluk 63, 64, 68, 73, 74, 76-78, 90
Mandeans 104, 124, 133
Mani 154
Manicheans 26, 38
Mansur, al- 24, 34, 37, 47, 48
manufacture 89, 107, 109
Manuschihr, head of Z 30
Manuschihr-i Goshn-Yam 30
Maqrizi 61
Mar Abd Ishu 54
Mar Eliyya 133
Mar Mattai 12
Mar Mikail, convent 65
Mar Samuel of Nehardia 7
Mar Shallita, church 70
Mar Shamun 133
Mar Ya'kub of Salh, Monast 91
Maraba 11
Maragha 63, 68, 70, 71, 78, 85, 132
Marbanan 113
Marco Polo 63, 68
Mardanshah, Bahram b. 31
Mardin 67, 90
Mariam 12
Marikha II 59
market 100, 110, 114-116, 118, 162
Marquzan 98, 99
Marrar, Jahwar b. 22
Marta 95
martyrs 105
Marutha 10
Marwan II 20
Marwan, Fadl b. 39
Mary 11
marzuban 19
Mas'ud of Bar Qatwa 66
Mas'ud, Jewish convert 74
Mas'udi 36, 49
Masawayh, Yuhanna b. 49
masnavi 141, 143
Mathieu of Avaniac 122
Mattatiah 137
Maurice, Byzantine Emperor 12

mawalis 20
Mawlana Yusuf Yahudi 144
Mawsili, Ishaq al- 29
Mayyafariqin 67, 74
Mazandaran 84, 113
Mazda-worship 25
Mazdaism 154
Mazdakis 24
Maziyar 25, 39, 48
Mecca 97, 99, 142
Medes 140
Media 7
medicine 30, 48, 50, 160
Mediterranean coast 110, 114
Megillat Antioch 144
Mehuza 9
Melkites 34, 48
Merv 14, 19, 49, 54, 76, 83, 87, 151, 160
Mesopotamia 1, 14, 15, 33, 37, 38, 41, 43, 45-47, 55, 63, 65-68, 74, 77, 85, 88, 90, 93
messiah 37, 105
messianic movement 8, 37, 105
metropolitans 11, 13, 87
Michael VIII Palaeologus 64
Midrash 83, 144
Midyat 89
Mihr Hormuz 13
Mihraban, Rustam 81
Minasench family 119
Mino Khirad 97, 100, 147
Minozes, Hodshe 135
miqdash 139, 140
Mir Vays 156
Miran Shah 89
Mishnah 46
Mishneh Torah 138
missionaries 35, 54, 59, 65, 75, 78, 101, 104, 108, 124-127, 130-133, 161
mithva 140
Mo'ed Qatan 7
monastery 12, 90, 91
Mongke 57, 58, 63
Mongols 2, 4, 52-56, 59-69, 71, 74-77, 79, 81, 85-88, 93, 95, 100, 111, 151, 152, 160-162

Monophysite 12
Moors 102
Moreen, Vera 107
Morgan, David 67
Moses, Joseph b. 83
Moses, katholikos 120
Moses, physician from Nisibi 11
Moses, Prophet 83, 144, 145
mosque 55, 60, 71, 73, 90, 134, 145
Mosul 35, 48, 62, 65-67, 69, 91, 133
mother of Shah Abbas I 130
Mrkuz, Yovhannes 135
Mu'awiya 17
Mu'tadid, al- 40
Mu'tasim, al- 28, 39, 48, 50
Mu'tazid, al- 49
Mu'tazila 46
mu'tazilis 46
Mubid Azar Kayvan 101, 153
Mubid Farzana Bahram b. Farshad 154
Mubid Hush 154
Mubid Khudajuy 154
Mubid Kushi 154
Mubid Sorush b. Kayvan b. Kamgar 154
Mubid-i Mubidan 21
mubids 149, 150
Mughal
  authorities 118
  court 135
  Emperor 145, 153
  Empire 152
  India 154
  monarch 152
Mughals 152
Muhammad Beg 104, 105, 110, 120, 121, 127
Muhammad, Prohpet 40
Muhammad, Prophet 18, 66, 97, 99, 102, 150
Muhtadi, al- 40
mujtahid 94, 153
Mukammas, David al- 37
Mukhammas 144
Mukhtas, Isa b. 66
mule 36, 112
mulhid 62

Mulla Abu Hasan Lari 103
mulla bashi 156
Mulla Massih 108
Mulla Sadra 153
Munshi, Iskandar Beg 107
Muqanna, al- 23
Muqtadir, al- 34, 42, 46, 49
Muqtafi, al 43
Muqtafi, al- 53
Musa, Yusuf b. Ishaq b. 143, 144
Musa-nama 83
Musilaya, Abu Sa'ad al- 43
Muslims 2-4, 15, 18, 19, 21, 24, 26, 31, 34, 36, 37, 40, 43, 49-54, 56-75, 81, 82, 87, 89, 93-96, 98, 99, 101, 103, 105, 107, 108, 110, 112, 113, 115, 120, 124, 129, 133, 140, 143, 146, 149, 150, 153, 155, 156, 161
Musta'in, al- 40
Musta'sim, al- 60
Mustanjid, al 43
Mustanjid, al- 44
Mustansir, al- 44
Mutawakkil, al- 26, 27, 39, 40, 49
Muthanna, Abu Ubayda al- 46
Muti, al- 44
Muttaqi, al- 44
Muwaffaq al-Dawla 64
Muzaffar, Izzidin Muhammad b. 61
Muzaffarids 88
Muzakkir al-Ashab 145
mythology 147
nabi 99
Nadir Shah 111
Nahawandi, Benjamin b. M 46
Nahrawan 90
Naimans 54
Najara, Israel 83
najasat 115
Najib al-Dawla 70, 72
najis 142
najjarbashi 121
Najran 13
Nakhchevan 91, 113, 115, 122, 125, 129
Napet 125
Naples 121

Index

naqqashbashi 121, 135
Nariman Hushang 92, 100, 146, 148
Narseh 7
Narses, physician from Nisib 11
nasi 104
Nasir al-Din, Grand Vizier 71
Nasir Khusraw 47
Nasir, al- 44, 53
Nasraye 8
Nasrullah 157
Nawbakht 29
nawruz, festival 139, 155
Nawruz, Mongol Amir 69-71, 86
nazir 121
Nebuchadenezzar 139, 140
Nedarim 9
neday 149
Nehardia 160
Nehardia, Academy of 9
Nehemiah 41, 83
Nehormizd 13
neo-Mazdean 154
neo-Zoroastrian 26
Nestorians 8, 11-13, 33, 38, 43, 48,
    54, 60, 75, 77, 78, 85, 87, 88,
    91, 93, 94, 113, 122, 124, 131,
    132, 160
Nestorius 11
Netherlands 118
Netira II, Abraham b. 41
Netzer, Amnon 64, 145
New Testament 46
Newbury, John 108
Nicolas IV, Pope 76, 78
Nicolas, Arghun's son 66, 76
Nihavand 46, 87
Nikirsi of Gurgan, Jacob al- 47
Nimruz 151
nisba 140
Nishapur 31, 84, 87
Nisibis 10-12, 26, 35, 90, 160
Nizam al-Mulk 42, 43
Nizam, family al- 44
Nizami 83, 136, 141, 147
Noah 141
non-Arabs 46
non-Christians 126
non-Iranians 6, 148

non-Jews 7
non-Julfan Armenians 129
non-kosher 71
non-Muslims 1, 2, 4, 15-17, 19, 20,
    26, 27, 33, 39, 40, 42-45, 48,
    50, 51, 53, 56, 58, 62, 68, 69,
    73, 78, 79, 81, 86, 88, 89,
    93-97, 103, 112, 128, 132, 134,
    142, 156-158, 161, 162
non-Shi'ite elements 156
non-Zoroastrians 30, 148
North Africa 3
Nushirvan (Anushiravan) 84, 99
Odenarth 9
Odoric of Pordenone 76
Ohrmazddatan, Martan Farr 30
Olearius, Adam 107
Oman 143
Orie, Israel 122
Ottoman Empire 4, 94, 105, 107,
    108, 112, 114, 117, 120, 121,
    123, 124, 133
Ottoman occupation 106, 110
Ottoman-Safavid wars 130
Ottomans 5, 91, 93, 95, 103, 112-114,
    116, 117, 122, 124, 131
padyab 18, 149
pagan 36, 54, 70, 96, 139, 140
pagodas 69
Pahlavi 2, 8, 29-32, 37, 49, 79, 97, 160
painter 121, 135
paintings 83, 134, 135
Palestine 7, 108
Palmyra 9
Papa, wealthy Jewish figure 9
Papacy 66
Pargard 149
parsangs 149
Parsis 92, 100, 146, 150, 152
Parthians 7
pasul 142
Patna 153
patriarch 34-36, 52, 70, 71, 90
patriarchate 120, 131
Paul, Pope 118
peasants 113
Pentateuch 83, 137, 142
Pereyra de Paiva, Moses 108

perfume 149
persecution 3-8, 10, 14, 16, 26, 32, 33, 43, 94, 100, 103, 121, 125, 127-129, 132, 141, 147, 158, 159, 162
Persian-speaking 4
Perush Ha-Milot 83
Pesah 9
Philippe le Bel 76
Philippos, katholikos 120
philosopher 49, 142
philosophy 4, 15, 154
physician 3, 4, 10-12, 15, 20, 34-36, 38-45, 47, 49-51, 56, 63, 64, 67, 73, 82, 85, 109, 142, 160
physicist 49
pigs 115
Pinchas, Joseph b. 41
Piruz 18
Pishabur 65
Pius IV, Pope 91
poetry 4, 83, 136-138, 141, 142, 145, 147
poets 31, 32, 62, 83, 136, 141, 145, 152, 160
Poland 74, 122, 125
Poll-tax 9, 16, 44
polytheists 58
Pope 56, 66, 73-78, 91, 118, 122, 124-127
Portugal 124
pre-Islamic Iran 31, 33
priests 6, 11, 30, 35, 36, 52, 58, 64, 70, 82, 101, 122, 124, 131, 152
princes 74-77, 122, 131, 138
printing house 117, 134
proselytizers 54
pseudo-Zoroastrian 26
Ptolemy 48
Pumbedita, Academy of 9, 41
Qa'an 82
Qabus-nama 32
Qadaq 56, 57
Qaimaz, Qutb al-Din 44
Qandahar 101, 130, 156, 157
Qara Bogha 64
Qarabagh 114, 115
Qarakhanids 28

Qarchay Beg 120
Qarin, Mazyar b. 39, 48
qazi 57, 58
Qazi, Haji Muhammad al- 91
Qazvin 122
Qazwini, Muhammad Tahir 104
Qazwini, Shams al-Din 57
qibla 142
Qirqisani, al- 42
Qirqisani, Ya'qub al- 46
Qissa-ya Haft Baradaran 139
Qizilbash 96
Qubad 150
Qubilai 58, 66, 69, 76
Qudama 51
queens 86
Qum 37
Qumisi, Daniel b. Moses al- 37, 46
Quran 25, 46, 55, 58, 97, 151
Qurqura, Kaykhusraw 96
Qutai Khatun 65
Rabbanim 37, 46
Rabbanites 37, 40
rabbi 8, 44, 106, 128, 138, 142
Rabbi Yose 138
rabbinical schools 10
Radi, al- 28, 42, 80
Rahat al-Insan 32
Ram Hormizd 40
Ramadan 61
Rashid al-Din 54-58, 60, 64, 68-73, 81, 82, 86, 89, 105
rasul 99
Rayy 19, 23, 32, 37, 87
Razi, Abu Zakariya al- 48
relics 124, 130
Resh Galuta 7, 8, 106
Resh'aina 26
rivayats 101, 146-149, 151
Romans 7, 13
Rome 56, 66, 75, 76, 78, 118, 122, 140, 143, 144
rubais 145
ruby 110
Rudaki 30
Rumi 83
Russia 112, 117, 122, 129
Russians 129

Index

Rustam Khan 130
Rustam, epical hero 144
Rustam-i Dastan 27
Ruzbih 19
Sa'ad Vaqqas 151
Sa'd al-Dawla 67, 78, 86, 105
Sa'd al-Din 70, 72, 73, 77
Sa'ib of Isfahan 136
Sa'id, leader of the Jews 110
Saadia 41, 47
Sabians 25
Sadid al-Dawla 73
Sadiq, Ja'far al- 155
Safavid capital 113
Safavids 2, 4, 88, 91-96, 101, 106, 112-114, 116, 121, 130, 131, 134, 153, 155-157, 161, 162
Saffah, al- 19, 35
Saffarids 28, 30, 32
Safi Sulaiman, physician 62
Safi, Shah 104, 109, 115, 116, 118, 120, 123, 130, 135
Sahib al-Diwan 65, 67, 86
Sahl b. Raban of Tabaristan 48
Sahl, Fadl b. 27, 28
Sahl, Hasan b. 27
Saint Sargis 112
Salama, Da'ud b. 86
Saljuk Turks 32
Saljuks 42, 43, 54, 111
Salmos Davte 134
Samanids 28, 32
Samaria 7
Samarqand 55, 59, 83, 87, 112
Samarqandi, Muhammad 145
Samuel Mar Judah 8
Samuel, Judah b. 41
Sanhedrin 9
Sanskrit 153
Sar Shalom 44
Sarah bath Asher 104
Sarakhs 54
Sarbadars 88
Sarghaghtani Beki 59, 60
Sargon II of Assyria 7
Sariya, Masha'allah b. 45
Sarmad 135, 145
Sartaq 58

Sasan 30
Sassanian
    administrative system 14
    bureaucratic system 2
    court 8, 34
    government 7, 8, 18, 34
    monarchy 13
    state 10, 13
Sassanian Empire 8, 10, 160
Sassanians 2, 3, 6-9, 12, 14, 15, 17, 22, 26, 28, 30, 33, 34, 45, 48, 155, 159
satellites of New Julfa 120
Sayyar, Nasr b. 19
Sayyid Anan 37
sayyids 82
School
    of Ctesiphon 12
    of Edessa 12
    of Gundishapur 51
    of Isfahan 153
    of Nisibis 12
science 2, 4, 10, 15, 16, 50, 53, 79, 81, 82, 87, 160
scribes 53, 134
sculptors 86
Sebaste 90
sects 26
Sefer Muratowicz 122
Seleucid era 139
Sennacherib 7
seraglio 130
Serge, bishop of Elam 36
Sergius 35
Sezavvol 143
Shabbatai Tzvi 105
Shabbath 9
Shabbetai Tzvi 37
Shafi'i 25
Shafraz family 119, 120, 129
Shah Jahan 135, 145
Shah-nama 33, 139, 143, 147
Shahanshah 8
Shahin 83, 84, 137, 142
Shahrastani of Ghazna 47
Shahriha i Eran 6
Shahrimanian family 119
Shahta, Farat b. 34

Shalutha, Isa b. 34
Shamanism 72
Shamanists 70
Shamta 13
Shapur I 7
Shapur II 8
Sharestan 154
sharia 56
Sharifabad 92
Shayba, Shabib b. 34
Shaykh Haydar 95
sheikhs 55
Shengar 26
Sherley, Anthony & Robert 121
Sheroe 13
Shi'ism 72, 93-95, 153
Shi'ites 5, 26, 39, 60, 62, 95, 142, 155-157
Shi'itization of Iran 95
Shiraz 83, 105, 108, 109, 111, 113, 121, 131, 136, 153
Shirazi, Falzlallah 154
Shirazi, Sadr al-Din 153
Shirin 12
Shirvan 114, 115, 121
Shirvanshahs 96
Shkand Gumanik Vicar 30
Shoftim-nama 141
Shu'ubis 46
Shu'ubism 46, 51
Shu'ubiyya 46
Shush 8
Shushandukht 8
Shushtar 8, 14, 105
silver 58, 107, 115, 119
silversmiths 86
Simeon, physician 56, 63
Simon Tov Mumin 104
Sirishk 87
Sistan 29, 55, 81, 101, 151
Sivas 90
Siyar Muluk al-Ajam 31
Siyasat-nama 42
Siyavush 147
slaughtering of animals 56, 58
Solduz 132
Som of Nariman 144, 147
Spain 3, 42, 46, 83, 108, 119, 142

Spitaman 148
St John Baptist, convent 68
Sublime Porte 117
suffragans 78
Sufi ideas 138
Suhrab 144
Suhravardi, Shaykh al-Ishra 153, 154
Sulayman, Abdallah b. 40
Sulayman, Shah 103, 122, 126-130, 155-157
Sultan Husayn 101, 102, 123, 126, 129, 156
Sultan Muhammad 89
Sultan Sanjar 54
Sultaniya 78
Sunbad 22
Sunna 102
Sunnism 73, 77, 93, 94
Sunnites 5, 60, 72, 95, 103, 113, 156
Sura, Academy of 10, 38, 41, 46, 47
Surat 119, 120
Surb Astuacacin 112
Surin 35
Surpa Kroop 134
Surpa Tomafa 134
Susa 65
synagogues 44, 69, 109
synod 11
Syria 33, 64, 77, 88, 90
Syriac 45, 47-49, 62, 65, 70, 84, 85, 160
Ta'anit 8, 9
Ta'i, al- 49
Tabari, al-
    Ali b. Sahl b. Rabban 39, 48
    Muhammad 13, 14, 39
Tabaristan 22, 24, 25, 40, 46, 48, 84
Tabriz 63, 67, 70, 71, 73, 75-78, 82, 85, 88, 92, 112, 121, 130
Tabrizi, Muhammad Husayn 154
Tadjik 52
tafsir 144
Tagachar 76
Tagrit 12, 55
Tahir, Abdallah b. 24, 29
Tahir, Muhammad al- 40
Tahirids 27-29, 32
Tahmasp Quli Khan 106, 111

Index

Tahmasp, Shah 96, 130
Taj al-Din Isa 67
Taj al-Ru'asa 43
Tajis 25
takhallus 141
Takrit 43, 89
Talmud, Babylonian 7, 9
tamiims 140
Taoist priests 58
Taqvim al-Yehudah 142
Tarikh-i Sistan 28, 32
Tarmashirin 87
tarsas 62
Tavernier, Jean-Baptiste 102, 107, 108, 110, 116, 121, 127, 132
Tawus, Jacob b. Joseph 136
Tayfuri, Isra'il b. Zakariya 39
Tella 26
Tenreiro, Antonio 108
textile 89, 100, 101, 107, 110, 142
Thévenot, Jean de 101
Thomas, apostle 36
Tibet 64, 70
Tiflis 60, 76, 96
Tiglath-Pileser III 7
Tigris 143
Timothy I 35, 36, 48, 59
Timothy II 73
Timur Lang 88, 90, 91, 94, 95, 113, 131, 161
Timurids 111
Tobiah 141
Tolayq, Ishaq b. 19
Tolui 54
Toma, Theophile 48
Torah 46, 47, 138, 139, 143
traders 78, 110, 118, 121, 122
tradesmen 45, 116, 119, 123, 162
translators 45, 48, 49, 82, 154
Transoxania 22, 23, 35, 54, 59, 83, 88, 90
treasurer 13, 39, 66
treasury 18, 30, 42, 62, 68, 70, 151
treaties 117, 123
treaty 13, 73, 78, 118, 123
Tsar 123
Tsar Alexei Mikhaelovich 129
tumans 105, 110, 115, 127, 128

Tur Abdin 89
Turfan 54
Turkabad 92
turkeys 117
Turkmen
    dynasty 95
    military arictocracy 96
    military aristocracy 116
Turkmens 130
Turks 6, 22, 32, 80, 87
Tus 84
Tusi, Nasr al-Din 60
Tustar 42
Ubaydallah, Qasim b. 49
Ugeday 56, 57, 63, 82
Uighur script 54
Uighurs 54
Ukba 41
ulema 104, 128
Uljaytu 71, 72, 78
Ulu David 60
Umar b. al-Khattab 18, 151, 156
Umar, Jazira b. 63, 64
Umar, Yusuf b. 19
Umayyad rule 20
Umayyads 17, 19, 22, 33, 37
uncircumcised 137, 139, 140
unclean 58, 142, 149
Uniat Status 78
Urban IV, Pope 75
Urgenj 83
urine 36
Uruk Khatun 71
Urumia 132
Ustadhsis 23, 24
Uthman 5
Utrar 90
Uzun Hasan 91, 95
Vakhtanga 156
Vamiq-u Adhra 29
Vartan 60, 75
Vassaf 67
vassal 7, 80
Vatican 122
Vays 152
Vecchietti, Giambattista 136
Veh-Ardashir 73
Velijian family 119

Vendidad 149
Venetians 91, 112
Venice 114, 118, 121, 129
Venus 141
vessels 117, 118, 123
viceroy of Naples 121
village 12, 65, 72, 89-91, 112, 113
Vine, Aubry 14
vineyards 107
vizier 27, 33-35, 39-42, 44, 48, 50, 51, 56, 60, 66, 70, 77, 90, 96, 105, 120, 121, 128, 156
Wakhush 96
waqf 70
Wasiq, al- 49
Western Asia 69, 78, 85, 114
whores 102
Wilhelm von Rubruck 54
wine 101, 110, 142
wives 12, 23, 52, 121, 130
wood of aloes 149
Ya'qub b. al-Layth 29, 30
Ya'qub, Armenian envoy 122
Ya'qub, Prophet 140, 141
Yahballaha III 65, 70, 73, 76, 77, 85, 160
Yahudi of Ghaznin, Isaac 42
Yahudiyya, al- 8
Yahushu' ben Nun 141
Yahya, Ubaydallah b. 41
Yakobian 121, 135
Yaqut 39
yarligh 57, 69
yasa 55, 56
Yazd 88, 92, 101, 102, 105, 106, 109, 110, 141, 157
Yazdanbokht 38
Yazdankhwast 45
Yazdgird I 8, 10
Yazdgird II 8
Yazdgird III 14, 17, 151
Yazdi
  Abraham 106
  Behdin Kavus 102
  Sharaf al-Din 89
Yazdin 13
Yazid II 19
Yebamot 9

Yoma 10
Yormia 141
Yuhanna, Masawayh b. 48
Yussuf Khan 121
Yusuf, Prophet 141
Yusuf, Umar b. 40
Zadan Farrukh 18
Zafar-nama 137
Zagam (or Zagrum) 103
Zagros 6
Zakariya, wealthy Armenian 120
Zaki 63, 65
Zakkai, David b. 41, 42, 46
Zar-i dast afshar 154
Zarathusht 148
Zarathusht-nama 31
Zarathushtra 22, 36, 97-99
Zardusht 97
Zartusht Bahram 79, 80
Zawra-ye bastan 154
Zheng He 92
Ziarid prince 32
Zindiqs 26
Zohar 142
Zoroastrian books 32
Zoroastrianism 6-8, 11, 12, 16-20, 22, 24, 30-32, 80, 91, 97, 99, 149, 150, 155, 159
Zoroastrians 1-4, 7, 10, 15-20, 22, 23, 25, 26, 29-33, 35, 37, 40, 49, 50, 53, 55, 57, 62, 64, 80, 81, 86, 87, 89, 92, 94, 97-102, 110, 111, 128, 129, 131, 132, 138, 140, 145-148, 150-157, 159-162
Zubdat al-Tawarikh 72
Zuqnin 26
Zygmunt III Waza 122

Printed and bound by CPI Group (UK) Ltd, Croydon, CR0 4YY
20/03/2026
02075557-0020